Developments in German Politics 3

Developments **titles available from Palgrave Macmillan**

Laura Cram, Desmond Dinan and Neill Nugent (eds)
DEVELOPMENTS IN THE EUROPEAN UNION

Patrick Dunleavy, Andrew Gamble, Richard Heffernan and
Gillian Peele (eds)
DEVELOPMENTS IN BRITISH POLITICS 7

Alain Guyomarch, Howard Machin, Peter A. Hall and Jack Hayward (eds)
DEVELOPMENTS IN FRENCH POLITICS 2

Paul Heywood, Erik Jones and Martin Rhodes (eds)
DEVELOPMENTS IN WEST EUROPEAN POLITICS 2

Stephen Padgett, William E. Paterson and Gordon Smith (eds)
DEVELOPMENTS IN GERMAN POLITICS 3

Gillian Peele, Christopher Bailey, Bruce Cain and B. Guy Peters (eds)
DEVELOPMENTS IN AMERICAN POLITICS 4

Stephen White, Judy Batt and Paul Lewis (eds)
DEVELOPMENTS IN CENTRAL AND EAST
EUROPEAN POLITICS 3

Stephen White, Alex Pravda and Zvi Gitelman (eds)
DEVELOPMENTS IN RUSSIAN POLITICS 5
of related interest

Ian Holliday, Andrew Gamble and Geraint Parry (eds)
FUNDAMENTALS IN BRITISH POLITICS

If you have any comments or suggestions regarding the
above or other possible *Developments* titles, please write to
Steven Kennedy, Palgrave Macmillan, Houndmills,
Basingstoke RG21 6XS, UK or e-mail s.kennedy@palgrave.com

Developments in German Politics 3

Edited by

Stephen Padgett
William E. Paterson
Gordon Smith

First published 2003 by
PALGRAVE MACMILLAN
Houndmills, Basingstoke, Hampshire RG21 6XS and
175 Fifth Avenue, New York, N.Y. 10010
Companies and representatives throughout the world

PALGRAVE MACMILLAN is the global academic imprint of the Palgrave
Macmillan division of St. Martin's Press, LLC and of Palgrave Macmillan Ltd.
Macmillan® is a registered trademark in the United States, United Kingdom
and other countries. Palgrave is a registered trademark in the European
Union and other countries.

ISBN 0–333–96201–X hardback
ISBN 0–333–96202–8 paperback

This book is printed on paper suitable for recycling and made from fully
managed and sustained forest sources.

A catalogue record for this book is available from the British Library.

10 9 8 7 6 5 4 3 2 1
12 11 10 09 08 07 06 05 04 03

Printed and bound in Great Britain by
Creative Print & Design (Wales), Ebbw Vale

Contents

List of Maps, Figures and Tables

Map

Figures

Tables

Preface

Our purpose in *Developments in German Politics 3* is to provide an integrated and systematic assessment of current trends in the Federal Republic as it confronts the challenges of the early twenty-first century. All chapters are entirely new and specially written for this volume. Its two predecessor volumes focused on the repercussions for German politics and society of unification. Although Germany has not yet fully absorbed the 'shock' of unification, its effects are now compounded by the effects of globalization. The effects are manifested internally through increasing pressure on the distinctive German model of political economy and the welfare state. Economic constraints, in turn, have implications for external relations. The role that the Federal Republic has played within the European Union has been predicated on economic *strength*. With the economy in crisis, it is by no means clear that it can sustain its traditional role in Europe, or that it can live up to the more activist role that it is expected to play in the post-September 11 security order. Thus the problems and perspectives of this book are very different from those addressed in *Developments in German Politics 2*, which was published in 1996.

In drawing largely on current material that is often available only in journal articles or German language publications, the book seeks to give up-to-date accounts of leading issues. Nevertheless, the discussion of each topic is combined with sufficient background information to make the book accessible for readers who do not have a detailed knowledge of German politics. It is designed, therefore, to be used either as a complement to a basic textbook or on its own, depending on course requirements; indeed, it should be accessible to interested global readers or political/policy practitioners.

As on previous occasions, we wish to thank our contributors – German, American and British – for their willing cooperation, despite all their other commitments. We would also like to thank the publishers of *West European Politics* (Frank Cass) for allowing Martin Seeleib-Kaiser to draw substantially in his chapter on his article published there.

January 2003   Stephen Padgett
                                                     William E. Paterson
                                                     Gordon Smith

Notes on the Contributors

David P. Conradt is Professor of Political Science at East Carolina University (Greenville, North Carolina). He is the author and editor of numerous books on German and European politics including *The German Polity, Power Shift in Germany, Politics in Europe* and *The Civic Culture Revisited.* He has been a Guest Professor at universities in Mannheim, Konstanz and Dresden. Currently, he is preparing a book on the 2002 German parliamentary election.

Russell J. Dalton is Professor of Political Science and Director of the Center for the Study of Democracy at the University of California, Irvine. His scholarly interests include comparative political behaviour, political parties, social movements, and empirical democratic theory. His recent publications include *Democratic Challenges, Democratic Choices* (2003), *Citizen Politics* (2002), and *The Green Rainbow: Environmental Interest Groups in Western Europe* (1994).

Kenneth Dyson is Research Professor of European Politics at the University of Cardiff. He is a Fellow of the British Academy and member of its research grants committee as well as an Academician of the Learned Societies of the Social Sciences and member of its Committee of Academicians. He has published, *The Road to Maastricht* (1999, chosen as an outstanding academic book of the year by the US library journal Choice), *The Politics of the Euro-Zone* (2000) and *European States and the Euro* (2002). He was an adviser for the BBC2 series on the making of the euro.

Klaus H. Goetz is Senior Lecturer in German Politics and Government at the London School of Economics and Political Science (LSE), where he convenes the MSc in European Politics and Policy. He has written widely on institutional policy in Germany and post-Communist Central and Eastern Europe, and is co-editor of the journal *West European Politics.* His most recent publication is *Germany and Europe: How Europeanized is Germany?* (co-editor, 2003).

Simon Green is Lecturer in German Politics at the Institute for German Studies, University of Birmingham. As well as writing widely on immigration in Germany, he has recently been researching the links between citizenship and integration.

Adrian Hyde-Price is Professor of Politics and International Relations at the University of Leicester. He studied politics at the University College of Wales, Aberystwyth, and was awarded his doctorate from the University of Kent. He has held lecturing posts at the universities of Birmingham, Southampton and Manchester, and a research fellowship at the Royal Institute of International Affairs, London. He is currently visiting Research Fellow at Lund University, Sweden.

Charlie Jeffery is Professor and Deputy Director of the Institute for German Studies, University of Birmingham. His recent work on German federalism and the European Union includes the co-authored volume *Germany's European Diplomacy; Shaping the European Milieu*. His articles have appeared in *Political Studies, West European Politics*, and *Parliamentary Affairs*. He is co-editor of *Regional and Federal Studies*.

Stephen Padgett is Professor of Politics at the University of Strathclyde. He has written extensively on German and European politics and policy. His recent publications include *Organizing Democracy in Eastern Germany; Interest Groups in Post-Communist Society* (2000) and (co-edit) *Continuity and Change in German Politics; Beyond the Politics of Centrality* (2002). He is an editor of *German Politics*.

William E. Paterson is Professor of German Politics and Director of the Institute for German Studies at the University of Birmingham. He has published widely on various aspects of German politics. The theme of Germany and European integration has been an abiding preoccupation. His current interests include the management of bilateral relations in the European Union and policy transfer to the communist successor parties of East Central Europe. He was awarded an OBE in 1999 for 'Scholarship in German Studies' and in the same year was awarded an Officer Cross of the German Order of Merit.

Wolfgang Rüdig is Reader in Government at the University of Strathclyde, Glasgow, Scotland. His main research interest is the comparative analysis of Green parties, and he is currently conducting a project financed by the British Academy involving surveys of Green Party members in 12 West European countries.

Martin Seeleib-Kaiser is Senior Research Fellow at the Centre for Social Policy Research, Bremen University. His research interests are party politics, political economy, and comparative welfare state analysis. In addition to his recent book *Globalisierung und Sozialpolitik. Ein Vergleich der Diskurse und Wohlfahrtssysteme in Deutschland, Japan und den USA* (Frankfurt/and/New York, 2001), he has published numerous articles in journals including *German Politics, Politische Vierteljahresschrift, Social Policy and Administration, Zeitschrift für Soziologie*, and *West European Politics*.

Gordon Smith is Emeritus Professor of Government at the London School of Economics. He has written extensively on German and comparative European politics as well as party systems analysis. He is co-editor of the journal *West European Politics*.

Roland Sturm is Professor of Political Science at the Friedrich-Alexander University Erlangen-Nuernberg and head of the Political Science Department. He has published widely in the fields of German politics, comparative politics and comparative public policy, political economy, British politics and European integration.

List of Abbreviations

AWACs	Airborne Warning and Control Systems
BBU	Bundesverband Bürgerinitiativen Umweltschutz (Federal Association of Citizen Action Groups on Environmental Protection)
BMFT	Bundesministerium für Forschung und Technologie (Federal Ministry for Research and Technology)
BMU	Bundesministerium für Umwelt, Reaktorsicherheit und Naturschutz (Federal Ministry for Environment, Reactor Safety and Nature Protection)
BSE	bovine spongiform encephalopathy ('Mad cow disease')
BUND	Bund für Umwelt- und Naturschutz Deutschland (German Association for Environmental and Nature Protection)
B'90/ Die Grünen	Bündnis '90/Die Grünen (Alliance '90/The Greens)
CAP	Common Agricultural Policy
CDU	Christlich Demokratische Union (Christian Democratic Union)
CFSP	Common Foreign and Security Policy
CHP	combined heat and power
CJTF	Combined Joint Task Force
CSU	Christlich-Soziale Union (Christian–Social Union)
CSCE	Conference on Security and Cooperation in Europe
DNR	Deutscher Naturschutzring (German Society for Nature Conservation)
DVU	Deutsche Volks Union (German People's Union)
ECB	European Central Bank
ECJ	European Count of Justice
EMU	Economic and Monetary Union

ERM	exchange-rate mechanism
ESCB	European System of Central Banks
ESDP	European Security and Defence Policy
EU	European Union
FAZ	*Frankfurter Allegemeine Zeitung*
FDP	Freie Demokratische Partei
	(Free Democratic Party)
GDR	German Democratic Republic
ICLEI	International Consortium of Local Environmental
	Initiatives
IFOR	Implementation Force
IGC	Intergovernmental Conference
IT	Information Technology
NABU	Naturschutzbund (Nature Protection Association)
NATO	North Atlantic Treaty Organization
NEPA	National Environmental Policy Act
NPD	Nationaldemokratische Partei Deutschlands
	(National Democratic Party of Germany)
OECD	Organization for Economic Cooperation and
	Development
OSCE	Organization for Security and Cooperation
	in Europe
PDS	Partei des Demokratischen Sozialismus
	(Party of Democratic Socialism)
PISA	Programme for International Student Assessment
RuStAG	Reichs- und Staatsangehörigkeitsgesetz
Schill-PRO	Schill-Partei und Rechtsstaatliche Offensive
SEA	Single European Act
SED	Socialist Unity Party
SPD	Sozialdemokratische Partei Deutschlands
	(Social Democratic Party of Germany)
StAG	Staatsangehörigkeitsgesetz
UBA	Umweltbundesamt (Federal Environment Agency)
UMK	Umweltministerkonferenz (Conference of
	Environmental Ministers)
UMTS	Universal Mobile Telecommunications System
UNOSOM	United Nations Operation in Somalia
UNTAC	United Nations Transitional Authority in Cambodia
WEU	Western European Union

Glossary

Aussiedler	ethnic Germans
Aussitzen	'wait-and-see' attitude
Ausländer(gezetz)	foreigner (Foreigners' Law)
Bundesrat	representation of 16 Lander governments
Bundestag	Federal Parliament
Entflechtung	disentanglement
Erstimme	first vote
Grundgesetz	Basic Law
Kindernachzug	immigration of minor dependants
Leitantrag	main resolution
Leitkultur	dominant culture
Machtwort	last word
Modell Deutschland	model Germany
Neue Mitte	new centre
Neue Mittestand	new middle class
Optionsmodell	model of options
Politikverflechtung	political entanglement
Spataussiedler	ethnic German immigration
Stattpartei	'Instead' party
Volksparteien	people's parties
Wende	turnaround
Wechselwähler	change voters
Wirtschaftswunder	economic miracle
Zivilmacht	civilian power
Zweitstimme	second vote
Zuwanderungsgesetz	Immigration Law

MAP 1   *Map of the Federal Republic and the Länder*

Introduction

The publication of this book coincides with a critical juncture in German politics. Once an exemplar of economic dynamism, Germany is currently the 'sick man of Europe', staggering under the massive cost burden of unification whilst at the same time struggling to come to terms with global economic change. Economic malaise is reflected in politics. Failure to confront underlying economic weakness discredits political institutions and patterns of political behaviour that were once regarded as the 'efficient secret' of economic success. The 2002 election sharpened perceptions that Germany stands at the crossroads between economic reform and a spiral of economic decline with unpredictable political fall-out. The contributors to this book are thus preoccupied with the unfolding crisis of German political economy over the last decade, its repercussions for polity, politics and policy, and the consequences for Germany's role in Europe and the wider world.

The economic success of the Federal Republic is encapsulated in the phrase *Model Germany*. The concept denotes a distinctive set of economic institutions combining the dynamism of the market with traditional German values of order and stability, and a particular emphasis on the state as guarantor of social solidarity. Its implications, however, extend far beyond this narrow definition. The German economic model is inseparable from the political institutions that define the Federal Republic and that have shaped the patterns of political behaviour and policy-making which are characteristic of post-war Germany. More broadly still, with the Deutsche Mark serving as a symbol of 'economic patriotism', the German model provided the focal point for national identity, compensating for the truncated political stature of the 'semi-sovereign state'. Finally, the economic and political institutions of the German model have dovetailed so closely with those of the European Union (EU) that it is difficult to distinguish a Europeanized Germany from a German Europe. Given the 'anchor' role that the German model of political economy has played in the Federal Republic, the consequences of its failure could be, in the words of the political weekly *Der Spiegel* (21 September 2002), 'a crisis so elemental that it could endanger the whole future of the country'.

1

Economy and State in Crisis

The most visible manifestation of the decline of the German model is unemployment, standing at over 4 million at the end of 2002. Unemployment reflects a wider syndrome of underperformance in the economy: stagnant growth, the foreign migration of German investment, and escalating state debt. The underlying structural causes of decline are complex. At a general level, however, it is clear that economic and political institutions have failed to adapt quickly enough to the complex forces of globalization.

In contrast to Anglo-Saxon capitalism, in which *markets* play the decisive role, the German model is characterized by coexistence between markets and institutionalized networks of cooperation and coordination. The model emerged from the manufacturing sectors that constitute the foundation of the German economy. Success here depends on competitive advantage in markets where quality matters more than price. This type of quality production relies on a supportive infrastructure of knowledge and skill, supplied through intensive programmes of research and development and a comprehensive system of vocational training. To give employees and employers the confidence that investing in skills will yield long-term rewards, labour markets and industrial relations are regulated by social institutions, empowered by the state. Characterized by stability and order, the German model of coordinated capitalism has undoubted long-term strengths. As we shall see in Chapter 6, however, it lacks the flexibility to adapt to the fast-changing product markets in the contemporary global economy.

A second factor behind Germany's loss of international competitiveness is the cost burden of an oversized and inefficient welfare state. Dating back to Bismarck and reinforced by the post-war settlement between capital and labour, the welfare regime maintains the social cohesion that underpins the German model. In so doing, however, it places an unsustainable burden on the productive economy. The problem is twofold, encompassing both the scale of social expenditure and the manner in which it is financed. Based on the principles of social equality and a uniformity of living standards, social security entitlements and pensions have an unusually high 'replacement value' in relation to former earnings. These generous entitlements are funded by insurance contributions that fall heavily on employers, with non-wage levies constituting over 40 per cent of employment costs. The result is a mutually reinforcing syndrome of increasing social insurance levies and rising unemployment.

Other aspects of the social state are also both expensive and inefficient. Germany pays more for its healthcare than any other country apart from the USA, placing a massive burden on sickness insurance funds. On almost every indicator, the intensity of healthcare exceeds other European Union countries. The average German consults a medical practitioner 6.6 times per year; the duration of hospitalization averages ten days; referrals for therapeutic health cures proliferate. In the absence of effective measures for cost-containment, healthcare expenditure has increased by almost 50 per cent in the last ten years. In a recent cross-national comparison of life expectancy, however, Germany ranked 15 out of 22 comparator countries. In education, by contrast, poor performance reflects underfunding. Education expenditure as a proportion of GDP lags behind the Organization for Economic Cooperation and Development (OECD) average. Cross-national performance comparisons of 15-year-olds' reading competence place Germany in lower mid-table. Even more disturbingly in a self-professed 'social state', a 32-country comparison of differentials in educational achievement between privileged and underprivileged showed Germany in last place, seven places behind the USA.

Interests and Institutions

How are we to explain the recurring patterns of underperformance that now characterize so much of economic and social life in the Federal Republic? One answer lies in the neo-corporatist nexus of social interests that permeate the institutions of economic and political life. Labour markets, social security and healthcare are bound by rigid legal frameworks which define rights and entitlements. Administrative responsibilities are devolved to social institutions spawning large bureaucracies in which the representatives of both service providers and beneficiaries are entrenched. For trade unions, the web of employment regulations that protect labour market 'insiders' are sacrosanct. The 'lobby in white' occupies a similar position in the health services. This nexus of interests and institutions 'has created fixed patterns of social and labour market inclusion and exclusion that protect certain groups ... from market based performance indicators at the expense of other groups who suffer high permanent unemployment' (Kitschelt, 2000, p. 208).

The interests of service providers and beneficiaries are also deeply embedded in the main political parties and in Parliament. Labour market reform and the overhaul of the welfare state are effectively precluded by 'clientelism' within broadly inclusive *Volksparteien* (people's parties), both of which contain strong trade union and social policy lobbies. More generally, the political class is dominated by public sector bureaucrats and employees. Over half the 1998–2002 Parliament was made up of civil servants, party and interest group officials and education professionals.

The nexus of interests and institutions at sectoral level intersects with the broader institutional framework of the German polity. A system of institutional pluralism sets the parameters of policy-making. In a decentralized federal system, institutional interdependence is far more deeply rooted and sophisticated than in older constitutional systems of checks and balances. Interdependence has a number of profound effects. One has been to make the process of policy formulation and policy implementation subject to intensive and complex negotiation and adjustment. The consensus-inducing mechanisms of the institutional structure have left a strong imprint on the style of German politics, with an orientation towards compromise rather than confrontation. In the 'golden years' of the post-war *Wirtschaftswunder* (economic miracle), the depoliticization of the economic order could be regarded as the efficient secret of the Federal Republic. In the face of structural economic decline, however, consensus can quickly translate into 'risk aversion' and a reluctance to embrace change.

Institutional Pluralism

The neo-corporatist nexus of interests and institutions is compounded by the institutional pluralism of the German polity. Characterized by the reconciliation of *interlocking* social interests within a decentralized and open political system, the German model performed well in an era of economic stability and social consensus. In the harsher economic environment in which Germany now finds itself, however, institutional pluralism simply multiplies the opportunities for self-interested actors to veto structural reform. As we shall see in Chapter 1, a decentralized political system places multiple constraints on executive decision-making. First, government at the centre implies party government; parties are themselves governing institutions. Second, a chancellor's powers of patronage and agenda-setting are circumscribed by coalition government. Third, the German federal system requires close cooperation between government and the Länder in legislation. Finally, not only does cooperation encompass Länder, it also extends upwards to the European Union. Chapter 8 shows how almost every field of domestic public policy is characterized by dense interaction between national policy-makers and EU actors. Thus the scope of federal government for flexibility and innovation in setting the policy agenda is severely restricted.

Chancellors are not without resources with which to assert their authority. The Chancellor's Office provides an institutional base from which to assert the leadership prerogatives contained in Article 65 of the constitution. Many informal practices have evolved to meet the need for coordination, especially in coalition and chancellor–party relations. Externalization provides a further source of flexibility, allowing the chancellor to by-pass the formal framework of the executive by establishing commissions or working groups to prepare the ground for policy initiatives. Helmut Kohl made extensive use of these practices and (as we shall see in Chapter 5) Gerhard Schröder has extended them further, in what some have characterized as a centralization of executive authority.

Ultimately, however, the experience of the Schröder government and that of his predecessor do not suggest that these expedients can offer an escape route from the constraints of interdependence. In both cases the rhetoric of economic liberalization failed to translate into effective reform. Key aspects of Schröder's modernizing *neue Mitte* (new centre) agenda were either shelved (labour market reform), or weakened by the intervention of social interests (pensions). As we shall see in Chapter 5, policy-making under Schröder has been characterized by a culture of dialogue and deals with social and economic interests, exemplified by the withdrawal of proposals to control the price of pharmaceutical products in the health service in return for a one-off contribution by the manufacturers to health insurance funds. Thus 'the institutional context of German politics tends to ... grind down radical policy initiatives so that the end product, if one emerges at all ... represents the lowest common denominator between those corporate actors which command the potential to crush the initiative completely' (Webber, 1992, p. 174). The result is 'situational government': short-term decisions which avoid underlying policy problems.

The federal system is similarly plagued by conflicts of interest. Federal systems express a trade-off between territorial social differences and membership of a common state. One of the pillars of the German system of 'cooperative federalism' was a commitment to uniform policy standards and a uniformity of living conditions, underpinned by economic and social homogeneity. As we see in Chapter 2, however, economic decline has hit some of the Länder harder than others. Divergent economic performance has created growing political cleavages between western and eastern and richer and poorer Länder. The result is a trend from cooperative to competitive federalism, associated over the last decade with conflicts over the complex system of financial equalization between the federal states. The pursuit of territorial self-interest can also

be seen in divergent policy agendas, and in initiatives for a regionalization of healthcare, unemployment insurance and pensions to decouple
the richer Länder from the structural economic problems of their poorer
neighbours. The new territorial politics of competitive federalism exemplifies the malign syndrome of economic decline and institutional
malfunction currently confronting Germany. Economic decline creates
or exacerbates tensions in a pluralist institutional system, reducing
the capacity of institutions to respond effectively to the challenges of
economic reform.

Party System Developments

Similar questions hang over the party system. Until the 1998 election the
German party system had remained exceptionally stable, with two major
parties, the Christian Democratic Union (CDU) and the Social
Democratic Party (SPD), alternating in government, with the Free
Democratic Party (FDP) holding the balance between them. This 'triangular' pattern of government came to an abrupt end in 1998 when the
SPD was first able to share government with the Greens. The SPD–Green
formation held firm – somewhat against expectations – and was narrowly
successful in the 2002 election. It thus appeared that a two-bloc party
system had become established, with the SPD and Greens on the one
side, and the CDU with the FDP on the other. The stability of the two-
bloc party system, however, remains questionable. In principle, the 'right
bloc', CDU and FDP, should be cohesive, but the FDP may have become
an unreliable partner, judging by its rather bizarre performance in the
2002 campaign. On the left, the SPD and Greens appear to have found
much common ground but, with the German economy increasingly
under pressure, difficult decisions will have to be made over the next few
years, and there is no guarantee that the coalition will hold firm until the
next federal election scheduled for 2006. Uncertainties on both left and
right make it clear that the continuation of a two-bloc system cannot be
taken for granted. But it is difficult to see at this stage what might take its
place, especially since electoral behaviour is far less certain than it was in
the 'old' Federal Republic, and it is likely to become even more fluid in
the face of Germany's economic difficulties.

The Fluidity of Electoral Behaviour

Electoral ties to political parties have weakened generally in Western
democracies and Germany is no exception to this process. In the Federal

Republic two of the most reliable indicators in the past were social class and religious affiliation, but both have been steadily weakening influences. Since German reunification, however, analysis has become more complex, as shown in Chapter 3, because eastern and western Germany display different patterns of development and, of course, radically different starting-points.

In western Germany, there has been a convergence of middle- and working-class voting behaviour, with the growing 'new' middle class dividing its vote between left and right. Moreover, underlying factors such as the levels of education and income have become less certain guides than in the past. In eastern Germany to begin with there was, in the first elections, actually a reversal in the direction of class-based voting, but by the time of the 2002 election a more normal linkage had become apparent.

Religious persuasion is still an important guide to political loyalty in western Germany, particularly among Catholics and generally for those attending church; only a relatively small minority count themselves as non-religious. The religious factor is far less significant in eastern Germany, since some two-thirds of the electorate regard themselves as 'non-religious'. There is a paradox here: the strong support given to the 'Christian' CDU in the east is at variance with the prevailing non-religious sentiment.

Despite the sharp contrast between electoral behaviour in the two parts of Germany, there is an important similarity. In the west there has been a continuing decline in partisanship; in the east, it has been weak from the outset. Thus, party attachments are either weakening or already weak. In the west, the process is one of dealignment, but in the east still one of pre-alignment. With the German electorate less 'structured' than in the past, voters are more 'free' to make their own choices, seen in the rise in the number of voters switching between parties from one election to another and in the growth of 'split-ticket' voting. There is also evidence that voters are making their decisions later during the course of an election campaign. They are more likely to be influenced by the campaign itself and the issues raised that are most salient to their own interests. In reaching a decision, voters are increasingly influenced by the 'image' presented by the rival candidates for office in successfully incorporating those issues. All these factors were in evidence during the 2002 election. Chancellor Schröder's success in being able – at least temporarily – to meet the concerns of voters, especially in eastern Germany, must account for the governing coalition's ability to hold on to office.

As Kitschelt (2000) has pointed out, the German alignment of electoral competition is particularly unconducive to liberalizing economic reform. Despite modernization and a re-orientation towards the *neue Mitte* under Schröder, the SPD retains residual ties to the labour movement and an important electoral constituency of trade union member manual workers committed to 'solidaristic' labour markets and the welfare state. The CDU/CSU (Christian–Social Union) electorate is a complex coalition of social groups, including a not inconsiderable constituency of trade union members. In a fluid electorate in which voting decisions revolve around issues and policies, for either of the *Volksparteien* to break away from the orthodoxies of the social market economy in favour of liberalization would be a high-risk strategy bordering on electoral suicide.

Political Culture in a Unified Germany

Political culture relates to a common set of values, beliefs and attitudes towards the political system. Democratic institutions rely for legitimacy on supportive citizen attitudes towards the principles of democracy. A distinction is often made between 'diffuse support' – a reservoir of goodwill towards democracy – and a more pragmatic type of 'specific support' related to economic well-being. Unsurprisingly, given their different histories, east and west Germans exhibit different attitudes towards democracy and democratic institutions.

Contrary to initial expectations, East/West differences in political culture have persisted in the decade since unification, to the extent that it may appear that two distinctive cultures exist alongside one another. Integral to any explanation of the differences is the contrasting economic development of the two parts of Germany. In the west, rapid economic growth, full employment and widespread affluence served to anchor liberal democracy by the 1960s. In the east, by contrast, the post-unification economy remains heavily dependent on continuing state subventions. Unemployment continues to be around 18 per cent, almost three times the western level, and GDP per capita is still only some three-fifths of that in the west.

This persistent economic imbalance underlies the analysis made in Chapter 13, which examines the problem of the 'two cultures' by drawing on the evidence provided by opinion poll data. They show that despite the efforts of the federal government, both unemployment and the fear of unemployment are dominant themes expressed by easterners. Their concerns mean that they have a largely socio-economic conception of democracy rather than, as in the west, a liberal democratic one.

It is important to bear in mind that the impact of unification has been far greater in the east than in the west, and it would be more accurate to describe easterners as 'dissatisfied democrats' rather than as being against the political system. Nevertheless, support for democratic institutions depends on a continuing high level of state intervention and redistributive policies. It remains to be seen whether this specific support will broaden into more diffuse endorsement in line with the political culture of western Germany. (One very positive indication is that, in contrast to older people, the younger generation of under-30s expresses itself satisfied with democracy.) In the meantime, support for democratic institutions is heavily dependent on the 'output' of the system, and the response of east Germans to a sustained period of decline in the national economy is somewhat unpredictable.

The End of the Virtuous Circle

The remarkable success of the Federal Republic was built on its prowess in the export field. This is, perhaps, less surprising (given the historical strengths of key sectors in German industry) than the manner in which successive governments of the Federal Republic fashioned a statecraft which allowed Germany access to export markets and made the progress of the German economy acceptable to its partners and competitors. By combining a readiness to contribute German budgetary resources with a commitment to collective goals and institutional structures (reflexive multilateralism), Germany became a very significant international actor and the European and international systems learnt to live with (and, indeed, welcomed) a strong and powerful Germany. The resource crunch occasioned by German unity and declining economic prowess now calls this into question. A Germany forced to take on an increasingly bottom-line view of its contributions to the EU and constrained in playing its 'civilian power' role in the stabilization of conflict and in collective defence risks breaking the virtuous circle that existed between the internal and external dimensions of the German model. Other states have a positive interest in the multilateral fora which have been built in no small part on German economic strength. Living with a weak Germany is now imposing more strains than living with a Germany that some regarded as too strong.

A German Europe or a European Germany?

The interaction between Germany and its European environment has been crucial both for Germany and for the character of European integration. In the founding decades of the Federal Republic its identity was profoundly affected by its commitment to European integration. European integration acted as a very powerful force on a divided and defeated Germany seeking to re-establish its capacity to act internationally in order to lift the restrictions placed upon it after the war. It saw in European integration a policy which would give its neighbours enough confidence to lift these provisions. An export-orientated economic structure gave West Germany a fundamental interest in the creation of frameworks for opening up trade at the European level.

Participation in European multilateral fora was complemented and deepened by the development of a privileged bilateral relationship with the European state which had originally been keenest to limit the external capacity of the Federal Republic: France. Focused initially on reconciliation, the Franco–German relationship became a vehicle for collective action bilaterally and in multilateral fora, which made growth in German economic capacity acceptable. Economic growth in turn helped internally to strengthen popular attachments to the Federal Republic; initially conditional on economic success, these gradually diffused into a more fundamental allegiance to the West German state. Those attachments were 'post-national' and in part projected outwards into 'Europe'. This Europeanized state identity increasingly resonated in affiliational terms at both mass and elite level. The consensus on the desirability of European integration became a central element in the wider political consensus that developed in the Federal Republic. It was widely perceived as part of a virtuous circle which transformed the Federal Republic into a stable, liberal democratic state embedded at the heart of a wider (West) European stability.

The creation of a European Germany was a central aspiration and to a very considerable extent an achievement of the old Federal Republic. These factors had greatly increased trust in Germany and were a central element in making German unity, when the opportunity arose, acceptable to Germany's European neighbours. In the early post-unity years the commitment to a European Germany continued, and even to some extent deepened as Germany became even more European. At the same time Germany began to visibly shape its surrounding European environment. In the reconstitution of Europe post-Wall there was a considerable element of institutional export, most notably in relation to Economic and Monetary Union (EMU; see Bulmer, Jeffery and Paterson, 2000). This process of Germanization was aided greatly by Germany's readiness to undertake cheque-book diplomacy and to lubricate agreements by side-payments.

In recent years the interaction between Germany and Europe has become more complex. There is a resource crunch occasioned by the costs of unification, Germany's declining economic prowess and the imperatives of the Stability Pact. This reduces Germany's reach and shaping capacity and makes it much readier to advance an explicit national interest. Generational change also has the effect, especially marked in the transformation from Kohl to Schröder, of increasing the readiness to speak in terms of national interest, although this continues to be accompanied by a commitment to long-term institutional change (see Chapter 10). In the European Union liberalization is starting to bite deeply into embedded interests in a much weaker Germany characterized by high levels of unemployment and is now quite often resisted by a whole range of German political actors from Minister-Presidents through to the Chancellor. Germany is now becoming less European. Continuing Europeanization in some sectors coexists with resistance in others, and 'a European Germany might look more contingent and precarious' (see Chapter 8). Germany will remain committed to the European Union as a framework but its economic weakness will reduce its shaping capacity. In a worst case analysis it will export this economic weakness throughout the European area in a new vicious circle.

Germany and the New Europe: Paying for Enlargement

From a German perspective enlargement brings both costs and benefits. The economic benefits are a much wider market and greatly increased opportunities to evade the labour market rigidities that have depressed German economic performance in a new division of labour where low-value processes are outsourced by German firms. The political benefits are associated with pushing the border of western Europe further eastwards and creating a zone of stability on Germany's eastern flank. This would be especially helpful in relation to Justice and Home Affairs.

There are, however, a number of costs. The budgetary threat to the Federal Republic is the most palpable. The ability of the Federal Republic, always the largest net contributor to the EU budget, to bear any marked increase in contribution must be seriously in doubt. The new government, already confronted with a large budget deficit, will overshoot the 3 per cent limit on budget deficits allowed under EU rules but is under huge pressure to keep this margin as small as possible. At a political level there is a danger that a wider Europe would lead to gridlock.

As we shall see in Chapter 10, the reaction of the German government to these dangers has been less convincing than the consistent leadership it displayed on EMU. The institutional dilemmas were only very partially tackled at the Nice Summit of EU leaders in 2000. Since then, the Federal Government has been the leading player in the debate, and hopes to instrumentalize the European Convention on institutional reform to shape the outcome at the Intergovernmental Conference (IGC) that will conclude reform in 2004. This policy was reflected in the nomination of Joschka Fischer as the official German representative to the Convention after the Federal election. It is sometimes assumed that enlargement would restructure preferences in the EU in a German-led direction given the marked economic interdependence between Germany and the accession countries and Germany's role as the main contributor to the budget. Whilst this argument has some current plausibility, two caveats must be entered. Germany's increasing inability and unwillingness to adopt the paymaster role constrains the exercise of budgetary power by Germany. Second, in the area of European Security and Defence Policy (ESDP) the enlargement of the North Atlantic Treaty Organization (NATO) will ensure that the post-EU enlargement will have a higher proportion of NATO members than the present EU, and this is likely to strengthen Atlanticist tendencies in security policy and decrease pressure for ESDP.

One difficult and unresolved issue for Germany is the status of the Turkish application for membership of the EU. On budgetary, movement of labour and human rights grounds the German government would find Turkish membership very difficult. On the other hand, given the large number of Turks in Germany who will be increasingly enfranchised (see Chapter 11), the rejection of a Turkish application on incompatibility of culture grounds in the manner advanced by Chancellor Kohl in the past is clearly not possible. There is also very strong pressure from the USA which is keen to stabilize NATO's eastern flank against Islamic fundamentalism by admitting Turkey to the EU. This will be a difficult issue for the EU but the large number of Turkish citizens in Germany and the need to repair relations with the US administration render it especially difficult for Germany.

On the question of paying the financial costs of enlargement the German government has continued to favour externalizing the costs by supporting a lowish level of support for applicant countries in the area of the Common Agricultural Policy (CAP) and regional and structural funds. New member states will be offered 25 per cent of the direct farm aid received by existing EU farmers in 2004, rising to 40 per cent in 2007 and by 10 per cent per annum thereafter. Without substantial cuts in the basic levels of agricultural support, the expanded CAP will entail massive costs. Enfeebled by conflict on too many fronts, Chancellor Schröder acceded in 2002 to a French proposal to freeze rather than cut agricultural support for existing member states for six years after 2007. This decision was arguably necessary in order to secure enlargement, but the price is potentially high. The level of protection offered to Western European farmers will continue to block the entry of Third World agricultural products into the EU, and the low level of support offered to the Central European applicants will further alienate significant elements of the electorate in these states.

Defence and Security: Still a Civilian Power?

Defence and security policies in West Germany were structured by the imperatives of the Cold War and territorial defence. The Federal Republic was a consumer rather than a producer of security, and the defence of Germany was embedded in wider NATO strategic doctrines The assumptions that underpinned the wider West German consensus on the relationship between territorial defence and wider NATO doctrines were beginning to erode at the end of the 1980s in the face of Gorbachev's policy of detente. As we shall see in Chapter 9, the post-Cold War Federal Republic was often identified as 'a civilian power': one that embraces military force as an *ultima ratio*, and then only multilaterally on the basis of a clear mandate from a legitimate source of international authority such as the UN. There was also a fairly widespread assumption that NATO would not occupy the central position as the key security provider in the future though there was disagreement as to whether the OSCE, a broad pan-European organization (the Organization for Security and Cooperation in Europe), or the EU would be the focus of security in the future.

The last decade has turned out quite differently. The security and human dilemmas faced by the long-drawn-out agony of former Yugoslavia have led to a redrawing of German security doctrines and it is now prepared to take part in a wide range of peacekeeping interventions, even when (as in Kosovo) the international legal basis was partially flawed. The crisis in former Yugoslavia also quickly exposed the limitations of the EU and the OSCE as security providers while NATO continued to be central. Indeed, Defence Minister Volker Rühe was the principal European exponent of NATO enlargement.

The incremental but steady increase in Germany's propensity to employ force has led many to question whether Germany is still a 'civilian power'. It may be argued that ultimately Germany remains a 'civilian power' because it continues to be reluctant to employ force, and even then only once all other methods have been exhausted and in pursuit not of national interests but of wider international public goods (Maull, 2000, pp. 1–24). It is certainly the case that Germany remains a civilian society where there is little public enthusiasm for armed intervention. Power is seen in the context of some wider goal, not as an end in itself. The changes are, however, equally manifest. First, Germany, like other states, increasingly employs coercive diplomacy. Second, civilian power relied very heavily on soft power, and the size of German financial resources. The state of the German economy would now seem to preclude extensive use of the cheque book.

Germany's Role in the Wider World

In the post-war era Germany's relations with (and impact on) the wider world have been highly constrained. The aim of foreign policy throughout much of the old Federal Republic was to overcome the disadvantages of Germany's divided and semi-sovereign status. Its interest in the wider world lay in securing American backing for its security needs and wider international support for its claims to legitimacy as against those of the rival German state, the German Democratic Republic (GDR). By the 1980s West Germany, underpinned by a massively successful economy, was a key member of the European Community and NATO and had become a leading regional power. Germany's role as regional power has increased in importance since unification and there are few who would question that it is *the* leading power within the European Union. Ultimately, however, Germany's foreign policy depends on a high-performance economy. The resource crunch created by the costs of unification and the weak performance of the economy is beginning to erode that position.

Although Germany is perceived within Europe as being a more significant power than the UK or France, unlike them it has had very little global reach. It is, of course, the case that France and the UK exaggerate the global role conferred on them by Permanent Membership of the Security Council, possession of nuclear weapons and the institutionalized links they have with their former colonies. In the present system there is, after all, only one superpower: the USA. Nevertheless it is difficult to deny that France and the UK are powers of a different order from Germany. In the recent Iraq crisis their Permanent Membership of the United Nations Security Council conferred on them a crucial role, whilst Germany as a non-permanent member was largely absent; a marginal player.

Given the huge power disparities between the USA and Europe, a global role for a European power can only exist in relation to the USA. The UK has sought to maximize its international influence by acting as the USA's most reliable partner. France possesses a greater degree of autonomy and often occupies a symbolic position of distance from the USA. In 1989, President George Bush offered Germany 'a partnership in leadership' in which Germany would increasingly play a global role, commensurate with its economic strength. This was an option Germany turned down in the Gulf Crisis. In the intervening decade, it has dropped many of its objections to playing a greater extra European role but the results have been very mixed. It is true that Germany now makes a contribution to a large number of peacekeeping operations, but there is very little appetite for increasing such intervention, much less tying it to a global strategy. Three factors militate against such a development: first, a resource crunch now constrains German possibilities; second, Germany remains a civilian society with little appetite for military intervention; and finally, Germany as a trading nation tends towards a mercantilist neutralism in interstate relations.

In its attitude towards the war on terrorism Germany has followed a somewhat erratic course. Initially, after 11 September Chancellor Schröder promised full solidarity to the American administration and, in November 2001, he led a governmental initiative to facilitate the deployment of German troops in Afghanistan. In the election campaign of 2002, however, the Chancellor indicated his strong opposition to German intervention in the Iraq crisis even if it were supported by a UN mandate. Chancellor Schröder's position was novel in two senses. First, it is unprecedented for a German Chancellor to attempt (and, indeed, to secure) electoral advantage through distancing himself from the USA. The Chancellor's lack of readiness to back an intervention legitimized by the United Nations is equally unprecedented and marks a significant retreat from Germany's traditional posture of 'reflexive multilateralism'. Both responses indicate a more self-confident Germany which is more prepared to decide its own priorities. The downside is a loss in influence in multilateral fora such as NATO and the United Nations.

German preferences now differ more widely from the USA across a range of issues. Germany remains a state where environmental policy is important. Here it was hoped that Germany could play a global role through the European Union. The strong unilateral focus of American policy, its brusque rejection of the Kyoto Agreement and its resistance to multilateral initiatives in environmental policy have been perceived as deeply disappointing in Germany. The rejection by the USA of a proposed International Criminal Court engendered deep unease in a country whose disregard of international legal norms had rendered it a universal object of criticism after the Second World War. All of these tensions surfaced in 2002–03 in the wider debate surrounding the question of German intervention in the Iraq crisis where Germany was caught between Iraq and a hard place. Given the centrality of the German relationship to the USA and Germany's dependence on exports, it had been assumed that Germany would use its non-permanent role in the Security Council to offer increased support for the USA. As the Iraq crisis deepened, however, the German Government ruled out armed participation in Iraq even if such an intervention was mandated by the Security Council. Its stance (taken in close alignment with France) inflicted very serious damage on US–German relations and polarized the European Union, thereby threatening to undermine the central purpose of post-war German diplomacy.

The Future of the German Model

The close connection between the internal and external dimensions of the German model makes the long-term future of German political economy a matter of grave concern to its European Union and international partners. It is difficult to take an optimistic view of Germany's economic prospects. In the face of negative economic forecasts in the immediate aftermath of the 2002 election, and in the absence of any real impetus for 'supply side' reform, the new government's austerity programme of spending cuts and tax increases seems likely to prove counter-productive. Many fear that the country is running out of time: whilst there is still a 'window of opportunity' to tackle the root cause of economic weakness, procrastination could result in irreparable structural damage.

The weak start to Schröder's second term in office suggests that his government lacks a clearly defined reform agenda. With stirrings of unrest within the government parties, leadership manoeuvres in the opposition CDU/CSU, and a funding scandal in the FDP, the political class does not appear to be shaping up to the challenge. What does seem clear, however, is that German politics is set for a more conflictual course in the medium-term future; either conflict accompanying belated attempts to reform labour markets and the welfare state, or recriminations over policy failure and economic decline. The crucial question for German politics will be how effectively a political system geared to consensus will be able to absorb the polarizing conflicts that lie ahead.

1

Government at the Centre

KLAUS H. GOETZ

According to Article 65 of the German Constitution – the Basic Law – the Federal government consists of the Federal Chancellor and the Federal ministers: together they form the political apex of the Federal executive. The provisions of the Constitution and political conventions as they have developed since the foundation of the Federal Republic in 1949 have placed the executive firmly at the centre of the German political system. Konrad Adenauer's election as the first Chancellor of the Federal Republic on 15 September 1949 (with the narrowest of majorities) might, at the time, have seemed like a throwback to the Weimar Republic, the democratic state that had come into being in 1919 and had been liquidated by the Nazi regime in 1933. Not only were there striking parallels between the Weimar Constitution and the Basic Law in respect of the definition of the powers and responsibilities of the Chancellor; even the person of Adenauer himself – who, at the time of taking office, was already 73 – seemed to point to the past, for Adenauer's political career had begun during the Wilhelmine Empire. Yet, in retrospect, it is clear that links with the Weimar past notwithstanding, the executive led by Adenauer heralded a new departure in the history of German government. Its defining features included an unambiguous concentration of executive authority in the government and its members, which restricts the indirectly elected Federal President to a largely ceremonial role; full parliamentary accountability of the government; and a remarkable degree of stability in government institutions and leadership personnel. Executive authority, parliamentary accountability and stability have thus characterized the experience of government at the centre since 1949.

The following discussion defines the position of Federal government in the wider context of the key political institutions; clarifies the

17

relationships between the government as a collegiate body (the Cabinet), the ministers and the Chancellor; and concludes with rival scenarios for the future of government at the centre. To understand how the government operates, it is necessary to take account of three basic tensions in executive organization: between politics and bureaucracy; institutions and people; and formality and informality. The Federal government is an eminently political body but, at the same time, it is an administrative authority, composed of the Federal ministries and the Chancellor's Office. It is a political and administrative institution with deeply entrenched ways of doing things; yet key individuals are able to reshape the offices that they hold, as is demonstrated by the impact of successive incumbents on the chancellorship. And while many aspects of the operation of the Federal government are highly formalized, unofficial arrangements regularly complement, and sometimes supersede, formal institutions and operating procedures.

The Federal Government in Context

Government at the centre implies parliamentary, party, coalition, federalized and Europeanized government. This fivefold characterization not only helps to locate the Federal government in the wider political system, but it also points to the nature of the key relationships the government entertains with other political institutions and gives a first indication of the chief political constraints under which it operates.

Parliamentary Government

The Federal government bears the hallmarks of a classical parliamentary government. Thus the Federal Chancellor, as the head of government, is elected by the Bundestag, the Federal Parliament. The Chancellor must be a member of the Bundestag and may, at any time, be replaced through a constructive vote of no confidence, through which a successor is elected by a majority of the members of the Bundestag. Ministers are formally appointed (and dismissed) by the Federal President upon the binding proposal of the Chancellor rather than being elected by the Bundestag; but they must take their oath of office before Parliament. Both the Chancellor and the ministers are fully accountable to the Bundestag, its committees and to individual MPs, who enjoy extensive rights of information, consultation, scrutiny and control *vis-à-vis* the Federal government, in addition to very extensive legislative powers (von Beyme, 1997). Parliamentary accountability is secured through formal means, such as the right of Parliament to elect the Chancellor, regular reporting requirements imposed on the government, parliamentary questions and interpellations, the exhaustive scrutiny of bills introduced by the government, and the detailed parliamentary monitoring of the implementation of the Federal budget, but also through many informal mechanisms by which Parliament reaches into the executive process (Saalfeld, 1998), such as regular meetings between ministers and MPs from the governing parties to consider forthcoming legislative initiatives. The majority parliamentary parties and the government are, accordingly, said to constitute a 'composite actor' (*Handlungsverbund*: von Beyme, 1997, p. 358). Early close cooperation may also be required with the opposition, as in the case of fairly frequent constitutional amendments, which can only be passed by two-thirds majorities in both the Bundestag and the Bundesrat (the representation of Germany's 16 Länder governments: Helms, 1997).

Party Government

While parliamentary government is an expression of constitutional norms, party government has developed as a constitutional convention. The concept of 'party government' may, indeed, be 'nebulous if not wholly obscure', as Blondel (2000, p. 1) has observed, but it serves to emphasize the close link and mutual dependence between the government and the governing parties that are typical of most Western democracies. The Federal government is constituted after the quadrennial Federal elections on the basis of coalition negotiations between the main representatives of the national parties and their parliamentary groups; majority party leaders typically join the government as ministers or, in the case of the largest party, Chancellor; major political initiatives are usually approved by the governing parties' national decision-making bodies prior to their submission to Cabinet; and the withdrawal of support by one of the political parties that make up the governing coalition inevitably spells the end of the government. Political parties do not just decide on the formation and termination of the government; given the interlinkage between government and majority parties the latter can themselves be regarded as governing institutions.

Coalition Government

Coalitions have been the rule throughout the history of the Federal Republic, as a proportional electoral system has prevented either of the two main political camps – the CDU/CSU and the SPD – from gaining an absolute majority. Only once, in 1957, did the CDU/CSU win an outright majority in the Bundestag, but Chancellor Adenauer chose to invite two ministers from the small German Party (DP) to join the government (see Table 1.1). With the exception of three very brief interludes of minority caretaker governments in 1966, 1969 and 1982 – in each case after the breakdown of a coalition – the Federal government has always been based on a coalition commanding a majority in the Bundestag. Coalitions have not only been compatible with stable government; they have underpinned continuity in executive institutions and personnel. Chancellor Konrad Adenauer headed CDU/CSU-dominated coalitions between 1949 and 1963, and his last coalition, which included the Free Democrats, was continued by his successor, Ludwig Erhard, until 1966. After the brief experience of a 'grand coalition' between the CDU/CSU and the SPD from 1966 to 1969, under Chancellor Kurt-Georg Kissinger, the Social–Liberal pact between the SPD and the FDP lasted from 1969 until 1982 (following the resignation of Willy Brandt as Chancellor in 1974, Helmut Schmidt was elected head of government).

TABLE 1.1 *Federal governments since 1949*

Legislative period	Cabinets/Chancellors	Coalition partners
1949–53	1 Adenauer	CDU, CSU, FDP, DP
1953–57	2 Adenauer	CDU, CSU, FDP, DP, GB/BHE
1957–61	3 Adenauer	CDU, CSU, DP
1961–65	4 Adenauer (until 1962)	CDU, CSU, FDP
	5 Adenauer (1962–63)	
	1 Erhard (from 1963)	
1965–69	2 Erhard (until 1966)	CDU, CSU, FDP
	1 Kiesinger (from 1966)	CDU, CSU, SPD
1969–72	1 Brandt	SPD, FDP
1972–76	2 Brandt (until 1974)	SPD, FDP
	1 Schmidt (from 1974)	
1976–80	2 Schmidt	SPD, FDP
1980–83	3 Schmidt (until 1982)	SPD, FDP
	1 Kohl (from 1982)	CDU, CSU, FDP
1983–87	2 Kohl	CDU, CSU, FDP
1987–90	3 Kohl	CDU, CSU, FDP
1990–94	4 Kohl	CDU, CSU, FDP
1994–98	5 Kohl	CDU, CSU, FDP
1998–2002	1 Schröder	SPD, Greens
2002–	2 Schröder	SPD, Greens

DP = Deutsche Partei
GB/BHE = Gesamtdeutscher   Block/Bund   der   Heimat-vertriebenen   und
Entrechteten

Schmidt was succeeded by Helmut Kohl who, together with the FDP, won four successive Federal elections in 1983, 1987, 1990 and 1994. The Federal elections of 1998, which brought to power an SPD–Green coalition headed by Chancellor Gerhard Schröder, broke the link between coalition and continuity. For the first time in its history, the Federal Republic experienced a complete rather than partial change of government, since none of the three former coalition partners – the CDU, the CSU and the FDP – were represented in the new government. But the re-election of the Red–Green coalition in September 2002, which had seemed unlikely until a few weeks before the elections, once again proved that coalition and durable government go hand in hand.

Federalized Government

Germany is a federal polity, and decentralization of policy-making powers, responsibilities and resources is one of its fundamental constitutional principles. The Federal government is thus only one among 17 governments, as each of Germany's 16 Länder has its own fully-fledged executive (see Chapter 2). Combined with a tradition of strong non-executive institutions, such as the independent Bundesbank or the Federal Constitutional Court, federalism gives Germany the character of a polycentric polity, in which the scope for unilateral action on the part of the Federal government is closely circumscribed (Katzenstein 1987).

Yet the constitutional principle of a vertical division of powers conflicts with the political principles of Federal involvement and responsibility. Federalism does not equal effective political decentralization. There are at least two points to note here. First, the Federal government tends to be held politically responsible, even where the Constitution envisages problem-solving by the Länder or local government. The range of political matters with which the Federal executive deals is scarcely less extensive and popular demands and expectations no less urgent than in unitary systems. Politically, the Federal government can rarely afford to neglect a particular policy issue, even if its relevant formal powers might be very restricted. Second, the German practice of 'cooperative federalism' requires close cooperation between the Federal government and the Länder, most notably in legislation. The Basic Law grants the Länder the power to participate in the Federal legislative process via the Bundesrat, through which all Federal legislation must pass. Depending on the nature of the matter to be legislated, the Bundesrat either enjoys an absolute veto over legislation approved by the Bundestag or it may exercise a suspensory veto, which must then be overturned with an absolute majority in the Bundestag (or a two-thirds majority, if the Bundesrat vetoes the draft law with a two-thirds majority). Federal–Länder cooperation is, therefore, often a key prerequisite for the successful realization of the Federal government's political and legislative ambitions.

Europeanized Government

The Federal government is part of a multi-level governance structure that extends both 'downwards' to the Länder and local government, and 'upwards' to a host of international and transnational organizations in which Germany participates and which increasingly share in the governance of the country. Of these, the European Union is the most important (in the field of defence and security policy, this distinction belongs to NATO); but there are many others, such as the Council of Europe, the United Nations with its many suborganizations, the OECD, or cooperation in the form of the G-8 summits. The orientation towards European integration and the concomitant 'opening of the state' (Wessels, 2000) constitute defining features of the German polity (see Chapter 10 below). Partly as a result of the historical co-evolution of the Federal Republic and the European integration project, German statehood has become progressively Europeanized (Knodt and Kohler-Koch, 2000; Dyson and Goetz, 2003; also see Chapter 8 below), so that there is a very intensive interaction between national policy-makers and EU actors, extending to virtually all fields of domestic public policy and, increasingly, also to foreign and security policy. Policy impulses coming from the supranational level have to be synchronized with national preferences and priorities. For example, it is estimated that approximately one-fifth of all laws passed by the Bundestag are the result of EU-level initiatives, with a much higher average in some fields (von Beyme, 1997, p. 186). The national legislative agenda is, accordingly, only partly under the control of national law-makers, let alone the Federal government.

   What follows from the political and institutional embeddedness of the Federal government and the permeability of boundaries between the government, political and parliamentary parties, the Länder and the Bundesrat, and EU institutions? The autonomy of the Federal government in the German political system is low. Unilateral action is rare; even when it might be legal, it is seldom politically feasible. Managing cooperative ties is, therefore, a preoccupation of both the political and the administrative parts of the Federal executive. The need to cooperate should not, however, be confused with a lack of executive authority, for the government's power resides in its capacity to shape and drive the agenda, to negotiate, persuade, cajole and, if necessary, 'bribe' other decision-makers on whose cooperation, or at least acquiescence, it depends. A telling example of the latter tactic were the last-minute promises of Federal financial assistance made by Chancellor Schröder to a number of Länder governments in July 2000 in an attempt to secure the adoption of the government's tax reform legislation in the Bundesrat (Günter Bannas, 'Dominospiel in einer langen Bonner Nacht. Wie Schröder und Eichel ihre Mehrheit zusammenbrachten', *Frankfurter Allegemeine Zeitung* (*FAZ*), 15 July 2000). In the event, Schröder was able to 'buy off' key states, thus achieving a political success that had long eluded the Kohl government. Government at the centre is not about the untrammelled exercise of power, but about the creative use of institutions and people, political and administrative resources, and formal and informal governing devices in the service of realizing the executive's political objectives.

Inside the Federal Executive

Three principles shape the internal life of the government, as laid down in Article 65 of the Basic Law. First, the *cabinet* principle states that 'the Federal government resolves differences of opinion amongst ministers' and decides on matters of political importance. Second, the *departmental* principle gives ministers independent responsibility for conducting the affairs of their departments. Finally, the *Chancellor* principle means that the Chancellor 'determines and is responsible for the general guidelines of policy' (these guidelines must be observed by ministers in conducting their departmental, business). As the following discussion will seek to show, these principles are open to political interpretation; their relative importance has varied over time and across policy areas, and a degree of tension amongst them is inevitable.

Cabinet

As of October 2002, the Federal government consisted of the Chancellor and the 13 Federal ministers (the smallest government since 1949: see Table 1.2). The government as a collegiate body is often referred to as the Cabinet. In addition to the Chancellor and the ministers, non-voting participants in the weekly Cabinet meetings, usually held on

Wednesdays, include the Chief of the Chancellery, the ministers of state in the Chancellery, the heads of the Federal President's Office, the Federal Press and Information Office, the Chancellor's Office (i.e., the Chancellor's personal office in the Chancellery), and a scribe. Others who are customarily in attendance are the minister of state in the Foreign Ministry dealing with EU affairs, the deputy press spokesman of the Federal government, and the heads of division in the Chancellery. Still others attend more irregularly. For example, the head of the Bundesbank is usually present at the meeting at which the government adopts the Federal draft budget; and key members of the coalition parliamentary parties might be asked to come to a Cabinet meeting to speak to a particular point (Busse, 2001a). Moreover, in his absence, a minister can nominate a parliamentary or administrative state secretary as substitute, although the latter are not allowed to vote in the minister's place.

Cabinet is pre-eminent in that it has wide-ranging prerogatives to consider and decide matters. By law or custom, many issues must formally be settled by Federal government as a collegiate body rather than individual ministers or the Chancellor. In addition to a number of specific matters reserved for Cabinet decision-taking on the basis of constitutional and statutory law, the Common Standing Orders of the Government stipulate that all matters of political importance must be referred to Cabinet for consideration and decision-taking, including,

TABLE 1.2 *Composition of the Federal government as of October 2002*

Office title	Name of holder
Chancellor	Gerhard Schröder (SPD)
Minister of Foreign Affairs	Joschka Fischer (Greens)
Minister of the Interior	Otto Schily (Greens)
Minister of Justice	Brigitte Zypries (SPD)
Minister of Finance	Hans Eichel (SPD)
Minister of Economics and Labour	Wolfgang Clement (SPD)
Minister of Consumer Affairs, Food and Agriculture	Renate Künast (Greens)
Minister of Defence	Peter Struck (SPD)
Minister of Family, Senior Citizens, Women and Youth	Renate Schmidt (SPD)
Minister of Health and Social Security	Ulla Schmidt (SPD)
Minister of Transport and Construction	Manfred Stolpe (SPD)
Minister of Environmental Protection and Nuclear Safety	Jürgen Trittin (SPD)
Minister of Education and Research	Edelgard Bulmahn (SPD)
Minister of Economic Cooperation and Development	Heidemarie Wieczorek-Zeul (SPD)

inter alia, all bills and government ordinances; major ordinances by individual ministries; comments by the Bundesrat on government-sponsored bills; and disagreements between ministers, including major disagreements on plans for the Federal budget. Answers to major parliamentary interpellations and reports to the Bundestag must also pass through Cabinet, as do personnel matters in the case of top officials. Collective decision-taking is thus a fundamental feature of executive policy-making.

Yet Cabinet is not the place where conflicts are typically resolved, for both formal rules and informal conventions put a heavy emphasis on unanimous Cabinet decisions. To the greatest possible extent, interministerial disagreements should be resolved in advance, if necessary through meetings of the relevant Federal ministers under the chairmanship of the Chancellor. A matter is, in principle, only considered ripe for Cabinet consideration once interministerial agreement on all points has been reached. Given this understanding of what constitutes a *kabinettreife Vorlage* ('a proposal ripe for Cabinet'), meetings of the Federal government largely authorize decisions reached elsewhere. Despite an elaborate machinery for conflict resolution comprising both the administrative and the political levels of the executive, unanimity cannot always be secured, and there may be reasons to seek a Cabinet decision, even though substantial interministerial disagreements persist. The most notorious example dates from April 1993, when the then Chancellor, Helmut Kohl, asked the government to approve the participation of German soldiers in NATO observation flights over Bosnia. The FDP argued that the Basic Law did not permit such an operation. By way of a compromise, the coalition parties agreed that the CDU/CSU majority in Cabinet should approve the mission against the votes of the FDP ministers, and that the FDP parliamentary party would subsequently submit this decision to judicial review before the Federal Constitutional Court ('Die "peinlichste Kabinettssitzung des Jahres" ', *Süddeutsche* Zeitung, 2 April 1993). Dissent in Cabinet was not unexpected; rather, agreement to disagree had been reached in advance.

Ministries and Ministers

The rules concerning the demarcation of ministerial portfolios allow for a great deal of flexibility. Departmental organization is a prerogative of the Chancellor; he can establish and abolish ministries through a simple administrative ordinance, and he also determines the interministerial distribution of tasks. Only three ministries – Finance, Defence and

Justice – are, in principle, exempt from this far-reaching organizational power, since they are explicitly mentioned in the Basic Law. Despite the Chancellor's discretion, 'incremental changes' in ministerial organization that produce only 'small modifications of the status quo' have been the norm (Derlien, 1996, p. 564). During the long tenure of Chancellor Kohl, the only genuine innovation was the creation of a Ministry of the Environment, Conservation and Nuclear Safety in 1986 (Pehle, 1998), which has since developed into a high-profile Federal department. During the first Schröder government, no new ministry was created, although the Ministries for Transport and for Construction were merged and dispersed responsibilities for Federal cultural policy were concentrated in the newly-created office of the Federal Commissioner for Culture and Media, overseen by a Minister of State and directly subordinated to the Chancellor (a constitutionally sensitive development given the Länder's prerogatives in this policy domain). However, at the start of his second government, Schröder used his freedom in ministerial organization to signal key political priorities. He merged the ministries of economy and labour, thus creating a 'superministry' to push forward economic regeneration, and transferred the responsibilities of the Government Commissioner for the New Länder to the Ministry of Transport and Construction, to be led by a prominent SPD representative from the east, the former Minister-President of Brandenburg, Manfred Stolpe.

Under the Basic Law, the Chancellor enjoys the exclusive right to form the government. In some respects, the Chancellor's discretion in ministerial appointments is considerable. Federal ministers need not be Members of Parliament or have occupied any other elective office. In forming both his governments, Schröder made extensive use of this provision, for five of the 15 ministers he initially chose in 1998 were not members of the Bundestag; no previous Federal government had included so many ministers without a parliamentary mandate. His second government, too, included high-profile ministers recruited from outside, such as the new 'superminister' in charge of economics and labour, Wolfgang Clement, who up to his appointment had been Minister-President of North Rhine-Westphalia, Germany's most populous Land. In other respects, the Chancellor's room for manoeuvre is more closely restricted. With regard to ministers from the Green Party, Schröder accepted, in principle, the nominations from the coalition partner without question; in this, he followed a convention that had evolved over the decades, and had become an unwritten rule under Chancellor Kohl. Nonetheless, some constitutional decorum needs to be maintained. Following the resignation of Economics Minister Jürgen

Möllemann in 1993, the FDP's choice of successor, Günter Rexrodt, publicly reminded the Chancellor that he had no discretion over his appointment. Angered, Kohl reaffirmed, equally publicly, his prerogatives under the Basic Law, although this rebuke did nothing to change political realities and Rexrodt was duly appointed. Within his own party, the Chancellor's discretion is much larger. It has sometimes been suggested that a great deal of attention is paid to achieving a certain balance in terms of ministers' regional background, gender, religious denomination (especially in the case of the CDU/CSU) and political outlook; but is it difficult to determine the real influence of these factors, and the diversity of the Cabinet probably owes as much to the diversity of the pool from which ministerial appointees are selected as to any careful Cabinet engineering.

With the election of the first Schröder government, continuity in key political personnel, highlighted above as an important feature of postwar executives, was initially broken, as neither the Chancellor nor any of his ministers had previous ministerial experience at Federal level. This contrasted with the formation of earlier Federal governments, which had always included members of the previous administration, allowing some ministers exceptionally long periods in office. The best-known example is Hans-Dietrich Genscher, former FDP leader, who first became Foreign Minister in May 1974 under Chancellor Schmidt, having already been Minister of the Interior for almost five years. Genscher headed the Foreign Ministry for 18 years (with barely three weeks' interruption at the end of the last Schmidt government), until he unexpectedly resigned in May 1992. Schröder's first government was also unusual in that its four years in office saw the resignation or dismissal of no less than seven ministers. This included the resignation of Oskar Lafontaine as Minister of Finance and SPD party chairman less than five months after the formation of the new government, and, as something of a denouement, the dismissal of Rudolf Scharping, chairman of the SPD between 1993 and 1995, as Minister of Defence a few weeks prior to the 2002 elections. The formation of the second government in October 2002 saw the departure of a further five ministers. But the Red–Green coalition also bears out the stabilizing influence of the coalition principle, as the three Green ministers remained secure in their posts.

In running their departments, ministers rely on an administrative apparatus that follows a common blueprint. In addition to the minister, the leadership of the ministry consists of between one and three administrative state secretaries and one or two parliamentary state secretaries. Administrative state secretaries, who are civil servants, occupy the highest grade in the Federal administration, and are regularly amongst the key figures in the ministerial policy process. They deputize for the minister in running the department, and they operate directly at the interface between politics and administration. Their special position is recognized in their status as 'political civil servants' as defined by Article 36 of the Federal Civil Service Law. It is acknowledged that they need to be in permanent basic agreement with the government's views and objectives in order to perform their task of helping to transform the government's political will into administrative action. Political civil servants, who also include heads of division, need not be recruited from amongst career civil servants. Already by the early 1980s, some 40 per cent of political civil servants had been recruited to their position from outside the ministry in which they served (Mayntz and Derlien, 1989, p. 392); of these about half were genuine external recruits, not previously employed in the Federal administration. As political civil servants, they can also at any time be sent into early retirement by the political leadership, and ministers use this possibility frequently (Derlien, 1984; Goetz, 1997; Goetz, 1999).

While the function of an administrative state secretary is clearly defined as the administrative head of the department, the position of parliamentary state secretaries – first established in 1967 – has remained 'difficult' and 'nebulous' (König, 1992, p. 123). Parliamentary state secretaries must be members of the Bundestag (following the election of the Schröder government, the law was amended to allow for an exception to this rule in the case of parliamentary state secretaries serving in the Chancellery). They do not formally belong to the Federal government, yet in coalition negotiations these posts, too, are subject to intense bargaining. The Law on the Legal Status of Parliamentary State Secretaries defines their function only in the broadest of terms: to support the minister (or, in the case of parliamentary state secretaries in the Chancellery, the Chancellor) in his governmental functions. According to the Standing Orders of the Federal Government, the parliamentary state secretary generally deputizes for the minister in making official statements to the Bundestag, the Bundesrat and in Cabinet meetings. Beyond these stipulations, the parliamentary state secretaries' tasks are, in principle, determined by the minister. In general, the nurturing of relations with the parliamentary parties, committees and working groups, and often also with Länder governments and the Bundesrat, constitute a major part of their work. As politicians, they tend to focus their attention on the external relations of their ministry rather than its internal processes. Parliamentary state secretaries are sometimes referred to as 'junior ministers'. When the post was first established, there were hopes that it might develop into a training ground for future ministers. In the successive Schmidt governments, parliamentary state secretaries did, indeed, frequently climb up the career ladder, but this has rarely been the case since. Between 1982 and 2002, only four ministers were recruited from amongst parliamentary state secretaries.

There is no clear dividing line between politics and administration in the Federal ministries, either in terms of formal organization or personnel. Below the top leadership level, the ministries are hierarchically organized into divisions, subdivisions and sections. In the words of the Common Standing Orders of the Federal Ministries, 'The section constitutes the fundamental unit in the organizational structure of the ministry. Every task in a ministry must be allocated to a section.' Formally, the section has primary responsibility for policy development (Mayntz and Scharpf, 1975, pp. 67ff.). Heads of section must possess detailed policy expertise and, once they have been appointed to a particular section, they are unlikely to move again, unless they are promoted (the exception to this rule are sections that belong to the political support units: see below). It is not uncommon, therefore, to find the same official in charge of a particular policy issue for many years, if not decades.

However, the traditional picture of a policy process 'from below', in which policy development is driven by the experts at the 'working level' of the ministry, is increasingly in need of revision. Political support and coordination units, which are directly attached to the ministerial leadership and operate outside the main departmental line organization, have greatly gained in importance. The core of the political support units is typically made up of the personal assistants to the minister, the parliamentary and administrative state secretaries, and at least three further offices: the Minister's Office; the Office for Cabinet and Parliamentary Affairs, which is sometimes split into two; and the Press and Information Office, which is often divided into a press office and an office for public relations (Goetz, 1997). Increasingly, these support units do not just monitor the work of the mainline administration and structure access to the ministry's leadership; rather, they direct the work of the line divisions and ensure that the latter 'stay on message'. Thus, the ministerial policy process has, over the years, become more 'top-down', in that political support and coordination units increasingly direct the activities of administrative line units.

The decision to divide the Federal ministerial administration between Bonn and Berlin according to a 'combination model' has given a further impetus to the concentration of directive powers within political support units. There are now two categories of ministries: those with their principal residence in Bonn, and those who have most of their staff in Berlin (BT-Drucksache, 1999; Goetz, 1999). However, both the Federal government as a constitutional organ and the legislature reside in Berlin, so that ministers and their closest aides and advisers necessarily spend most of their time in the capital, regardless of whether they head a Bonn or Berlin ministry. As a result, the traditional model whereby ministerial line units rather than specialized French-style *cabinets ministériels* advise the minister is becoming further eroded.

Given the proximity of these units to the top ministerial leadership, it is not surprising that they should act as key informal training grounds for future top officials, for they cultivate expertise, access and 'political craft' (Goetz, 1997; Goetz, 2000): that is, the capacity to operate effectively in a politicized environment. This is not to say that the Federal senior civil service is comprehensively party-politicized in the sense that membership of the governing parties is a prerequisite for advancement (although the majority of administrative state secretaries and heads of division belong to the governing parties); rather, senior officials, including heads of subdivisions and many heads of section, need to be able to act in a way that maximizes the chances for the realization of the government's political objectives. This requires that they must be able to interact freely with, and enjoy the trust of, political actors not just in their own ministries, but also in Parliament, political parties and Länder governments. The importance of political craft is underlined by the fact that in a sample of Federal ministerial officials covering the top four ranks in 1987, some 86 per cent agreed that 'it is at least as important for a public manager to have a talent for politics as it is to have any special management or technical subject skills' (Aberbach, Derlien and Rockman, 1994, p. 282).

Against this background, it is not surprising that the first Schröder government effected far-ranging changes in ministerial personnel. Between taking office on 27 October and 18 November 1998, the new government sent 51 'political civil servants', mostly administrative state secretaries and heads of division, into early retirement ('Regierung hat 51 Beamte in einstweiligen Ruhestand geschickt', *FAZ*, 19 November 1998) and, by spring 1999, the two top tiers of the Federal ministerial civil service had been comprehensively recast. Staff in ministerial support units were substituted almost without exception; changes in line units were made easier by the fact that new heads of subdivisions and sections dealing with personnel issues were also quickly appointed in most ministries. The sweeping changes in personnel, in particular in political support and coordination units, personnel sections, and sections for general policy development were the result of a mixture of motives. Party-political patronage certainly played a role, as did the desire to promote officials who felt that their careers had been stifled during the long years of Christian–Liberal ascendancy. Arguably, however, political craft mattered more. The new constellation of political forces in the Bundestag and in the government meant that officials' political-administrative networks, nurtured during the long years of Kohl's chancellorship, became invalidated. As political craft depends on officials' access to politicians both within the executive and in Parliament, high-ranking civil servants known to be supporters of the new opposition were unlikely to serve the new government effectively, especially when it came to politically sensitive tasks.

Chancellor, Chancellery and Party

The roles of the Chancellor and the Chancellery have never been determinate (Müller-Rommel, 1997). During the first decade of Adenauer's chancellorship, many argued that the Federal Republic was developing into a 'chancellor democracy', distinguished by the concentration of formal and, in particular, informal political powers in the Chancellor (Ridley, 1966). Strong central coordination of government policy, chancellorial control over (and interference with) the activities of ministers, compliant coalition parties, an executive-dominated Parliament and a marginalized opposition, it was suggested, made the chancellorship into the unrivalled centre of power in the political system. As the last years of Adenauer's tenure and the experiences of his successors have shown, this concentration of powers in the Chancellor cannot be taken for granted (Mayntz, 1980). The strength of Chancellors Erhard, Kiesinger, Brandt, Schmidt, Kohl and Schröder within the Federal executive, and the political system more broadly, has depended on their capacity to mobilize constitutional, party political, coalitional, electoral and policy resources (Smith, 1991; Smith, 1994). In particular, it is the degree of domination that they have exercised over their own party that is often seen as key to their success or failure in office (Clemens, 1994; Clemens, 1998; Paterson, 1981).

However, to recognize the limitations of the Chancellor's powers is not to suggest that he is merely a moderator of conflicting interests and demands; neither should it be denied that the political weight of the Chancellor within the executive has increased during the 1990s and into the first years of the new century. In addition to the Chancellor's constitutional prerogative of determining the membership of the Cabinet, his power to define the 'guidelines of Federal policy' and to declare any such guideline binding on all members of the Federal government deserves highlighting. This constitutional privilege is rarely explicitly invoked; but it underpins the Chancellor's position as the paramount figure within the government. The 'guideline' power, in effect, allows the Chancellor to involve himself in any policy issue and to determine both the government approach and, if he so chooses, policy detail; ministers rarely have the political resources to repel such interference. Since the foundation of the Federal Republic, foreign policy and European integration policy have been policy domains in which chancellorial involvement and intervention have been especially pronounced and continuous (Paterson, 1994); indeed, this focus on foreign and European policy has been identified as a defining feature of 'Chancellor democracy' (Niclauß, 1999; Niclauß, 2001). Under Kohl, European policy was early on established as a pivotal chancellorial domain (Gaddum, 1994), and Kohl's intense engagement with European policy meant that he decisively shaped the course of European integration, including EMU (Dyson and Featherstone, 1999) and the Maastricht Treaty (Fröhlich, 2001). Chancellor Schröder thus followed historical precedent when he, too, chose to interpret his guideline competence very extensively in this field; as in the case of his predecessors, frictions with Cabinet colleagues intent on defending their turf, notably the Foreign Minister, proved inevitable (Bulmer, Maurer and Paterson, 2001; 'Schröder macht Fischer die Europapolitik streitig', *FAZ*, 19 March 2002; Eckart Lohse, 'Die Europapolitik als Streitobjekt', *FAZ*, 20 March 2002). And while Schröder did not create a Ministry for European Affairs, as mooted before the September 2002 elections, he did, for the first time, create a division within the Chancellery devoted exclusively to EU matters, asserting his claims in this policy domain.

The Chancellor is not first amongst equals but, according to the Constitution, the leader of a government whose composition he determines and whose policies he defines. During the long tenure of Chancellor Kohl, his capacity to turn these 'constitutional resources' into effective political power increased. Contributing factors included, in particular, Kohl's growing dominance, if not stranglehold, over his party (Clemens, 1998); the more cooperative stance of the CSU following the death of Kohl's arch-rival, the long-time leader of the CSU, Franz Josef Strauß in October 1988, and the inclusion of Strauß's successor, Theo Weigel, in the Cabinet from April 1989; and the weakness of the FDP, which, at least since the resignation of Foreign Minister Genscher in 1992, lacked both a credible alternative to the Christian–Liberal coalition and heavyweight ministers able to square up to the Chancellor. The 'third life' of Chancellor Kohl after unification (Smith, 1994) therefore saw a progressive centralization of executive power.

Under Schröder, this concentration of executive power in the person and the office of the Chancellor has advanced further. There have been several factors that have facilitated Schröder's dominance over his Cabinet. The single most important was the sudden resignation of Oskar Lafontaine as Minister of Finance and chairman of the SPD in March 1999. With Lafontaine, the only potential challenger to the Chancellor's authority departed. Schröder's subsequent election as party chairman was a foregone conclusion, in view of the absence of any credible alternative. Since then, none of the other SPD ministers has had a sufficiently strong constituency in the party to allow them to oppose Schröder. Schröder's grip has been less forceful as far as his Green coalition partners have been concerned, yet he has been keenly aware – as have been the Greens themselves – that they lack any credible alternative to the SPD–Green coalition (by contrast, the Liberals throughout the Kohl era sought to keep alive the option of switching their coalition partner, although this became less plausible as time went on). Some very public 'dressing downs' for the Green Minister of the Environment, Jürgen Trittin, early on during the first Schröder government, ensured that to the extent that coalition dissent persisted, it was resolved behind close doors, thus cementing Schröder's image as the undisputed leader of his government.

The Chancellery is the most important institutional resource of the Chancellor (König, 1989). It is at the heart of what in comparative executive studies is often referred to as the 'core executive': that is, 'all those organizations and structures which primarily serve to pull together and integrate central government policies, or act as final arbiters within the executive of conflicts between different elements of the government machine' (Dunleavy and Rhodes, 1990, p. 4). Its principal tasks include administrative and political support and advice for the Chancellor in his capacity as chief executive, member of the Bundestag and party leader; for the Chief of the Chancellery and the parliamentary state secretaries – with the title of Ministers of State – working in the Chancellery; and for the government as a collegiate body. The Chancellery is at the hub of interministerial coordination and the management of executive–external relations, with a special emphasis on relations with the governing parties, Parliament, interest groups and the media (Berry, 1989; Busse, 2001a). Several supplementary responsibilities may be added, such as policy planning and development, especially in domains that are of special interest to the Chancellor; monitoring the implementation of the Federal government's political programmes (for instance, the Chancellery is regularly asked to draw up 'political "balance sheets" documenting the results of government performance': König, 1985, p. 45); fire-fighting (i.e., political crisis and ad hoc emergency management in the case of major natural catastrophes, terrorist threats, or foreign policy emergencies); and special tasks that for political or administrative reasons are entrusted to the Chancellery rather than ministerial departments or non-ministerial agencies (an example is the direct supervision of the intelligence services exercised by the Chancellery).

The Chancellor's key aide is the Chief of the Chancellery, whose remit covers, in principle, the full breadth of Federal policies (Busse, 1998). For much of the Kohl chancellorship, a Minister without portfolio fulfilled this role. Chancellor Schröder departed from this model, initially installing a dual leadership consisting of Bodo Hombach as Chief of the Chancellery with the rank of a Minister without portfolio, and Frank-Walter Steinmeier, who was appointed administrative state secretary. Hombach was to focus on political planning and advice to the Chancellor and to deal with politically sensitive special tasks, such as the government's 'Alliance for Jobs' or the international negotiations on the compensation for Jewish slave labour under the Nazi regime. By contrast, Steinmeier was to have prime responsibility for coordinating general government policy ('Heye ist häufig bei Schröder, Schröder taucht oft bei Hombach und Steinmeier auf', *FAZ*, 4 December 1998).

However, the resignation of Hombach in March 1999 provided Schröder with the opportunity to do away with the dual leadership, which had been seen by many as contributing to coordination failures during the early months of the new government. Since then, Steinmeier has remained in sole charge, and although he has retained the rank of an administrative state secretary, his closeness to the Chancellor and his involvement in all aspects of public policy have meant that his power and influence surpasses that of most, if not all, Cabinet ministers. The last Chief of the Chancellery under Kohl, Friedrich Bohl, was once described as the 'man with the oil can', the Chancellor's 'messenger and adviser, servant and executor', a 'sort of prime minister' serving directly the head of government and 'thus a considerably more equal than his Cabinet colleagues' ('Der Mann mit der Ölkanne', *Der Spiegel*, 21 August 1995). The same description also captures Steinmeier's role (Günter Bannas, 'Politischer Beamter in Zentrum der Macht', *FAZ*, 15 December 2000).

In contrast to the Chief of the Chancellery, the remaining top personnel occupy much more narrowly defined roles. Under Schröder – and broadly in line with conventional practice – top appointments include the Press Spokesman of the Federal government, with the rank of administrative state secretary; a further Minister of State who is particularly closely involved in the coordination between the Federal government, the Länder, the Bundestag and the Bundesrat; and the Federal Commissioner for Culture and Media.

Institutions and People

It should have emerged from the preceding discussion that the Federal executive is a complex institution. Complexity is not so much a matter of intricate organigrams or elaborate standing orders; rather, it is found in the intricate interplay of politics and bureaucracy, institutions and people, and formality and informality. The previous sections have already noted the interaction in the governing process between the political and administrative components; Sturm (Chapter 5 in this volume) provides a survey of the use of informal governing devices under the Schröder government. Some comment is, however, warranted as regards the connection between institutions and people (Goetz, 2003). Political institutions, in general, and the political parts of the executive, in particular, are distinguished by the exceptionally close identification between office and office-holder (Göhler, 1994). Personalization is, accordingly, a defining feature of executive organization, especially at the level of top political offices. Comparative executive studies, notably of chief executives and ministers, regularly stress the importance of the personal qualities, dispositions and motives of incumbents and the extent to which individuals shape the office they occupy. At the level of heads of government and core ministers, 'man maketh the office' as much as the 'office maketh the man'.

Examples of this mutual dependence are not difficult to find. Recent writing on the 'governing' or leadership styles' of successive Chancellors underlines that one of the secrets of chancellorial success lies in exploiting the malleability of both the Chancellery and the majority governing party through organizational changes but also, more importantly, decisions on personnel so as to create institutions tailored to the Chancellor's personal needs, priorities and preferences (Korte, 1998; Korte, 2000; Korte, 'In der Präsentationsdemokratie: Schröder's Regierungsstil prägt die Berliner Republik', *FAZ*, 26 July 2002). Conversely, the example of Joschka Fischer, Foreign Minister in the Red–Green Cabinet, shows the extent to which the office may transform the office-holder. Not only did Fischer, upon taking office, decide to retain the overwhelming majority of senior staff in the Foreign Office (since all senior diplomats are classed as 'political civil servants', he had ample opportunity for 'purging' the ministry, which had after all been led by FDP politicians for 29 years). He also very quickly adopted the habits and mannerisms of a senior statesman acting at some remove from the squabbles of daily politics. This transformation extended to a new-found preference for sombre three-piece suits: a marked contrast to the jeans and trainers he famously wore when he was sworn in as minister in the Hesse Land government in 1985, and further evidence of the 'long run to myself' – the title of his memoirs-cum-fitness-guide (Fischer, 2000b) – that has characterized his political career.

What Future for the Centre?

What conclusions might be drawn about the future of government at the centre? More recent contributions disagree on the evolving role of the executive in the political system and power relations inside the Federal government. Indeed, political and academic comment supports two rival scenarios. The first may be described as 'dual concentration'. According to its proponents, power in the political system is becoming increasingly concentrated within the Federal executive at the expense of Parliament, political parties and the Länder. European integration makes national decision-makers become part of a multi-level governance structure; but the main domestic beneficiary of the resultant 'two-level game' is the executive. Europeanization and domestic executive preponderance go together. This development is mirrored by progressive concentration within the executive. The Chancellor's power in the Federal government has increased, whilst collegiate decision-making and departmental autonomy are progressively undermined. In Schröder's case, the potentially countervailing force of the SPD party apparatus has been effectively neutralized, partly through organizational reform, partly through careful elimination of rivals and detractors (Karl-Rudolf Korte, 'Das System Schröder', *FAZ*, 25 October 1999). As under Adenauer, Germany is still – or perhaps once again – a 'Chancellor democracy', characterized by the 'central role of the Chancellor in the preparation of political decisions in Cabinet'; the 'personal prestige of the Chancellor'; the 'close connection of the office of Chancellor and the leadership of the largest governing party'; the 'dualism of government and opposition camps'; and 'the personal engagement of the Chancellor in foreign policy' (Niclauß, 1999, pp. 37–8). Indeed, some have spoken of a 'presidentalization' of the political system (Korte, 2001).

The rival scenario – 'dual deconcentration' – stresses the constraining effects of the Federal executive's entanglement with political parties, Parliament, the Länder and the EU, which is thought to undermine the government's agenda-setting powers. Its 'governmentality' is seen to be under threat, as it is becoming an executive in the strict sense of the word, executing political decisions taken elsewhere, whether in informal circles of the governing parties and Parliament, in the institutional thicket of cooperative federalism, or at EU level. For example, concerning the influence of the governing parties and their parliamentary groups on the preparation of major legislative initiatives, it has been suggested that 'The Bundestag increasingly penetrates this preparation phase – informally, of course ... As regards the experts of the parliamentary parties one must by now not question the efficiency but rather the transparency of their influence' (Oberreuter, 1992, p. 169). Executive policy formulation is no longer followed by parliamentary deliberation. Rather, 'Today's political decision-making processes often follow an almost reverse order, in which coalition working parties negotiate political compromises, which are then passed on to the responsible ministry, in which they are put in the form of draft legislation' (Manow, 1996, p. 103). Under such conditions, the Federal executive as a whole, and the head of the government in particular, find themselves cast in the role of mediators of conflicting interests rather than powerful policy-shapers. Recourse to independent policy commissions (Sturm, Chapter 5 in this volume) is a reflection of the loss of executive authority. Germany is not a 'Chancellor democracy', let alone a presidentialized system, but rather a 'coordination democracy' (Jäger, 1994; Padgett, 1994) or a 'negotiation democracy' (Holtmann, 2001).

Neither scenario can be dismissed out of hand, but much depends on how the evidence is weighed. As the contributions to this volume underline, public policy-making in the Federal Republic takes place in a dense network of interests and institutions that extends deeply into organized civil society and in which the mass media appear to play an ever greater role. Decision-making by chancellorial fiat may occasionally be possible and attract special public attention, but it is the exception to the rule of consultation, negotiation, mediation, compromise and arbitration. The gloomy economic outlook at the start of the second Schröder government, combined with acute crises in the health and pensions systems, appears to have strengthened the Chancellor's resolve to take decisive measures, if necessary against vocal protests by affected interests. He also strengthened his Cabinet by retaining key figures, such as the Minister of the Finance and the Interior, dismissing weak ministers, and bringing in a 'heavy hitter' with a broad policy remit in the person of Clement. But while the rhetoric may be one of renewed resolve and determination, the second Schröder Cabinet is more likely to confirm than challenge historic patterns of government at the centre, marked by executive authority, accountability and stability.

2

Federalism and Territorial Politics

CHARLIE JEFFERY

Federalism is normally about territorial politics. Federal systems typically express some kind of trade-off between territorial social differences and membership of a common state. Those differences may be ethnic or linguistic (e.g., in Canada or Belgium). They may just reflect the diversity of circumstances and preferences in large states (e.g., the USA or Australia). In each case territorial political systems – provinces, regions, states, Länder – which express those differences are located within an overarching, statewide federal political system. The aim of federalism is to reconcile territorial diversity with statewide integration.

The Federal Republic of Germany is an exception to this rule. It is neither ethnically diverse nor especially big. It is clearly federal, with 16 Länder combined in an overarching federal state. Indeed, some 47 clauses (out of 141) in the German constitution, the Basic Law, are needed to describe and specify the structures and mechanics of German federalism. But for most of the post-war era German federalism has not really been about *territorial* politics. The federal system evolved instead as a vehicle for producing more or less equal standards of public policy – 'living conditions' as the Basic Law puts it – *across all* of the Federal Republic.

That model of German federalism, focused on building common national standards rather than expressing territorial diversity, is now under challenge. The main cause of the challenge is German unification, though the roots of the challenge go back into the pre-unification era. The challenge is one of territorial politics. Increasingly, the German Länder have come to prioritize more narrowly defined, territorial interests ahead of the pursuit of nationwide common standards. And some of them, especially the economically stronger, politically conservative southern Länder – Bavaria, Baden-Württemberg and Hesse – have campaigned vigorously over the last few years for a reorganization of the federal system to reflect this new territorial dimension in German politics better.

This chapter explores and explains how German federalism has come to be about territorial politics. Its starts with a review of the constitutional framework of the federal system which, despite the territorial challenge, has remained largely unchanged since the late 1960s. It then looks at the political dynamics which produced out of that framework a federalism of 'uniform living conditions' over the period 1949–82. Those dynamics began to break down after 1982 and their breakdown was accelerated after German unification. The next sections of the chapter explain that breakdown and the new territorial politics which have resulted, focusing in turn on how new territorial sensitivities have come to pervade economics, party politics and social attitudes in the Länder. Finally the chapter explores some of the key issues which now face the federal system as it confronts the new territorial challenge.

Federalism in the Basic Law

Germany has a long federal tradition which was born out of the attempts to unify a German nation split across a large number of dynastic and republican states: there were 39 German states, or Länder, in 1815, and 25 in the German Reich founded under Bismarck and Prussian domination in 1871. The post-war Federal Republic of Germany, established in 1949 in what became known as West Germany, built on this tradition. It included a number of 'historic' Länder: Bavaria, the two city-states of Bremen and Hamburg, and the three south-western Länder (Württemberg-Hohenzollern, Baden and Württemberg-Baden) which combined in 1952 to form Baden-Württemberg. It also included a number of other Länder which were newly created after 1945: Hesse, Lower Saxony, North Rhine-Westphalia, Rhineland-Palatinate and Schleswig-Holstein. These were in part amalgamations of existing, smaller Länder, and in part subdivisions of the Land of Prussia which had been abolished and broken up by the occupying powers in 1945. Finally, West Berlin was also administered as a Land from the foundation of the Federal Republic, though it remained formally under the authority of the post-war occupying powers until 1990.

The Saarland, which had initially been under French administration after the Second World War, joined the Federal Republic in 1957; and then in 1990 the five 'new' Länder (in effect reconstructions of Länder established in East Germany from 1945 to 1952) joined the Federal Republic to bring about German unification. At the same time West and East Berlin were reunited and formally established as a full-fledged Land. Some of the key facts and figures on the 16 Länder that now make up the Federal Republic are given in Table 2.1.

Division of Powers between the Federal Level and the Länder

As Table 2.1 shows, the Länder are extremely varied in size and population. Each, though, has an equal status as a component unit of the German federation. Though Länder can be amalgamated – as happened in Baden-Württemberg, and as may yet happen with Berlin and Brandenburg – the division of Germany into Länder is one of the 'eternal' principles of the Basic Law. The Basic Law sets out in (at times) exhaustive detail what the constitutional responsibilities of the Länder are and how they relate to those of the federal level, in particular the Bundestag and the Federal government. The relation of the federal level and the Länder is regulated in three main ways.

First, the power to make law in different policy fields is assigned to one level or the other, or shared between them. The Basic Law sets out three types of legislative powers.

TABLE 2.1 *Data on the German Länder*

Land	Size (km²)	Population (million)	Bundesrat votes
Baden-Württemberg	37751	10.524	6
Bavaria	70548	12.230	6
Berlin	892	3.382	4
Brandenburg	29477	2.602	4
Bremen	404	0.660	3
Hamburg	755	1.715	3
Hesse	21114	6.068	5
Lower Saxony	47616	7.926	6
Mecklenburg-West Pomerania	23173	1.776	3
North Rhine-Westphalia	34041	18.010	6
Rhineland-Palatinate	19847	4.035	4
Saarland	2569	1.069	3
Saxony	18413	4.426	4
Saxony-Anhalt	20447	2.615	4
Schleswig-Holstein	15763	2.790	4
Thuringia	16172	2.431	4
Totals	358982	82.260	69

Source: www.destatis.de/jahrbuch/jahrtab1.htm

1 *Exclusive powers of the federal level.* These include foreign affairs and defence, citizenship and immigration, the framework conditions of the German internal market and important statewide services such as post and telecommunications.
2 *Concurrent powers.* These are areas where either the federation or the Länder can legislate, but where federal law takes precedence. They include civil and criminal law, employment and aspects of health, welfare, energy, industrial, transport and environmental policy
3 *Federal framework powers.* These are areas in which the federal level can establish a legislative framework into which Länder laws have to fit. They include higher education, regulation of the press and land use and planning.

In addition, there are *exclusive powers of the Länder.* These are not specified in the Basic Law. The assumption is that any field of policy not explicitly assigned to the other categories listed above is 'residually' assigned to the Länder. Among these residual powers are pre-university education, broadcasting, regional economic policy, local government and most aspects of policing and some of healthcare. Over the life of the Federal Republic the scope of the residual power of the Länder has narrowed. In part powers have 'migrated' through a succession of constitutional amendments into one or other of the categories mentioned above. Moreover, federal precedence has been established in most areas of concurrent power and the federal level has used framework powers in a way which has left the Länder little discretion in their own legislation. The role of the Länder as law-making authorities has as a result shrunk.

This does not mean that the Länder have lost relevance or, indeed, political weight. The Basic Law sets out a further, functional division of labour between the federal level and the Länder. While the federal level now *makes* most laws, the Länder as a rule are responsible for *implementing* those laws 'in their own right': in other words without close federal supervision. Because of this responsibility, most of the Federal Republic's civil servants are employed by the Länder; the federal level only has administrative authorities in the field of its exclusive powers, and even there it can delegate administrative responsibility to the Länder. All this gives the Länder a high degree of administrative expertise and knowledge of how policies work 'on the ground'. This expertise and knowledge is vital in formulating effective legislation and helps create an interdependence of the federal level and the Länder in the federal legislative process. And as the scope of federal legislation has widened, so has the scope of that interdependence.

That interdependence is also strengthened by the role of the Bundesrat in the federal legislative process. The Bundesrat is the German second chamber. It is made up of delegations representing the governments of the Länder. Each Land has a number of votes (see Table 2.1) which have to be cast en bloc. The Bundesrat may introduce federal bills (12.4% of all federal bills from 1949 to 2001), but more usually responds to bills introduced by the Federal government (54.2%) or the Bundestag (33.3%: see Bundesrat, 2002). Its legislative authority lies more though in its capacity to reject Federal government or Bundestag bills. It has an absolute veto over any federal legislation which impacts on the Länder and their administrative functions; in all other areas it can suspend, but not ultimately block, federal bills. The significance of the Bundesrat absolute veto has grown over the life of the Federal Republic. The growth of federal legislative powers has on the one hand widened the scope of the administrative role of the Länder. Moreover, constitutional practice has supported a wide interpretation of just what affects the Länder in their administrative role, so that even if a federal bill has just a single clause that impacts on Länder administration, then the whole bill is subject to the Bundesrat veto. In the legislative period 1949–53 just 41.8 per cent of all federal laws fell under the scope of the absolute veto. By the period 1983–87 this had risen to 60 per cent and has remained since at over 55 per cent (Bundesrat 2002).

Cooperative Federalism

Clearly the Federal government and the Bundestag have an interest in getting their legislation through the Bundesrat, so usually a basis for compromise is negotiated before the introduction of the bill in order to incorporate Länder concerns (assuming the Länder can build a collective view in the Bundesrat; this point is discussed further below). The interdependence and compromise-orientation between the federal level and the Länder/Bundesrat has led German federalism to be described as 'cooperative' federalism. The cooperative, interdependent character of German federalism has been strengthened since 1949 in three ways.

First, in a set of constitutional reforms in 1969–70, a number of Länder responsibilities were redefined as *joint tasks* of the Länder and the federal level. These included university construction, regional economic policy and agriculture. These areas became subject to joint planning, decision-making and financing. Other reforms passed as part of the same package made possible federal co-financing of major infrastructure projects in the Länder and shifted a number of exclusive powers of the Länder into the catalogues of concurrent and framework powers. The overall effect was to take federal–Länder interdependence to a new level, captured in Fritz Scharpf's term *Politikverflechtung*, 'political entanglement' (Scharpf, Reissert and Schnabel, 1976; Scharpf, 1988).

Second, parallel constitutional reforms in 1969 reorganized the process of raising and then distributing tax revenues 'vertically' between the federal level and the Länder and 'horizontally' among the Länder. Following this reform all the main taxes – income tax, corporation tax and VAT – became 'shared' taxes, with revenues distributed in agreed proportions to the federal level and the Länder. A system of *fiscal equalization* was also introduced to ensure that Länder with below-average tax revenues were brought up to the average by transfers from the above-average Länder (plus, where necessary, top-ups from the federal budget). In this way cooperative federalism was reinforced by an explicit duty of financial solidarity between the two levels and, crucially, between richer and poorer Länder.

A third and final set of reforms to cooperative federalism followed after German unification in 1992. These had to do with a *European integration* process which had begun to accelerate in the mid-1980s and which 'deepened' further with the agreement on the Maastricht Treaty in 1991. Accelerated integration meant the transfer of member-state policy powers to the European level. In Germany that meant the transfer of both federal and Länder powers. This was problematic for the Länder in two ways. First, they were losing even more of their already shrunken set of exclusive powers. Second, European integration policy was considered foreign policy, and therefore an exclusive power of the federal level. The Länder were therefore both losing powers to 'Europe' and being shut out of the European decision-making process. A long and skilfully managed campaign which reached its peak during the Maastricht negotiations allowed them to 'strike back' (Jeffery, 1994) in a constitutional amendment in 1992 which introduced a new 'Europe Article' to the Basic Law. This – Article 23 – gave the Bundesrat a veto over any further transfer of powers to the European Union. It also gave the Bundesrat rights of involvement in German EU decision-making broadly equivalent to those it has in the domestic legislative process. In this way EU policy was also integrated into the structures and practice of cooperative federalism.

Cooperative Federalism 1949–82

Constitutional structure is a necessary but not sufficient condition for a particular style of politics such as cooperative federalism. Constitutions can be interpreted in different ways, and tend to 'flex' over time to accommodate changes in circumstance and opinion. It was suggested in the introduction to this chapter that post-war German federalism was less about expressing territorial differences than about delivering common standards of public policy nationwide. That orientation of German federalism was certainly facilitated by a set of constitutional structures which favoured nationwide, federal legislation over regionally differentiated Land legislation, and which 'entangled' the federal level and the Länder in close cooperation in the federal legislative process and later in joint tasks, fiscal equalization and EU policy. But cooperative federalism developed in this way also, and perhaps more importantly, because there was a normative agreement among the main political actors (and, indeed, the general public) that it should do so.

National Standards as the Goal of German Federalism

There are a number of reasons why this agreement on a cooperative federalism of nationwide standards developed. The western occupying powers provided one as they set out some framework conditions for the Basic Law in 1948–49: they wanted federalism not to promote social diversity, but to introduce checks and balances on the power of German central government after central government power had been abused so arbitrarily in the Third Reich. For them federalism was more about limiting power at the centre than enabling territorial distinctiveness. Another 'founding' condition for cooperative federalism lay in the circumstances of a state bearing the devastation of war, conquest and occupation, divided in two by Cold War politics, and struggling to absorb 12 million or so refugees and expellees. The overwhelming priority was one of national integration: rebuilding what the war had damaged, compensating the eastern parts of West Germany for the effects on economy and society of the new East–West German border, and housing and employing the massive flow of refugees.

These were circumstances that favoured national responses, a sense of nationwide social equity to generate common purpose in national reconstruction. They were circumstances in which the growth of federal legislative powers made sense. Even where the Länder retained exclusive powers, there developed an instinct for coordination also directed at producing common, nationwide standards. The most well-known example of this 'self-coordination' of the Länder is the Conference of Ministers of Culture, which sets common frameworks for school education from primary school through to school-leaving qualifications. In most fields of responsibility of the Länder, this kind of 'self-coordination' became the norm. A survey across the Land Government of North Rhine-Westphalia in 1989, for example, showed that its ministries were involved in 137 self-coordination committees which in aggregate held around 350 meetings annually (Sturm, 2001, p. 80).

In this atmosphere of agreement on the need for nationwide standards – even where no constitutional foundation for common standards existed – one particular phrase in the Basic Law assumed an importance which the framers of that law had undoubtedly not anticipated: the 'maintenance of legal or economic unity, especially the maintenance of uniformity of living conditions beyond the territory of a Land'. That phrase was used in Article 72 of the Basic Law which sets out when the federal level can make use of its concurrent and framework powers. 'Uniformity of living conditions' became something of a mission statement for German federalism. It became a powerful justification for the growth of federal legislative powers, the shrinkage of the role of the Länder as law-making bodies, and thus for the weakness of territorial politics in the Federal Republic.

The Grand Coalition and the Era of the 'Big Government'

The weight of the notion of 'uniform living conditions' as a normative goal for the Federal Republic then increased further during the 1966–69 Grand Coalition, which brought the Social Democratic Party (SPD) into the Federal government for the first time. The SPD brought into Federal government a new, Keynesian policy approach and with it a growing confidence in the capacity of government intervention to secure social and economic goals. This confidence was expressed in a commitment to new instruments of policy planning, including the 'joint tasks' mentioned above. By the mid-1970s German government had become interventionist 'big government', dealing through cooperative federalism with major issues of taxation policy, economic management, infrastructural investment, and educational and health policy. And the fiscal equalization process also introduced by the Grand Coalition ensured that big government translated into uniform outcomes: all the

Länder – now of course implementing a much wider federal legislative portfolio – were to have an equalized financial capacity so that they could deliver policies of common scope and quality across the federation.

There were three conditions for the operation of cooperative 'big government'. One was a sufficiently buoyant fiscal situation. As Fritz Scharpf (1988) showed, carrying out major interventionist policies through cooperative procedures was inefficient and wasteful of resources (it was easier to get agreement to build a new hospital in every Land than to make more selective decisions based on actual healthcare needs!). However, national economic growth, a relatively loose budgetary situation and a wider contentment with relatively high levels of taxation 'lubricated' the system sufficiently. A second precondition was that national economies were still precisely that: *national*, not yet subject to the competition and fiscal rules which now apply in the EU, and not yet subject to the tougher competitive disciplines which accompanied the technological shift to the global, 'microchip' economy.

Party Politics and Public Opinion

A third precondition lay in the political attitudes of the West Germans. These were not strongly differentiated by territory. The main political cleavages – social class and religious beliefs – played out nationwide. Only in Bavaria was there a strong sense of territorial difference; in a survey in 1958 only 54 per cent of Bavarians preferred remaining in the Federal Republic over independence (Grube, 2001, p. 106). Otherwise – and even increasingly in Bavaria – public opinion surveys showed a growth in expectations that living conditions should not vary significantly from one Land to the next (Grube, 2001, p. 109). As the Federal government put it in 1969 as justification for the new system of fiscal equalization: 'Public opinion no longer accepts significant differences in performance and obligations as the price for the Länder delivering wide-ranging public services under their own responsibility' (cited in Clement, 2002, p. 17). Though the Federal government no doubt exaggerated the point, the main contours of political debate were clearly about alternative views on how *national* living conditions should be regulated, not about how the Länder might do things differently on their own territory.

This nationwide frame of reference for political debate was reflected in voting behaviour and party competition. After an initial period of party system concentration, West Germany developed a highly streamlined, nationwide party system. Two large parties – the SPD on the centre-left and the CDU/CSU on the centre-right – and the smaller, centrist FDP competed on more or less the same terms across the Federal Republic. Though each of the bigger parties had particular regional strongholds they were strong everywhere and their strength did not vary greatly in any one Land in Bundestag or Land elections. There was a high degree of congruence between party systems at the federal level and in the Länder.

Federal–Länder congruence was important for the relationship of the Bundesrat to the Bundestag and the Federal government in the federal legislative process. As was noted above, the Bundesrat comprises representatives of Länder governments. In a congruent party system those governments were made up of the same parties as those forming national government and opposition in the Bundestag. This made it easy to ensure effective party-political coordination between the two chambers to the extent that the Bundesrat became less a chamber of territories than a second party-based chamber. This did not mean there was no conflict between Bundestag and Bundesrat. During the 1970s competing majorities in Bundestag (SPD–FDP) and Bundesrat (CDU/CSU) led to periodic partisan conflict between the two bodies (Lehmbruch, 1976). Nonetheless, the Bundesrat was still engaged in the same national debate as in the Bundestag about what kind of nationwide living conditions the Federal Republic should have. Territorial issues were clearly subordinate.

The Changing Parameters of German Federalism after 1982

The parameters surrounding German federalism began to change in the 1980s. There are three key dates: 1982, 1986 and 1989. In 1982, a CDU/CSU–FDP Federal government under Chancellor Helmut Kohl replaced Helmut Schmidt's SPD–FDP government. Kohl promised a *Wende*, a 'turnaround', from the interventionist politics of the SPD. The models were the market-driven, neo-liberal administrations of Margaret Thatcher in the UK and Ronald Reagan in the USA. Compared with Thatcher and Reagan, Kohl's *Wende* was a whimper. Kohl was not as ideologically committed to 'rolling back the state', and neither was he able to push far-reaching reforms through a political system with a large number of veto points (not least the interdependence of the federal level with the Länder: see Webber, 1992). The *Wende* did, though, signal a shift in the political terrain away from confidence in 'big government'. One of the outcomes were some marginal shifts in the operation of federalism, with Kohl's government promising (rather more than delivering) legislative self-restraint and, by implication, fewer national standards and more room for manoeuvre for distinctive policies in the Länder (Klatt, 1991). These marginal shifts opened up a debate about the *Entflechtung* or 'disentanglement' of the federal level and the Länder which simmered away during the 1980s and burst into life after German unification.

The year 1982 is significant, too, for the reason why Kohl came to power. This had much to do with the recession of 1979–80. On the one hand the recession damaged Helmut Schmidt's reputation for economic policy competence; on the other – and following an earlier recession in the mid-1970s – it shook confidence in the steady economic growth to which the West Germans had become accustomed. There was two implications for cooperative federalism. First of all, the inefficiencies and waste of joint decision-making processes now began to look unaffordable (Kohl's attempts at 'disentanglement' characteristically focused first and foremost on the 1969 joint tasks; see Klatt, 1991).

Second, the effects of the more uncertain pattern of economic growth were territorially asymmetrical; they affected the economies of some Länder more than others. Northern Länder had a disproportionate share of industries now in rapid decline: coal, steel, shipbuilding. Some of the southern Länder which lacked this heavy industrial tradition were at the same time emerging as new centres of technology-led growth. Widening economic disparities placed new strains on the fiscal equalization process. New territorial sensitivities about 'our money' emerged: how much the economically stronger Länder (unjustly) had to give away to their weaker counterparts; and how much the economically weaker Länder were (rightly) due from their stronger counterparts. The idea of interterritorial solidarity weakened and new sense of territorial self-interest led to a wave of complaints to the Federal Constitutional Court about the effects of fiscal equalization (Exler, 1991).

The next key date was 1986, when the Single European Act (SEA) came into force. The SEA ended a period of 'Euro-sclerosis' and breathed new life into the European integration process. At its core were measures to liberalize the operation of national markets, to produce a level playing field for competition across the EU (then still the EC), and bring into effect the genuinely single European market that had been the founding aim of European integration in the 1950s. The SEA above all limited the scope for state intervention in national economies (e.g., in supporting declining industrial sectors). New tools of European-level intervention offered only partial compensation. A by-product of all this was a new economic policy prominence on the part of regional governments, which increasingly stepped in to find new ways of restructuring, regenerating or attracting industries in their regions. Some German Länder joined this trend, with Baden-Württemberg (Götz, 1992) and North Rhine-Westphalia (von Alemann, Heinze, Hombach, 1990) leading the way. In regional economic policy at least, Länder began to carve out for themselves niches for autonomous policies beyond the traditional frameworks for joint decision-making and Länder self-coordination.

The final key date was 9 November 1989, when the Berlin Wall began to be dismantled and the route to German unification opened up. Unification has radically shifted the terms of the debate about German federalism. There are now more Länder, and there now exists a sharp east–west divide between them. The costs of unification have been immense and have both sharpened territorial sensitivities over equalization transfers and slashed the resources available for federation-wide joint decision-making. Some of the Länder have responded by pushing to expand the scope for autonomous Land policies beyond regional economic development. In other words, unification has reinforced the changes which began to filter through in the operation of cooperative federalism in the 1980s and has opened up the field for a more territorial federalism.

The New Territorial Politics

Economic Disparity

West Germany was, in relative terms, economically homogeneous. Only in the 1980s did territorial economic disparities become a politically sensitive issue; until then cooperative federalism had been able to reduce disparities or, at least, provide for sufficient resource redistribution for them to be adequately compensated. As Table 2.2 shows, post-unification disparities, even a decade on, have been stark and, perhaps, unbridgeable.

Table 2.2 gives a clear indication of the east–west divide in prosperity following unification. All of the eastern Länder have unemployment close to (and in the case of Saxony-Anhalt, more than) double the national average. All of them except Berlin have a GDP/head of around two-thirds the national average. And all of them, including Berlin, are dependent on massive financial transfers in the fiscal equalization process.

The divide is not just east–west, however: within the 'old west' there are considerable disparities. Lower Saxony, Rhineland-Palatinate, Schleswig-Holstein and Saarland are each at best at around 90 per cent

TABLE 2.2 Economic disparities among the German Länder

Land	GDP/head (2001; € thousand)	Unemployment rate (2001; %)
Baden-Württemberg	28.75	4.9
Bavaria	29.22	5.3
Berlin	22.39	16.1
Brandenburg	16.27	17.4
Bremen	33.92	12.4
Hamburg	42.88	8.3
Hesse	30.56	6.6
Lower Saxony	22.63	9.1
Mecklenburg-West Pomerania	16.29	18.3
North Rhine-Westphalia	25.52	8.8
Rhineland-Palatinate	22.75	6.8
Saarland	22.96	9.0
Saxony	16.79	17.5
Saxony-Anhalt	16.18	19.7
Schleswig-Holstein	22.57	8.4
Thuringia	16.41	15.3
Germany	25.08	9.4

Note: Fiscal equalization data includes 'pre-equalization' of VAT revenues, horizontal equalization and federal supplementary allocations.
Sources: Statistisches Bundesamt at www.destatis.de/jahrbuch/jahrtab1.htm, www.destatis.de/jahrbuch/jahrtab13.htm, www.destatis.de/jahrbuch/jahrtab65.htm (viewed on 20 August 2002) and Sturm (2001, p. 104).

of average GDP/head, while North Rhine-Westphalia just makes it to the average. Only Bavaria, Baden-Württemberg and Hesse are comfortably above average (note that the Bremen and Hamburg GDP figures are skewed by their nature as major seaports and can be discounted). On unemployment, Baden-Württemberg, Bavaria and Hesse and Rhineland-Palatinate are the only Länder with a rate of less than 7 per cent. Only five of the Länder are significant net contributors to the fiscal equalization process; North Rhine-Westphalia, Hesse, Baden-Württemberg and Bavaria all contributed from six to seven billion DM in 1999, while Hamburg chipped in around a billion. All the others were net recipients, with the six eastern Länder receiving the most, but with Bremen, Saarland and Lower Saxony in the west also receiving significant sums.

In simplified terms there is a three-way divide here: Baden-Württemberg, Bavaria and Hesse are doing well, with North Rhine-Westphalia and Hamburg struggling to keep pace. The six eastern Länder are doing badly. An intermediate group of Bremen, Lower Saxony, Rhineland-Palatinate, Saarland and Schleswig-Holstein stretches across the gap, with only Rhineland-Palatinate within striking distance of the 'premier league' and with Bremen and perhaps Saarland close to 'relegation'. This is a very wide set of disparities. United Germany is economically heterogeneous, and the Länder at either end of the scale clearly have divergent economic interests and needs.

Political Differentiation

Alongside this greater territorial heterogeneity of regional economies, regional politics in Germany have become more differentiated. This can be seen in two ways. First the trend initially evident in the 1980s of Länder seeking out greater policy autonomy – and less nationwide coordination – has grown. The idea of tailoring regional economic policy to specific Länder needs is now an unchallenged orthodoxy in the Länder. Facing up to the competitive demands of increasingly border- less EU and global economies has made national policy rules increas- ingly redundant. As the North Rhine-Westphalian Minister-President, Wolfgang Clement (2002, p. 18), put it: 'In today's conditions – a competition between regions for investment and jobs – inflexible and uniform federation-wide regulations are more than anything a hindrance.'

What has emerged since the mid-1990s is a growing tendency to pur- sue territorially differentiated policies in other fields too, including higher education (Zehetmair, 1998), rural policy (Mehl and Plankl, 2002) and labour market policy (Blancke and Schmid, 2000). Perhaps most significant have been the controversial attempts by the 'rich three' southern Länder to play ideas about territorial policy differentiation into fields of social policy considered until now as touchstones of the idea of uniform living conditions. Hesse's Minister-President Roland Koch (CDU), has argued for the right in Hesse to transform *Sozialhilfe* – the main nationwide form of welfare payments to those whose entitlement to unemployment benefit has expired – into a US-style 'workfare' pro- gramme in Hesse. This would oblige all claimants fit to work to take up a form of work or training offered by the Hessian authorities (Koch, 2001; Jeffery, 2002). And Bavaria (CSU), with support from Baden- Württemberg (CDU) has set out plans for a 'regionalization' of health insurance and suggested similar solutions for unemployment insurance and pension contributions (Stamm, 1998; cf. Münch, 1998; Sodan, 2002). The various social insurance funds in effect operate equalization mechanisms to reduce the variation in contributions made and benefits drawn around the country, which is of course consistent with the idea of uniform living conditions. The effect is, however, that some of the contributions made by individuals in Länder with fewer healthcare needs/unemployed/pensioners end up paying for care/benefits/pensions in others. In proposing to regionalize contributions and benefits Bavaria is seeking to introduce a new, territorial principle: 'to make clear the causal relationship between the policies of a Land and their impact on its citizens' (Stamm, 1998, p. 240).

Bavaria has not succeeded in advancing that agenda far, and neither has Hesse on workfare. Both initiatives conflict with residual attachments to the idea of maintaining uniformity of living conditions and, implicitly, social solidarity. It is striking, though, that these ideas have been put forward. They point to a new capacity to 'think outside the box' and try out different policy solutions in different places. Though the most prominent examples of territorialized policy thinking have been CDU/CSU Länder, SPD or SPD–Green Länder have also begun to develop more territorially 'tailored' policy portfolios (Sturm, 2001, pp. 89–90; cf. Schmid, 2002).

A contributory factor underlying this new territorial politics has been the pattern of Länder election results since unification. Federal and Land party systems are now much less congruent. There is on the one hand an east–west divergence. Only the CDU and SPD can claim to be parties of national integration, with a roughly even pattern of support in west and east. The FDP and the Greens are parties with an essentially western base; and the PDS is clearly a regional party for the east that has minimal resonance in the west. In this situation government–opposition formations at the federal level and in the Länder no longer map neatly on to one another (see Table 2.3).

The pattern is complicated by a growing differentiation of party performance in Bundestag and Land elections, with the two major parties SPD and CDU periodically losing ground in the Länder even in traditional strongholds, and with protest parties on the far right or from citizens' movements at times scoring well. This electoral volatility in the Länder has made government formation more difficult and led both the SPD and CDU to enter unusual coalition agreements. The SPD, for example, has been in Länder coalitions since 1990, not just with the established parties, the Greens, CDU and FDP but also with:

- the PDS (in Mecklenburg-West Pomerania 1998–)
- the Greens and the FDP *together* (the 'traffic-light' coalitions in Brandenburg 1990–94 and Bremen 1991–95)

- the citizens' protest group *Stattpartei* ('instead of a party'!) in Hamburg 1993–97
- the Greens in a minority coalition 'tolerated' by the PDS in Saxony-Anhalt (1994–2002).

Table 2.3 shows the current set of Land coalitions. Their variety has an important implication for territorial politics. It is now much less the case that the political arenas in the Länder are all engaged in the same debate about how national living conditions should be shaped as they were, say, 20 years ago. The volatility of Land election results, and the varied coalition formations that they have thrown up, suggest a growing territorialization of political debate. This is important as an indicator of social attitudes (see below); but it is also important for political dynamics within parties. It makes uniform debates and priorities within parties more difficult to bring about if electoral trends are leading, say, the CDU in Hamburg or the SPD in Mecklenburg-West Pomerania to stress different priorities from those of the national CDU or SPD. This dislocation of national and Länder party politics has the effect of facilitating some of the territorially distinctive policy agendas in the Länder that were noted above.

TABLE 2.3 *Coalition alignments in the Länder, May 2003*

Land	Aligned with the federal govt (SPD–Green)	Cross-cutting federal govt and opposition	Aligned with the federal opposition (CDU/CSU–FDP)	Other
Baden-Württemberg			CDU–FDP	
Bavaria			CSU	
Berlin				SPD–PDS
Brandenburg		SPD–CDU		
Bremen		SPD–CDU		
Hamburg				CDU–FDP- Schill
Hesse				
Lower Saxony			CDU	
Mecklenburg-West Pomerania				SPD–PDS
North Rhine-Westphalia	SPD–Green			
Rhineland-Palatinate		SPD–FDP		
Saarland			CDU	
Saxony			CDU	
Saxony-Anhalt			CDU–FDP	
Schleswig-Holstein	SPD–Green			
Thuringia			CDU	

Source: Own calculations.

Social Attitudes: Uniformity or Diversity?

How far are widening economic disparities and growing political differentiation reflected in social attitudes? There are clearly new patterns of territorial diversity. Most immediately this new diversity is about eastern Germany. Over and above the differences of objective need indicated in Table 2.2, there is also a collective sense of difference in the east, an east German identity whose roots lie in the GDR past, and which has been recast and reaffirmed by the material dislocation of the post-unity era (Hough, 2002, pp. 77–80). As Dan Hough (2002, pp. 106–7) has shown, the net outcome is the emergence of eastern Germany as a distinctive political 'space' which is more egalitarian and more statist than the west.

The territorial impact of unification cannot be limited just to an east–west dimension, however. Measures taken to address the socio-economic needs of the east – higher taxation generally, and higher equalization transfers within the federal system more specifically – have heightened wider territorial sensitivities about the allocation of resources. An era of budgetary restraint has added spice to the mix. Debate about the costs and benefits of social equity has become more vivid and, in part, polarized between donors and recipients. In some places political rhetoric about 'our money' has resonated with social identities. Bavaria is the most obvious example. Bavaria might be said to have shared Margaret Thatcher's response to German unification: 'Germany got bigger, but we didn't.' Being a smaller part of a larger Germany has reduced Bavaria's 'weight' in the federal system. It has also increased its obligations (Germany, on average, also 'got poorer', but Bavaria did not). It is no surprise in these circumstances that in Bavaria discourses of regional distinctiveness – based in traditions of independent statehood, political Catholicism and rural nostalgia – have become more prominent and have helped to underpin the Bavarian government's distinctive policy approach.

In other Länder – those with better economic situations in the west, and eastern Länder which claim historical tradition, such as Saxony and Thuringia – claims to social distinctiveness have also strengthened. More generally voters, as discussed above, have begun to use Land electoral arenas to express different judgements on parties from those they express in the national electoral arena. However, though voters act differently in different places, and though territorial identities have become more important in some parts of Germany, opinion polls still show that Germans favour uniform policy outcomes across the whole of Germany. An Allensbach poll in 1995 showed that Germans in east and west favour common standards not just in fields where nationwide solutions seem obvious (e.g., policy on nuclear energy, drink-driving or pollution limits) but also where Land-to-Land differentiation might seem more natural given the distribution of powers in the Basic Law (e.g., policy on universities, schools, local government elections and policing: Grube, 2001, pp. 109–10). There was also strong support (even more so, for obvious reasons, in the east than in the west) for a system of fiscal equalization in which 'rich Länder give money to poorer Länder' (Grube, 2001, p. 110).

The discrepancy between what Germans think is right according to Allensbach and what they actually do in Land elections is puzzling. It suggests a residual attachment to traditional ideas about uniformity and social solidarity which resonate in the abstract and warn against a more territorial politics, but which is outweighed by other, more immediate factors in the polling booths. It perhaps equates to the paradox in British social attitudes whereby voters agree in opinion polls that more tax should be levied to pay for better education or health standards, yet they fail to vote for parties which promise to do just that. Nevertheless popular ambiguity about greater territorial diversity remains a potential obstacle to those committed to pushing further a territorial agenda for German federalism.

Issues in the New Territorial Politics

Competitive Federalism

There has been a remarkable debate in Germany over the last five or six years about how a more territorial federalism might look and whether or how far it should be implemented. That debate has revolved, often rather emotively, around the idea of a 'competitive' as opposed to a 'cooperative' federalism. The idea of 'competitive federalism' has been pushed on most strongly by the 'rich three', Christian Democratic Bavaria, Baden-Württemberg and Hesse. It has clearly been inspired and developed by reference to debates in the USA about the states acting as 'laboratories of democracy' (Osborne, 1988; cf. Jeffery, 2002). The basic premise is that if the scope of Federal government is limited, and cooperative policy arrangements linking the federal level and the Länder are cut back, the greater Länder autonomy that results will lead to innovative policy thinking and, through a competition of ideas, 'benchmark' policy solutions better than those that would come forward in a more circumscribed federation-wide policy process. As the Bavarian Minister,

Barbara Stamm (1998, p. 237) put it:

> Only through innovative ideas can prosperity and Germany's social sys-
> tems be developed further. That is only possible when the opportunity
> for reward exists alongside the risk of failure. A precondition is courage
> to be individual and seek freedom as well as courage to take risks and
> to fail. And precisely in smaller units new and unconventional ideas can
> be tested through 'trial and error' and identified as right (or as wrong).

These ideas are challenging in a society that has been risk-averse and
a political system which has been slow to embrace change. Their
emphasis on individualism clashes with norms of solidarity and equity.
In some quarters they have been strongly rejected as offensive to the traditions of the Federal Republic, not least in a paper by nine of the
Länder in 1999 entitled 'The strong would get stronger' (Berlin *et al.*,
1999). Their view was that demands for a 'competition-oriented federalism have to receive a clear rejection because of the strongly divergent
social and economic structures in the Federal Republic. A fair competition would not be possible; the starting positions of the Länder are
all too diverse.'

This contest of visions of federalism – between cooperation, solidarity and equity on the one hand and competition, individualism and
difference on the other – has become one of the key themes in political
debate in the Federal Republic (Grosse Hüttmann, 2000; Fischer and
Grosse Hüttmann, 2001). It raises a number of key issues.

Reforming the Federal System

The first two concern how far the federal system can be reformed to support a more territorial federalism. Some see the likelihood of reform as
low. A series of reform projects since unification have come to little
(e.g., the post-unification constitutional reform discussions in 1992–93,
or the proposed merger of Berlin and Brandenburg in 1996). 'Path
dependencies' in a political system with a high number of veto points to
impede change mean that they are likely to continue to come to little
(Lehmbruch, 2000).

Another argument is that the disjunctions between a set of federal
structures geared to producing standard, nationwide outcomes and
growing territorial diversity in economics, politics and society are now
so great that reform pressures will persist and will steadily nibble
away at the edges of cooperative federalism. Hesse and Bavaria have in
different ways tried since 1990 to find ways of 'rolling back' the federal

role in concurrent and framework legislation and to boost the policy autonomy of the Länder. Hesse pushed this theme strongly in the Bundestag–Bundesrat Joint Commission on Constitutional Reform in 1993. The results were tougher hurdles before the federal level can claim the right to legislate and the possibility of rescinding established federal precedence in fields of concurrent powers. In 1995 Bavaria led an initiative, which led to a draft bill published together with Baden-Württemberg and Hesse in 1998 (which was ultimately shelved) to concretize the possibility of rolling the federal level back out of concurrent and framework powers (Männle, 1998, pp. 181–218; Jeffery, 1999, p. 334). More recently Bavaria has pushed for a different approach based on individual Länder opting out of federation-wide legislation in concurrent and framework powers (Münch 2001, pp. 121–2). This approach may prove more acceptable than one which imposes on all Länder an obligation to legislate autonomously (Schulze, 2000, pp. 696–8), although this has not yet borne fruit.

The point is: the 'rich three' keep coming back for more. One can see a similar pattern regarding the fiscal equalization process. Table 2.7 shows the scale of equalization transfers and the net impact on the budgets of the 'rich three'. There are long-standing arguments (Jeffery and Mackenstein, 1999) that the scale of transfers is iniquitous, penalizing economically stronger Länder for their success and failing to give sufficient incentives to weaker Länder to improve their performance. These arguments led to constitutional complaints (among others by Hesse and Baden-Württemberg) in the 1980s and an acrimonious debate about how the eastern Länder could be incorporated into the equalization process in the Solidarity Pact negotiations of 1993. The Länder finally accepted a proposal in 1993 made by the Bavarian government (which pushed most of the additional costs on to the Federal government). The same Bavarian government then launched a new constitutional complaint together with Baden-Württemberg in 1997 (which Hesse subsequently joined), and the Constitutional Court's decision in 1999 was followed by an acrimonious debate about how richer and poorer Länder interests could be reconciled in the Solidarity Pact II negotiations of 2001. The Solidarity Pact II outcomes nibbled a little at the edges of the incentives question, allowing the contributor Länder to keep a little more of their above-average revenues. That outcome did not go far enough in buying off the underlying pressures caused by widening economic disparities. If the acrimonious debate on Solidarity Pact II was a replay of the acrimonious debate on Solidarity Pact I, it seems only a matter of time before acrimony – or, to put it another way, unalloyed territorial politics – flares up again.

The Character of the Bundesrat

The Bundesrat has now become much more a chamber of territorial interests. The diversity of party systems across the Federal Republic and the differentiation of voting behaviour from Land to Land have increasingly prised free the Bundesrat from the national political debate as conducted in the Bundestag. As Table 2.3 shows, the Bundesrat simply does not have the same party-political dynamics as the Bundestag. The Länder governments represented in the Bundesrat frequently cut across the Federal government–opposition divide. The scope to apply party discipline and coordinate between parties in Bundestag and Bundesrat is weakened; cross-cutting coalitions normally have an 'abstention clause' if, say, the SPD and CDU in Bremen cannot agree on their position on a federal bill. In this situation coalitions of interest in the Bundesrat are built as much (or more) around shared territorial concerns as around shared party-political loyalties. The most prominent recent example was the success of Chancellor Schröder in 2000 in constructing a cross-party coalition in the Bundesrat to support his tax reform package (a coalition constructed through generous application of financial incentives for individual Länder: Sturm, 2001, pp. 65–6). The Bundesrat is, more than ever before, a genuinely territorial chamber.

The Länder and European Integration

Territorial politics has also 'spilled over' into the EU policy of the Länder. It was noted earlier that the Länder had been successful in 1993 in extending the practice of cooperative federalism to EU policy through the new Article 23 of the Basic Law. There is a sense, though, that Article 23 was immediately anachronistic. It was the culmination of a campaign launched by the West German Länder and focused on how West Germany engaged with the European-level policy process. As such it focused on the collective representation of Länder views in European decision-making through the Bundesrat. But just as in domestic politics, it is far more difficult to build collective views now that the post-unification Länder are economically, politically and socially much more diverse. Two tendencies emerge from this. The first is that Article 23 tends to generate modest, lowest common denominator positions which – after they have been negotiated alongside Federal government views into a German policy position – have relatively little impact in shaping what happens in European decision-making.

The second is that the Länder have placed a growing emphasis on limiting the scope of European regulation and therefore preserving as wide a space for autonomous decision-making as possible. All have united behind a commitment to preserve what they call *öffentliche Daseinsvorsorge* (i.e., public funding for so-called 'essential services' such as small business development funding or local radio) from EU regulation (Pielow, 2002). Some of the bigger Länder – Bavaria, unsurprisingly, but also North Rhine-Westphalia and Lower Saxony – have taken the principle further by pushing for a clearer delineation of competences between the EU and the member states. This approach would, on the one hand, limit the scope for further Europeanization of member state competences (and that means in Germany federal *and* Länder competences); on the other, it has been used to argue for the re-nationalization (in Germany also re-*region*alization) of some fields of competence, in particular agricultural policy, regional policy and subsidy controls (Jeffery, 2003). The effect would be to increase the autonomy of each of the Länder in the management of their territorial economies. Whether they succeed in these aims will not be clear until the next EU Intergovernmental Conference (IGC) scheduled for 2004.

Conclusion

It is clear from this discussion that the German federal system is in flux. The structures of cooperative federalism, developed in the period of post-war reconstruction and extended by the 1969 constitutional reforms, were fine-tuned in and for a West German society with a high degree of economic and social homogeneity and – as a result – a nationwide political arena with the same concerns at play in federal as in Länder politics. Those structures now clash and grind in a united Germany in which economics, politics and society are increasingly differentiated by territory. The assumptions of cooperative federalism – nationwide policy standards and uniformity of living conditions, equity and solidarity – are now challenged by a new territorial politics. Though the constitutional framework of German federalism remains by and large unchanged, the meaning given to it by those involved in the practice of federalism clearly is changing. As was noted above, constitutions can be interpreted in different ways and tend to flex over time to accommodate changes in circumstance and opinion. The character of German federalism has clearly changed as territorial concerns have come more and more to the fore. It remains to be seen how far the new circumstances and ideas of territorial diversity and territorial 'competition' can bend the old constitution to fit the new reality.

3

Voter Choice and Electoral Politics

RUSSELL J. DALTON

The 2002 Bundestag elections demonstrate the emerging new style of German electoral politics. Where once a stable basis of party competition seemed to determine electoral outcomes, the catchword for 2002 was the *Weschelwähler*, or the changing voter. The traditional bonds to social groups, such as class and religion, have steadily eroded across Bundestag elections in the late twentieth century, and these ties had only a limited impact in 2002. Similarly, affective party ties that once connected citizens to their preferred party have also weakened. Certainly some voters remain connected to social milieu or a habitual party tie, but the number of these voters has been steadily decreasing.

Instead of relying on such long-term party bonds, more Germans are entering each election with an open mind and deciding their vote based on the issues and candidates' performance during the campaign. This was clearly evident in 2002. Both the Social Democrats and the Greens – the Greens of all parties – waged campaigns that focused on the personal characteristics of their respective party leaders. The Social Democrats told voters to trust in Gerhard Schröder to lead the country through the difficult times ahead, though it was not exactly clear where he would lead them. The Greens tried to convince voters that their second vote (*Zweitstimme*) was the 'Joschka vote' for Joschka Fischer, the party leader and Germany's foreign minister.

Issues, too, played a very visible role in the 2002 campaign, illustrating the dynamism of current electoral politics. For most of 2002 the CDU/CSU focused the policy debate on the economic problems facing the nation, and the government's inability to address these issues. For most of 2002 the governing parties trailed in the polls. Then in

August Schröder led the government into action to help citizens and businesses that had suffered from a disastrous flood in eastern Germany; this demonstration of government competence swung many voters towards the Social Democrats. Perhaps no one since Noah has benefited more from a flood than Schröder. The televised debates between Schröder and Edmund Stoiber, the chancellor candidate for the CDU/CSU, further personalized the campaign and injected new policy claims. The campaign closed with a flurry of claims and counter-claims regarding Germany's foreign policy towards Iraq and its relations with America. Reflecting these dynamic forces, public opinion polls shifted back and forth during the last weeks of the campaign, tracking ebbs and flows of party support that were much greater than normally observed in German elections.

While this trend of growing electoral change has been developing over a long period in the West, the situation is different among voters in the East. Since unification easterners have celebrated their new democratic freedoms of democracy and have begun to exercise their new voting rights. Easterners lack the historical experiences with political parties that westerners have, thus precluding the type of long-term party ties that guide some western voters. Similarly, the social and economic dislocations of German unification have attenuated the social group bonds that historically provided a framework for electoral politics in the West. In short, easterners are trying to develop their understanding of electoral politics and their party preferences in this dynamic political environment. Thus, in comparison to westerners, easterners are even more changeable in their partisanship.

This chapter focuses on the electoral behaviour of the German public and examines the political differences between westerners and easterners. Elections are a useful setting in which to study political attitudes and behaviours, because they require that citizens think about political issues and make political choices. During elections, citizens express their judgements about the past accomplishments of the political parties, and make choices about the future course of the nation. Elections also mobilize and display the political cleavages existing within a society. Thus, a study of the voting behaviour can tell us a great deal about how citizens think about politics and the political legacy of Germany's divided history.

We begin by examining the factors that are normally described as stable and long-term influences on electoral politics: social group ties and partisan identifications. These factors provide the enduring basis of party competition, and voters often use them to simplify their choices. Then, we study the role of issues and candidate images in guiding voting behaviour, and in defining policy contrasts between easterners and westerners. In the conclusion, we discuss the implications of these findings for the German party system and German democracy.

The Erosion of Traditional Party Loyalties

Electoral research in the early history of the Federal Republic often viewed parties and elections in terms of relatively stable and enduring patterns of political competition. Party systems normally arise from the social divisions existing within a nation, and the strategic choices social groups make in courting party allies (Lipset and Rokkan, 1967). Because of this, people use their social position or their judgements about the social group leanings of the parties as a guide to their voting choices. A Ruhr steelworker who votes for the Social Democrats, or a Bavarian Catholic who supports the CSU, is reflecting his or her own values as well as the political choices available at election time. Thus, social characteristics often provided a good surrogate for studying differences in political values within a nation, and the influence of alternative social networks on political behaviour.

Similarly, many people developed long-term, affective attachments to a specific political party (often a party that represented their social milieu or that was supported by their parents). Card-carrying SPD members, for example, began each election knowing who they would support, just as self-identified Christian Democrats habitually endorsed the CDU/CSU. With continued support for their preferred party at successive elections, such affiliations strengthened during the early history of the Federal Republic. Thus, each election typically pitted the same social groups and same partisan camps against one another, with most voters supporting the same party as in the previous electoral battle.

Yet recent electoral research documents the gradual erosion of these partisan alignments across the history of the Federal Republic. At each subsequent election it appears that fewer and fewer voters in the West are following the guidance of social cues such as class or religion, or partisan attachments.

At the same time, the citizens in the East have experienced a very different electoral history. Many of the social group ties that structured traditional partisan politics in the West were unfamiliar or inapplicable to eastern voters as they began their new experience with democratic elections in the 1990s. And while western voters might have inherited their parents' partisan preferences or developed their own partisan identities over a lifetime of voting experience, the party system and electoral politics of the Federal Republic was a new experience for easterners. For different reasons, therefore, the new voters in the East also lacked long-term, stable ties to guide their electoral behaviour.

This section compares the impact of these long-term sources of voting behaviour for western and eastern voters. We examine the role of class, religion and social divisions, as well as the influence of party preferences as a guide for voting choice.

The Narrowing of Social Class Voting

The Federal Republic's party system is partially built upon the traditional class conflict between the bourgeoisie and proletariat, and more broadly on the problems of providing economic well-being and security to all members of society. These economic conflicts were important in defining the initial structure of the party system. Moreover, the CDU/CSU and SPD are embedded in their own network of support groups (business associations and labour unions) and offer voters distinct political programmes catering to these group interests.

Despite the historical importance of the class cleavage, four decades of electoral results point to an unmistakable decline in class voting differences within the FRG's party system (Dalton, 2002, ch. 8; Schmitt, 1993). At the height of class-based voting in 1957, the SPD received a majority of working-class votes (61 per cent) but only a small share (24 per cent) of middle-class votes. In overall terms, this represented a 37 percentage point gap in the class bases of party support, rivalling the level of class voting found in Britain and other class-polarized party systems (see Figure 3.1). Over the next two decades, the level of class voting steadily decreased in Germany, as in most other advanced industrial democracies. By the 1980s, the percentage point gap in class voting averaged in the teens. In other words, over time there has been a general convergence in the voting patterns of the middle class and the working class in the West. Voting differences based on other class characteristics, such as income or education, display a similar downward trend in their influence.

The top panel of Table 3.1 displays the voting patterns of social class groups within the western electorate for the 2002 election. Reflecting the shadow of past class alignments, a bare majority of the working class supported the Social Democrats (52 per cent). Indeed, one of the SPD's strategic goals has been to broaden its social base beyond the party's traditional support in the working class, essential since the number of working-class voters has declined over time. In contrast, middle-class

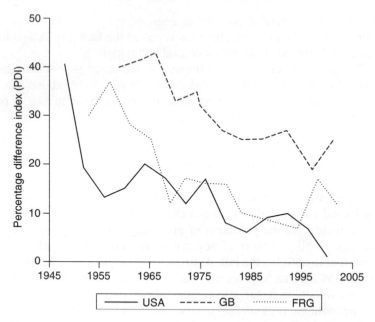

FIGURE 3.1   *Trends in class voting in Western Germany, Britain and the USA*
Sources: Germany, 1953–2002: German Election Studies (Western Germany only 1990–98);
USA, 1948–2000, American National Election Studies; Great Britain, 1955, Heath *et al.*
(1985); 1959, Civic Culture study; 1964–97, British Election Studies. Figure entries are the
Alford Class Voting index: that is, the percentage of the working class preferring a leftist
party minus the percentage of the middle class voting for the left. American data are based on
congressional elections, except for 1948 which is presidential vote.

voters in the West give the largest share of their vote to the CDU/CSU
(42 per cent). If we simply calculate the difference in the percentage
leftist vote (SPD and Greens) between the working class and the
combined middle class, the 12 per cent gap in party support in 2002 is
narrower than in 1998 and close to the average of elections in the
1980–90s.

Past research stresses the emergence of a new class in the West, a
modern middle class (*Neue Mittelstand*) of salaried employees and government workers that differs in social position and political behaviour
from the traditional middle class (the self-employed and professionals)
and the working class. The new middle class now represents the largest
sector of the labour force, and in recent elections they have split their
votes between left and right parties. This pattern is also repeated in
2002, with only a 1 per cent difference in the CDU/CSU and SPD vote
share within this stratum.

TABLE 3.1 *Social class and party support (%)*

	Working class	Middle class		
		Combined	Old	New
Western voters				
PDS	1	1	1	1
Alliance 90/Greens	8	12	15	12
SPD	52	36	19	39
FDP	6	9	13	8
CDU/CSU	34	42	52	40
Total	100	100	100	100
(% of voters)	25		14	61
Eastern voters				
PDS	10	13	9	15
Alliance 90/Greens	4	7	9	6
SPD	52	43	23	47
FDP	7	9	18	6
CDU/CSU	27	29	41	26
Total	100	100	100	100
(% of voters)	37		12	51

Note: Social class is based on the occupation of the respondent where this information is available.
Source: 16–20 September 2002 German Election Study (*Forschungsgruppe Wahlen*).

The persisting impact of social class on voting choice becomes even more blurred when we consider the voters in the eastern Länder (see Table 3.1). In the first democratic elections in the early 1990s, it was difficult to apply western notions of social class to a society that was in the midst of transition from socialism to capitalism. Moreover, the political ties between the parties and class-based interest groups in the East was equally unclear. The GDR was ostensibly a system intended to benefit workers and farmers, but members of the intelligentsia and upper class were actually more likely to subscribe to the values of the regime.

Due to these complications, the elections of the early 1990s displayed a *reversal* of class voting patterns among Easterners (Dalton and Bürklin, 1996; Dalton, 2002, ch. 8). The eastern CDU won most of the working-class vote, and fared less well among the middle class. Conversely, the leftist-oriented parties – SPD and PDS – garnered more votes among the middle class than among their 'normal' working-class constituency. The Alliance 90/Greens (B'90/Die Grünen) also gained greater support from the middle class. The few self-employed professionals in the East supported the CDU, but white-collar salaried employees in the East disproportionately endorsed leftist parties.

The class cleavage in the eastern Länder returned to the 'normal' pattern in the 1998 election, as the SPD and PDS won new support from the working class in the East. Kohl's promise of blooming landscapes in the East and a new economic miracle had confronted the grim reality of economic transformation and dislocation. Faced by continuing high unemployment levels in the East, and what appeared to be a permanent income gap between East and West, eastern workers supported the leftist parties in growing numbers.

The lower panel of Table 3.1 displays the patterns of class voting for eastern voters in 2002. The working class now leans toward the left (SPD, Green and PDS), while the middle class gives disproportionate support to the Christian Democrats. Yet the size of these differences is quite modest (a 3 per cent gap).

In summary, while social class once was a potential political cue, guiding how many citizens voted, the impact of this cue has steadily eroded in the West, and the new voters in the East have not been integrated into this class voting structure. Thus, when votes there are added to the weakened pattern of class voting in the West, this further obfuscates the impact of social class cues on German voting choices.

This blurring of class lines occurs because citizens are less likely to rely on the guidance of labour unions, business associations and other economic groups in deciding how to vote. It is not so much that the voters cannot recognize these cues; indeed other evidence suggests that voters are now better able to perceive these cues. In addition, it is not so much that economic and class issues are less important, as these issues still routinely dominate election campaigns; rather, voters are making their own choice on these issues, examining the candidates and issues of the campaign instead of voting on habitual class loyalties. This is the first piece of evidence to show how voters are beginning to choose.

The Erosion of Religious Influences on the Vote

Historically, religion has been another basis for partisan division with the Federal Republic. Political debates on the separation of church and state, and persisting differences between Catholics and Protestants, had a formative influence on the party system of the Federal Republic. Religion is often a silent issue in German politics, although it occasionally becomes visible in conflicts over religious or moral issues, such as abortion, state support of church programmes, and policies towards the family.

Religion still exerts a strong influence on voting patterns in the West. The top panel of Table 3.2 describes the pattern of religious voting in the

TABLE 3.2 *Religious denomination and party support (%)*

	Catholic	Protestant	No religion
Western voters			
PDS	–	1	7
Alliance 90/Greens	11	10	20
SPD	35	45	39
FDP	5	9	13
CDU/CSU	49	36	21
Total	100	100	100
(% of voters)	42	42	16
Eastern voters			
PDS	1	3	16
Alliance 90/Greens	8	7	10
SPD	38	52	49
FDP	8	7	4
CDU/CSU	46	30	21
Total	100	100	100
(% of voters)	7	31	62

Source: 16–20 September 2002 German Election Study (*Forschungsgruppe Wahlen*).

West in 2002. A 9 per cent gap separates Protestants and Catholics in their support for leftist parties (SPD and Greens). The voting gap between religious and non-religious westerners displays a similar divide. Both patterns are similar to results for other recent Bundestagswahlen. Furthermore, other public opinion data suggests that citizens perceptions of the Catholic Church's leanings towards the CDU/CSU remain distinct.

The impact of the religious cleavage on eastern voters is uncertain because of the GDR's history. Although the GDR followed the policy of separation between church and state, the government had replaced formal religious rites (such as *Taufe*, or baptism, and *Konfirmation*) with secular rites (e.g., *Jugendweihe*, an initiation rite which marks the passage of 14-year-olds to adulthood). The churches' existence were not questioned, but they were under strict government control. It was unclear whether religious cleavages could persist in such an environment. In addition, unification changed the religious balance of FRG politics; Catholics and Protestants are roughly at parity in the West, but the East is heavily Protestant. Thus, unification significantly altered the religious composition of the new Germany.

The lower panel of Table 3.2 displays the religious voting patterns among easterners. In the East, Catholics and Protestants disproportionately support the CDU. The voting gap between denominations is 13 per cent in leftist voting preferences (similar to the pattern within the western electorate). The more relevant dimension for easterners involves the secular/religious divide or religious attachments such as church attendance. Secular voters favour leftist parties by a large margin; the size of this gap is similar to the West.

Religious voting apparently follows a similar pattern in West and East, yet this commonality overlooks a basic difference in the composition of the two electorates. The GDR government created a secular society during its 40-year rule. For instance, the 1999 World Values Survey finds that 77 per cent of westerners believe in the existence of God, compared to 32 per cent in the East; 62 per cent of westerners consider themselves religious, but only 29 per cent of easterners. The vastly different composition of the two electorates is seen in Table 3.2. Only one-sixth of the western public say they are non-religious, compared to almost two-thirds of easterners! In summary, the East is a much more secularized society than West Germany, even though the West had experienced its own secularization trend.

The sharply different religious preferences of easterners and westerners illustrates the distinct electorates across the two regions. The western electorate is still relatively religious; the eastern electorate is predominately secular. The different religious composition of the two electorates creates two distinct constituencies within the major political parties. In the West, the majority of CDU/CSU voters are Catholics; in the East, the majority of CDU's voters describe themselves as having no religious attachment. Among Western democracies, this is probably the only example of a party explicitly espousing religious values that has such a secular voter base.

These large regional differences can create sharp intraparty tensions. Because CDU voters in the new Länder are significantly less religious and less Catholic than their western counterparts, their attitudes towards abortion and other social issues conflict with the policy programme of the western CDU. If Christian Democratic politicians from the East represent these views, they come into conflict with the party's official policies. If eastern CDU deputies do not reflect these views, this produces a representation deficit for easterners.

Despite the evidence of a persisting relationship between religious values and partisan preferences, the religious cleavage is following the same pattern of decline as the class cleavage. Social modernization can disrupt religious alignments in the same manner that social-class lines have blurred. Changing lifestyles, and religious beliefs, have decreased involvement in church activities and diminished the church as a focus of social (and political) activities. The Federal Republic, like most Western nations, displays a steady decline in religious involvement over the past 50 years (Franklin *et al.*, 1992, ch. 1). In fact, comparisons of the voting patterns of religious denominations include only those voters with religious attachments. Individuals who attend church regularly remain well integrated into a religious network and maintain distinct voting patterns. But there are fewer of these individuals today, and the growing number of secular voters by definition do not turn to religious cues to make their electoral choices. Thus as the number of individuals relying on religious cues decreases, the partisan significance of religious characteristics and their overall ability to explain voting are also decreasing.

The Weakening of Party Attachments

Social cleavages may provide the foundations of modern party systems and electoral choice, but they are only one factor in electoral decision-making. Electoral research finds that people develop direct personal attachments to their preferred political party, which guides their voting and other aspects of political behaviour (Dalton, 2002, ch. 9). Researchers call this a sense of 'party identification'. Party identification is generally socialized early in life, often as part of a family political inheritance or derived from social group cues, and then reinforced by adult electoral experiences.

These party ties are important because they can structure a person's view of the political world, provide cues for judging political phenomena, influence patterns of political participation, and promote stability in individual voting behaviour. For instance, 80–90 per cent of partisans routinely support their preferred party at election time. The concept of party identification has proved one of the most helpful ideas in understanding the political behaviour of contemporary electorates (Holmberg, 1994).

Prior research has tracked two distinct phases in the post-war development of the party attachments in the Federal Republic. The stabilization and consolidation of the party system during the 1950s and 1960s strengthened popular attachments to the political parties (Baker, Dalton and Hildebrandt, 1981; Norpoth, 1983). In the late 1970s, however, this trend towards partisanship among western voters slowed, and then reversed. A decreasing proportion of westerners expresses strong feelings of partisan identity, and a growing number do not feel attached to any political party.

Several factors seemed to account for this decline in partisanship. After the decades of post-war growth and policy accomplishments, the political parties have struggled with economic recession and the rise of new political issues (Zelle, 1995). Other political institutions – such as citizen-action groups or public interest lobbies – arose to represent these new political interests and challenge the political parties. In addition, a series of political scandals at the national level and state levels tarnished party images (e.g., a series of party finance scandals and exposés on party collusion). The parties appeared to be self-interested and self-centred organizations, which created feelings of partisan antipathy among the public. In short, these developments created doubts about the ability of political parties to represent the public's interests effectively.

In addition, the growing sophistication of the western electorate weakened individual party ties. Similar to the decline of partisanship in the USA and Britain, dealignment is concentrated among politically sophisticated and better educated citizens (Dalton and Wattenberg, 2000). With growing interest and knowledge about politics, people are better able to make their own political decisions without depending on party attachments. Furthermore, as voters begin to focus on issues as a basis of electoral choice, they are more likely to defect from their normal party predispositions, which then erodes these predispositions and makes further defections even more likely. This general pattern is described as a *dealignment* of long-term party attachments in the Federal Republic.

German unification has accelerated this process of dealignment. Unification created major policy challenges for the Federal Republic, and often the reality of politics fell short of the rhetoric from party elites. In addition to the problems of German union, continuing scandals further undermined the parties' stature and contributed to these negative images. A series of political scandals in the early 1990s led President Richard von Weizsäcker to take the unusual step of criticizing the political parties for being obsessed with power (von Weizsäcker, 1992). Instead of pursuing the nation's interests, he reprimanded the parties for pursuing their own self-interest. Then, after Kohl left office he was convicted of accepting illegal contributions to the CDU while he was in office and, despite public criticism, he refused to declare the amount of these contributions or the sources. Another series of financial scandals occurred during the run-up to the 2002 election, touching politicians from several different parties. For many westerners, this pattern of poor performance and party scandals confirms their doubts about the vitality of the German party system, and even their own partisan loyalties.

For many easterners as well, these events raised fundamental questions about how democracy really functions. In fact, we should expect the partisan orientations of easterners to be very different from westerners (Kaase and Klingemann, 1994). Easterners were just beginning their democratic experience with the Federal Republic's parties, so few easterners should (or could) display the deep affective partisan loyalties that constitute a sense of 'party identification'. Although some research suggests that many easterners had latent affinities for specific parties in the Federal Republic, these were not the sort of long-term attachments born of early life experiences that we normally equate with party identification.

Table 3.3 monitors this dealignment trend by tracking party identification among western voters (1972–2002) and easterners (1991–2002). The western data indicate a slight erosion in the strength of party attachments during the 1980s, which accelerates in the 1990s. In the 1972 election, for instance, 75 per cent of the electorate felt an attachment to their preferred party. By 1990 this group of partisans amounted to 71 per cent of the public, and by 2002 to 65 per cent. In 1972 a majority of westerners expressed strong party ties (55 per cent), but by 2002 only a third express such strong party bonds (37 per cent). Clearly party ties are eroding in the West.

Regular measurement of partisan attachments did not begin in eastern surveys until early 1991. By then, most voters already had significant electoral experience with the FRG parties. They had participated in two national elections (the March 1990 Volkskammer and December Bundestag elections) as well as regional and local contests. Still, eastern voters were significantly more hesitant about expressing a sense of party attachment. By 2002, eastern partisanship remained weak. Only 28 per cent of easterners claimed to hold 'very strong' or 'strong' party ties, and two-fifths of the public (45 per cent) are explicitly non-partisan. The first decade of democratic experience with the Federal Republic's party system has not developed partisan ties.

In summary, citizens in both east and west display evidence of weak psychological ties binding them to the political parties, and thus a diminished role of partisanship in structuring vote choices. But we interpret these findings differently for the two regions. The decrease in partisanship among westerners is similar to several other advanced industrial democracies (Dalton, 2001). This suggests a general pattern of partisan dealignment in contemporary democracies, and Germany's special problems of unification may simply reinforce this general process.

In contrast, we might describe easterners as a pre-alignment electorate. Democratic politics is still a relative new experience for eastern voters. Party attachments normally strengthen through repeated electoral experiences, especially in newly-formed party systems (Kaase and Klingemann, 1994). Thus, the current situation in the East might be

TABLE 3.3 *The strength of partisanship* (%)

	Western votes									Eastern votes			
	1972	*1976*	*1980*	*1983*	*1987*	*1990*	*1994*	*1998*	*2002*	*1991*	*1994*	*1998*	*2002*
Very strong	17	12	13	10	10	11	12	9	12	4	6	7	7
Strong	38	35	33	29	31	29	24	22	25	22	19	17	21
Weak	20	35	29	35	31	31	31	31	27	35	34	30	26
No party; don't know	20	16	19	22	25	27	31	36	32	37	40	44	45
Refused	5	3	6	4	3	2	2	2	3	3	1	2	2

Source: Data from German election studies collected by the *Forschungsgruppe Wahlen*; several pre-election surveys and a post-election survey are included for most timepoints.

closer to the Federal Republic in the immediate post-war period. We should expect the partisan attachments of easterners to strengthen over time, but the dealigning forces of the contemporary party system may slow this process. The rapidity with which easterners develop party attachments is an important measure of their development of stable political orientations and their integration into the Federal Republic's party system.

From Habituation to Voter Choice

Although many voters continue to support the same party from election to election, a mounting body of evidence points to the increasing fluidity of electoral choice. In the 1980s, the Greens and the issues they espoused introduced new political choices and new volatility in the electoral process. Unification has continued this process, with the introduction of the PDS and the issues flowing from unification. Moreover, the electorate itself is changing, placing less reliance on the stable social and partisan cues that once guided their behaviour.

Evidence of this shift from habituation to voter choice is apparent in a variety of statistics. For instance, in the 1960s and early 1970s the party system was characterized by a fairly stable pattern of party competition between the CDU/CSU, SPD and the FDP. During this period, barely 10 per cent of the voters reported switching their party choice between elections (Figure 3.2). This pattern of electoral stability changed in the 1980s, during which elections were characterized by more intense political and personal rivalries between the parties. By the end of the 1990s, roughly a quarter of the western electorate reports they switched votes, which is probably an underestimate of the actual amount of volatility. In the September 2002 Forschungsgruppe survey election, 23 per cent of westerners and 22 per cent of easterners reported that they had shifted votes since 1998.

Split-ticket voting is another possible indicator of the rigidity of party commitments. When Germans go to the polls they cast two votes. The first vote (*Erstimme*) is for a candidate to represent the electoral district; the second vote (*Zweitstimme*) is for a party list that provides the basis for a proportional allocation of parliamentary seats. A voter may therefore split his or her ballot by selecting a district candidate of one party with the first vote and another party with the party-list vote.

The amount of split-ticket voting has also inched upward in recent elections (Schoen, 2000). Up until the late 1960s, less than 10 per cent of all voters split their ballots (Figure 3.2). The proportion of splitters

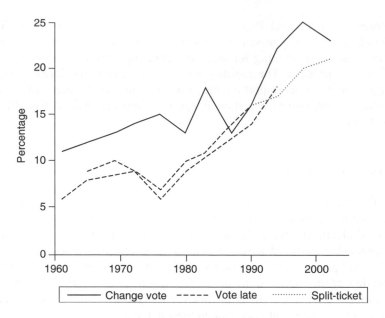

FIGURE 3.2   *Indications of increasing fluidity of voting choice*
Sources: 1961–2002 German Election Studies (Western Germany only to ensure the comparability of the trends).

increased in the 1980s, and by the 1990s one-sixth of voters claimed to cast a split ballot. In 2002 this reached 21 per cent in the West. The growth of split-ticket voting partially reflects the increased strength of minor parties which siphon off second votes from the major parties. In addition, split-ticket voting exemplifies the increasing fluidity of contemporary voting choices.

Another sign of the changing pattern of electoral choice is the timing of voting decisions. We have argued that most Germans once began election campaigns with strong predispositions to support their preferred party of the past. But as these predispositions weaken, more voters should be making their decisions on the issues and candidates of the campaign, and thus making their decisions later in the election cycle. If this is correct, fewer voters will say that they decided how to vote before the campaign, and more will claim that they decided during the campaign or even on election day itself.

Figure 3.2 indicates that an increasing percentage of western voters say they are making their decision during the last few weeks of the campaign. The percentage of self-defined late deciders has doubled over time, from less than one-tenth of the electorate in the 1960s to nearly one-fifth in the 1990s. In the 2002 election, one-third of voters reported that they had decided during the election period.

In summary, fewer Germans are approaching each election with their decision already made. Instead of habitual or inherited party preferences, or those directed by external group cues, more voters are apparently making their decisions based on the content of the campaign and the offerings of the parties. While one might attribute this pattern to the political disruptions caused by unification, it is a general pattern occurring in virtually all advanced industrial democracies (Dalton and Wattenberg, 2000, ch. 3). Politics is shifting from habituation to voter choice.

The Changing Basis of Electoral Choice

If the long-term sources of voting choice are weakening in influence, this raises the question of what voters now use to make their electoral choices. Inevitably, the erosion of social group and partisanship cues must lead to increased reliance on shorter-term factors, such as the issues and candidates of each campaign. Moreover, the evidence of increased party switching between elections suggests that such short-term factors are having an increasing weight on voter choice.

Issue positions are the currency of politics, and the choice of parties or the choice of governments is closely linked to the policies they will enact. Each campaign, however, has its own set of issues that reflect the political controversies of the day, and the parties' choices about what themes to stress in their campaigns. Moreover, we are more interested in the total impact of issues, rather than the specific set of issues that have affected each Bundestagswahl.

We can provide a general illustration of the role of issue preferences in voting choice by examining the relationship between left/right attitudes and vote. Left/right attitudes are a sort of 'super issue', a statement of positions on the issues that are currently most important to each voter. For some voters, their left/right position may be derived from views on traditional economic conflicts; for others, left/right position may reflect positions on New Politics controversies such environmental quality or gender issues. The issues of German unification can also be translated into a left/right framework. The specific issues might vary across individuals or across elections, but left/right attitudes provide a summary measure of each citizen's overall policy views (Dalton, 2002, ch. 9).

Table 3.4 displays the relationship between left/right attitudes and party choice in the 2002 election for voters in both West and East.

TABLE 3.4 *Left/right attitudes and party support (%)*

	Left	–	Centre	–	Right
Western voters					
PDS	8	4	1	0	0
Greens	21	23	11	3	5
SPD	55	58	41	10	30
FDP	3	5	9	10	10
CDU/CSU	13	10	38	78	55
Total	100	100	100	100	100
(% of voters)	(5)	(17)	(63)	(12)	(3)
Eastern voters					
PDS	35	21	6	3	13
Greens	5	15	5	1	0
SPD	46	56	45	20	45
FDP	2	3	10	13	0
CDU/CSU	12	4	34	62	42
Total	100	99	100	99	100
(% of voters)	(7)	(24)	(60)	(9)	(1)

Source: 16–20 September 2002 German Election Study
(*Forschungsgruppe Wahlen*).

In both regions there is a close fit between left/right position and vote. The PDS, for example, gets disproportionate support from leftist voters, especially in the East where the party receives more than a third of the vote from leftists. Virtually no one on the right side of the political spectrum supports the PDS in either region. The PDS bases its appeal on a combination of economic issues and advocacy of a separate eastern identity. The Greens are also a predominantly leftist party, with an appeal that is noticeably stronger in the West. The Greens appeal to voters on cultural and social issues, rather than economic issues.

The ideological basis of support for the two large established parties is also clearly apparent in Table 3.4. In eastern Germany the SPD and PDS divide the support of leftist voters, and the SPD garners a large majority among leftist voters in the West. In both regions the Social Democrats vote steadily erodes as one moves right. The CDU/CSU's voting base presents a mirror image: high among conservative voters and steadily declining as one moves left. Finally, as a party standing between the two large established parties, the Free Democrats get most of their support from voters in the centre and just right of the centre.

Table 3.4 thus indicates that left/right attitudes, and thereby the specific policy issues that define left/right, have a very strong relationship to party preferences. This has long been the case in German elections, but the role of left/right attitudes and issues have apparently increased over time as voters focus more on what candidates and parties are emphasizing in each election (Franklin *et al.*, 1992). This is one consequence of the shift from stable voting dispositions to more fluid party choice.

In addition to issue voting, candidate characteristics may function as another short-term basis for voting choice. Since the German ballot is divided between a party vote and a district candidate vote, one might assume that candidate voting was always part of the electoral calculus. But early voting studies demonstrated that many voters were unaware of the candidates running in their district, and cast their candidate vote as a simple extension of their party preference. Moreover, since the Chancellor was selected by the parties in the Bundestagswahl, the image of the Chancellor candidates played less role in Bundestag elections than in the candidate-centred direct election of the US president.

As voting choice has become more fluid, however, the importance of candidate image has increased. First, there is evidence that party and candidate preferences are not as closely related as they were in the past (Dalton and Wattenberg, 2000, p. 53). Second, images of the chancellor candidates are more strongly related to party choice in the elections (Anderson and Zelle, 1995; Ohr, 2000). German chancellor candidates have turned to television to personalize the campaigns, arranging campaign events for their video appeal and using televised town hall meetings to directly connect to citizens. The growth of private television broadcasting in Germany over the past decade further accelerated these trends. The 2002 contest probably accentuated the importance of candidate image; candidates played a prominent role in party campaign advertising and the Schröder/Stoiber television duel focused attention on the two chancellor candidates. Indeed, because of the centrality of the chancellor candidates one leading political analyst called 2002 the first 'presidential election' in Germany.

When all of these factors – long-term and short-term – come together, they determine the voting choice of Germans. Current voting decisions reflect a mix of these factors. In the 2002 election, despite the dealignment trend described above, partisanship still weighed heavily on the vote choice of westerners. This is the strongest single factor shaping vote choice, and we should expect that those with partisan ties will generally follow them at election time. Candidate image also had a large impact in 2002; comparable analyses of 1998 suggest that the influence of candidates increased. Left/right attitudes, and the issue positions represented by this super issue, play a secondary role.

The electoral calculus is somewhat different for easterners. For those easterners who have party ties, partisan preferences have significant influence on vote choice. However, eastern voters place greater weight on the issue and ideological factors summarized by left/right attitudes. Candidate image influences voter choices in the East, although less than in the West (if the CDU/CSU had kept Angela Merkel as their party leader, candidate influences in the East would probably have become even more important).

The Two German Electorates

This chapter has highlighted two broad characteristics of electoral politics in contemporary Germany. First, considerable potential for electoral change exists. For the past two decades, long-term sources of voting choice have diminished in influence among voters in the West. Social class, religion, residence, and other social characteristics have a declining impact on voting behaviour. Similarly, a dealignment trend signals a decrease in the influence of enduring partisan loyalties on voting decisions. Fewer westerners now approach elections with fixed party predispositions based either on social characteristics or early-learned partisan ties. It is not that voters lack partisan predispositions, but that the nature of these predispositions is shifting from *strong ties* (group and party attachments) to *weak ties* (issues, candidate images, and perceptions of party performance). Much like the findings of American or British electorate research, this erosion in the traditional bases of partisan support has occurred without producing new, enduring bases of support that might revitalize the party system (e.g., Rose and McAllister, 1989; Wattenberg, 1996). Indeed, it is the lack of a new stable alignment that appears to be the most distinctive feature of contemporary party systems.

Citizens in the five new Länder, of course, have a very different electoral history. Rather than an erosion of previous social and partisan ties, the eastern electorate is still learning about democratic politics and the rough-and-tumble life of partisan campaigns. Easterners understandably begin this experience with weaker party ties and less certainty about the general structure of political competition. One factor to watch is how quickly they adapt to the political structures of the west, or whether they remain only weakly tied to the party system. Little has yet changed in these patterns over the past decade (e.g., Dalton, 1996a).

The modest impact of long-term determinants of party choice is likely to strengthen the role that policy preferences play within the German electoral process. Although most voters still habitually support a preferred party, the tentativeness of these bonds will increase the potential

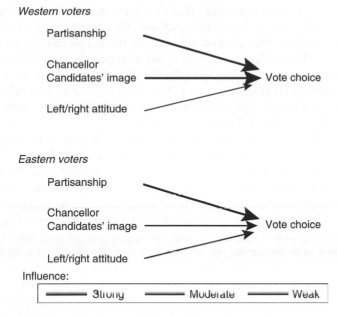

FIGURE 3.3   *The factors influencing voter choices*

that a particular issue or election campaign may sway their voting choice (at least temporarily). More and more, party issue positions and political images will influence voter choices, as a substantial group of floating voters react to the political stimuli of the election campaign. There is even some evidence that candidate images are playing a growing role in voters' decision-making, especially among easterners. This shift toward issue-based voting behaviour is likely to make policy considerations a more important aspect of elections while injecting considerable fluidity into electoral politics, or at least until (if ever) a new stable group basis of party support forms.

A second implication of our findings concerns the contrasts between western and eastern Germans. There are two distinct electorates within the one German nation. The sharply different religious preferences of easterners and westerners is the most distinctive evidence that two separate electorates now exist. The western electorate is fairly religious, as well as conservative on economic and social welfare issues; the eastern electorate is secular and liberal on social issues. In addition, easterners are more likely to describe themselves as leftist on the left/right scale to a greater extent than westerners.

The concerns of easterners that they were not well represented by either of the two major parties undoubtedly contributed to the PDS's success in the 1990s as spokesperson for the disenfranchised east. In 2002 the SPD made a conscious effort to appeal to these PDS voters, and this is one reason why the PDS fell below the 5 per cent hurdle. But it is uncertain whether the Social Democrats will be able to effectively represent these new supporters in the east, and balance their preferences against those of the SPD electoral in the west.

It is also clear that the minor parties are developing distinct regional clienteles. The PDS remains a party of the east, and it is likely to remain active in state and local governments in the new Länder. Conversely, the Greens and FDP are based in the west. The Greens split the leftist vote with the SPD in the west, but have limited appeal to eastern voters. The Free Democrats present themselves as a reasonable centrist alternative to the SPD and CDU/CSU, but this appeals appears distinctly more attractive to westerners.

Regional differences in the patterns of party support also can create sharp intraparty tensions. For instance, because CDU voters in the new Länder are significantly less religious and less Catholic than their western counterparts, their attitudes towards abortion and other social issues conflict with the policy programme of the western CDU. If CDU politicians from the east represent these views, it places them in conflict with the party's official policies. If eastern CDU deputies do not reflect these views, then this produces a representation deficit for easterners. The SPD and the other parties face similar problems in representing contrasting constituencies in west and east. Thus, the complex relationship between horizontal integration with the national party elite, and vertical integration between party elites and their social constituencies has been unbalanced by German unification.

Conclusion

Taken together, these patterns of partisan fluidity and contrasting political alignments across regions do not lend themselves to a simple prediction of the future of the party system. A situation that was already complicated in the 1980s has become even more complex in the 1990s. It appears that electoral politics will be characterized by continued diversity in voting patterns. A system of frozen social cleavages and stable party alignments is less likely to develop in a society where voters are sophisticated, political interests are diverse, and individual choice is given greater latitude. Even the new political conflicts that are competing for the public's attention seem destined to create additional sources of partisan change rather than recreate the stable electoral structure of the past. This diversity and fluidity may, in fact, be the major new characteristic of German electoral politics and the contemporary electoral politics of other advanced industrial societies.

4

The 'New Model' Party System

GORDON SMITH

Even though it was only by the slenderest of margins, the SPD–Green coalition was able to hold on to office at the September 2002 election. Thus Chancellor Gerhard Schröder's venture in turning to the Greens as the SPD's preferred coalition partner in 1998 proved to be a winning strategy. Indeed, had the coalition been defeated, it would have been the first occasion in the history of the Federal Republic that an incumbent government had lost an election after its first term in office.

In one sense, the 2002 election represented no more than a continuation of an existing coalition. At the same time, however, other developments were becoming apparent that could have significant effects for the parties and the system as a whole. Before considering the course of possible development, we should first take account of the enduring characteristics of the party system because they have long been integral to its functioning.

Core Persistence and System Stability

Judged on several criteria, the German party system has proved to be highly stable, and it mirrors the wider stability over the years enjoyed by the Federal Republic. The lasting features of the party system have been: the two-party dominance exercised by the CDU/CSU and the SPD; their periodic alternation in office; the durability of governing coalitions; the maintenance of a 'restricted' party system; and the failure of extremist parties to gain representation at the federal level. That the established system proved to be highly resilient was shown by its ability to withstand the shock of German reunification, when it could have been expected that a divisive splintering would occur.

Of course, most of these features are subject to qualification in one way or another. Thus, the 'alternation' of the major parties in government has in practice meant that one or the other has been excluded for many years at a time, as happened to the SPD for the long 'Kohl era', from 1982 to 1998. Exceptionally a coalition has broken down, as when the FDP deserted the SPD in 1982 to put the CDU into government. The pattern of coalitions and the chancellors holding office since the founding of the Federal Republic are shown in Table 1.1 (p. 20).

It is also a 'restricted' multi-party system, but its long-lasting three-party format – CDU/CSU, SPD and FDP – changed to a five-party one with the arrival, first, of the Greens on the federal stage in 1983 and then with the PDS in 1990 following reunification. The continuing absence of other small and/or extremist parties, which could lead to a flourishing multi-party system, must largely be ascribed to the 'restrictive' nature of the electoral law with the 5 per cent threshold normally necessary to secure parliamentary representation.

Whatever characteristics – and qualifications – are brought into the overall portrayal of the party system, the one that dwarfs all others is the long-term dominance wielded by the two major parties. Together, they constitute the bulk of the party system, and are of overriding importance for its operation as well as for the pattern of coalition alignments. These are the characteristics of the 'core' parties in a party system (Smith, 1990). In the German case, the two *Volksparteien* (people's parties) have a wide electoral appeal, a pragmatic outlook, and an integrative drive that makes it difficult for ideological or sectional parties to compete. In sum, their political strategies and style of electoral competition imply a centripetal party system rather than a polarized one.

As Russell Dalton has already shown in detail (see Chapter 3), the German electorate has become increasingly fluid in its behaviour. This decline in partisanship means that the parties can no longer be assured of the support that they could rely on in the past. Moreover, the two-party aggregate, combining the SPD's and CDU/CSU's vote, has gradually declined over the years. Thus in the 1970s their share of the total vote was over 90 per cent, but by 1998 and 2002 it had fallen to around 76 per cent. If this decline were to continue, then one or other party could eventually forfeit its 'core' status, and the system would be open to fundamental change.

The 'Triangular' System

As far back as the early 1960s, the party system took on what was aptly depicted by Franz Urban Pappi in terms of a 'triangular' formation, a patterning which persisted for more than 30 years (Pappi, 1984). In essence, this model required either the CDU or the SPD to form a governing coalition with the Free Democrats or, exceptionally, as with the 'grand coalition' from 1966 to 1969, one between the CDU/CSU and the SPD. The FDP thus became the pivot of the party system and was able to ensure itself a place in government. So successful was the FDP in this pivotal role that it has actually held office for longer than either the CDU or the SPD. From this perspective, the FDP was able to impose a 'centripetal bind' on the party system.

Pappi's formulation makes clear that the basis of the model was the presence in the three parties of partially shared features. Thus the FDP had in common with the CDU 'bourgeois values', chiefly those favouring a market economy. With the SPD, the FDP found common cause on 'social-liberal' issues against the religious traditionalism associated with Christian democracy (for instance, over such issues as divorce law reform and abortion). Underpinning the whole framework was the strong link between the CDU and the SPD by what Pappi termed 'corporatist issues'. This common ground for the two parties met, on the one side, the CDU's commitment to a 'socially-responsible market economy' (*soziale Marktwirtschaft*), and, on the other, the SPD's 'class compromise' as spelt out in the party's Godesberg Programme of 1959, in which the party adopted the *Volkspartei* description of itself.

At the time he wrote, Pappi argued that 'one should give up the simple framework of a left–right dimension underlying the German party system' (Pappi, 1984, p. 12) and instead proposed his model of an 'isosceles triangle' linking the parties. Even so, he stressed that the parties themselves did not thereby relinquish their defining political orientation, or *tendance*. Implicitly, therefore, the way was left open for them to be reasserted in the future.

Towards a New Geometry

Helmut Kohl's long domination of German politics came to an end with the election of 1998. Although it was not readily apparent at the time, that election also signalled the demise of the triangular system. The SPD's vote rose substantially to 40.9 per cent, and that of the CDU/CSU then fell to 35.1 per cent (its lowest share since 1949). This sharp decline

TABLE 4.1 *Elections to the Bundestag, 1994–2002*
(% list vote)

	Seats[1]	2002	1998	1994
SPD	251	38.5	40.9	36.4
CDU/CSU	248	38.5	35.1	41.5
Greens	55	8.6	6.7	7.3
FDP	47	7.4	6.2	6.9
PDS	2	4.0	5.1	4.4
Others	0	3.0	6.0	3.5
Turnout (%)		79.1	82.2	79.0

[1] For the 2002 election the number of Bundestag seats was reduced to 603, with the inclusion of 4 *Überhangmandate* (surplus seats). The purpose of the change was to reduce the number of *Überhangmandate* because they distort the proportionality of the electoral system (Roberts, 2000a).

Source: *Der Bundeswahlleiter.*

did not, in fact, presage an imminent decline in the two-party aggregate. Nevertheless, the movement in 1998 was sufficient to allow for a re-ordering of possible coalition alignments (see Table 4.1).

With its substantial lead over the CDU/CSU, the SPD was in a strong position to decide on the make-up of the new government. In theory the SPD had several options available. One was the resurrection of a grand coalition with the CDU, while another was to go back once more to coalition with the FDP, or just possibly also an oversized coalition to include the PDS as well as the Greens. None of these combinations was at all attractive for the incoming chancellor and his choice of governing with the Greens – although viewed as problematic by many at the time – gave Schröder a clear majority in the Bundestag.

At that stage, it was by no means certain which direction the party system would take: the Red–Green coalition might easily have fallen apart, and then what would have happened? This eventuality was only one possibility. Even if it did survive the full four-year term, the experiment with a diverse left-leaning government seemed unlikely to be repeated.

In examining several indicators, Stephen Padgett, subsequent to the 1998 election, pointed to a number of complicating developments that indicated an uncertain future. These were: the mounting uncertainties affecting electoral behaviour, the growing diversity of the party system, and the increasing ideological complexity of the parties themselves. Taken together, these developments would lead to strategic dilemmas for the individual parties and further complicate interparty relations. He concluded: 'Indeed, most of the evidence points to a much more fluid pattern of inter-party relations, and a high potential for flux' (Padgett, 2000, p. 106).

As yet this potential remains unrealized, as the outcome of the 2002 election was to show. What became clear, however, was that the party system was set on a new course and that the familiar triangular party constellation was unlikely to be resurrected.

The 2002 Election

In the run-up to the 2002 federal election, the prospects for the SPD/Green coalition looked grim, with the SPD trailing behind the CDU/CSU in opinion polls; in the Saxony-Anhalt Land election held in April 2002, the SPD's vote plummeted to below 20 per cent, to give control of the government to the CDU and FDP.

Saxony-Anhalt is one of the poorest regions, and that result was most likely related to the generally deteriorating economic situation. Throughout Germany, rising unemployment and a stagnant economy were major causes of concern and they had become increasingly so in the latter part of 2001. Over the whole period since the 1998 election, the economic situation had been an ever-present issue. In 1998, Schröder had made employment and economic growth the prime aim of the new government. He then declared that the level of unemployment would be cut to 3.5 million by the time of the next election. Rather rashly, he added that if this aim was not achieved, his government would not deserve to be re-elected; this pledge must have returned to haunt him subsequently, for by the time of the 2002 election the figure still stood at the 4 million mark.

By January 2002, Germany had adopted the euro as its currency. This constraint along with the conditions of the Growth and Stability Pact, as well as ceding control over interest rates to the European Central Bank restricted the Federal government's freedom of action to stimulate the economy. If these constraints held back a German recovery, then one surprising aspect of the campaign was that there was no discernible anti-euro backlash, and certainly not a party-based one. This party–elite consensus over what in other countries could become a sharply divisive issue says much about the consensus mechanisms in the German political system (Lees, 2002).

Throughout the campaign, Schröder's personal rating in opinion polls stood high and above that of his own party. The CDU/CSU, in contrast, had been dogged by leadership crises since the previous election, and it was not until January 2002 that the matter was settled when

Edmund Stoiber, the CSU Minister-President of Bavaria, was adopted as the chancellor-candidate for the CDU/CSU.

The SPD was not helped by the case of 'sleaze' involving Rudolf Scharping, the defence minister, and formerly the party leader and chancellor-candidate. Scharping was accused of receiving substantial bribes from a private firm. Scharping refused to resign, and was then summarily dismissed by Schröder in July. With the economy stagnant and the SPD trailing in the opinion polls, the party was left, rather like Charles Dickens's character, Mr Micawber, hoping that 'something would turn up'.

Turn up it did. In early August, barely six weeks before the election, devastating floods affected central Europe and parts of Germany, particularly along the course of the River Elbe in the east. All at once this catastrophe gave the Chancellor a chance to show leadership and take decisive action. He immediately called a 'summit' meeting of the countries affected, and also promised that no one in Germany would be any the worse off as a result of the widespread flood damage, setting aside the equivalent of some £5 billion (€7 billion) in compensation. From that point onwards the opinion polls began to move in the government's favour. This episode also helped the Greens, since their concerns with the environment naturally found a response in the electorate. Furthermore, Schröder's actions were appreciated in eastern Germany and boosted the SPD's standing.

The opposition parties were understandably wrong-footed by the dramatic turn of events. Even though Stoiber and the CDU/CSU continued to attack the government's economic record, this theme lacked sufficient impetus in the closing stages of the campaign. Schröder clearly grew more optimistic, and by the second of the television 'duels' between the two contestants it was apparent that Stoiber, as sound as his arguments were, was unable to match his opponent's new-found confidence.

One other event helped to tip the balance in the SPD's favour. Schröder came out strongly against any German involvement in a future American-led military attack on Iraq. This sharp rebuff to the USA immediately soured the relations between the two governments. It appeared to be a foolhardy position to adopt; yet, seen solely from the perspective of the election campaign, Schröder's move appealed to the pacifist sentiments of many Germans who had no wish to be caught up in another war. In a way, there was an echo of the *ohne mich* ('count me out') reaction when German re-armament first came about in the early years of the Federal Republic.

In the September election, the SPD and the CDU/CSU finished on almost level terms, with the SPD somewhat down on its 1998 share of the vote and the CDU/CSU recovering from its previous low point, largely thanks to the very strong support in Bavaria. In fact, it was the contrasting performance of the smaller parties that proved decisive: the Bündnis'90/Greens increased their vote by some two percentage points, which was sufficient to compensate for the losses of the SPD. In contrast, the failure of the PDS to clear the 5 per cent hurdle or to win at least three direct mandates (they secured only two) was helpful to the SPD. Thus in east Germany, the SPD vote rose significantly, from 34.1 to 39.7 per cent, but largely at the expense of the PDS.

How should the results of this election be interpreted? Given the narrow margin of a few thousand votes between the two parties, it can hardly be described as a 'victory' for the SPD, and neither was it in itself a 'defeat' for the CDU/CSU. At the first meeting of the new Bundestag in October, with the task of electing a new chancellor, Schröder secured 305 votes out of 603, just three more votes than the absolute majority required by the Basic Law. Close as the whole campaign and election had been, the outcome nevertheless served to confirm the changing nature of the party system that had begun to become apparent in 1998.

Party Perspectives in a Two-Bloc System

The SPD

Evaluation of the SPD in office largely depends on the assessment made of Gerhard Schröder's performance. The lacklustre record of the SPD throughout most of the Kohl era can in part be put down to the quality of SPD leadership, at least in contrast to Kohl's dominating authority in the earlier years. That had been the fate of Oskar Lafontaine, the party's chancellor-candidate in 1990, and of Rudolf Scharping in 1994. For the 1998 election, the choice of candidate was made by party members, and their preference was for Schröder, the successful Minister-President of Lower Saxony (where the SPD had won an absolute majority in the 1998 Land election) rather than Scharping. The former favoured a coalition with the Greens, and the latter probably one with the FDP. Schröder's success in 1998 owed much to the belief among voters, especially those weakly attached to parties, that the SPD had greater competence in dealing with economic problems, particularly the high level of unemployment.

There was certainly an element of boldness in opting for the untried experiment of governing with the Greens. However, the more pressing problem at first was dealing with opposition within Schröder's own party. It centred on the figure of 'Red Oskar' Lafontaine, SPD party chairman, who also became finance minister in the new government. He stood for neo-Keynesian reflationary policies to boost employment and for the defence of traditional social democratic interests. In sharp contrast, Schröder favoured a conventional economic policy, being concerned not to fuel inflation and to be business-friendly. Their mutual antagonism soon became acute and led to Lafontaine's bitter resignation in March 1999, with Schröder then assuming the party chairmanship as well. This showdown had echoes a few years later when he dismissed Scharping. Thus two of the party's former chancellor-candidates had fallen by the wayside.

Schröder was also committed to creating a German version of the 'Third Way', a party of the *neue Mitte* to straddle the middle ground, a policy that his critics within the party feared would take the party away from its old roots. Nevertheless, Schröder was in a strong position to embark on a new course. One important way he did so was by modifying the influence of the party within government and relying on business and other external expertise (Padgett, 2003). Significantly, too, four of the party's nine ministers were not members of the Bundestag (one, the Economics Minister, was not even a member of the SPD). The party was not exactly 'sidelined', but in Schröder's push to 'modernize' the SPD there were hints of old-style 'chancellor democracy'.

That Schröder could be decisive and face down opposition was also clearly shown in November 2001 in the dispute over the government's agreement to deploy military units in Afghanistan in support of the 'war against terrorism'. This move led to considerable opposition from within the Greens, but Schröder took up the challenge and made the issue subject to a vote of confidence in the Bundestag to ensure that the Greens stayed in line: the motion was passed by only the narrowest margin. It was a risky step to take but, despite speculation that the coalition would fall apart in consequence, the Greens accepted the outcome and the alliance held firm.

During the 2002 election campaign, Schröder's decisiveness was also laced with a ready opportunism. He was able to gain much-needed support by seizing the opportunity offered by the crisis of the floods to take immediate action. His opportunism was also clearly displayed in his rejection of the Federal Republic taking any part in a possible war against Iraq. On one interpretation, Schröder's declaration could be regarded as a turning-point in Germany's foreign policy, for no previous chancellor would have countenanced an open breach of American–German relations.

Both pre-election episodes were of benefit to the SPD, especially in winning support from uncommitted voters with weak partisan loyalties (i.e., those who vote more on the basis of emotion and sympathy rather than, in this case, on economic issues: see Noelle, 2002). With the increasing dealignment of the electorate, Schröder's personal qualities proved to be a winning asset for the SPD.

As successful as the SPD proved to be in holding on to office, the government's failure to deal with Germany's flagging economy was carried over to the second term of office. Just prior to the election, a commission set up by the government issued its findings in the so-called Hartz Report, detailing measures that could cut unemployment by two million in three years (Hartz Kommission, 2002). The report was enthusiastically welcomed by Schröder. A reduction in unemployment and in the national debt became the central planks in the new SPD/Green new coalition pact, and a new super-ministry was established to coordinate both economics and employment. However, the underlying problems remained, in particular the overregulated labour market and the burdensome complexity of the welfare state, and these issues were not tackled during the SPD's first term.

The Greens

As proponents of the New Politics – including minority rights, a participatory democracy and radical environmental policies – the Greens are in principle opposed to the materialist backbone of the left/right dimension. Originally, too, the Greens were anti-establishment, against inner-party elitism, perhaps even an 'anti-party party'. But after first entering the Bundestag in 1983, the Greens were soon to experience the 'parliamentary embrace' and become a more conventional political party. In the intervening years there has also been a change of political orientation, from 'eco-socialism' to 'eco-capitalism', a shift that was to draw the party towards the centre-left.

Even more profound in its effects was the 1998 decision to join the SPD in government, succumbing to the 'coalition embrace', and so taking responsibility for government policies. The fact that the coalition remained intact and was renewed in 2002 is evidence of the party's changing character.

The Greens' strong attachment to grass-roots activism does not fit easily with the requirements of serving in government and being forced to make compromises unwelcome to ordinary members; yet the tensions have been contained. A case in point was the decision finally reached on a timetable for ceasing nuclear energy production, which was naturally a high priority for the Greens. In the face of legal threats from the industry, Schröder negotiated an agreement for the closure to take place over an extended 30-year period. That the coalition survived this critical juncture – as well as the issue of Germany's involvement in the American-led Afghan campaign – was thanks in part to the calibre of Green ministers. It was, however, Joschka Fischer, Vice-Chancellor and Foreign Minister, a figure both urbane and charismatic, who did most to unify and steer the Greens. It has been argued that the Greens have no strategic concept and no adequate organization (Raschke, 2001). Yet it is precisely because the party is still evolving and having to accept the constraints of coalition that this style of leadership is perhaps the most suitable. In fact, the Greens had lost support at every Land election between 1998 and 2002, so that the party's federal success was largely thanks to that leadership.

At one time the Greens, belonging neither to left nor right, toyed with the possibility of forging links with the CDU. That option is now remote since it appears to be firmly harnessed to the SPD, and even accorded the status of a 'client party'. However, the reality is that the two parties have come to depend on each other in a reciprocal relationship which is both competitive and cooperative. If they do not hang together, they could hang separately.

The PDS

Although the PDS competes on a federal-wide basis, its natural constituency is eastern Germany where it has been able to attract around 20 per cent of the vote, in contrast to below 2 per cent in the west. This imbalance means that the party is never assured of winning Bundestag representation. In 1998 the PDS just cleared the 5 per cent threshold with 5.1 per cent, but in previous elections the party had to rely on the alternative route of winning three mandates in the single-member districts so as to obtain seats according to its overall share of the vote. However, for the 2002 election there was a substantial re-drawing of constituency boundaries and a reduction in the size of the Bundestag. This change adversely affected the PDS. It secured only 4 per cent of the vote and won only two single-member districts. With just two members in the Bundestag, and unable to form a party group or *Fraktion*, the PDS lacked the parliamentary powers of the other parties.

On one level the PDS still has to live with the reputation of being the successor-party of the former Socialist Unity Party (SED) in the communist regime; yet, although it is in the mould of the old-style left, the PDS is by no means to be labelled 'extreme' or 'anti-system'.

It naturally identifies itself with east German interests, and has sizeable support among younger voters. Moreover, the PDS has been grudgingly accepted by other parties, and as 'coalitionable' (*koalitionsfähig*) by the SPD in the new Länder, most notably by serving in the Berlin government with the SPD since 2001, but only after the latter's negotiations with the FDP and Greens, to form a so-called 'traffic lights' coalition, came to nothing.

The failure of the PDS in 2002 (see Table 4.2) was only partly due to changes in constituency boundaries. In the east, the party's list vote (*Zweitstimmen*) also fell sharply, from 21.6 per cent in 1998 to 16.9 per cent, to an extent arising from internal party discord over the direction the party should take. Further disarray prior to the election was caused by the sudden resignation of Gregor Gysi (the former party leader) as economics minister in the Berlin coalition, ostensibly over a minor sleaze allegation. Gysi had been significant in giving the PDS a more acceptable and modernizing image. The SPD was the main beneficiary, largely because of Schröder's adept handling of the floods crisis, and not least in demonstrating solidarity with east Germans which – from their point of view – is too often lacking in the west.

What kind of future can the PDS expect? It will remain a viable force in the eastern Länder, but it will be difficult for the party to regain a federal footing. Electoral behaviour in the new Länder is still relatively unstructured in moving away from the impress of communist rule. Whether it will eventually develop a patterning similar to that in the west is uncertain but, if it does, then the PDS would forfeit its ability to foster a distinct east German identity, and that would perhaps signal the final step in the process of German reunification.

TABLE 4.2 *Elections to the Bundestag, East and West Germany, 1998 and 2002: % of list votes* (Zweitstimmen)

	East[1]		West[2]	
	2002	1998	2002	1998
SPD	39.7	35.1	38.3	42.3
CDU/CSU[3]	28.3	27.3	40.8	37.0
The Greens	4.7	4.1	9.4	7.3
FDP	6.4	3.3	7.6	7.0
PDS	16.9	21.6	1.1	1.2
Others	3.9	8.6	2.8	5.2
Turnout %	72.9	80.0	80.7	82.8

[1] Includes East Berlin.
[2] Includes West Berlin.
[3] In the East, only the CDU.
Source: *Der Bundeswahlleiter*.

The CDU/CSU

From its origins in the aftermath of German defeat in 1945, Christian Democracy has consistently sought to make a wide social appeal. Its long-term success over several decades came to an abrupt end in the debacle of its 1998 election defeat. The CDU/CSU has little room for ideological manoeuvre: a sharp shift to the right would destroy its cherished reputation for social inclusiveness as a party of the moderate centre-right. It has no real alternative but to tempt back those voters who, in 1998, opted not to give Helmut Kohl a fifth term as chancellor.

Subsequent to 1998, the CDU recovered in Länder elections and was successful at the 1999 elections to the European Parliament. Kohl, however, left a bitter legacy to the party: his repeated refusal to reveal the source of huge donations secretly made to the CDU led to him and his party being found guilty of not publishing the donations in the party's accounts (Clemens, 2000). Morale in the CDU sunk again when Wolfgang Schäuble – Kohl's successor as party leader after the election – stood down in April 2000, admitting that he, too, had received secret donations (Roberts, 2000b).

The CDU was thus afflicted by a long-term difficulty in settling on a suitable leader. The problem was made more pressing by the question of who could take the party into the 2002 election as a convincing chancellor-candidate. Angela Merkel had succeeded Schäuble as CDU party leader yet, despite her competence and her east German credentials, it was widely doubted within the party whether she had sufficient drive and presence to present a real challenge to Schröder in the forthcoming election. It was not until January 2002 that the issue was resolved when she stood aside in favour of Edmund Stoiber, leader of the CSU and Minister-President of Bavaria. Merkel, however, still retained the position of CDU party leader.

Within Bavaria, the Christian-Social Union is a dominant force, and in the previous Land election in 1998 it had won 52.9 per cent of the vote. The party's Bavarian 'homeland' image serves it well within Bavaria but, by the same token, it has a rather negative connotation in northern Germany. Furthermore, there were uneasy echoes of 1980 when Franz Josef Strauß – with his reputation of being a right-wing demagogue – had led the CDU/CSU to defeat. However, Stoiber's recommendation was rather that he presided over that part of Germany that had the most successful economic record in the Federal Republic. To the extent that the party was able to focus on economic issues during the 2002 campaign, the choice of Stoiber was a sound strategy, but it is doubtful whether he will be chosen again in the future (in which case, the CDU faces a prolonged period of uncertainty until a new leading figure emerges).

The Free Democrats

For a party that had long sought to occupy the middle ground of German politics, the FDP's campaign in 2002 took on unaccustomed features. That its electoral strategy changed fundamentally was chiefly the responsibility of the party leader, Guido Westerwelle, and Jürgen Möllemann, deputy leader. Their aim was to move the party sharply to the right, a stance that Hans-Dietrich Genscher, former party leader and foreign minister, sharply criticized, especially as this new course was taken without the approval of the FDP at the party's conference earlier in the year.

With what appeared to be a totally unrealistic aim of securing 18 per cent of the vote – far more than the party had ever achieved previously – the FDP campaign sought to attract voters who might otherwise support the extreme right, perhaps hoping to emulate Jörg Heider's success in Austria: he had much earlier taken the previously moderate Freedom Party in that direction, and Heider gave Möllemann his support. Möllemann also stirred up controversy on his allegedly anti-semitic stance, angering Germany's Jewish community.

That the FDP seemed to have 'lost its way' was further shown by Westerwelle's refusal to commit the FDP to a coalition with the CDU prior to the election. This, along with the nature of the party's campaign, estranged many voters, and in these circumstances even the modest rise in the FDP's vote was perhaps surprising. The problem the FDP has still to resolve is how to re-position itself in the new two-bloc system, as it is no longer able to straddle between the CDU and SPD, or apparently able to garner votes on the extreme right.

The Extreme Right

Understandably, in view of Germany's past history, manifestations of right-wing extremism are of concern at home and abroad. Yet if there is a potential, its impact has been modest in the Länder and almost non-existent at the federal level: the best performance in a federal election was that of the National Democratic Party (NPD) in 1969 with 4.3 per cent. Subsequently, the *Republikaner*, in three federal elections in the 1990s, averaged around 1.9 per cent of the vote. In early 2002 there were upsurges in support for far-right parties in both the Netherlands and France, but nothing remotely similar later in the year for Germany: the *Republikaner* had just 0.6 per cent and the NPD 0.8 per cent.

As could be expected, the picture in the Länder is somewhat different, with the far right occasionally gaining representation, but at a level insufficient either to enter government or to destabilize the established parties. In fact, it is misleading perhaps to include them under a heading of extreme right parties. They have also been unable to maintain their initial momentum from one election to another. For example, in 1992 the *Republikaner* won 10.9 per cent in Baden-Württemburg, but in 2001 failed to win representation. The same applied to the DVU (German People's Union): after its 12.9 per cent share in 1998, the party was unsuccessful in the 2002 Land election, where the FDP was probably the beneficiary due to its appeal to the far right.

The most interesting and exceptional case is that of the 'Schill-Partei und Rechtsstaatliche Offensive' (Schill-PRO). In Hamburg at the 2001 Land election, coming from nowhere, it took almost one-fifth of the vote and then joined the CDU and FDP in a centre–right coalition. The party was founded by a Hamburg judge, Ronald B. Schill, dubbed 'Judge Merciless' for his harsh sentencing. The Schill-Partei won strong support through its platform highlighting popular concerns relating especially to crime levels, drugs, immigrants and traffic problems (Fass and Wüst, 2002). While some of these issues have been used by the extreme right, sizeable support came from previous SPD voters as well as the CDU. The fact that the SPD in Hamburg had held power for no fewer than 44 years was an additional factor.

Can the Schill-Partei be labelled 'extremist'? At least in its Hamburg context the party appears to have acted as a broadly-based protest party. For the 2002 federal election, the Schill-PRO competed throughout Germany but, away from its home base, the party could only muster 0.8 per cent in Germany as a whole, a fate no different from other parties on the far right.

Party Systems in the Länder

With their considerable powers, the Länder are obviously important in their own right. But for the federal parties, their ability to control the political complexion of Länder governments has direct consequences for the federal balance of power: they alter a party's weight in the Bundesrat, so changing the balance between the government and opposition forces. Thus, in 2002 the CDU/CSU and its allies had gained a controlling voice in the Bundesrat with which the successful SPD–Green coalition had to contend.

The mixed pattern of party systems and governments in the Länder obscures the government/opposition division because some coalitions span the divide. These 'cross-cutting' coalitions inevitably complicate Bundesrat voting patterns, as is evident in Table 4.3.

There are all kinds of possible connection between the results of a Land election and what happens subsequently at the federal level. A Land contest and the resulting coalition may be a precursor for a later federal line-up, as was the case with the SPD and the Greens prior to 1998 and, much earlier, for the SPD and the FDP. Such Land coalitions are in the nature of 'trial marriages' which may or may not work out. Certainly, Länder contests do act as a warning or an encouragement to federal parties, not least the incumbent ones, and they may presage what will happen in a federal election.

Yet despite the importance of Land politics, it is difficult to find a definite relationship between the federal party system and the performance of federal parties in the Länder. It is an elusive quest because conflicting conclusions can often be drawn as to the possible federal–Land effects. At times federal-wide issues dominate and make Land contests focus principally on them and hence on the federal protagonists; yet Land elections have much to do with local and regional issues as well as the qualities of provincial leaders. The long tenure of Kurt Biedenkopf (CDU) in Saxony is an example.

TABLE 4.3 *Composition of Land governments and Bundesrat votes, Jan 2003*

Land	Election year	Governing parties
Baden-Württemberg	2001	CDU/FDP
Bavaria	1998	CSU
Berlin	2001	SPD/PDS
Brandenburg	1999	SPD/CDU
Bremen	1999	SPD/CDU
Hamburg	2001	CDU/Schill/FDP
Hesse	2003	CDU
Lower Saxony	2003	CDU–FDP
Mecklenburg-West Pomerania	2002	SPD/PDS
North Rhine-Westphalia	2000	SPD/Greens
Rhineland-Palatinate	2001	SPD/FDP
Saarland	1999	CDU
Saxony	1999	CDU
Saxony-Anhalt	2002	CDU/FDP
Schleswig-Holstein	2000	SPD/Greens
Thuringia	1999	CDU

Two other factors weaken the case for a direct linkage. One is the lower turnout for Land elections in comparison with federal contests; another is the support given to small parties that have little or no impact on the federal stage but which make a reasonable showing in a Land election. For example, in Hamburg (1999) the Schill-Partei achieved a remarkable 19.4 per cent of the vote, while in Saxony-Anhalt (1998) the extreme right-wing DVU scored 12.9 per cent, but neither had a significant support in the following federal election.

A further complicating factor is the divided nature of the party system as between east and west after reunification, since different factors affect party performance in the two parts of Germany, and it has not been just a transitional phase. The most striking contrast is the weak showing of the PDS in west Germany and the party's solid following in the east. In the west, its 'best' Land performance has been just 2.9 per cent in Bremen. In the six eastern Länder (including Berlin) it has ranged from 20 to 25 per cent. In contrast (now excluding Berlin) both the FDP and B'90/Greens are fortunate if they can score much more than a few percentage points apiece, though the FDP's striking 13.7 per cent in Saxony-Anhalt (2002) is a strange exception. The weakness of these two parties means that the eastern Länder are mostly functioning three-party systems.

Berlin, with its amalgam of both east and west, combines both elements in the make-up of its five-party system. As well as the FDP and the Greens, there are the three large parties, CDU, SPD and PDS; hence the need for some form of 'grand coalition', as with the SPD–PDS coalition formed in 1999, replacing the former SPD–CDU coalition. The format of Berlin's party system is akin to the federal one, but government formation is radically different.

Despite the problems of finding an unambiguous relationship between the federal performance of parties and their counterparts in the Länder, one approach takes the *timing* of a Land election within the federal 'electoral cycle' as the important variable. The argument is that the incumbent federal parties are likely to perform better if a Land election occurs either at the beginning or the end of the electoral cycle, with the poorest results coming in mid-term (Reif and Schmitt, 1980).

This finding can be applied to earlier years, but it was not evident for the SPD–Green coalition's first term from 1998 to 2002. Thus, in no fewer than seven Land elections held in 1999, the CDU wrested control of two, Hesse and the Saarland, from the SPD. In four others it substantially increased its share of the vote, and only in Saxony, where it was in sole control of the government in any case, did the CDU lose ground, though less than the SPD. A key factor in the CDU's 1999 successes was its mobilization of huge popular support – by means of signed petitions – against the government's proposed reform of the citizenship law, and in particular the granting of dual nationality (Cooper, 2002).

Then in 2000 and 2001, broadly in mid-term, the SPD performed strongly, retaining Schleswig-Holstein where it had fully expected to be defeated, and also retaining power in North Rhine-Westphalia. The SPD also performed better than the CDU in Baden-Württemberg, the Rhineland-Palatinate and Hamburg. Then in the Berlin election of October 2001, the CDU vote collapsed, falling by 17 percentage points, and the SPD share rose by seven points.

The most striking case came right at the end of the electoral cycle, in April 2002. In Saxony-Anhalt, at the last Land contest prior to the September federal election, the SPD's vote fell dramatically to 18.7 per cent (from 35.9 per cent in 1998), and that of the CDU rose to 37.4 per cent compared with just 22.2 per cent previously.

At least in this electoral cycle, the view that the federal governing party performs worse during the mid-term and better shortly after and before a federal election was not borne out. Indeed, the whole prognosis was completely reversed. Two kinds of explanation can be offered. One is that during this period some special factor affected the mood of Länder electorates, with changes in the prevailing economic outlook being particularly significant during these years. Another explanation – reinforcing the first – is that Länder contests are ceasing to be 'second order' elections, but instead are coming increasingly to reflect specific Länder concerns and circumstances (Jeffery and Hough, 2002).

A Stable System?

As evident from the pattern in the Länder, various governing formations are feasible, even an exceptional three-party combination. It is important to bear this possibility in mind, and also remember that a Land coalition may foreshadow a later link-up at federal level. For instance, although a CDU–Green coalition, say, seems remote at present at either level, it could be a feasible development at some stage; all parties have to keep future options open and allow for changing circumstances.

For these reasons, the continuation of the Red–Green coalition after the 2002 election was still far from showing that a two-bloc party system had become consolidated. For that to be the case, a requirement would be for a shift in governmental power between blocs *and* on more than one occasion; in other words, with the passage of another two federal elections.

It could be that the merits of a clear division between party blocs, the lack of distortion in electoral choice, and the choice between two sets of distinctive policies quickly take root. After all, the CDU/CSU and SPD have long provided the choice and have alternated in government. The only difference – though a critical one – is that a choice of coalition 'options' for both major and minor parties would no longer be available.

Yet there are many uncertainties. Even though the SPD and the Greens have found common ground, will this amity persist in different circumstances? How will the future of the PDS affect the left bloc? If it regains its position as a federal force, or is strengthened, how will the cohesion of the bloc be affected? On the right, the questions largely concern the role that the Free Democrats choose to play: should they limit themselves to being the partner of the CDU, or rather act as maverick players, much as their performance in 2002 indicated?

Questions such as these cannot be answered in the abstract, since they depend on the nature of problems facing the Federal Republic over the next few years and the policies the parties adopt in consequence. The overriding issue concerns the economy, not merely, say, the level of unemployment or the rate of economic growth, but rather the whole future of *Modell Deutschland*, whether or not the individual parties choose to see it in these terms.

The deep-seated nature of the problems became increasingly apparent during Schröder's first term. There was widespread agreement among German economic experts that the rigidities of the labour market and the burdensome welfare state both needed fundamental structural reform, otherwise there would be a downward spiral of depression and deflation. With the election over, the gravity of the economic problems – highlighted by the government's plans to increase taxes and impose higher social welfare contributions – became widely apparent, and the popularity of the SPD–Green coalition sank quickly to a low ebb.

In circumstances such as these, the merits of a two-bloc system ought to become apparent: such a system provides clear alternatives both of policies and of a government to implement them. Yet it is by no means the case that the CDU/CSU and FDP themselves have a thought-out strategy, still less the determination to carry it through. In fact, there might be little difference in practice from the record of the SPD–Green coalition.

One important reason for the similarity between the CDU and the SPD is the presence in both parties of two distinct constituencies, typical of broadly-based *Volksparteien*: one is 'modernizing' and the other is anxious to maintain the security of the status quo. Carrying through fundamental reforms on the lines that have been advocated could well spell electoral disaster for the governing parties before any benefits became apparent.

It is tempting at this point to refer to a possible solution of a political impasse, namely the formation of a grand coalition between the CDU/CSU and the SPD. Such a move would give neither a party-political advantage, and despite the unrest they would experience from sections of their electorates, their governing position would be secure. It can also be argued that a grand coalition would be in tune with German corporatist traditions.

In this context it is instructive to refer to the CDU/CSU–SPD coalition of 1966–69, not so much for the policies pursued at the time, but for the negative effects. In this short period, the extremist NPD performed strongly in Land elections and only narrowly failed in the subsequent federal election; just as worrying for the established parties was the rise of the *außerparlamentarische Opposition* (Extra-Parliamentary Opposition) on the left. That is precisely the kind of risk the major parties would now run: the mushrooming of right-wing radicalism on one side and, on the other, growing support for the Greens as well as the prospect of a resurgent PDS. Faced with these possibilities, the attractions of a grand coalition seem far less convincing. It is too soon to judge whether the two-bloc system will be stable and whether it can provide answers to Germany's economic malaise; but it is doubtful if any 'grand coalition' or other model would be better able to cope.

5

Policy-Making in a New Political Landscape

ROLAND STURM

The change of government in 1998 transformed Germany's political landscape. For the first time in the country's history a Red–Green coalition government, led by a Social Democrat, Chancellor Gerhard Schröder, came to power. The government was re-elected in 2002. Though Schröder had announced in the 1998 election campaign that it was not his aim to revise all the major policy decisions of his predecessor Helmut Kohl, many supporters of his government expected new directions in policy-making. Policy innovation was, however, the exception, and incremental policy changes remained the rule.

To explain the constraints which force German decision-makers to be content with incremental policy changes and often to celebrate them as successes, it is necessary to start with some thoughts on institutional pluralism as a background for policy-making in Germany. After that, strategies to overcome the constraints institutional pluralism generates will be discussed. The Schröder government's successful strategies by-passed institutional routines and substituted traditional methods of decision-making for a social dialogue of the most powerful interests involved. Strategies do not tell us much about priority-setting, however. The next topic we look at, therefore, is what the Chancellor's policy preferences were, and how he organized the Chancellor's Office to provide guidance for his government. This leads us also to the observation that an important aspect of policy-making in Germany is the process of negotiation between those parties which form government coalitions. Coalition partners agree on policy priorities before a new chancellor is elected. In addition to the analysis of the direction given by parties in government we then need to look at the wider context of policy-making to understand political outcomes. For Germany, EU membership (Sturm and Pehle, 2001), the important political role of the Constitutional Court (Helms, 2000) and the veto power of the quasi-Second Chamber of Parliament, the Bundesrat (Sturm, 2001), are influences which restrict a Chancellor's political choices. Finally, our analysis of policy-making in Germany will concentrate more specifically on the Schröder chancellor-ship and we will discuss both policy style under Schröder and the policy record of the Schröder government.

Institutional Pluralism and the Culture of Dialogue

Chancellor Schröder's predecessor, Helmut Kohl, was often criticized for his lack of resolve and a tendency to avoid necessary decisions. It has been argued, however, that his 'wait-and-see' attitude (*aussitzen*) was only partly due to his style of leadership. It can also be interpreted differently (März, 2002, p. 179): namely, as the best way to steer a com-plicated political system which is designed to produce many checks on political power. Every German Chancellor has to develop a strategy to cope with a wide range of institutional constraints confining his decision-making powers.

The Basic Law in Article 65 formally structures the executive by vest-ing decision-making powers in the chancellor, the cabinet and individual ministers (Padgett, 1994). Though the chancellor has the right to control the policies and the direction of government, this does not mean that individual ministers do not initiate policies themselves. For individual ministers this is not only important for their political careers, but also for their reputation in government. Cabinet is in practice only a weak clear-ing house for differences in political preferences which regularly arise between the chancellor and individual ministers. Decision-making on policies is further complicated by the need to balance the party-political interests of the coalition partners in government. Though German chan-cellors, and this is above all true for Helmut Kohl and Gerhard Schröder, have shown an inclination to act as a kind of 'president' who is above political wrangles and is therefore not necessarily involved in the nitty-gritty of policy-making (Korte, 2000, p. 14), they cannot avoid dealing with the problem of alternative power centres in government. To secure the Chancellor's leadership in policy-making, both a crude and a subtle method of policy control are used. The crude method is a public attack by the Chancellor on one of his ministers telling him that no further dis-cussion is needed and that the Chancellor's decision is the last word in the matter under dispute (*Machtwort*). The subtle method is based on additional institutional competition in government. For decades now German chancellors have expanded the Chancellor's Office to be able to draw on intellectual resources for policy-making which rival those of individual ministers. Chancellors have acquired the capacity to reserve for themselves the most important political issues (*Chefsache*). For Gerhard Schröder these were, for example, strategies for the economic development of East Germany, the fight against unemployment, or European integration policies.

Outside the institutional boundaries of the executive, too, institutional pluralism provides a challenge to the Chancellor's decision-making power. Governments are well advised not to rely on the Constitutional Court as final arbiter of policy conflicts with the opposition if they want to control political outcomes. And when the opposition controls the Bundesrat, governments often need the support of their political opponents to pass legislation. In addition, in some policy areas (such as labour market policies, social policies, health policies or income policies), no far-reaching political decision is possible without the support of the most influential interest groups. Institutional pluralism inside and outside government has created a complicated web of political power which typically produces at best incremental change, and in the worst case gridlock. Douglas Webber (1992, p. 174) observed with regard to several reform projects in the Kohl era:

> All these features of the institutional context of German politics tend to have the same impact, namely to grind down radical policy initiatives so that the end product, if one emerges at all in the form of an authoritative decision or policy output, represents the lowest common denominator between those corporate actors which command the potential to crush the initiative completely.

It is not surprising therefore that the search for consensus has long been a central feature of policy-making in Germany. One aspect of this consensus is an informal 'grand coalition' of the major political parties in government and opposition, especially with regard to legislation which needs the consent of the Bundesrat. Another aspect of this consensus is the organization of decision-making processes outside Parliament in dialogue with the relevant social and economic interests. Under the Kohl government it was an open secret that policy-making in Germany could no longer rely on the superior knowledge of the government and the law-making power of Parliament. In many important policy areas politicians had to learn to find partners in society (e.g., companies, interest groups, churches, doctors in the health service) with whom solutions for social problems could be discussed and who were willing to contribute to problem-solving, often using their own resources. German democracy is based on the need for extensive coordination in order to be successful in policy-making.

For the role of the state in policy-making this means that there is no longer a hierarchy of actors with the government in a leadership position when it comes to the solution of social problems. The new reality is that of a level playing field on which governments have to negotiate with the relevant interests involved if they want to be able to set priorities. This ongoing social dialogue (which, in the old neo-corporatist model, used to bring together both sides of industry and the state) has now been extended and includes a wide range of social and economic interests. The re-arrangement of power in society affects the role of the state in policy-making therefore in a more general way. The state in Germany has become a 'cooperative state' (Voigt, 1995): that is, a state which relies on negotiated policy solutions and a permanent discourse with the representatives of interest groups and companies.

This kind of deal-making has been christened the 'culture of dialogue' (*Dialogkultur*) by Franz-Walter Steinmeier, the head of the Chancellor's Office (Niejahr, 2001, p. 25). Steinmeier justifies the neglect of democratic institutions and decision-making outside Parliament, which is central to the new culture of deal-making, with the argument that political institutions are too complicated. They cannot react swiftly and adequately to new challenges. If policy-making relies too much on them, Steinmeier argues, traditional institutions become a problem instead of being a tool for solving problems (*Der Spiegel*, 28 May 2001, p. 50). His hope is that top-level arrangements of the relevant actors in a policy field will be better suited to producing efficient and quick results.

If policy-making relies on a 'culture of dialogue', the capacities as well as the limits of the cooperative state become clear. Such dialogue often produces political deals which demonstrate political activism, but avoid the substance of policy problems. The OECD (2001, pp. 107ff.) regularly criticizes, for example, the German governments' lack of courage in confronting the problems of the welfare state and to remodel social policies. In the government's dialogue with relevant interest groups, solutions for policy problems have in the past often been postponed; then, at the end of the breathing-space won by official declarations and other forms of symbolic politics, these problems returned to the political agenda. Symbolic short-termism of this kind usually has two sets of winners: industry and other social and economic interests, which avoid political regulation, on the one hand, and politicians on the other who can present solutions which (with luck) will last until the next general election is due. Losers are all those who are negatively affected by non-decisions, especially when those relating to long-term structural reforms, including the pension system in Germany's ageing society, Germany's ossified labour market (Nativel, 2002), or the country's inefficient health (Bandelow, 2002) and education systems (Ostermann, 2002), are avoided.

Chancellor and Government

Situational Government

German chancellors are no ideologues. This is not to say that they were never guided by a political vision, but the successors of the first Chancellor, Konrad Adenauer, had to accept that the consolidation of the German political system over the course of time constrained reforms of Germany's domestic institutional and social status quo. Only under the exceptional circumstances of the grand coalition in the late 1960s, with a two-thirds majority in Parliament, could incrementalism in policy innovation be overcome. As Paterson (1998, p. 21) has argued:

> The overwhelmingly consensual nature of domestic politics, the inclusive character of the Volksparteien, federalism and the dual majority Bundestag/Bundesrat hurdle, the prevalence of coalitions, the manner in which interests are mediated, and the role of para-public institutions, taken together, narrow the space for the articulation of an alternative domestic vision very considerably in contrast, say, to the United Kingdom.

Helmut Kohl, as well as his successor, Gerhard Schröder, soon discovered that priority-setting was easier and much more politically attractive in foreign than in domestic policy-making. During Helmut Kohl's chancellorship European integration and German unification challenged the Chancellor's ability to make strategic choices, but provided him also with the opportunity for fairly radical policy innovation. At home, the conditions for a political fresh start were much more difficult. Schröder inherited from the Kohl years the dilemmas of the German 'economic disease'. As a consequence of the German economic crisis (which started in the mid-1990s) and the even older unemployment problem, economic policy-making is trapped between competing demands. Industry wants reforms of the welfare state and new tax policies which increase industrial competitiveness, whereas most ordinary Germans do not want to see the welfare state reduced (for East Germans, who were socialized into a paternalistic socialist state, this is even less conceivable). The situation is further complicated by the fact that the state at all levels (federal, Land, local government) has a massive budget deficit which restricts its ability to cut taxes and to invest at the same time in social and employment policies. Chancellor Schröder came to accept what, since the 1970s, other chancellors have had to learn before him: policy changes which affect the core of the welfare state are the most difficult ones in Germany.

Helmut Kohl used to look, above all, for short-term solutions to this kind of policy problem. This had the advantage that the impact of the policies was limited and therefore the government did not have to invest too much political capital in creating a new political and social consensus. But it turned out that a lot of this short-termism was dysfunctional and created new problems without really solving the old ones (Wewer, 1998). Chancellor Schröder's policy style is in many respects similar to the approach his predecessor Helmut Kohl preferred. Neither Schröder nor Kohl has been interested in all the complicated details of policy-making and neither of them shied away from pragmatic non-ideological solutions. Schröder sees his role as being responsible for political results which generate consensus in society. This includes U-turns in policy decisions if necessary.

The pragmatic orientation of the Schröder government towards policy outcomes has led to 'situational government' (Raschke, 2001, p. 94). 'Situational government' is characterized by a lack of obligation for the decision-maker to keep promises, to be consistent, or to accept rules. Situational government is driven by a short-term cost–benefit analysis without much thought about future consequences. An example of policy-making which follows this pattern are Chancellor Schröder's attempts to save some big companies from bankruptcy. Chancellor Schröder chooses such interventionism in the economy at will and with a populist instinct. A typical case is the rescue effort made in 1999 to save the Philipp Holzmann construction company. The government offered credits and guarantees as the final part of a DM4.3 billion rescue plan mounted by the banks. Gerhard Schröder, at that time at a low point in his approval rates, was celebrated by the press as the man who saved thousands of jobs. His approval rates improved. Holzmann, however, could only be kept in business till 2002. The company first had to make more workers redundant and then went into bankruptcy; this time, however, it was ignored by the government.

Cabinet, Chancellor's Office and Party

Like Kohl, Schröder has put some distance between himself and the cabinet, and also between himself and the cabinet members of his own party. Even when there were spectacular confrontations of cabinet ministers the Chancellor often watched these confrontations from the side-lines almost as if he was only a political observer and not the key actor. Such rhetorical battles have, for example, been fought in his government between Jürgen Trittin, the environment minister of the Green Party, and Werner Müller, the economics minister with no official party affiliation, on the phasing-out of nuclear power plants. Whereas Trittin first advocated an immediate end for nuclear power in Germany, Müller wanted to give industry a chance to recover sunk costs and therefore supported a transition period of several decades for the closing down of power stations. There was also a public confrontation between the defence minister, Rudolf Scharping, who complained about the lack of funds for the Bundeswehr, and the finance minister, Hans Eichel, who defended the planned public expenditures on the defence budget. At some stage Schröder saw himself, however, forced to demonstrate that his was to be the last word (*Machtwort*). In doing so he exercised his constitutional right to determine the direction of politics.

One can debate whether the constitutional text really implies the right of the Chancellor to decide every policy detail rather than more general principles to guide policy-making. And one could argue that the debate between ministers should have its place in cabinet and not in the media. For the ministers in conflict such legal niceties are less important than the fact that when the Chancellor closes such debates he mostly does so for strategic reasons. In this context the public image of the government takes precedence over the substance of policies. The end of the debate on policies is therefore difficult to foresee for the departmental ministers. It depends to a great deal on the Chancellor's political instincts and the kind of advice he listens to. In the Schröder years cabinet discipline in policy-making was (and this was different from the Kohl years) relatively weak, but at the same time the Chancellor tended to centralize decision-making without much prior warning in order to keep control; sometimes this was because of conflicts of interest in the cabinet, sometimes also because he made promises to interest groups outside cabinet which he wanted to see honoured in the wording of bills. Kohl was often criticized for being 'only' a policy coordinator, but Schröder tried hard for a long time for a greater efficiency in this role.

In its first years in office Chancellor Schröder's government not surprisingly went through a period of political activism. At first, however, it did so with completely inadequate institutional support. There was not even a chart which listed the responsibilities in the Chancellor's Office. Everything was guided on an ad hoc basis by the minister responsible (at that time, Bodo Hombach). After the long years in opposition (for the Greens it was the first time that they had been a coalition partner in Federal government), the reform impetus of the Red–Green coalition was great. The price which had to be paid for the early activism was a number of defeats, policies that did not make it on to the agenda and weak compromises (e.g., no introduction of a low wage sector in industry, no new policies to deal with smog problems in summer, no law to support equal opportunities for women in the workplace, and no reform of the rail transport system which separates responsibilities for passenger and freight transport on the one hand from the railway tracks on the other). The new government had great difficulties in learning to govern efficiently, to write laws which did not constantly need revisions (*Nachbessern*, revisions, became a household world in the legislative process), and also found it hard to avoid an overload of the political agenda because of the amount of legislation it had initiated at the same time.

The Schröder government had to learn the hard way that for budgetary reasons, and in order to mobilize social support for its legislation, it needed a more focused policy style. This insight found its organizational expression in a reorganization of the Chancellor's Office. Here a battle was fought between the pragmatists and political administrators headed by Franz Walter Steinmeier (who had worked for Schröder before when the Chancellor was Lower Saxony's prime minister), and a group behind Bodo Hombach. Hombach was the successful manager of Schröder's first election campaign and had political ambitions himself. He was often compared to Peter Mandelson, Tony Blair's political adviser. Hombach admired Blair and wanted to import 'Third Way' thinking into Germany in order to give social democracy there a new face. For Schröder the conflicts this strategy provoked within the Social Democratic Party, together with the chaotic style of leadership which Hombach practised, were good reasons to dismiss Hombach in June 1999 and to appoint Steinmeier as his successor. Under Steinmeier the Chancellor's Office was reorganized and became an efficient tool of government.

Schröder found a phrase to describe his new style of more cautious policy initiatives which in substance means exactly the same as Helmut Kohl's *aussitzen*: namely, policy-making on a steady course (*Politik der ruhigen Hand*). In the last two years of his term in office Gerhard Schröder at first did not have the ambition to initiate major new policies. The government concentrated on legislation in some of the policy fields for which reforms had been promised when there was a change in office in 1998. These were, above all, the law on immigration and a law on homosexual partnerships. Initially other reforms were postponed until after the 2002 election with the argument that the unresolved policy problems were so complicated that satisfactory solutions could not be found during the government's first four years. But two pre-election shocks – the results of the international Programme for International Student Assessment (PISA) education study, which documented the low quality of Germany's educational standards, and the dramatic development of unemployment rates – once again provoked 'situational government'. Ad hoc solutions and legislative proposals unrelated to older discourses in either the SPD or government were produced. The Chancellor blamed German federalism for Länder differences in educational achievements and proposed a more centralized education system as a panacea for Germany's educational ills. A quick fix for the unemployment problem was found with the appointment of an expert commission chaired by Peter Hartz, staff manager of the Volkswagen car company. The proposals of the Hartz Commission were presented to the public as a fast-track solution for the most serious unemployment problems.

Since 1999 Chancellor Schröder has also been chairman of the Social Democratic Party. He succeeded Oskar Lafontaine who represented the left wing of the SPD and who had been Minister of Finance. For Lafontaine, the defence of social policies was not only an ideological priority, but it also had the advantage of strengthening mass income and, by implication, the demand side of the economy. Lafontaine's vision was of a Keynesian-style managed economy both in Germany and in the European Union which guaranteed social justice and full employment. Lafontaine's intention to return to political interventionism to steer the economy came into conflict with the economic convictions of Chancellor Schröder, who can be vaguely described as compassionate supply-sider. As long as Lafontaine was in office Schröder saw himself in a position fairly distant from the policy preferences of his party. And even in the first few months after Lafontaine had left, Schröder had difficulty listening to his party, which was in complete contrast to his predecessor, Helmut Kohl, who had turned his party into an efficient personal support base. Only after the more ideological representatives of the SPD's left wing had lost their jobs in government (the last one was the transport minister, Reinhard Klimmt, in 2000), and after a rapprochement between the party, the unions and the government which was facilitated by the end of the 'Third Way' rhetoric in the SPD, did the influence of the party and the unions on policy-making increase. The informal ties between union leaders and the Chancellor (who had, in his first year in office, portrayed himself as close ally of the captains of industry) were strengthened. Schröder even tried to return to old-style neo-corporatism, at least in economic and social policy-making, by guaranteeing not only the employers but also the unions a role in the informal decision-making process.

Coalition Relations

The political agenda of the first Red–Green coalition was defined during the negotiations on the coalition treaty. Coalition treaties summarize (often in great detail) those policies on which the parties in government have agreed and what their political priorities are. These treaties are given political legitimacy by special party congresses of the parties in government. Coalition treaties have become the rule for coalition governments in Germany at both the federal and the Land level (Kropp and Sturm, 1998). They are, however, not binding for the new government. For the Red–Green coalition their coalition treaty of 1998 very soon lost all practical value for the initiation of politics, not only because the world had changed with the war in Kosovo and against Serbia, but also because of the changes in ministerial offices in mid-1999, and especially because Hans Eichel, a fiscal conservative who sees his priority in balancing the budget, became the next minister of finance after Oskar Lafontaine, and he is still very much in the tax and spend tradition of the old social democratic left-wing. This last factor definitely changed the political climate.

In 1998 the Green Party was in a relatively weak bargaining position in the negotiations on the coalition treaty, because the Social Democrats also had the option of either the Christian Democrats or the Liberals (FDP) as a coalition partner. The Social Democrats were not willing to compromise their electoral promises which meant that the Green Party's only chance was to champion topics which the Social Democrats did not see as essential for their own image. Where the Greens had ideas for economic reforms, they had to find compromises with Oskar Lafontaine; where they suggested new ecological policies they often found resistance from Chancellor Schröder's camp. The Greens could not profit for the purpose of agenda-setting from the differences of opinion in economic and ecological matters between the party chairman, Lafontaine, and Chancellor Schröder (Raschke, 2001, pp. 91ff.). Still, a number of new policies reached the political agenda: dual citizenship to integrate the German-born foreigners, the phasing-out of nuclear energy and an ecological tax reform as a first stage in the introduction of a tax system based on taxing the consumption of energy instead of economic growth.

Policy coordination in the Red–Green coalition is different from the coordination process which was the rule in Helmut Kohl's Christian Democrat/Liberal coalition. The Green ministers have no official leading position in their party, because until 2002 their party statutes did not allow Green representatives to hold several political offices at the same time. Those who speak for the party are sometimes not even MPs. In the first Schröder cabinet the three Green ministers were lonely defenders of the interests of their departments. Policy coordination between them was also made difficult due to the fact that the 'uncrowned' party chairman, Foreign Minister Joschka Fischer, headed a department which was not interested in domestic policies. The consequence was that the policy coordination between the two parties in government, which traditionally had its place also in cabinet, moved more or less out of cabinet into informal circles or to the ranks of the parliamentary parties.

The Greens in government do not form a political bloc. Chancellor Schröder was quite successful with isolating Green ministers in policymaking, whether we consider the first health minister, Andrea Fischer, whom he did not protect against the negative campaigns of the health lobby, or Jürgen Trittin, the minister of the environment, whom he portrayed in public as arrogant and inefficient. Schröder could even say to the press that it would be good for his government if there was more of Fischer (the foreign minister) and less of Trittin. The Green Party did not react to this provocation. Trittin's role in government is an extreme, but in substance it is a typical case of the isolation and political emasculation of Green ministers. Trittin not only lost the battle for an immediate shut-down of nuclear power stations, but in the end he even had to change sides. He was seen to support the transport of nuclear fuel through Germany, which placed him in opposition to supporters of the Green Party who tried to stop rail transport.

The Wider Context of Policy-Making

As mentioned, constraints on policy-making in Germany also originate from the checks of political institutions which have their own role in the political system of the country and, in addition, increasingly from the Europeanization of policy-making in Germany. There are at least two institutions, the Bundesrat and the Federal Constitutional Court, whose role in policy-making needs to be looked at in this context. Germany has no second chamber of Parliament. When laws are made, the Bundesrat (the chamber of the German Länder) performs a role which is fairly similar to that of a second chamber. It can even veto legislation which affects the interests of the Länder (i.e., between 50 and 60 per cent of all bills). A 'yes' vote in the Bundesrat needs the absolute majority of seats of the chamber (Article 52(3) of the Basic Law): at present 35 out of 69. For the Schröder government it was difficult to secure such a majority, not only because of the problems the parties in government in Berlin experienced in successfully contesting Land elections, but also because in the Länder they were often forced into coalition arrangements with parties in opposition at the federal level. For voting behaviour in the Bundesrat this had the consequence of neutralizing the respective Land. Abstentions count in the Bundesrat, however, as 'no' votes, a fact which further weakened the position of the government parties there.

Since 1999 Chancellor Schröder has been in the awkward position of having no secure majority in the Bundesrat. For the legislative process this can prove a severe obstacle. Prestige projects, such as tax reform, can be blocked by the opposition. The Social Democrats themselves, when in opposition in 1998, succeeded in stopping a big tax reform project of the Kohl government in the Bundesrat, because at that time they controlled sufficient votes here. To avoid a similar fate for his own tax project Chancellor Schröder tried to introduce his strategy of deal-making in the Bundesrat as well, and when it turned out that this was successful (because enough votes could be won over from Länder governments with opposition parties as coalition partners), deal-making in the Bundesrat became the rule.

For a 'yes' vote in the Bundesrat on tax reform the Schröder government revised the bill to further reduce the tax burden of small and medium-sized enterprises. This pleased the Liberals (FDP) and guaranteed the support of the SPD–FDP government of Rhineland-Palatinate. A promise of financial support to solve some of the Land's budgetary problems won over the grand coalition (SPD–CDU) in Bremen. Berlin's grand coalition (CDU–SPD) was promised subsidies for its expenditures on culture and the extension of Berlin's Olympic stadium. Brandenburg (with an SPD–CDU coalition) voted for the government in the Bundesrat in exchange for new roads. For Mecklenburg-West Pomerania governed by a Red–Red coalition (SPD–PDS), the Chancellor could offer a new railway tracks, and equal treatment for the ex-Communists of the PDS whenever contact between political parties and the Chancellor's Office becomes necessary. (Until that point, the PDS had usually been excluded from all-party talks with the Chancellor.)

Package deals of this kind, which connect political projects which are logically unconnected but which create benefits for everybody, have become the rule as last resort for securing majorities for important legislative projects that might otherwise not survive the Bundesrat.

The 2001 pension reform is a further example (the decisive votes here were those of Berlin and Brandenburg), and the 2002 reform of the organization of the Bundesbank is another. Though North Rhine-Westphalia first opposed the idea that with the new Bundesbank law it should lose its representative on the Bundesbank board, the Land gave the federal government the majority it needed in exchange for an increase of subsidies paid by the federal government for the introduction of a new high speed railway system in the Land (*Transrapid*).

The Federal Constitutional Court, when asked to adjudicate, can also constrain policy-making. Often its judgements are fairly specific with regard to the substance of policies, so that policy initiation is another by-product of decisions of the Constitutional Court. Although it is a constant theme of German politics as to whether the Court should not be more cautious when it defines rules for policy-making, one should not forget that decision-making is mostly forced on the Court by the unwillingness of political parties to come to (or accept) political solutions. One example for policy initiation by the Court is its 1999 ruling on financial equalization policies concerning financial transfers between the Länder in favour of the poorer ones. When asked to decide whether current rules for financial equalization violated the constitution, the Court forced Parliament to make a law on the ground rules for financial transfers (*Maßstäbegesetz*). The idea here was to find a set of rules which cannot be drawn into the bargaining process between the Länder, and between the Länder and the Federal government, when it comes to the sharing-out of tax income. In this way the Court wanted to force the Länder and the federal government to agree on neutral procedures in order to ensure that the fair treatment of the richer or the poorer Länder did not depend on non-transparent ad hoc agreements with a strong party political component. Another example concerns the revisions of legislation the Court initiated with its 2001 ruling concerning the law on the care for the elderly. It stipulated that the financial contributions of families without children to the insurance system which finances these services should be higher than that of families with children.

Another source of new policies was the European Union, which sometimes had far-reaching political consequences, as the following examples show. The Basic Law in its Article 12a(4) explicitly excluded the armed military service of women. Based on an EU directive of 1976 against sexual discrimination, the European Court decided that the German constitution was violating EU rules. German politicians avoided the problematic question of whether an EU directive has a legal status superior to that of a national constitution. With a two-thirds majority in the Bundestag and the Bundesrat the Constitution was changed and armed military service for women on a voluntary basis was introduced (Janisch, 2000).

The EU also rewrote Germany's budget rules. Germany's budgetary policy-making was forced into the straitjacket of a balanced budget to be presented not later than 2004 by the EU's threat to censure Germany for a violation of the Stability and Growth Pact which sets limits for annual budget deficits. On a more positive note, one could mention that one of the EU's policy initiatives helped German customers because it led to the liberalization of trade practices and ended restrictions (*Rabattgesetz and Zugabeverordnung*) regarding special offers for sales (Jahreswirtschaftsbericht, 2001, p. 56).

Policy Style under Schröder

In addition to Chancellor Schröder's above-mentioned inclination to resort to 'situational government' and his reliance on the 'culture of dialogue' for consensus-building, his policy style had three more distinct features which have to be included and evaluated for a full picture of his policy style: neo-corporatism, government by expert groups and government via the media.

Neo-Corporatism

At the core of neo-corporatism (i.e., of institutionalized negotiations between the partners of industry and the government) is the 'Alliance for Jobs' (Schroeder and Esser, 1999). From the start this was a complicated negotiation experiment. Whereas Oskar Lafontaine saw in the Alliance for Jobs a mechanism which would allow him (in coalition with the trade unions) to put pressure on industry to create more jobs and more industrial training opportunities for entrants in the job market, industry saw in the Alliance a tool for modernizing Germany's economy in order to make Germany more attractive for investments (see Figure 5.1). So far, this latter hope has only materialized in part (e.g., with regard to tax policies). The level of direct taxation has been reduced by the Red–Green government. Starting in 2002, companies were even allowed to sell shares of firms they owned tax-free. The ecological tax reform of 1999 contributed to a reduction of costs per employee to the firms, because it reduced the social security contributions for the employers. The ecological tax reform was a typical compromise of Green ideas (the taxation of energy), support for industry (exemptions from the tax for

Alliance	Industry Presidents of interest groups	Government Chancellor, Cabinet Ministers	Trade Unions Chairpersons
Steering Committee	General Secretaries BDI (Federation of German Industry) BDA (Federation of German Employers) DIHK (Chambers of Commerce) ZDH (Artisans)	Chancellor's Office Ministries of Finance, Employment, Economics, Health (Education on an ad hoc basis)	Top representatives of: DGB (German TUC), IG Metall (Engineering Union), Ver.di (Services Union), IG Chemie (Chemical Workers' Union)
eight working groups (Ministry in charge)	education and training (Research) tax policies (Finance) pension age and early retirement (Employment) reform of social security (Employment)		work hours (Employment) East Germany's economy (Chancellor's Office) redundancy payments (Employment) Benchmarking (Chancellor's Office)

FIGURE 5.1   *The institutional set-up of the Alliance for Jobs*
Source: *Das Parlament,* 30 July 1999, p. 5.

big industrial energy consumers), and social policies (tax income is used to subsidize the national pension fund).

The employers were less successful when they tried to stop those political reforms which were not in their interest, such as the reform of the law on workers' representatives at the firm level, which strengthened the role of the unions (M.M. Müller, 2001). Some of the reforms were even seen fairly sceptically by both sides of industry, the unions *and* the employers. This was the case with the new law to strengthen employment which was passed in 2001, the so-called 'job-aqtiv Gesetz' (*aqtiv* stands for *a*ctivate, *q*ualify, *t*rain, *i*nvest and help with finding a job, or *vermitteln*). The employers had hoped for a much greater restructuring of the job market, and the unions criticized possible income reductions and the introduction of contracts with a time limit (Hartwich, 2002).

For the government the Alliance for Jobs mostly had disappointing results although the Alliance certainly helped to convince industry that the government was prepared to listen to its needs. But although dialogue between both sides of industry was secured and the Schröder government was willing to try out new strategies, its biggest problem, unemployment, remained unsolved. This was particularly awkward because the Chancellor himself had said that when going to the polls at the next election he wanted German voters to take the reduction of the number of the unemployed as a yardstick for their voting decisions. The government could only list five achievements resulting from the

Alliance for Jobs (Jahreswirtschaftsbericht, 2002, pp. 29ff.): an agreement to make an effort to reduce overtime work, an agreement to support the training of entrants to the job markets, and to support life-long learning, an agreement to help older employees to keep their jobs, and the expectation that suggestions would be made as to how companies could contribute to a new old-age pensions model (e.g., with pension funds).

Integrated in the Alliance for Jobs is the benchmarking group in the Chancellor's Office which has the task of finding the best practices worldwide for the solution of policy problems in Germany and which supports decision-making in the eight working groups. It is based on the work of outside experts who have investigated, so far, a number of policy strategies in other countries, such as the Swiss pension model or the Dutch method of fighting unemployment. Though these studies had some impact on the intellectual debates in Germany their practical consequences were very limited. It has proved harder than imagined to integrate foreign experience into national policy-making in Germany.

The decision-making process of the Alliance for Jobs is based on deal-making. The unions may agree, for example, to tax reductions for industry if in exchange they are promised that industry intends to reduce overtime work. Such deals are facilitated if their costs are to be paid by a third party (most of the time the taxpayer, or all those who pay into insurance systems). An example of this kind of solution is the 1999 reform of rules for part-time work by older employees (Hank, 1999), the costs of which were off-loaded on to the social security system. If it is impossible to find a compromise on new policies, the role of the Alliance for Jobs can also be to negotiate a non-decision. This has been the case with the trade unions' idea to create employment opportunities for entrants into the job market through the early retirement of 60-year-old employees. The plan was to finance early retirement by an extra fund in which industry pays if the unions agree to accept lower pay rises. Chancellor Schröder negotiated in the Alliance for Jobs an empty compromise which said that industry, according to the individual needs of companies, will do its best to find ways to facilitate early retirement (Knelangen, 2000).

When the Federal Accounting Office criticized the methods by which the Federal Labour Office calculated its unemployment figures, the debate on the reform of the labour market won a new life of its own. The Alliance for Jobs was no longer the centre of the debate. Instead, situational government took over. First the Schröder government put its political weight behind the ideas of the new head of the Federal Labour Office, Florian Gerster, and then the proposals of the Hartz Commission became official government policy. This demonstrates very clearly the relative importance of neo-corporatism for policy-making in Germany today. It is no longer, as it still was in the 1970s, the institutionalized expression of the balance of economic power in Germany. Today the Alliance for Jobs is just another forum for the culture of dialogue, and not even a privileged one, as its complicated set-up seemed at first to imply.

Government by Expert Groups

The institutional framework of the legislative process has not been changed through initiatives of the new government. Germany has, however, gone through a debate about whether in policy-making Parliament has become side-lined to an extent which is dangerous for democracy (Thierse, 2001). Never before have there been so many joint action groups, networks, working groups, round tables, commissions and initiatives for the future (Leicht, 2001; Heinze, 2002). About 100 can be counted. A debate on the negative effect of policy-making by non-parliamentary committees was started in 1991, but surprisingly this has not led to claims that policy-making based exclusively on the work of these specialized small groups is less legitimate than traditional policy-making.

The role of specialized groups has to be seen in perspective (see Table 5.1). They are on the one hand an instrument of government to provide intellectual support and legitimacy for decisions which most of the time have already been made by the government, and on the other hand they are frequently very limited in their role. They were created to prove that the government pays attention to a problem (such as the above-mentioned Hartz Commission), but whether it wants to deal with this problem and which proposals of expert groups find their way into new legislation is, however, another matter. So it seems that decision-making in specialized groups is more like an extension of the decision-making process of government (not Parliament!) than a removal of the decision-making process from the sphere of political discourse.

Chancellor Schröder listens to experts, but he does not believe in the neutrality of expert advice. He is quite capable not only of by-passing Parliament, but also experts and his ministers, if he believes this is nec-essary to strengthen political support for his government. When the experts had spoken on pension reform and his employment minister, Walter Riester, had already presented a new pension bill, Schröder

TABLE 5.1 *Examples of specialized expert groups created by the Red–Green coalition*

Category	Task	Number of meetings (1998–2001)	Ministry responsible
Joint action groups	Against Extremism and Violence	6	Home Office
	Against Sex Tourism	5	
	In support of the Film Industry	4	Chancellor's Office
Networks	Integration of ethnic Germans from Eastern Europe	meetings at a local level as necessary	Home Office
Working groups	Human Rights and the Economy	6	Foreign Office
	Cross-border illegal drug traffic	2	Home Office
	Environment and Direct Investments Abroad	2	Environment Ministry
Round tables	Phasing-out of nuclear energy	several times per year (from 2002 once a year)	Economics Ministry
	Building industry against illegal employment	2	Employment Ministry
	Reform of the health system	2	Health Ministry
Commissions	Future of the Bundeswehr	12	Ministry of Defence
	Developing Berlin's Historical Centre	7	Transport and Housing
	Housing in East Germany	6	Ministry
	Reform of company taxation	11	Finance Ministry
	Immigration	14 plenary sessions, 30 working group sessions	Home Office
Future initiatives	Education Forum Innovations	12 (2–3 meetings annually)	Education and Research Ministry

Sources: Deutscher Bundestag: Übersicht über Aktionsbündnisse, Netzwerke, Kooperationen, Runde Tische, Kommissionen, Zukunftsinitiativen, Offensiven und Allianzen, Bundestagsdrucksache 14/7722, 4 December 2001.

reopened the discussions in Parliament to accomodate pressure from the unions. The final deal between Schröder and the unions was made in a restaurant in Hannover, the Chancellor's home town. The relevant parliamentary committee afterwards made its decision based on the advice of the leadership of the Social Democrats in Parliament without any input from the minister responsible (the employment minister, Riester, who was in Australia at that time). When he returned the only task left for him was to explain the new law to the general public.

Government via the Media

New to Schröder's policy style, compared to the way his predecessor presented himself (at least in his first years in office), was his relationship with the media (Meng, 2002). Whereas Helmut Kohl often demonstrated how he despised certain members of the press, Schröder not only went through a honeymoon period with the journalists who were happy to see new and friendly faces in government, but he also tried to integrate the world of show business and its rules into his political style. The media campaign after the election victory of 1998 was a strategy to compensate for the policy failures of the first six months. His media campaign implied that to support Schröder was trendy in itself. Schröder won himself the title of 'lifestyle chancellor' when, dressed in a Brioni suit and a cashmere coat, and smoking Cohiba cigars, he described politics as sheer fun.

Political communication as such may be more important today than it ever was before, and for Germany there is certainly no exception to this rule (Korte and Hirscher, 2000). But Chancellor Schröder had to learn that political communication without a policy message was empty and could become politically useless, and even dangerous. In mid-1999 Schröder himself saw this risk and reduced his presence on television game shows and talk shows. Also, as a reaction to the political funding scandal which engulfed the opposition Christian Democrat Union and former Chancellor Kohl, he tried to convey the message that the future of Germany was at stake and that he had a serious job to do (Weischenberg, 2001).

Conclusion

The policy record of the Schröder government has its strengths in non-economic reforms, such as the law on homosexual partnerships and immigration. The latter certainly has an economic component because immigration is now geared to some extent to the German labour market. Whether the immigration law will survive the test of the Federal Constitutional Court is, however, uncertain, because it is being contested whether the votes in the Bundesrat were counted correctly (Adamski, 2002). The phasing-out of nuclear power signals a profound change in industrial policy. But the big policy problems – reform of the health sector, of the pension system and unemployment – have at best been touched upon lightly by the first Red–Green coalition. The Schröder government is shying away from a radical reform of the welfare state which, as industry keeps telling government, is the only recipe for curing the 'German disease'.

Substantial political reforms also meet procedural obstacles. It has proved extremely difficult to gain efficiency in policy-making in by-passing traditional institutions. The limits of the culture of dialogue, government via the media and expert advice are met whenever hard choices have to be made. Neo-corporatism is today no longer attractive to companies and other powerful interests in society, because the state has little to offer. Companies and organized interests know that the state needs their advice and support and that the state has difficulty in mobilizing resources even for financing the status quo. Situational government and symbolic politics have often been the hectic and short-term reactions to new social problems. In the end non-decisions or policies based on the smallest common denominator of competing interests have, however, frequently been the result.

With Gerhard Schröder Germany has a chancellor who is a passionate deal-maker, a coordinator and political fixer, who believes in consensus as the best strategy for successful policy-making (Hofmann, 2000). This consensus is mostly not found in Parliament, but in special decision-making circles outside Parliament. The reputation of interest groups in political life has gained as a consequence. In his Red–Green coalition Chancellor Schröder has no counterpart who wants to restrict his ability to govern pragmatically. The representatives of the Green Party have no team spirit or joint vision that could provide the glue for joint policy initiatives to force the Chancellor to listen. The 2002 election result has strengthened Joschka Fischer, the Green foreign minister, however; he is now inclined to play a political role in domestic policy-making too.

Whether the old art of muddling through which finds expression in Schröder's pragmatism can produce the policies Germany needs today to reform its welfare state, to cope with the financial and intellectual problems of its education system, and to solve Germany's budgetary problems, to name just a few of the most pressing challenges, can be disputed. With corruption scandals in both political camps, and growing cynicism among the general public with regard to the role politicians play in society, it has become extremely difficult in Germany to organize rational discourses on policy changes. The paradoxical situation is that expectations in society concerning policy outputs are high, but trust in those who are supposed to deliver results – the politicians – is spectacularly low. As the status quo is not an option, however, a more open debate on the policy responsibilities of the state and the necessary degree of social reform in Germany seems to be unavoidable.

6

Political Economy: The German Model under Stress

STEPHEN PADGETT

Plagued by low growth, structural unemployment and a crisis of state debt, the travails of the German economy in the 1990s and 2000s intersect with a wider debate about the relative merits of different models of capitalism. An exemplar of the Rhineland model of 'institutionalized' capitalism, the ailing German economy is compared unfavourably by many with the market-driven 'dynamism' of the Anglo-Saxon variant. For others, however, the dichotomy between markets and institutions is a false one. Far from imposing rigidities on markets, they argue, economic institutions can facilitate adaptation to changing market conditions and the challenges of globalization. This chapter examines the characteristics of the German model of political economy, its recent performance record and the steps being taken to 're-invent' the model in response to changes in the economic environment. The underlying question is whether the model is doomed to underperformance until it conforms to the orthodoxies of its Anglo-Saxon counterpart, or if it can reinvigorate itself from within, drawing on the traditional virtues of German political economy? First, however, we will locate the question in the wider context of the debate about globalization, national economic institutions and varieties of capitalism.

Globalization, Institutions and Varieties of Capitalism

The response of national economies to globalization has become a central focus for scholars of political economy. Approaches differ between three schools of thought. The first sees globalization as a juggernaut sweeping away the distinctive models of capitalism embedded in national institutions. This school predicts that national economies will inevitably gravitate towards the liberal market model exemplified by North America and the UK. Institutionalists, on the other hand, see the patterns of behaviour and values that make up national political economies as more persistent and durable. From this perspective, the 'stickiness' of national institutions gives them an inbuilt resistance to change in the international economy, even at the cost of some loss of performance. The 'varieties of capitalism' school suggests a more dynamic interplay between economic change and institutions. National economies continually adapt to technical and economic change, but they do so in accordance with their own traditions of capitalism. This approach distinguishes between the *liberal market economy* model and the *coordinated market economy* found in the northern part of continental Europe. Neither is intrinsically superior to the other, and both have their strengths and weaknesses. The flexibility of the liberal model equips it for exploiting short-term opportunities in sectors characterized by rapid innovation and fast-changing markets. Endowed with strong social institutions supporting stable relations between economic actors, on the other hand, the coordinated model performs better in those sectors which rely on a longer-term accumulation of capital and skills, and where change therefore needs to be orchestrated and negotiated between economic actors (Crouch and Streeck, 1997).

Germany is a prime example of the coordinated market economy. Market forces co-exist with economic institutions which regulate economic life. Cooperative relations between firms are embedded in networks of cross-shareholdings and interlocking directorates, with especially close relations between firms and their banks. Key aspects of economic life are coordinated by industry or employer associations. Industrial relations are managed jointly by the 'social partners' – management and trade unions – within a framework of rules set out by the state. These institutionalized relations provide a strong platform for coordination in company finance and investment, research and development, programmes of vocational training to upgrade workers' skills, and the labour market. For its part, the state has combined discipline in monetary and fiscal policy with the promotion of economic growth and employment. The balance in the German model between market forces and institutional coordination has not always been easy to maintain; there have been periodic tensions between the two tendencies. Nevertheless, the model had an enviable track record of dynamism and stability.

More recently, however, the lustrous reputation of the German model has been tarnished by its faltering economic performance. In the 1980s it appeared to have lost much of its *dynamism*; in the 1990s and 2000s its aptitude for *stability* has been under scrutiny. A common diagnosis of the malaise of the German model focuses on the capacity of its institutions to respond to rapid change in the global economy. This chapter examines the effects of changes in the international environment on the German model of coordinated capitalism, and the ways in which the model is responding to change. Are its institutions being swept away by international market forces, as globalization theory predicts, or are they resisting the forces of change – at the cost of declining economic performance – in line with institutionalist expectations? Alternatively, can we see Germany from the 'varieties of capitalism' perspective, engaged in a gradual process of 'coordinated adaptation', and reinventing its traditional institutions to regain its competitive advantage?

The German Model of Political Economy

The German model was synonymous with the post-war *Wirtschaftswunder* (economic miracle). For three decades it provided the foundation for an outstanding economic performance, exemplified by economic growth, employment, monetary stability and fiscal balance. The annual increase in GDP averaged 8.2 per cent between 1950 and 1960, and 4.4 per cent between 1960 and 1973. Exports were a major driving force of economic growth. In only seven years between 1949 and 1990 did the economy suffer a current account trade deficit.

The structure of the post-war German economy reflects an industrial tradition reaching back to the nineteenth century. Its strengths lie in manufacturing, especially in the mechanical engineering, automobile, chemical, pharmaceutical and electrical sectors (Matravers, 1997, pp. 37–51). In these sectors, German companies are amongst the world leaders. In electricals and electronics, Siemens ranks second in size to the US General Electric; in motor manufacturing BMW and Volkswagen lie seventh and eighth in world rankings, and in chemicals and pharmaceuticals, BASF, Bayer and Aventis are amongst the leading players (Harding and Sorge, 2000).

Success in these sectors has been based on deriving a competitive advantage from what Streeck (1992) has called 'diversified quality production'. Specializing in product markets where *quality* matters more than *price*, German companies have pursued the formula of *Vorsprung durch Technik* (technical advantage), turning technological excellence into product leadership, which enabled them to compete very effectively in international markets. International competitiveness is crucial, since the domestic market for quality competitive products cannot sustain German companies. Thus the German economy is heavily export-oriented; exports accounted for 35 per cent of GDP in 2000. Germany is second only to the USA in its share of world exports.

The ability of German manufacture to maintain a competitive advantage in quality production relies on a supportive infrastructure of knowledge and skill. One of the traditional strengths of the German economy is its capacity for product innovation through scientific research and development, and a cascade system of technology transfer to ensure that research is applied in production (Cantwell and Harding, 1998). A second strength is a comprehensive system of vocational training to deliver the 'human capital' of highly skilled labour that is an essential component in quality production. The counterpart to a skilled labour force is a high wage structure to provide incentives to workers to undertake vocational training. High wage levels, however, have been supported by the high 'value added' component in quality competitive production (Coates, 2000).

Institutions

In contrast to Anglo-Saxon capitalism, in which *markets* play the decisive role, the German model is characterized by coexistence between markets and more or less institutionalized *networks* of cooperation and coordination embedded in the structure of corporate ownership and governance. *Intercorporate* networks are overlaid by an intermediate tier of *associational* institutions which serve to organize and coordinate the various sectors of the economy and to mediate relations between capital and labour. Finally the *state* combines the liberal role of maintaining the framework conditions for a successful market economy with the regulatory function of maintaining economic and social equilibrium in a system of 'managed capitalism'.

The foundations of the German model lie in a distinctive pattern of corporate ownership. Individual shareholding is limited, with less than 15 per cent of German equity in the hands of private households as against almost 30 per cent in Britain. Insurance companies and pensions funds account for just 12 per cent of total equity (40 per cent in Britain). The largest shareholders in German companies are *other* companies, accounting for 42 per cent of total equity, and banks, with a 10 per cent stake (Vitols, 2001, p. 342). Cross-shareholding accounts for a huge slice of German equity with an estimated value of around €270 billion. Corporate equity-holders have strategic business interests in the company, and therefore tend to take a longer-term view of its performance than pension funds and insurance companies with more aggressive investment strategies driven by quick returns. Intercorporate ownership networks generate mutual trust and stability in corporate governance, discouraging predatory takeovers, especially by non-German buyers. However, it is also a closed and somewhat insular system, sometimes referred to as 'Germany PLC' (Funk, 2000, p. 27), which tends to favour incremental change in established industries rather than rapid innovation in dynamic new sectors.

The interlocking networks of corporate ownership also help to support a pattern of corporate governance emphasizing *stakeholder* as opposed to *shareholder* values. The stakeholder principle treats companies as social institutions, responsive not merely to short-term fluctuations in their share prices, but also to the longer-term interests of related firms and banks as well as their employees. All of these interests are represented in the company via the supervisory board in which the strategic decisions of corporate governance are taken. Employees are also represented at shop-floor level through works councils, which have extensive rights of consultation and negotiation in matters of recruitment and redundancy, the organization of production, and some fringe remuneration issues such as bonuses and holiday pay. Legally obliged to work with management in the common interest of the company, works councils can facilitate adaptation to the demands of quality production but may also be a constraint on management agendas for corporate restructuring (Lane, 1994a; Lane, 1994b).

Interwoven with the structures of corporate governance are the dense networks of *associational* activity which are a further distinguishing feature of the German model. Both business and labour are intensively organized on the lines of industrial sector and region, with coordination exercised by relatively cohesive 'peak' associations. A striking feature of the German model is the way in which associations are empowered by the state to undertake a range of regulatory functions. Streeck (1997, p. 39) has shown how associational institutions support quality competitive production by enforcing high product standards and by orchestrating the vocational training programmes that provide the requisite skills base.

Above all, employer associations and trade unions regulate wages through industry-wide negotiation leading to legally binding agreements that prevent the sort of low-wage competition which might otherwise undermine quality competitive production. Geared to the quality manufacturing sectors, however, the architecture of wage regulation may be less well equipped for the more differentiated labour markets elsewhere in the economy. Industry-wide bargaining leads to 'flat' wage structures, with significantly less differentiation between skilled and unskilled workers than is found in most other countries. There is also a tendency towards wage 'pull', with rates of pay geared to the most profitable companies.

The third level of institution supporting the German model is *the state*, where the tension between liberal principles and managed capitalism is at its most intense. As Dyson (1996, pp. 197–8) has shown, the post-war West German state was based on the principles of ordo-liberalism, in which the state 'limited itself to designing an "economic constitution" of general rules ... whilst avoiding detailed meddling in economic processes'. Rules revolved above all around commitments to competition and a stable monetary order, enshrined in the Cartel Law and the Bundesbank Act of 1957. Whilst the former had mixed results in achieving its objective of preventing the concentration of economic power, the latter was spectacularly successful in providing the bedrock for the economic success of the German model.

At the same time, the state has been more regulatory and inter-ventionist than its ordo-liberal architects intended. First, the endowment of economic and associational actors with statutory competencies has generated the regulations that (as we saw above) circumscribe labour markets and industrial relations. Second, key sectors (such as agricul-ture, banking and insurance, coal and steel, the public utilities and trans-port) were exempted from competition law. Third, since the 1970s there has been a proliferation of state subsidies to declining sectors, rising to about DM133 billion (6 per cent of GDP) in 1988 and increasing exponentially since unification (Smyser, 1993, pp. 113–17). Finally, a commitment to the *social* market economy has seen the rise of a wel-fare state which, whilst maintaining the social cohesion that underpins the German model, now constitutes an unsustainable burden on the productive economy (see Chapter 7).

Policy

Tensions between ordo-liberalism and managed capitalism are seen in sharp relief in economic policy. A central tenet of ordo-liberalism is a clearly defined division of labour in economic management, with spe-cific responsibilities assigned to particular institutions. Monetary policy should be the responsibility of a central bank committed to monetary stability and low inflation, and insulated from political pressure by independent status. Fiscal policy – balancing tax revenue against government expenditure – is the domain of government, whilst macro-economic policy is the preserve of employers and trade unions (Funk, 2000, pp. 20–1; Dyson, 2001, p. 141). Managed capitalism, on the other hand, entails coordination between these three areas of economic policy, with government exercising a steering role, often in collaboration with its social partners.

In monetary policy, the Federal Republic has adhered very strongly to ordo-liberal principles, with monetary stability institutionalized in the Bundesbank. With its statutory independence reinforced by its public prestige the Bank was unwavering in the single-minded pursuit of its monetary responsibilities. The emulation of German design principles in the European Central Bank should ensure the continuation of monetary stability. In other respects, however, Germany has tended towards managed capitalism. The balanced (or surplus) budgets of the early years of the Federal Republic gave way in the late 1960s to the practice of using fiscal policy as an instrument of macro-economic management: that is, attempting to promote economic growth and employment through deficit budgets. At the same time, the economic steering capacity of the government was stepped up through the 1967 Law for Promoting Stability and Growth. The nexus between fiscal and macro-economic policy has periodically been institutionalized in social pacts between government and the social partners: *Concerted Action*, 1967 and 1977; Helmut Kohl's *Chancellor Round* (1992–98); and Gerhard Schröder's *Alliance for Jobs* (Timmins, 2000).

The Challenges

In the last two decades or so, the structural, institutional and policy components of the German model have come under challenge from the processes of technological and economic change commonly referred to as 'globalization'. Revolutionized by micro-electronic technology, financial and product markets increasingly transcend national boundaries, outstripping the capacity of national economic institutions to control and shape them in line with long-standing policy preferences. The German economy is particularly vulnerable to the effects of globalization because, as we have seen, it is heavily dependent on the capacity of domestic institutions to balance the demands of a high performance economy with high-wage labour markets and high levels of social protection in the welfare state. As social institutions are overtaken by global market forces it has become increasingly difficult to sustain this 'balancing act'. The resultant tensions are exacerbated by the burden imposed on the economy by the massive ongoing costs of unification.

Globalization and Technological Change

Globalization and technological change impact upon on the institutions of the German model in a number of ways. The first relates to the structural shift from mid-technology manufacturing, the traditional strength of the German economy, towards the service sector and to high-technology sectors such as micro-electronics and bio-technology. The institutionalized uniformity of industrial relations and labour markets in Germany is ill-adapted to the more differentiated structures of pay, productivity and skill in a service sector ranging from McDonald's to information technology (Funk, 2000, pp. 23–4). Specialized and fast-moving product markets in the high-technology sectors put a premium on post-Fordist forms of lean and flexible organization at the level of the firm. The German model of institutionalized cooperation between works councils and management has some capacity for organizational adaptation. Being geared to incremental technological advance, however, it is cumbersome in the face of rapid technological change. Doubts have also been raised about the capacity of rigidly organized research and development structures to match the pace of innovation and product development in the high-technology sectors (Vitols, 1997, pp. 31–2).

In the core sectors of the economy, a second challenge emanates from the growing ability of mass-manufacturing to undercut highly-skilled quality production by using sophisticated technology to match its product standards whilst exploiting the low-wage advantages of relatively low-skilled labour to beat it on price. The so-called 'Lexus effect' places pressure on quality competitive manufacturers to be attentive to price as well as quality competition in international markets. Inhibited from reducing labour costs by the institutional rigidities of the domestic labour market, German manufacturers are losing their international market advantage which, as we have seen, sustained the high wage economy. The resultant employment losses have been compensated in part by the 'redistribution of employment' through reductions in the working week. Expedients of this kind, however, have a limited capacity to offset the effects of international competition.

A third challenge relates to the mobility of capital, and the tendency of industry and finance to 'migrate' to parts of the globe offering the most favourable economic conditions. Sustaining the performance of

German high-wage capitalism, it has been argued, required continuous intervention on the part of domestic economic institutions to 'police the boundaries' between the national economy and its international environment. Globalization dissolves these boundaries, increasing the transnational mobility of capital, and enabling German companies to exit from restrictive labour markets in favour of countries that have embraced deregulatory agendas (Streeck, 1997, pp. 48–50). Over the last decade a succession of flagship German manufacturers such as BMW, Mercedes and Siemens have located quality production in low-wage economies in South America or Eastern Europe (Amoore, 2000, p. 59), intensifying concerns about *Standort Deutschland* (Germany as an investment location).

'Footloose capital' and the tendency of German producers to relocate abroad can also be related to changes in the financial sector which feed through into *corporate governance*. Globalization has undermined the commitment of financial capital to 'Germany PLC'. The big banks are less willing than previously to play the role of 'prefects' in the national economy, and are loosening their ties to German industry as they adopt a more international role. Manufacturing companies redefining themselves in global terms are attracted to international rather than national sources of capital. Moreover, with the liberalization of the German Stock Exchange, equity capital is beginning to play a larger role in company finance. Networks of cross-shareholding between companies are showing signs of unravelling. All these tendencies have contributed to the gradual emergence of a shareholder culture which has slowly begun to erode traditional stakeholder values.

Globalization has thus had an uneven effect on German capitalism, loosening up some of the financial institutions and forms of corporate governance that protected the economy from international competition whilst leaving the organization of production, industrial relations and labour markets relatively untouched. As we shall see, the consequent exposure of the latter to international market forces has far-reaching implications for economic performance.

The Costs of Unification

The German model has in the past proved its resilience in the face of external shocks, and might have been able to absorb the pressures of globalization had it not been for the huge cost burden of unification. Rebuilding an eastern economy capable of self-sustaining growth has proved elusive. The collapse of the GDR economy, combined with a programme of 'shock therapy' privatization, led to a massive contraction of economic activity in 1990–91. Economic collapse was followed by a post-reconstruction boom with growth rates of up to 10 per cent, but this was short lived, and since 1997 growth has hovered at just over 1 per cent. Even if the east achieved growth rates of 4 per cent (as against 2 per cent in the west), it has been estimated that it would take 30 years for it to catch up (*The Economist*, 12 May 2001). In the absence of self-sustaining growth, reconstruction programmes, along with social transfers to cushion east Germans against economic hardship, amounted to some DM1,400 billion in the first decade after unification. Representing around 4 per cent of GDP, this 'blood transfusion' to the eastern economy has had a catastrophic effect on state debt.

Apart from the cost burden, the failure of economic reconstruction in the east has damaged the credibility of the German model. Unification by 'institutional transfer' involved the introduction in the east of the whole range of social, economic and political institutions operative in the Federal Republic. Most controversially, these included the institutionalized wage bargaining and labour market arrangements that were already being questioned in the west. The logic of industry-wide wage structures led to a rapid pay equalization between the two parts of Germany, despite a yawning gap in productivity. Artificially inflated pay rates prevent eastern Germany from exploiting the competitive advantage of a low-wage economy and carry the prospect of 'high rates of unemployment lasting for decades' (Hughes-Hallett, Ma and Mélitz, 1996, p. 538). Whilst 'official' wage rates are frequently circumvented through collusion between employers and employees anxious to preserve their jobs, this merely serves to erode still further the credibility of institutionalized wage bargaining. Eastern Germany is thus the Achilles heel of the German model.

Performance Indicators

In retrospect it may be argued that even during its supposed 'golden years' the performance of the German model was somewhat exaggerated. It was only in the 1950s that the economy produced growth rates in excess of other leading European countries, averaging 7.7 per cent against an average of 4.6 per cent in the UK, France and Italy. Between 1961 and 1973, German growth rates were on a par with their main European rivals. Thereafter, until the end of the 1980s, German performance slipped marginally behind that of its EU comparators, the comparative decline accelerating in the 1990s so that by the end of the millennium growth was significantly below the EU average. The growth performance of the economy since 1990 reflects unification effects (see below, where annual increases are shown as a percentage of the previous year). A post-unification boom in the west in 1990–91 was followed by recessions in 1993 and 1995–96, as the west absorbed the shock of unification. Growth patterns also reflect fluctuations in the international economy, recovering in line with international recovery in the late 1990s to reach a high of over 3 per cent in 2000 before falling back sharply to less than 1 per cent in 2001 following the slowdown in the USA. Fluctuations in response to external influences, however, cannot disguise a secular erosion in the underlying strength of the German economy.

The secular decline in growth rates is mirrored in employment. From a low of just 179,000 in 1970, unemployment rose sharply to 1 million in 1975 and 2.3 million a decade later, before abating in the economic recovery of the late 1980s to 1.7 million in the west German economy in 1991. The collapse of the eastern economy, along with post-unification recessions in the west, pushed unemployment to a peak of around 4.5 million, or 11.4 per cent of the labour market, in 1997. Economic recovery in the late 1990s saw the jobless total fall to 3.9 million in 1999, only to top the 4 million mark again in 2001. Table 6.1 shows the rise in unemployment in east and west Germany as a percentage of the labour force.

Cross-national comparison underlines the declining employment capacity of the German model. Unemployment rates overtook those of Japan in the decade 1974–84 and the USA in the years 1985–98. Set alongside other 'coordinated market economies in northern Europe', only Belgium had a higher jobless rate. OECD calculations of the standardized unemployment rate in March 2002 showed Germany at 8.1 per cent, significantly above the international average of 6.7 per cent and comparing unfavourably with liberal market economies in the USA (5.7 per cent) and the UK (5.0 per cent). Unemployment, it should be noted, was not an exclusively German problem. Both France (9.1 per cent) and Italy (9.0 per cent) had higher rates, and the euro-zone average lay

TABLE 6.1 *Average unemployment rates 1973–2001 (% labour force; unstandardized)*

	1973–89	*1991*	*1993*	*1995*	*1997*	*1999*	*2001*
West	5.0	5.7	7.3	8.2	9.8	8.7	7.4
East		10.4	15.1	13.7	18.1	17.6	17.5
All Germany		6.6	8.8	9.5	11.4	10.5	9.4

Source: Economist Intelligence Unit.

at 8.4 per cent. Cross-national comparison, however, does suggest that the labour market rigidities and welfare state burdens which Germany shares with many continental European countries have a negative impact on employment performance.

Attributing unemployment to a single cause risks oversimplification. One major factor, however, is the high cost of German labour. Labour costs in manufacturing in 1996 were the highest in the world, exceeding Japan by 50 per cent, the USA by 80 per cent and being more than double the cost of labour in the UK (Funk, 2000, p. 25). The disparity arises not merely from high wage rates, but from the non-wage costs attached to employment, made up largely by the very high social insurance contributions paid by employers to sustain the welfare state. Employer and employee contributions to social insurance and pension funds amount to some 40 per cent of wages and salaries. Even accounting for the high productivity levels of German manufacturing, this still means that unit labour costs (the cost of production) are around 25 per cent higher than their major international rivals. Although unit labour costs have fallen slightly since the late 1990s following more restrained wage settlements, they remain a drag on the employment capacity of German companies exposed to international competition.

In diversified quality production, German companies compensate for high labour costs by product leadership based on high skill and technical excellence. Competitive advantage depends on a continual process of product innovation and development. Patent office data suggests that Germany maintains a lead in product innovation in the mid-technology manufacturing sectors of engineering and chemicals, although even here its performance is uneven. In the high-technology sectors of new materials, bio-technology, semiconductors and information technology Germany's capacity for innovation lags behind that of its international competitors (Hall and Soskice, 2001, pp. 42–3). Research and development infrastructures, it has been concluded, are geared to incremental development of exiting technologies rather than radical new technology innovation (Harding, 2000, p. 84).

High labour costs also have an adverse effect on employment by reducing the attractiveness of Germany as an investment location. This is reflected in a long-term flight of German investment abroad. Investment decisions are complex, involving more than merely wage-cost calculations. For German companies engaged in quality manufacturing, access to highly-skilled domestic labour can be a more important factor in location decisions than the cost of labour (Allen, 2002). Nevertheless, a large part of direct foreign investment finds its destination in the USA and the UK, suggesting that liberalized economies with relatively low production costs are a magnet for German capital. Direct foreign investment peaked in the 1990s with net outflows equivalent to €65 billion in 1996 and €61 billion in 1998. Since then, outflows have abated somewhat. Indeed, 2000 saw a net *inflow* of investment, consequent on the influx of foreign capital involved in the takeover of the telecommunications company Mannesmann by the UK company Vodaphone. This alerts us to a second factor in the flight of German capital abroad. Outflows reflect in part foreign acquisitions by large German companies pursuing strategies of international expansion. The closed nature of corporate governance in Germany generally tends to discourage inward investment in the form of foreign takeovers.

Under the triple pressures of escalating unemployment, the continuing costs of unification and the financial burden of the health and pensions systems (see Chapter 7), state finances approached crisis by the turn of the millennium. Total state debt stood at over 60 per cent of GDP (almost double the 1980 level of 33 per cent). Much of the damage was inflicted by unemployment, which deals a double blow to state finances, since contributions to the social security system decline at the same time as the benefit burden rises with the number of jobless. During the 1990s unemployment drove budget deficits up to around €25 billion, with a peak of €34 billion in 1993 (see Figure 6.1). After stabilizing at the end of the 1990s, the deficit exploded in 2001 to an estimated €45 billion, perilously close to the ceiling of 3 per cent of GDP stipulated in EU rules (see Chapter 8). Under the terms of these rules, Germany is

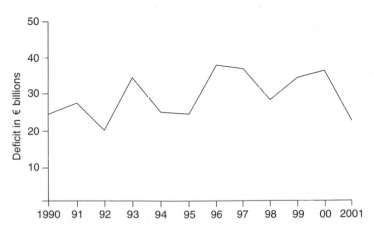

FIGURE 6.1   *Federal government deficit, 1990–2001 (€ billion)*
Source: Economist Intelligence Unit.

TABLE 6.2 *Trade and current account balance, 1996–2000 (€ billion)*

	1996	1997	1998	1999	2000
Exports	398.0	454.7	489.8	510.1	596.9
Imports	348.3	395.5	424.8	444.8	538.4
Trade balance	49.7	59.2	65.0	65.2	58.5
Current account	8.9	−2.5	−6.1	−16.8	−21.0

Source: Economist Intelligence Unit.

required to balance the government budget over the longer term. With fiscal policy subject to this constraint, and with monetary policy transferred to the European Central Bank, the management of the domestic economy rests increasingly with wage-setting and labour market policy. Tightly enmeshed in the 'institutional thicket' of the German model, these are relatively blunt instruments for economic management.

The pervading sense of economic gloom was relieved only by continuing strength in exports. The year 2000 was a record year in German trade history, the aggregate of exports and imports crossing the DM1,000 billion line for the first time. Germany remained the second largest exporting country in the world, with exports rising by an annual average of over 10 per cent between 1997 and 2000 (see Table 6.2). This was reflected in the consolidation of the visible trade balance in the late 1990s at around €65 billion, although the balance dipped in 2000 consequent upon a sharp rise in imports due to rising oil prices. Buoyant exports at the end of the millennium, however, should not be allowed to disguise more negative long-term trends. The German share of world exports declined from 12 per cent in 1988 to 8.5 per cent in 2001. Moreover, the strength of the visible trade balance is offset by a deficit in services and in investment incomes, resulting in an overall current account deficit which escalated steeply in 1999–2000. Almost all the economic indicators, then, show the German model losing performance in the face of the triple challenge of globalization, the costs of unification, and the burden of the welfare state.

Institutional Adaptation

At the beginning of this chapter we postulated three possible ways in which countries respond to change in the international economy; the capitulation of national institutions in the face of global markets, institutional resistance coupled with reduced performance, or flexible adaptation through mobilizing traditional institutional strengths. In this section of the chapter we examine recent developments in the institutions of corporate finance and governance, labour markets and industrial relations, asking which of these scenarios most accurately depicts the German response to international economic change.

In company finance, the last decade has been a period of quite significant institutional change, with important implications for corporate governance. The key development was the liberalization of financial markets, which triggered a strategic re-orientation on the part of the big commercial banks and a subtle change of business culture amongst large German companies. Designed to promote Germany as a finance centre, the liberalization of financial markets began in the late 1980s with opening-up of the Stock Exchange to new types of financial instruments and products. Between 1990 and 1998 three new laws were passed; the 1988 law alone contained over 100 different measures. Parallel to liberalization came a new approach to the *regulation* of financial markets. Opaque practices of self-regulation were replaced by a more transparent system of federal government supervision in an attempt to safeguard investors and thereby encourage stock market investment (Lütz, 2000, pp. 163–5).

Stock market liberalization has triggered a massive shake-up of the banking sector (Schröder, 1996). Responding to more open and diverse financial markets, the large commercial banks have expanded their involvement in securities trading. Seeking the know-how of their more advanced US and UK counterparts they have engaged in international mergers and acquisitions, Dresdner Bank joining Kleinwort Benson and Deutsche Bank merging with Morgan Grenfell and subsequently Bankers Trust. Reinventing themselves as international players and shifting their attention to securities markets, the commercial banks have loosened their relations with domestic companies. Top of their agenda has been divestment of the shares that banks and financial institutions hold in industrial companies which have little or nothing to do with their core business in financial services. The insurance giant Allianz is estimated to have €60 billion tied up in, amongst other companies, the BASF and Beiersdorf chemicals groups and the electricity utility Eon. Divestment of these holdings had hitherto been prevented by a punitive capital gains tax on share sales. One of the most important economic reforms of Gerhard Schroder's government was to abolish corporation tax on share sales from 2002. The reform was designed to provoke the unwinding of the incestuous network of cross-shareholding between companies that Chancellor Schröder has called 'the German disease'. Although its effects have not yet become clear, it has the potential for a seismic shift in German capitalism.

Global trends have not been restricted to the banking sector. A defining moment in the cultural transformation of German capitalism was the part-privatization of Deutsche Telecom in 1996, which triggered a wave of popular enthusiasm for equity ownership. Between 1988 and 2000, it has been estimated, the number of Germans owning shares doubled to 6 million. Along with the tendency of large companies to switch from bank finance to equity capital, the growth of 'popular share-holding' has triggered a change in cultural values, with an increased commitment to shareholder expectations of a healthy rate of return on their investment. One of the effects of these changes has been a wave of merger and acquisition activity which has broken with the traditional ethos of Germany PLC. Krupp's acquisition of Thyssen in 1997 had some of the hallmarks of a hostile takeover, which is unusual between flagship German companies. Merger activity in the 1990s also had a strong international dimension, with link-ups between Hoechst and Rhône-Poulenc, and Daimler-Benz and Chrysler creating global leaders in their respective sectors. The year 2001 saw two corporate marriages, the Veba–Viag and RWE–VWE hitch-ups, designed to establish European super-utilities in the liberalized electricity market. Other German companies, such as Siemens, shaped up for a more international presence through internal restructuring.

Above all, however, the winds of change in corporate finance and governance are symbolized by the hostile takeover of Mannesmann by the UK's Vodaphone–AirTouch, the world's biggest-ever hostile takeover. The battle for control of the engineering/telecommunications giant represented a head-to-head confrontation between the German economic model and Anglo-Saxon 'enterprise capitalism'. Whilst political leaders (including the Chancellor) denounced the attack on the social market economy, the financial and business community allowed Mannesmann shareholders to decide the issue, failing for the first time to mount a defence against a major 'cross-border raid' on Germany PLC (Garrett, 2001). The banks showed a similar reluctance to come to the assistance of the stricken construction giant Holzmann. On this occasion, Chancellor Schröder undertook the negotiation of a rescue package, announcing as he did so, however, that this would be the last time his government would bail out a struggling company (see also Chapter 5).

The unravelling of insider networks of corporate ownership, the explosion of merger and acquisition activity, and the emergence of an 'equity culture' of shareholder values signal a far-reaching transformation in German capitalism. The extent of change should not be exaggerated. First, it is not yet clear how fast the divestment of cross-shareholdings will proceed, following the lifting of corporation tax at the start of 2002. Second, it has been pointed out that beneath the top echelon of the corporate landscape there remains a *Mittelstand* consisting of tens of thousands of family-run, middle-sized companies where traditional practices and values remain strong. Third, a declining stock market in the early 2000s may have dampened the new-found enthusiasm of the Germans for share ownership. Despite all these caveats, however, it seems clear that Germany PLC is subject to irreversible changes that will gradually percolate through to the grassroots of the economy.

There is less evidence of change in the institutions of the labour market and industrial relations. Despite having come to office with a campaign theme of 'employment, innovation and social justice', the Schröder government has done little to relax the labour market rigidities that are blamed by many for restricting the employment potential of the German economy. Indeed, government legislation has had the effect of tightening labour law in a number of respects, as a quid pro quo for trade union cooperation in wider aspects of economic policy (see below). In an attempt to buttress welfare state finances, 'small jobs' paying less than DM630 per month, and pseudo-self-employment (a device to avoid social insurance contributions) were brought into the payroll tax net. Whilst this plugged tax loopholes, it did so at the cost of increasing the rigidity of the labour market. The Part-time and Temporary Jobs Act had a similar effect, giving employees the right to work part-time, and preventing the renewal of temporary employment contracts. Whilst the intention was to convert temporary jobs into permanent ones, critics claim that the inflexibility of the latter measure actually serves to discourage employment (Silvia, 2002, p. 18). Finally, revisions to the 1972 Works Councils Act strengthened the system of employee representation in the company, extending the practice to smaller firms and broadening the remit of the works councils to include environmental protection, training, equal opportunities and the fight against xenophobia.

In the labour market and industrial relations, the German model has been largely resistant to neo-liberal 'lessons' from other countries. Alert to the importance of lesson drawing, Schröder established a 'Benchmarking Group' attached to the Chancellor's Office with a brief to draw on 'best practice' in formulating proposals for freeing up labour markets and stimulating employment. Having given the group its brief, however, Schröder rejected its recommendations for a reduction in payroll taxes, the relaxation of rules protecting employees from dismissal and fewer restrictions on short-term contracts (Harlen, 2002, p. 77). Paradoxically, although they pointed in a similar direction, the findings of the Hartz Commission on labour market reform were offered by the government in the 2002 election campaign as an answer to unemployment.

In so far as industrial relations have adapted to global economic pressures they have done so gradually in ways that reflect traditional economic practices and values. Whilst the architecture of wage bargaining remains bound by the rigidities of sector-wide agreements, employers and trade unions have cooperated in the spirit of social partnership to preserve (or in exceptional cases to create) jobs. Landmark agreements in the chemicals and engineering sectors in 1993–94 saw employers offering commitments to maintaining jobs in return for trade union acceptance of wage restraint, reduced working time and flexible working practices (Bastian, 1995). New ground in this area was broken in 2001 with a deal between Volkswagen and the engineering union, IG Metall, in which the car-maker undertook to employ some 3,500 previously unemployed workers in return for union acceptance of an innovative employment contract involving performance and profit-related pay with working time geared to the company's order book. It is increasingly common practice for sectoral wage bargaining to be supplemented or superseded by local 'in-house' agreements of this kind, often negotiated directly between works council and management. Once little more than an extension of the trade union apparatus, works councils are becoming increasingly independent of the unions, identifying with the fate of the company and engaging in 'concession bargaining' (sacrificing wages for security of employment).

Whilst the institutional rigidities of wage bargaining may be mitigated at the margins by this type of local flexibility, a system of industry-wide wage tariffs remains a straitjacket on the productive economy. In its Annual Report for 2001, the Council of Economic Advisors was outspoken in their criticism of the system, advocating incentivized wage structures with more sensitivity to company profitability. In the absence of industrial relations reform, many firms seek an escape route of their own by learning the employer associations that negotiate wage agreements. Most large firms in the core industrial sectors continue to invest in the system as a source of order and predictability, but amongst smaller firms in the service sector the allure of wage autonomy is strong. Overall, the coverage of industry-wide agreements is gradually declining. In the west, around 65 per cent of firms adhere to collectively agreed norms, as against 50 per cent in east where company survival often takes precedence over legal niceties (French, 2000, p. 213). The exit of firms from the cost burden of wage regulation is mirrored by the exit of employees to a shadow economy where they can escape the oversized tax wedge (Schmidt, 2001, p. 9). The erosion of traditional wage bargaining structures can also be seen in declining trade union membership. The weakening of employer associations and trade unions signals a decline in the legitimacy and regulatory capacity of the social institutions on which the German model of industrial relations rests. In the absence of reform from above, it may be concluded, this aspect of the German model is being slowly subverted from below.

Macro-Economic Policy: The Record of the Schröder Government

The tension between markets and institutions that runs through corporate governance and industrial relations is reflected in government economic policy. As we saw earlier in this chapter, the role of the state is contested in German political economy. From the ordo-liberal perspective the state is restricted to establishing the ground rules of economic activity and maintaining a stable economic environment. The competing tradition of managed capitalism, on the other hand, casts government in a more active role, advocating the use of fiscal policy to promote growth and employment and the coordination of economic activity through dialogue with the social partners.

One of the main problems Chancellor Schröder faced in re-balancing the German model towards liberal principles was the strong attachment of his party and its trade union allies to the ethos of managed capitalism. His relationship with the SPD is somewhat distant, the party endorsing his candidacy in 1998 only because of his electoral appeal. Once in office, opposition to Schröder's programme of innovation and reform coalesced around Finance Minister Oskar Lafontaine, doyen of the SPD left. Lafontaine's formula for employment creation was rooted in the traditional social democratic belief in demand management, boosting consumer demand through deficit budgeting. This was flanked by criticism of the tight monetary policy of the European Central Bank and proposals for making the Bank more politically accountable (and thereby more sensitive to macro-economic objectives). Opposed to reductions in business taxes, Lafontaine advocated an alternative: the export of German tax levels through EU harmonization. The ensuing conflict with the Chancellor damaged the government's credibility and wasted most of its first year in office. Even though Schröder was able to outflank Lafontaine and force his resignation in March 1999, government policy still had to be sensitive to the concerns of social groups at the core of the SPD electorate. The Chancellor had to learn to live with the constraints. Following an ill-fated attempt at the programmatic reorientation of the SPD towards the Third Way exemplified by Tony Blair's New Labour,

Schröder has toned down his liberal rhetoric, preferring instead to pursue a strategy of 'reform by stealth' (Dyson, 2002a).

The effects of party constraints on Schröder's liberal instincts are very apparent in fiscal policy. One of the first major acts of the new government was the Tax Relief Act of late 1998 designed to reduce the tax burden on lower and middle income earners, and to free up consumer spending so as to stimulate economic activity and boost employment. Cuts in household taxation were paid for by closing some loopholes in business taxation, and by a one-off tax on the accumulated profits of electricity utilities and insurance companies. The combined effect of these reforms was a transfer of some DM30 billion from the company sector to households. A second front of tax reform was the introduction of 'ecological taxes' on petrol and energy. Ecology taxation was a condition of the coalition with the Greens on which the government was based. It was designed to 'kill two birds with one stone', reducing the consumption of environmentally damaging fossil fuels whilst at the same time raising revenue which would enable the government to reduce the payroll taxes that act as a deadweight on competitiveness and jobs (Silvia, 2002, p. 17). Fiscal policy manoeuvring along these lines ran strongly against the principles of order and predictability at the heart of ordo-liberal doctrine, provoking alarm and protests amongst business leaders, and severely denting the business-friendly image that the Chancellor had cultivated during the election campaign.

Schröder's record is not without reform achievements. Having seen off the challenge of Lafontaine, and with the more orthodox Hans Eichel as Finance Minister, he was able to follow his own instincts and reassert the liberal face of the German model. A second tax reform concluded in 2000 was designed to streamline the tax system by ironing out some of structural anomalies. It was also much more business oriented, including cuts in the higher rates of income tax along with large-scale cuts in company taxation. The combined effects of cuts in corporation tax and local business levies was to reduce taxation on company profits from 52 per cent to 37 per cent. At around the same time Eichel introduced a savings package cutting government spending by axing some social welfare benefits. Reform to the creaking pension system had the effect of linking entitlements to inflation rather than earnings (see Chapter 7). This attempt to rein in expenditure and curb a spiralling budget deficit was combined with a medium-term financial strategy, the Stability Programme, designed to reduce the federal government deficit to zero over five years to 2004. Reduced tax revenues resulting from a downturn in growth in 2001, however, meant that, despite these measures, the deficit continued to increase and the zero target remained a distant aspiration.

The scale of the government deficit, along with the constraints of the EU Stability and Growth Pact, leave little scope for the government to use fiscal policy to kick-start a stalling economy. At the same time, the transfer of monetary policy to the European Central Bank denies national policy-makers another instrument of economic control. Under these circumstances, the only effective instrument for managing the economy is labour market and wages policy. Thus a major front in Schröder's economic strategy was a drive for competitiveness through wage moderation and economic reform by agreement with the social partners. The institutional framework that was chosen for these tasks conforms very closely to the classical model of managed capitalism. Chaired by the Chancellor, the Bündnis für Arbeit (Alliance for Jobs) brings together the ministers of finance, economics, labour and health and the head of the Chancellor's Office, along with the leaders of the main business groups and trade unions. The central purpose of the forum was to deliver wage moderation in return for business commitments to employment creation. For Schröder, however, the wider objective was to build a consensus supporting his reform agenda (Timmins, 2000, pp. 46–9). Most observers emphasize the limited achievements of the Alliance for Jobs, ascribing to it little more than a symbolic function. It has been argued by others that it helped to create a consensual environment for the government's tax and pension reforms. It should be added, however, that the latter was weakened by concessions to the trade unions, and that the price of trade union consent was a tightening rather than a relaxation of some aspects of labour market regulation.

Conclusion

At the beginning of this chapter we posed three alternative perspectives on the response of national economic institutions to globalization. We may conclude that no single one of these perspectives accurately captures the German case. The institutions of German political economy have emphatically not *capitulated* to international market forces as globalization theory would suggest. Some aspects of the model, notably in corporate finance and governance, show unmistakable signs of internationalization and cultural transformation. In labour market organization and industrial relations, on the other hand, the persistence of traditional practices and values underlines the 'stickiness' of institutions. Does continuity simply reflect institutional inertia, with a consequent decline in economic performance, or can we see evidence of the German model undertaking a process of 'coordinated adaptation': that is, *absorbing* change by calling on existing institutional strengths to restore competitive economic advantage? This question hinges on whether strategies for incremental adaptation that draw on traditional practices and values are capable of matching the pace of change in the external environment.

Performance indicators suggest that the capacity of the German model for reconciling economic efficiency with traditional values may have reached its limits. The weak growth and employment performance of the 1990s was partly a reflection of cyclical trends, as well as the shock of absorbing the crippled economy in the east; it was also, however, a function of astronomical labour costs compounded by the inflexibility of regulated labour markets. To be sure, the stability and predictability of these institutional arrangements are prerequisites of the long-term investment in vocational training and research and product development that underpin diversified quality production. The increasing intensity of international competition in quality production markets, however, means that *price* competitition intrudes upon the logic of the high-wage, high-skill economy with disastrous consequences for the level of employment.

One potential source of change that we have observed in this chapter is the progressive transformation of corporate finance and governance. Developments here – a shake-up in the banking sector, the distancing of the banks from industrial companies, the gradual unwinding of cross-shareholdings and the progressive emergence of an equity culture – have the potential for opening up Germany PLC to international influences, thereby accelerating the pace of change elsewhere. At present, large companies in the core manufacturing sectors show little inclination to renounce the stability and predictability of German institutions for a more liberal system of industrial relations and labour markets. The tendency of smaller companies, however (especially in the service sector), to opt out of institutional arrangements may be indicative of the gradual erosion of the German model of industrial relations from below.

Attempting to steer the economy towards adaptation to its international economic environment, Chancellor Schröder has sought to maintain a balance between the traditions of ordo-liberalism and managed capitalism that compete within the German model. Political constraints, however, have meant that policy inclines strongly towards the latter, with government attempting to broker agreement between the social partners. Within this consensual framework, the more radical projects of labour market de-regulation and welfare state reform to create scope for reducing the pay-roll tax burden have been put on the back burner. There is a growing feeling amongst observers that until government tackles these politically intractable issues, the problems at the heart of the German economy will go unresolved and that the consequence may be a dangerous spiral of economic decline.

7

The Welfare State: Incremental Transformation

MARTIN SEELEIB-KAISER

Globalization is often viewed as a key challenge for continental European welfare states. High social insurance contributions and high tax rates, it is argued, undermine the international competitiveness of domestic companies. Consequently, changes in the financing structure and coverage of the welfare state is seen as a prerequisite of economic vitality. In the German context, however, the scope for reform is restricted by the 'semi-sovereign' character of the political system (Katzenstein, 1987), a welfare state consensus between the two major parties, and a majority of the electorate being clients of the welfare state. Reform thus tends to be incremental and gradual rather than comprehensive. Hence, a key question for political scientists is whether Germany is politically capable of social policy change. The aim of this chapter is to analyse social policy developments during the last two decades, seeking to establish the political determinants of change.

To analyse change we first have to define a time frame. The mid-1970s are a useful reference point because they mark the end of the so-called 'golden era' of welfare state capitalism. Second, we need tools or categories to be able to judge whether the sum of the many policy developments we have witnessed over the years constitute a *significant* change. Recent comparative welfare state analysis has focused on three dimensions of change: 're-commodification, cost containment, and recalibration' (Pierson, 2001). But how much alteration along these dimensions constitutes *significant* change? Hall (1993) differentiates between first, second, and third order changes. A first order change is defined as a change in the setting of instruments according to changed circumstances (e.g., an increase in the cost of living adjustment in an entitlement programme based on the inflation rate). A second order change can be understood as a change of policy instruments, while the overall objectives remain the same. Finally, we can speak of a third order change if the overall aims and instruments of a policy are newly defined and thus eventually constitute a new 'institutional logic' (Deeg, 2001, p. 36).

The Golden Era of the German Welfare State

In comparative research, Germany is characterized as the welfare state that resembles most closely the ideal category of a conservative welfare state regime (Esping-Andersen, 1990). One core element of such a welfare state regime is its strong emphasis on social insurance; consequently, Germany has also been characterized as a 'social insurance state' (Riedmüller and Olk, 1994). The other core element of a conservative welfare state regime is its reliance on the family and other communal groups in delivering social services.

According to the social insurance philosophy the primary function of the German welfare state was to provide wage-centred social policies. The precondition for receiving benefits was prior employment (Vobruba, 1990). Based on this institutional setting, social benefits were financed through equal social insurance contributions from workers and employers and *not* through general taxation. Consequently, the *main* aim was intertemporal redistribution within the life cycle and not interpersonal redistribution. The *leitmotiv* of post-war social policy was securing living standards through the replacement of a high proportion of income lost through sickness, unemployment and retirement. A prime example is the 1957 reform of old-age insurance which substantially raised the old-age benefits and indexed them to future wage increases. By the mid-1970s, the replacement rate had reached 70 per cent for the standard pensioner with a work history of 45 years on average income. In the 1950s, most senior citizens were dependent on means-tested social assistance. Now they could rely primarily on their old-age insurance benefits.

Unemployment insurance exhibited a similar design with standards of living insured against unemployment. The instruments to achieve this were twofold: (1) a replacement rate reaching 68 per cent of prior earnings in the mid-1970s to ensure a relatively stable income for workers during spells of unemployment; (2) suitable work was defined in such a way that an unemployed worker would not have to take a job offer, which – compared to the previous job – either paid less or was in a different occupational field. In addition, the active labour market policy was aimed at abolishing 'substandard' employment.

After strikes in the shipbuilding industry in the mid-1950s, income maintenance in the event of sickness became statutory for all employees. A further reform in 1969 made it obligatory for employers to provide 100 per cent of prior earnings during the first six weeks of a sickness; thereafter sickness insurance funds would provide 80 per cent for the duration of the illness. In the case of disability the law differentiated between those workers who, due to their disability, could no longer work within their profession or occupation and those who were fully disabled. The former could receive a benefit, which was only one-third lower than for those fully disabled. As in the case of old age and unemployment, these statutory regulations reflect the important role of guaranteeing the standard of living while sick or disabled.

Although financed through social insurance contributions, healthcare itself is provided based on the principle of solidarity. About 90 per cent of the population are insured through one of the more than 400 independent statutory health insurance companies. Aside from some very low individual contributions, the statutory health insurance companies cover all necessary medical-related expenses.

For the social policy expert of the 1960s and early 1970s, enhanced social insurance would eventually cover the standard social risks; social assistance in the sense of a minimum social safety net would ultimately become residual (Giese, 1986). Despite having a long tradition in Germany, fringe benefits provided by employers played only a minor role within the overall social policy arrangement.

The second core element of a conservative welfare state regime is its heavy reliance on the institution of the family, with the housewife cast in the role of a provider of social services. Based on the principle of subsidiarity, the state would support the family, in addition to a child allowance or the child tax credit, only if traditional self-help mechanisms had failed. Hence, in contrast to Scandinavian welfare states, the German welfare state provided public social services only in a very restricted way. The housewife and dependent children were entitled to social insurance benefits based on the employment history of the male breadwinner. The strong economic growth of the 1950s and 1960s, with its very low unemployment rate and the predominant acceptance by women of their role as caregivers for children and the elderly (Fröhner, von Stackelberg and Eser, 1956), contributed to a seemingly well functioning welfare state.

To summarize, one can argue that during the golden era, the German welfare state was mainly characterized by statutory insurance schemes which guaranteed previous living standards in case of old age, unemployment and sickness as well as providing grant-derived benefits to family members. The family itself had the important role as the primary provider of social services. From a normative perspective the German welfare state was primarily based on the principles of social integration and cohesion, not on redistribution between the classes, or fighting a war on poverty (cf. Goodin *et al.*, 1999).

Social Policy Expenditures and Financing

One way to measure social policy output is to analyse expenditures. Germany has a highly complex public financing structure through its federal system and the existence of para-fiscal institutions, such as social insurance funds. Hence, in order to grasp the overall development of social policy expenditures, we have to take a closer look at the 'social budget' or social policy expenditures. Figure 7.1 shows the overall social spending in relationship to GDP from 1975 to 2001. With the exception of the early 1980s, the data show a clear pattern of cost containment until German unification in 1990. Subsequently the social policy expenditures once again rose rapidly until 1996, after which the sharp increase was brought under control. Based on the overall spending data, the change in government in 1998 did not seem to alter the spending pattern substantially.

Spending by region between 1991 and 2001 shows continuity in the west and a gradual, but persistent, increase in the east since 1997 (Figure 7.2). The high level of social spending in the east is largely

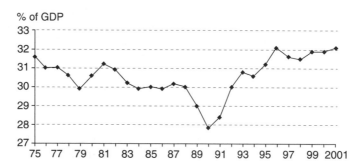

FIGURE 7.1   *Social spending in Germany as a percentage of GDP: 1975–2001*
Note: Starting 1991 data for unified Germany. Data for 1999 and 2000 preliminary, 2001 projections.
Source: BMAS (2002a), table I-1.

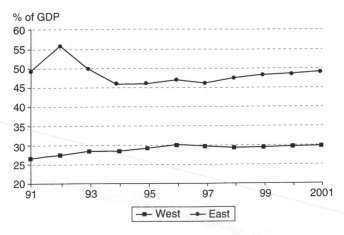

FIGURE 7.2   *Social spending in east and west as a percentage of GDP:*
1991–2001
Note: Data for 1999 and 2000 preliminary, 2001 projections.
Source: BMAS (2002a), table I-1.

financed through west–east transfers from the 'western' unemployment
and old-age insurance funds. Between 1991 and 1997 transfers amounted
to more than €100 billion, almost €65 billion in unemployment insurance (Tegtmeier, 1997). Transfers between 1996 and 2010 in old-age
insurance alone are projected to total almost €160 billion (Czada, 1998).
In 2001, approximately €27.9 billion were transferred from west to east
within the 'social budget' (BMAS, 2002a).

Instead of increasing taxation to finance the costs associated with
unification, the Kohl government chose to use the social insurance
system. Thus social insurance contributions rose sharply in the 1990s
(Figure 7.3). Without the west–east transfers the pension system in west
Germany would have accumulated surpluses of more than €10 billion
annually, which would have added to the surplus of about €20 billion
previously accrued. Consequently, looking at West Germany alone,
contributions to the retirement system could have been reduced in the
early 1990s without any increases until 2015 (Czada, 1998).

In order to reduce social insurance contributions the Red–Green government, which came into power in 1998, introduced an ecological tax,
the revenues from which – some €57 billion in the years 1999–2003 –
are earmarked by statute for the old-age insurance fund. Without the
revenues from the ecological tax the employers' contributions to the
old-age insurance fund would have been 0.75 percentage points higher

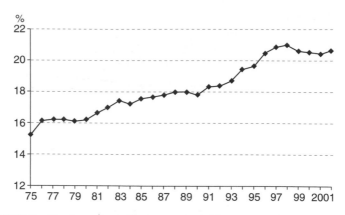

FIGURE 7.3   *Employers' contributions to social insurance schemes as a percentage of gross wage: 1975–2002*
Not included are premiums for accident insurance. Due to small differences between East and West, the data presented here are based on premiums in the West.
Source: BMAS (2002c), table 7.7; BMG (2002).

in 2002 (Truger, 2001a; Bundesministerium der Finanzen, 2002, p. 10). The rapid growth of social insurance contributions has put severe pressures on employers to control costs through productivity gains and close monitoring of wage increases. From 1991 to 1999 the productivity per hour has increased annually by an average of 6.6 per cent. Despite the steep increases in social insurance contributions, the productivity gains, coupled with modest wage increases, have led to a decline in unit labour costs by 3.3 per cent between 1991 and 2002 (BMAS, 2002c, Table 3.3). This has not, however, served to reverse the steady increase in unemployment which stood at 4 million in 2002–03.

Based on the quantitative data presented here it is clear that the Red–Green government did not follow a path of expansionary social policies. On the contrary, as proposed in party programmes and the coalition agreement of 1998, it further consolidated public finances and marginally reduced social insurance contributions. Nevertheless, the federal budget and social insurance funds, especially the healthcare as well as the pension funds, came under severe financial pressure during the fourth year of the Red–Green coalition government. This was largely the result of reduced government revenues, due to the effects of the 2000 tax reform, sluggish economic growth and increased social spending caused by rising unemployment (SVR, 2001; SVR, 2002).

Social Policy under the Christian Democrats 1982–98

The expansion of the welfare state came to a halt in 1975, with the first cutbacks in social policy legislated by the Social Democratic–Liberal coalition government. When the CDU came to power in a coalition with the FDP in 1982, not only did it promise to continue and strengthen the financial consolidation of social policy, but it also promised to shift the focus from the wage earner to the family. The institution of the family had allegedly been neglected by the Social Democrats (Bleses and Seeleib-Kaiser, 1999).

Social policy development under Christian Democratic government can be divided into four phases: the first two years were characterized by cutbacks, especially in the unemployment insurance programme, active labour market policies, and social assistance. In healthcare there were some relatively minor technical measures to control costs. Old-age insurance was largely left unchanged. Starting in the mid-1980s, the government expanded policy in some areas, although the overall goal remained budget consolidation and a reduction of social insurance contributions. Expansion took place in family policy, where the government reversed previous cuts in child allowance and child tax credits, recognized a limited time devoted to child rearing as equivalent to monetary contributions towards old-age insurance, and introduced parental leave and associated benefits. Finally in 1992, the conservatives passed legislation to expand the public provision of childcare facilities, which entitles every child between the ages three and six to a place in a kindergarten. The law went fully into effect in 1999 after a transition period, during which more than 600,000 places for children in public childcare facilities were created (Bäcker *et al.*, 2000, 212). The data in Table 7.1 reveal the significant expansion of public day care facilities for children between the ages of three and six during the 1990s.

The third phase came with German unification. As a matter of principle and in order to avoid chaos in the former German Democratic Republic the structure of the West German welfare state was extended eastwards. Without adequate financial provisions from general revenues and due to the magnitude of the social problems associated with the unification process, this inevitably led to a rapid increase in social spending and social insurance contributions (see Figures 7.1 and 7.3). Hence, it has to be stressed that these cost increases were not the result of programmatic social policy expansions.

After the process of unification was formally accomplished in late 1992, the Kohl government once again started to pursue a policy of retrenchment in social spending in order to bring social insurance

TABLE 7.1 *Supply of childcare facilities (no. of places as a percentage of age group)*

Year	Age		
	0–below 3 years	3–6.5 years	6–12 years
1965	n/a	33	n/a
1975	<1	66	n/a
1985[1]	1.6	69.3	3.0
1990	1.8 (54.2)	69.0 (97.7)	3.4 (32.4)
1995[2]	2.2 (41.3)	73.0 (96.2)	3.5 (22.6)
1998	2.8 (36.3)	86.8 (111.8)	5.9 (47.7)
	7.0	*89.5*	*12.6*

Note: The percentages given in the brackets are for former East Germany and the numbers in italic are for unified Germany. Data over the years are not fully comparable.

Sources: Alber (2001), 1975; Neidhardt (1978), 234; BMFSFJ (1998), 200; 1995–98: BMFSFJ (2002a), 129.

contributions under control. The various policy initiatives included changes in the unemployment insurance programme, a reduction of the statutory sick-leave benefit from 100 to 80 per cent of wages, a loosening of dismissal protection, and – for the first time in German history – a significant benefit cut for future pensioners. Through the implementation of the Labour Promotion Reform Law of 1997, an unemployed worker can no longer reject a work offer outside his or her occupation or level of qualification as unsuitable. In addition, he or she must accept any job offer that pays up to 20 per cent less than the previous job during the first three months of unemployment, and up to 30 per cent less during the following three months. After six months the unemployed will have to accept the offer of any job which matches the amount of unemployment benefit. It may be concluded from this that the state is increasingly relying on a means-tested approach and the market with regard to unemployment policy. Furthermore, various policy reforms at the local level since the mid-1980s and reforms at the federal level in 1993 and 1996 have put an increased emphasis on work-fare requirements within the social assistance programme. In 1998, approximately 300,000 (former) welfare recipients participated in welfare-to-work programmes, whereas the numbers for 1982 and 1993 were 20,000 and 110,000 respectively (Alber, 2001, Table 14).

Pension reforms proposed by the Kohl government in 1997 would have reduced the income replacement value of the standard pension from 70 to 64 per cent, leaving a substantial percentage of the elderly dependent on means-tested social assistance (Schmähl, 1999, pp. 417ff.). This was an implicit retraction of the principle of guaranteed living standards, which had been the *leitmotiv* of post-war policy.

To summarize: the conservative coalition government pursued a social policy approach, which scaled back on the principle of publicly guaranteeing the formerly achieved living standard, while at the same time expanding programmes for families. With the exception of the policy pursued during the unification process, the overarching goal was to limit and eventually reduce social expenditures and social insurance contributions, while at the same time acknowledging the overall need for an active role of government in social policy. The cumulative fiscal effect of the policy changes enacted by the Kohl government since 1982 – according to calculations based on figures by the Ministry of Labour and Social Affairs – reduced spending by almost 3 per cent of GDP in 1997 (Schmidt, 1998, p. 137).

The Red–Green Government and Social Policy

The first steps of the new government in late 1998 and early 1999 were to suspend the implementation of the Pension Reform Law, reinstate the 100 per cent replacement ratio of the sickness benefit as well as the 'old' dismissal protection regulations, and reduce some co-payments in the statutory health insurance schemes. However, these measures cannot be characterized as a sea change in policy development. The Pension Reform Law of 1999 was not revoked: its implementation was merely *suspended* until a comprehensive pension reform could be legislated. The reintroduction of the 100 per cent replacement ratio with regard to sick pay applied only to those workers who were not entitled to benefits (notwithstanding the statutory changes of 1996) as part of their collective bargaining agreements (Bäcker *et al.*, 2000, p. 455). Finally, the reinstatement of the 'old' dismissal protection affected only approximately 5 per cent of the workforce. Around 70 per cent of workers were still protected by the more stringent provisions even after the changes of 1996, which applied only to employees in very small firms (Seeleib-Kaiser, 2001a, p. 144).

During the first four years of the Red–Green coalition government no major reforms were legislated in the areas of healthcare, active labour market policy, unemployment insurance, and social assistance. In the field of healthcare all reforms in addition to the seemingly regular efforts to control costs failed (cf. SVR, 2002, pp. 237–63). Finally, the Health Minister, Ulla Schmidt, postponed a possible comprehensive reform until after the 2002 elections.

In November 2002 Schmidt appointed a blue-ribbon commission under the leadership of Bert Rürup (Chairman of the Social Security Council) to develop a comprehensive reform with the stated goal of reducing social insurance contributions. In regard to (re)integrating or activating unemployed workers, the Red–Green coalition supported the establishment of a limited number of pilot projects, initiated a programme against youth unemployment, and in early 2002 commissioned a report by a blue-ribbon commission (Hartz Kommission, 2002), which presented its findings shortly before the elections. One might have expected a significant expansion of active labour market policies in pursuit of full employment, the traditional hallmark of social democratic welfare policy. Instead the federal government embarked on implementing the Hartz recommendations, focusing on improving the effectiveness of labour exchange offices, increasing the scope for temporary employment and promoting small and medium-sized companies employing previously unemployed workers. Meanwhile, employment in workfare measures at the local level continued to increase from 300,000 (1998) to 400,000 in the year 2000, the last year for which figures are available (Deutscher Städtetag, 2001).

The work on a comprehensive pension reform started early in the tenure of the Red–Green coalition government. The first talks between the coalition parties and the Christian Democrats were held in the spring of 1999. In the summer of 1999, Walter Riester, Minister for Labour and Social Affairs, publicly announced the cornerstones of his proposal. In the autumn of 2000, the bill was put formally before Parliament. After further deliberations within the Committee for Labour and Social Affairs of the Bundestag, during which no consensus with the Christian Democrats could be reached, the coalition parties split the pension reform bill into two parts. The first part encompassed the provisions in regards to contributions and benefits within the public scheme, which did not require the consent of the CDU-controlled Bundesrat. Although the members of the opposition parties in the Bundestag had voted against the second part of the reform initiative, it finally passed the Bundesrat with some support from the opposition parties after further modifications. It was clear from this that the dispute between the governing coalition and the CDU was not about the principal direction of reform but merely over matters of detail.

At the centre of the reform – characterized by Chancellor Schröder as 'epochal' – is the limitation of future increases in social insurance contributions, accomplished by a significant reduction in the replacement ratio of the benefits to a level of about 64 per cent for the standard pensioner in 2030. (The government maintains that the replacement ratio of benefits will only decline to 67 per cent, but this is based on creative accounting.) In order to achieve higher levels of support during retirement, workers are encouraged through public subsidies to take up private old-age insurance. The level of subsidies for workers who enrol in private or company-based programmes depends on the level of income and the number of children in their household. Furthermore, the social partners are encouraged via the tax system to include old-age schemes in collective bargaining agreements. This will give unions a greater stake in shaping 'company' pensions with the possibility of including redistributive elements (BMAS, 2002b, p. 114). The overall effects of the 1999 Pension Reform will be to hold the old-age insurance contributions at around 20 per cent of wages to 2020 and 22 per cent in 2030 when baby boomers retire.

However, even if workers enrol in the various certified programmes, there is no *guarantee* of a defined benefit at the previous level because the companies offering the various financial products are legally 'only' required to guarantee the nominal amount paid into the system. Hence, the pension system in Germany is being transformed from a pay-as-you-go system based on the principle of defined benefits to a partially funded system based in part on the principle of defined contributions. According to estimates by the Bundesbank, a 50-year-old worker will have to save an extra 4 per cent of his or her gross pay in order not to witness any income loss in retirement; the additional saving ratio for a 20-year-old worker would have to be 1.5 per cent (Deutsche Bundesbank, 2002, p. 30). Through the progressive nature of the subsidies for those who enrol in the new programmes the state intends to reduce the negative effects for lower-income workers.

In addition, the occupational disability pension was reformed. In the future, workers can no longer draw disability pensions if they are unable to continue to work in their profession or occupation; they will have to rely on the labour market for an alternative occupation and/or on the regular disability programme. Although the reformed disability insurance programme now treats unskilled and skilled workers in the same way, it means a real change for skilled workers by ending the protection of their occupational or professional achievements in the event of specific disabilities (Wollschläger, 2001, pp. 283–4). Finally, the coalition government de facto introduced a minimum pension effective 1 January 2003, by revoking the income and wealth test of the relatives of low-income senior citizens when they apply for social assistance. The law requires the administrators of the old-age insurance fund to inform senior citizens with very low pensions about their entitlement to social assistance in addition to their insurance benefits (BMAS, 2002b, pp. 118ff.). Overall this pension reform leads to a re-commodification and marketization of the old-age and disability insurance system and to a withdrawal from the principle of publicly guaranteed living standards, while at the same time improving the conditions for very low-income pensioners.

The Red–Green coalition continued to expand the various family policies. The expansion of family policy developed along three dimensions: (1) increasing the child allowance and child tax credits; (2) strengthening the recognition of a limited time devoted to child rearing as equivalent to monetary contributions towards the old-age insurance; and (3) improving parental leave and the parental leave benefit, as well as introducing an entitlement towards part-time employment. The government also increased the monthly child allowance payment by stages to €154 per child (an increase of €41.50 per month since 1998) and the annual child tax credit to €3.648. Furthermore, parents can receive additional tax credits to defer some of the costs of childcare, if the childcare is deemed necessary due to the employment of the parents (BMFSFJ, 2002b).

Through the implementation of the Survivors' Pensions and Child Rearing Law of 1986, the state for the first time recognized the contributions of caregivers as equivalent to monetary contributions within the old-age insurance system. Currently, the time devoted to childcare will be recognized as a fictive contribution – equivalent to 100 per cent of the average contribution – to the old-age insurance system for the duration of three years per child. Moreover, if a parent chooses to combine part-time work with childcare, the state will contribute to the pension fund to make up for the 'lost' contribution. In this way the state reduced the dependence of the predominantly female caregivers on derived benefits of male breadwinners (Meyer, 1998).

Further legislation was introduced and consequently expanded to increase parental leave after the birth of a child. Since 1993, parents have been entitled to three years of leave; during the first two years, the government paid a flat monthly means-tested benefit of €307 (BMFSFJ, 2002b). The employer had to guarantee re-employment after the leave in a similar position and with equivalent remuneration. The Red–Green government made it easier for both parents to share the parental leave and substantially increased the earnings limit up to which parents are eligible for full benefits. The stated goal of the Red–Green government is that all parents with an average income shall once again receive the benefit (BMAS, 2002a, p. 228). During the tenure of the previous government the percentage of recipients declined substantially, since the earnings limit had not been adjusted since 1986 (Fuhrmann,

2002, p. 192). Furthermore, a new provision entitles parents with children born after 1 January 2001 to work part-time up to 30 hours per week during their parental leave.

During its first four years in power, the Red–Green coalition government did not pass any measures concerning the improvement and/or expansion of childcare facilities. It must be acknowledged, however, that education and childcare fall within the responsibility of the Länder; federal government can only intervene through regulatory policies or financial incentives to promote institutional change. Increasing spending for the establishment of new childcare facilities and schools with an all-day schedule is a top priority of the federal government during its second term. The Red–Green coalition has pledged to spend €1.5 billion annually for the expansion of day care for children under three years of age, starting in 2004. This programme is explicitly excluded from the continued efforts to reduce the budget deficit (SPD, Bündnis 90/Die Grünen, 2002, pp. 10, 29). The federal government estimates that after the full implementation of its programme, childcare facilities will be available for 20 per cent of the children under the age of three (compared to 7 per cent in 1998). Additionally, local and regional provision of all-day schools has increased significantly over the last two years. The Red–Green coalition government has promised to support the endeavour of establishing all-day schools with €4 billion between 2003 and 2007 (SPD, Bündnis 90/Die Grünen, 2002, p. 31).

The Dual Transformation of the German Welfare State

Overall welfare state expansion came to a halt in the late 1970s and early 1980s. Without the unification of the two Germanies, *ceteris paribus*, welfare state spending as well as social insurance contributions would be lower today than in the late 1980s. In the terms outlined at the beginning of this chapter, the changes occurring over the past 25 years constitute third order change in the normative aims and the institutional design of the welfare state. These findings are contrary to the stability often claimed in comparative welfare state analysis. In cases of disability, old age and unemployment the state no longer guarantees previous standards of living; the wage earner must rely increasingly on the market and means-tested benefits. Furthermore, the new emphasis within social policy on the 'needs' of the family amounts to a 're-commodification', but also (perhaps even more importantly) to a 'recalibration' of state responsibility. Increasingly, support for the family has become the new normative reference point for social policy, whereas in the past it was

primarily related to the risks of the wage earner. Although the family fulfilled a key function as a provider of social services and support within
the welfare system, it was assumed that the state should not (or only
minimally) interfere in its role.

Summarizing developments, it is no exaggeration to speak of a dual
transformation of social policy leading to a new institutional logic in the
welfare state. The processes of re-commodification and recalibration
have transformed the role of the state in social policy, establishing a new
normative framework. State social policy in Germany is decreasingly
aimed at securing the standard of living of former wage earners and
increasingly oriented towards meeting the needs of families.

Explaining the Dual Transformation

The process of transforming the German welfare state over the last three
decades can be explained in relation to four sets of factors: the changing
economic and social context, party politics, the changing terms of
political debate, and popular social and cultural attitudes.

Socio-Economic Context

Three contextual factors have shaped the recent development of the
German welfare state; the changing demographic composition of
German society; the economic fallout from unification; and the impact
of globalization. Demographic trends suggest that the percentage of
pensioners among the population will increase substantially over the
next 50 years. In 2030, 28 per cent of the population will be older than
65 years (i.e., two persons in the age group 15–64 will have to support
one pensioner: Alber, 2001, p. 14). Furthermore, recent decades have
seen changing preferences among women concerning the desire to work
outside the home and an – albeit slow – increase of female participation
in the labour market. Female labour force participation (aged 15–64
years) between 1970 and 1997 rose from 48.1 to 61.8 per cent (Scharpf
and Schmidt, 2000, p. 349). In 1998, both parents worked in 25 per cent
of families with children below 3 years of age, in 46 per cent of families
with children between 3 and 5, and in 60 per cent of families with
children between 6 and 17 (Bundesregierung, 2002, table III.4). These
societal developments have shaped key aspects of the welfare state,
particularly the retrenchment of pensions and the expansion of family
policies.

Welfare state reform has also been driven by the burden on the social insurance system following German unification. The annual GDP per capita in West Germany dropped from DM 40,200 in 1990 to DM 36,000 in unified Germany in 1991 (Czada, 1998). Furthermore, the economic restructuring in the former GDR led to unprecedented unemployment rates, which still hover close to 20 per cent ten years after unification. Due to the sharp decrease in employment in the East, huge transfers within the social insurance system from the west to the east are necessary, which concomitantly have led to a sharp increase in social insurance contributions (see above). In order to keep the system sustainable, one might argue, retrenchment within the social insurance programmes became a necessity.

Globalization, it is argued, restricts the autonomy of the nation state in social policy leading to a transformation of welfare states into competition states. The Achilles' heel of the West German economy since the 1950s has been its reliance on international markets (see Chapter 6). Since the 1970s, Germany has been increasingly vulnerable to change in the international economy. First, changes in the international monetary system led to a substantial appreciation of the German mark, with prejudicial effects on export capacity. Second, German companies supporting high wages and benefits have faced increasing competition from emerging economies in Asia with very low wage costs. Third, the liberalization of capital markets means that capital can move much more freely around the globe, opening up the 'exit option' of companies to relocate in low-cost economies.

Party Politics

Comparative welfare state analysis has identified political parties as a key variable in explaining development and change in the welfare state. According to a simplified version of the 'parties matter' theory, we would expect retrenchment during Christian Democrat government and expansion under the control of Social Democrats. In Germany, however, as we have seen, both Social Democrats and Christian Democrats identify with the 'social state' (Schmidt, 1998, pp. 168ff.). Under such conditions of party competition, if policy change occurs at all it will take the form of gradual incremental change. Incrementalism, it is often argued, is reinforced by the 'semi-sovereign' character of the German political system – especially the role of the Bundesrat and the Constitutional Court in social policy – which forces political actors into an almost permanent 'hidden grand coalition' (Schmidt, 1996).

The Terms of the Political Debate

Since the 1970s the Social Democrats have acknowledged the challenge to the welfare state from globalization. Whilst acknowledging the benefits of a comprehensive social policy in times of increasing inter-nationalization, they perceived the necessity to make changes in unemployment insurance and labour market policy in order to preserve the overall system. By 1980 the Christian Democrats had also come to terms with the view that high social insurance contributions had a nega-tive effect on the international competitiveness of German companies and therefore should be reduced. The theme was particularly prominent in the election campaign of 1986/87. During the process of German uni-fication, however, the primary concern of the Kohl government was to transfer the West German social insurance system to the East with scant regard for the costs. Arguments about the international competitiveness almost vanished from political discourse. The theme resurfaced in 1993, with the the Christian Democrats/Liberal coalition using competi-tiveness as a justification for the policy changes it pursued during the rest of the decade. By the second half of the 1990s, all the major parties – with the exception of the Party of Democratic Socialism (PDS) – perceived the stabilization of the social insurance contributions as a precondition for economic growth, employment, and keeping the economy internationally competitive. Nevertheless, it should be emphasized that the welfare state consensus remained intact. Whilst they questioned its financial structure and the levels of benefit it pro-vided, both Social Democrats and Christian Democrats continued to support the main principles of the welfare state.

Political discourse relating to family policy greatly differed from the pattern so dominant in wage-earner welfare policies. Since the 1970s, there has been a growing consensus that families need *more* support from the state. Traditionally, Christian Democratic social policy was strongly influenced by their strong commitment to the family as the core institution of society and to the idea that it was the responsibility of mothers to take care of the children. For Social Democrats, on the other hand, family policy was primarily focused on the 'working' mother as a wage earner. From the 1970s, however, Christian Democratic discourse began to change, advocating an expansion of family policies so that mothers could choose whether to work or to commit themselves to child rearing. The wage earner-centred social policy of the past had neglected the needs of the family. Through this change in their programmatic stance the Christian Democrats were able to position themselves politi-cally as capable of modernization. Since the second half of the 1980s, the Social Democrats and Greens have progressively accepted the CDU's argument that the state should take more responsibility for supporting the family.

Thus, at the turn of the century, it is accepted among the political elite that families need more support from the state. During the 2002 federal election campaign the various political parties attempted to exceed each other in family-friendliness. Both parents should be able to reconcile paid work and family obligations, while at the same time one parent should have the opportunity to commit him- or herself either full- or part-time to child rearing for a limited number of years. Increased child allowances, more flexible work arrangements, and an improved supply of childcare facilities are on the agenda of all political parties. The question is no longer whether social policy in the Federal Republic of Germany will become increasingly family oriented, but how fast the change can be accomplished (*Die Zeit*, 2002).

Social and Cultural Factors

Social or cultural support for the welfare state among the population could be considered as a further causal factor. Over the last four decades there has been a steady increase in the electoral strength of the welfare state clientele. Around 50 per cent of the German electorate could be considered as welfare state clientele in the mid-1990s (Pierson, 2001, p. 413). Survey data show a strong continuous overall support for the welfare state which was further strengthened by German unification, since the electorate in the east has a significantly higher support rate (cf. Roller, 1999; Andreß and Heien, 2001). Support for state responsibility for healthcare and pensions remained undiminished over the decade from 1985 to 1995, with only a modest decline in support for state responsibility for maintaining the living standards of the unemployed and for creating jobs (see Table 7.2). Thus policy-makers are caught between the socio-economic pressures for welfare state retrenchment and a political consensus that resists change.

Conclusion

Compared to the German welfare state of the 'golden' post-Second World War era, we have seen clear evidence of change along the dimensions of retrenchment, re-commodification and recalibration. The new social policy paradigm at the turn of the century embodies two main

TABLE 7.2 *Public support for state responsibility in various policy areas of the Welfare State (%)*

	Healthcare	Living standard of the elderly	Living standard of the unemployed	Create jobs
1985	98 (n/a)	97 (n/a)	85 (n/a)	82 (n/a)
1990	96 (99)	95 (99)	79 (94)	74 (95)
1995	97 (99)	96 (98)	80 (92)	74 (92)

Percentages for West Germany; numbers in brackets are percentages for East Germany.
Source: International Social Survey Programme (1985, 1990, 1996), cited in and calculated by Andreß and Heien (2001, p. 171).

trends. First, there is clear evidence of a gradual retrenchment of wage earner-centred benefits in the interests of economic competitiveness. Wage earners at risk will increasingly have to rely on the market and/or means-tested benefits and cannot depend any longer on the state alone in guaranteeing the previous standard of living. At the same time, traditional family responsibilities are being increasingly socialized in a reorientation towards a more family-oriented welfare state. The institutional logic of the German welfare state today clearly differs from the logic during the golden era of welfare state capitalism.

The dual transformation of the welfare state was not the result of one big bang, but of many seemingly incremental changes that have accumulated over the past decades. Socio-economic challenges – however perceived – inform political actors in the process of developing new policies, but they do not predetermine the path of change. Changes in the norms and values of political parties take time to accomplish. Along with the 'semi-sovereign' structure of the German political system this largely explains why the dual transformation of the welfare state has been so protracted. Nevertheless, the political discourse of the past decades has led to the emergence of new interpretative patterns, setting the boundaries for future welfare state development in Germany.

8

The Europeanization of German Governance

KENNETH DYSON

Though Helmut Kohl had disappeared from an active role in the German political scene, the federal elections of 2002 demonstrated the extent to which the European policy of his successors was defined by the need to grapple with his effects both as a European statesman and as the architect of German unification. Both Gerhard Schröder and Edmund Stoiber sought to avoid issues of European policy in the campaign. But it was clear that the performance of the Schröder government of 1998–2002 and the prospects for a Stoiber government were bound up with the historical constraints that were Kohl's legacy. These constraints stemmed externally from the European internal market and Economic and Monetary Union (EMU) and from the prospective enlargement of the European Union (EU) to east central Europe. Internally, they were associated with the economic burdens and the territorial diversity of interests that followed from German unification. European-level constraints may have remained largely unspoken in the 2002 elections, but they were no less real, for instance, in severely delimiting the room for manoeuvre of competing political parties in making electoral promises. Domestic changes were expressed in a different understanding of what was desirable and possible in Germany's European policy.

Routinizing European Integration: From Historical Vision to Muddling Through

There were two implications for European policy. First, European policy seemed to be defined by a phase of routinization that follows a period of bold creativity. The talents that were called for from German political leaders were those of 'muddling through', of negotiating an accommodation of German interests within a European framework that had been subjected to wide-ranging and rapid changes and which impacted differentially on these interests. Second, interweaving effects from the EU level and domestic changes created a new political dynamic of redefining Germany's European policy, not least to protect the policy competences of the Länder and their autonomy in exercising their powers. Schröder and Stoiber were marked by this historical context and notable more for what they shared with each other than anything that either of them had in common with Kohl. They were pro-Europeans in principle, but very pragmatic and cautious in approach. Both reflected and shaped a gradually emerging elite consensus from the mid-1990s onwards that – post-German unification and with the risks and uncertainties attending the eastern enlargement – exhibited more conditionality in attitudes to European integration. The 'big bang' of EU enlargement to east central Europe elicited 'muddling through' by Schröder and Stoiber rather than bold creativity, sustained historical legitimation and firm domestic political leadership.

In examining the effects of European integration on German governance it is important to distinguish two separate, albeit interdependent, questions. The first (dealt with in Chapter 10) asks about the kind of Germany to which Germans aspire and which they believe European integration is intended to bring about; the second, about how European integration is actually affecting Germany. As this chapter argues, the concept of Europeanization deals with a process rather than an end condition. Its preoccupation is with the mechanisms, cognitive and material, direct and indirect, by which European integration influences domestic institutions, politics and policies. At the same time there is an important interaction between the kind of Germany to which politicians and policy-makers aspire and how Germany is affected by European integration. Aspirations for Germany's role in Europe have implications for macro-political strategy towards Europe and how German interests are defined and identities conceived. They condition the degree of engagement of German elites in pushing forward European integration and in 'uploading' their own institutional arrangements and policy paradigms to the European level. Effective 'uploading' makes for a process of Europeanization that is relatively smooth and accommodating. Conversely, the complex political dynamics of the Europeanization process – for instance, influenced by greater territorial diversity consequent on German unification – can put in question what kind of Germany is emerging and foster a redefinition of macro-political strategy.

The Dynamics of Multi-Level Governance

Germany's freedom of manoeuvre in European policy is constrained by the need of its policy-makers to play a complex, multi-level game in which institutional self-interests at the EU, federal and Länder levels have to be reconciled. In particular, they have to pay close attention to domestic ratification difficulties, for instance in negotiating EMU where German public opinion was opposed to giving up the Deutsche Mark. The utmost political attention had to be devoted to 'binding in' the Bundesbank at every point in EMU negotiations (Dyson and Featherstone, 1999). German negotiators also have to contend with assertive Länder that jealously guard their policy competences, as for instance in EU justice and home affairs and in regional economic policy. These policy competences can be directly defended at the federal level through the Bundesrat in which the Länder governments are directly represented. Again, the federal government has made increasing efforts to bind both the Bundestag and the Bundesrat into EU policy-making and negotiations. Games of institutional self-interest in a semi-sovereign polity in which powers are shared, create the potential for veto politics. This potential was manifested at the Amsterdam European Council where – in response to Länder fears about loss of policy competence – Chancellor Kohl dropped his support for qualified majority voting in justice and home affairs.

German European policy is caught up in a complex, reciprocal and dynamic interplay between two ongoing political processes. There is an 'uploading' process of seeking to integrate Europe around Germany's own institutional models, policy preferences and ways of doing things. Examples of past success in 'uploading' to the EU level include competition policy, environmental policy, EMU (e.g., the design of the European Central Bank, or ECB) and the Schengen provisions on policing freedom of movement (including the design of Europol). In these areas Germany has acted as a policy leader. This process has been facilitated by Germany's reputation as a policy model of competence from which others could learn and by the organizational capacity of German interest groups which have been disproportionately successful in playing an effective role as multi-level players. To the extent to which this 'uploading' has given rise to a German Europe it is based on a combination of voluntary emulation of German policy success by others with persuasive German argument in EU-level negotiations. It manifests the effective use by Germany of the instruments of 'soft' power within the EU.

This 'uploading' process is complemented by a 'downloading' process of domestic adaptation to European integration, reinforced by the doctrines of primacy and direct effect enshrined in Community law. These adaptational pressures range from liberalizing energy and telecommunications markets to meeting the strict requirements of the EU's Stability and Growth Pact on fiscal deficits. But the 'downloading' of EU institutional models and policy paradigms often confronts powerful, well-organized sectoral interests. Examples include competition policy where the German book trade defended its right to regulate the book market, and electricity and gas where the key players preferred to negotiate market regulation rather than accept an independent regulator.

The degree of smoothness of domestic adaptation to these 'top-down' pressures is conditioned by the extent to which German negotiators are successful in the 'uploading' of German institutional models and policy preferences to the EU level and are able to influence the timing and tempo of EU-level change. Thus they proved able to match the scope and pace of EU telecommunications liberalization to the capacity to absorb change at the domestic level. They were also able – in tandem with the French – to maintain a margin of uncertainty and manoeuvre about the substance of EU energy liberalization so that domestic interests could be accommodated.

Congruence of Modes of Governance

Playing and winning these games of multi-level governance is facilitated by an underlying congruence between EU and German modes of governance. Katzenstein (1997, p. 33) has noted a basic similarity between what he calls the EU's 'associative' sovereignty – pooled competences in overlapping domains of power and interest – and domestic 'semi-sovereignty'. For Scharpf (1985) there is a symmetry in the practice of 'interlocking' politics at the EU level and within the German federal system. In both the challenge is similar: how to manage the potential for powerful interests to act as veto players? Most strikingly, governance within the EU and within Germany shares the characteristics of 'negotiation democracy': building and maintaining coalitions, managing a complex territorial politics and bargaining with powerful sectoral interests (Holtmann and Voelzkow, 2000). Managing Germany's relationship with the EU is made easier when 'ways of doing things' seem similar.

At the same time the 'fit' between EU and German modes of governance is by no means perfect, creating the potential for adaptational difficulties. Competitive majoritarian politics is more deeply entrenched in German politics simply because – unlike at the EU level – there is a direct electoral competition for office. 'Harder' forms of coordination in fiscal policy at the EU level – backed by the sanctions of the Stability and Growth Pact – than at the domestic level and tougher EU-level anti-subsidy policies represent tightening constraints on domestic majoritarian politics. The diminished room for electoral manoeuvre threatens to create a domestic political backlash. Neo-corporatist forms at the level of the powerful economic interest groups in Germany are not replicated at the EU level where peak associations are much weaker, power is more pluralistically organized, and American-style public affairs consultants are emerging as a new species of interest broker (Bührer and Grande, 2000). In this context the value for German interest groups and firms of working through the traditional peak associations such as the Federation of German Industry (*Bundesverband der deutschen Industrie*, BDI) is more questionable, and exit strategies more attractive. Finally, the increasing policy scope of European integration threatens to undermine trust and mutual confidence between the federal and the *Land* levels, shifting German federalism from cooperative to competitive forms of behaviour.

From Coexistence to Co-evolution and Contest

The above analysis suggests the degree both of stability and of conditionality that underpins Germany's role in Europe. There are dynamics at work that could disturb the foundations of this role. Up until the 1980s Germany's role in Europe was secured not just by powerful historical memories but also by a limited agenda of European integration which meant that for most policy sectors coexistence sufficed. Quite simply, domestic policy and politics in so many sectors were very little affected by the EU. Following the Single European Act of 1987, the Maastricht Treaty of 1993 and the Amsterdam Treaty of 1998, the broadening agenda has meant that coexistence has given way to either 'co-evolution' or to contest. Co-evolution involves the mutual adaptation of both EU and German levels; contest occurs when there is conflict about what should be done, how and when. Germany has been characterized by both more co-evolution, aided by the structuring from an historical memory that still resonates and more contest, reflecting changing conditions. These changing conditions include a greater self-confidence and self-assertiveness associated with generational change, and typified by Chancellor Schröder. They also involve a loss of 'soft' power consequent on Germany no longer playing the 'paymaster of Europe' role and on the loss of status as a model for Europe consequent on relative economic decline. Germany's role in Europe under Schröder is caught up in this paradox between a new self-confidence and diminished power.

What is Europeanization?

Following Dyson and Goetz (2003) Europeanization can be defined as: 'a complex interactive "top-down" and "bottom-up" process in which domestic polities, policies and politics are shaped by European integration and domestic actors use European integration to shape the domestic arena. It produces either continuity or change and potentially variable and contingent outcomes.' This definition focuses on process rather than on attempting to specify what kind of Germany will result. It does not involve pre-commitment to what the empirical consequences of Europeanization will be; in short, some view of an end result. The definition also avoids attachment to any particular hypothesis about the mechanism, or precise combination of mechanisms, through which Europeanization affects the domestic level (cf. Green Cowles, Caporaso and Risse, 2001). It is a matter for empirical research whether the mechanism is a 'misfit' of institutional models between the EU and the domestic levels, creating adaptational pressure; effects on the domestic political opportunity structure, empowering some actors over others; or effects on cognitive framing of how domestic problems and solutions are conceived. In addition, the definition does not specify the precise linkage between interests, ideas and institutions but again leaves that issue to empirical research. Finally, the definition does not contain the presumption that the effects of Europeanization are expressed only in domestic change: they may also be important in reinforcing continuities (again, cf. Green Cowles, Caporaso and Risse, 2001).

This definition highlights the dynamic political interactions that shape the Europeanization process. In consequence, and this bears reiteration, 'coexistence', 'co-evolution' and contest can be found simultaneously across institutional arenas, policy sectors and issues and succeed each other over time. Though the definition focuses on 'downloading' in order to distinguish Europeanization from concepts such as European integration and political unification, the context of 'uploading' cannot be ignored. The way in which European integration affects a state is shaped by how effective it has been in 'uploading' its institutional models, policy preferences and 'ways of doing things' to the EU level. Faced with adaptational pressures, domestic political elites can respond by seeking to renegotiate the terms of 'fit'. An example is the efforts of the German Länder to launch a constitutional reform debate within the EU, aimed at gaining a more precise delimitation of the respective powers of the EU, national and regional levels (Jeffery, 2003). Europeanization is an aspect of a two-way process.

In addition, the definition takes on board important changes in the nature of the European integration process, especially from 'hard' integration and the traditional Community method to an increased reliance on 'soft' integration. In parallel, one can distinguish between 'hard' and 'soft' Europeanization. 'Hard' Europeanization involves direct institutional effects (for instance, on how telecommunications are regulated). 'Soft' Europeanization involves ideational effects through policy transfer and learning. This process has been promoted by the so-called 'open method' of coordination with its stress on guidelines, peer review and 'benchmarking' best practice (notably in economic policies to improve growth and employment). For this reason the definition has to include the 'horizontal' dimension of policy transfer and learning. This 'horizontal' dimension has featured in debates about how to reform German labour market and social policies in order to create the kind of European 'knowledge society' outlined by the Lisbon European Council in 2000, and to improve employability.

The Impact of European Integration on Germany

The definition of Europeanization that is offered above addresses two important questions: what is Europeanized, and how? The 'what' embraces not just policies and the polity but also the wider effects on German politics, including the party system, interest groups and the media and the interaction of elites with the public. The broad consensus in the literature on Europeanization is that the most discernible effects are seen in public policies (Radaelli, 2000), though these can be linked to changes in institutional structures (e.g., the regulation of telecommunications) and institutional interactions (e.g., the federal system).

The 'how' draws attention to different types of effect: direct and indirect, and cognitive and material (Dyson, 2002b, pp. 13–16). Direct effects refer to institutional rules and policy objectives and instruments that are transposed to the domestic level. They may prescribe what governments may do, as in the EU fiscal rule requiring a budget of 'close to balance' over the economic cycle. Alternatively, they may proscribe governmental behaviour. Examples include loss of an independent monetary policy or of an independent exchange-rate policy or prohibition of state aids to industry that distort competition in the internal market. Indirect effects refer to changes in the larger context of economic, social and political behaviour, induced by EU-level action, which affect what governments can do. An example is the effects of the internal market and EMU on behaviour in collective bargaining and wages policy or on the room for manoeuvre of governments in business taxation. Indirect effects also include unintended or unanticipated consequences of an EU policy for other policy sectors. Thus an internal market in services and the EU Stability and Growth Pact's stipulations on budget deficits have implications for German social policies such as health and pensions.

Material effects operate by changing the parameters of state action. Thus the internal market and EMU jointly conspire to create transparency of prices and costs, more intense market competition, and accelerated merger and acquisition activity. In this way they affect the nature and scope of taxation policy as well as judgements about how fiscal policy is best used and social policy best designed. Cognitive effects are seen in the way in which domestic policy is framed, in what discourse reveals about what is judged desirable and possible, and also what is to be avoided and what is impossible. These effects may reinforce traditional German policy beliefs, for instance about the importance of 'sound' public finances, with the German-initiated Stability and Growth Pact serving as an added discipline on the federal government, Länder governments and local authorities. Conversely, they may help to spur policy change, for instance by diffusion of the idea of promoting 'employability' through new labour market and educational policies and by benchmarking German policies in this area (e.g., against Denmark, the Netherlands and the UK).

Effects on the Polity: Institutional Incentives to Europeanize

Europeanization of the German polity has been demonstrated in complex, dynamic and interactive ways. Institutions such as the federal executive, the Bundestag and the Bundesbank have undergone internal restructuring. The distribution of power both within and amongst institutions has changed (for instance, between ministries within the federal executive, between the federal executive and the Bundestag and between the federation and the Länder). There has been evidence of a new activism in 'bottom-up' processes as German actors, notably the Länder, seek to 'upload' German domestic models and preferences to the EU level. Also, reflecting its nature as a 'semi-sovereign' state with a high degree of institutional pluralism, the German polity has experienced Europeanization, and sought to adapt to it, in very different ways. Central to the nature of the effects of European integration on the

German polity has been the extent to which there have been institutional incentives to Europeanize.

At the level of the polity the institutions most bound up in Europeanization have been the federal executive, the Länder and the Bundesbank. The federal executive is most directly and intensively engaged because of its day-to-day involvement in the work of the Council of Ministers and its associated deadlines. But even here evidence of significant structural change is limited and more apparent at administrative levels than the level of executive politics (Goetz, 2003). More ministries have divisions and sections (*Referate*) specializing in European policy, a total of nine of the former and 99 of the latter by 2001 (Sturm and Pehle, 2001, p. 45). The effects are, however, differentiated, with Defence lacking any European policy unit and the Transport, Family, Environment and Health ministries having just one to three sections. In contrast, the Finance Ministry had 28 sections specializing in Europe, and the Foreign Ministry 18. The main coordinating structures for European policy – the Committee of State Secretaries for European Questions and the 'Tuesday' Committee of division heads – date back respectively to 1963 and 1971 and have altered little in functioning. Though their work is more formalized than is typical of interministerial committees, they reflect a German administrative tradition of horizontal coordination rather than the emergence of a strong central coordinating mechanism on the British and French models. Before 2002 no serious attempt had been made to enhance the status of European coordinating units, though there was a debate about whether a European minister – perhaps in the Federal Chancellor's Office and perhaps with responsibility for chairing these committees – was required. The Federal Chancellor's Office chairs neither committee and maintains a relatively low complement of relevant administrative expertise, with only two sections specializing in European policy. Coordination is characterized by a division of labour between the Foreign Ministry (which chairs the Committee of State Secretaries) and the Finance Ministry (which chairs the 'Tuesday' Committee), with the Chancellor's Office seeking to play a role especially in preparing the Chancellor for the meetings of the European Council. Overall, the primacy of the principle of departmental autonomy, aided and abetted by the effects of coalition politics, has closed off opportunities to emulate more rigorous systems of European policy coordination in other member states.

Europeanization has more clearly manifested itself in the way in which political and administrative actors in the federal executive have exploited the associated opportunities to augment their own power and profile. This process was seen with the new Red–Green government in 1998. Oskar Lafontaine as the new Finance Minister created a new European division by bringing in key European policy officials from the Economics Ministry and gained the main coordinating responsibility for European policy alongside the Foreign Ministry. A key part of the rationale was provided by the need for Germany to match the administrative capacity of the French Finance Ministry and of the British Treasury with the establishment of the final stage of EMU on 1 January 1999. EMU was accordingly associated with empowerment of the Finance Ministry and disempowerment of the Economics Ministry, a phenomenon that was generally discernible across the EMU (Dyson, 2000).

Otherwise, outside the realm of seeking out the opportunities offered by Europeanization to enhance domestic power and profile, the political level of the federal executive showed limited and intermittent evidence of the effects of European integration. This relatively low level of involvement from executive politics reflects the weakness of institutional incentives when European issues have low electoral saliency and when the links between European engagement and making a visible difference to what the electorate perceives to be the pressing problems are tenuous and uncertain. Hence executive politics has been little engaged with such issues as European policy coordination and then principally in terms of problem avoidance (e.g., for Schröder ensuring that the German automobile lobby was not damaged by EU actions and that a 'warning letter' from the European Commmission about the German budget deficit was avoided).

The relevance of institutional incentives is clear in the case of the Bundestag. In one respect, the Bundestag has an institutional interest in strengthening its role in the European integration process. It has seen an erosion of its legislative competence to the EU, an enormous growth in EU-related legislation, and a European integration process that has empowered the federal executive at the expense of its own disempowerment. These are important and real effects of Europeanization, and yet members of the Bundestag have not on the whole actively exploited opportunities to Europeanize their work. The Bundestag has been slow to develop a structural specialization on European policy, with the Committee for EU Affairs dating only from 1994. The ratification of the Maastricht Treaty in 1993, notably the associated new Article 23 of the Basic Law (which gave the new committee constitutional status), and the Amsterdam Treaty strengthened the information rights of the Bundestag. But these developments were linked more to active political lobbying by the German Länder than to independent initiatives by the Bundestag, and they produced only limited behavioural change. The Committee on EU Affairs has improved the potential for control over what German politicians are doing in the EU and for better quality plenum debates on EU matters, but it has proved difficult to realize this potential because of the lack of institutional incentives to Europeanize and exploit their new information rights. Members of the Bundestag tend to see the democratic legitimation function of the EU as a matter for the European Parliament rather than for themselves (Katz, 1999). They also have little incentive to specialize in Europe when it has low electoral uncertainty, when there is a high opportunity cost in doing so, and when the connection between this engagement and policy outcomes is tenuous and uncertain (Saalfeld, 2003).

The institutional incentives to Europeanize have been greater in the case of the Länder and of the Bundesrat. As with the Bundestag the Bundesrat has lost legislative competences to the EU and has had an incentive to defend its power and status by acquiring new rights. The federal government has had a particular incentive to listen because the Bundesrat could threaten to veto treaty change. Thus at Maastricht the German government pressed the case for a new EU Committee of the Regions to cement the role of the Länder at the EU level; whilst at Amsterdam Kohl reversed the German position of arguing for the retention of unanimity in Council voting on justice and home affairs matters, again to pacify the Länder. Hence in order to safeguard ratification of the Single European Act and of the Maastricht Treaty it was willing to tolerate new rights of both information and participation for the Länder in EU policy, including the right to represent Germany in Council meetings dealing with matters falling into the Länder sphere of competence. Because European integration has had wide-ranging effects on the distribution of competences, it has introduced increased sensitivities into Federal–Länder relations. Above all, it has driven the Länder, led by Bavaria, to seek to redefine and clarify the proper constitutional balance of powers between Brussels, Berlin and themselves, with the objective of securing more freedom of manoeuvre, notably in internal market and competition policy. The result has been an increasingly proactive role by the Länder in seeking to shape the debate about the future EU.

Perhaps the most startling example of Europeanization was provided by the Bundesbank, however. Under the old European exchange-rate mechanism (ERM) the Bundesbank effectively dictated the terms of monetary policy to other ERM members because of the Deutsche Mark's role as the anchor currency, but it was a case of the Bundesbank 'Europeanizing' its own monetary policy through the ERM rather than of the ERM 'Europeanizing' the Bundesbank. Consistent with the institutional incentives created by the Bundesbank Law of 1957, it only took account of domestic monetary stability. This changed after the

Maastricht Treaty committed Germany to realizing EMU by 1999 at the latest and following the ERM crises of 1992–3 which threatened this timetable. In particular, the logistics of working as part of the European Monetary Institute from January 1994 in preparing the final stage three placed the Bundesbank firmly in a framework of Europeanization. Institutional incentives pointed to it playing the role of loyal and constructive player in this treaty-driven process, not least to shape the specific features of EMU on its own terms and to underwrite its own long-term interest. The transfer of monetary policy to the new European Central Bank in January 1999 was the final catalyst in prompting a domestic debate about reform to both the structure and functions of the Bundesbank. This reform engaged the interests of the Länder in maintaining an influence on the future Bundesbank and of the big banks and financial institutions which wanted a new integrated financial services authority to combine regulation of banking with insurance and the stock markets. Both found themselves ranged against the Bundesbank, which wanted a streamlined single-tier Bundesbank board in place of the old two-tier structure to ensure more coherent policy, and also to strengthen its own position in banking supervision. The outcome of the reform in 2002 was a smaller single-tier board, with scope for the Länder to share in appointments, and also a new integrated financial services authority in which the Bundesbank was given guarantees of a role in banking supervision. Crucially, as it was now an operating part of the European System of Central Banks (ESCB), institutional incentives pointed to a thorough Europeanization of the Bundesbank.

In many ways more problematic have been the effects of European integration on the Federal Constitutional Court. The Court has been extremely reluctant to recognize the primacy of the European Court of Justice (ECJ) in matters of European law, especially where they touch on basic rights. In the process – especially after its ruling of 12 October 1993 on the constitutionality of the Maastricht Treaty – it has been drawn into considerable controversy. It was seen to be challenging the right of the ECJ, under Article 234 of the Treaty of Rome, to interpret the treaty in favour of stressing its own role in ensuring an interpretation that was consistent with the German Basic Law. This view of a judicial activism of the Court on matters of European law went back to the so-called 'Solange I decision' of May 1974 which saw EU and national law as 'independent of each other' and standing 'side-by-side'. This reluctance seemed to have been qualified in the 'Solange II decision' of October 1986 when the Court argued that as long as the ECJ provided an effective protection for basic rights its jurisprudence on matters of European law was not necessary. But the element of conditionality was revealed in the Maastricht ruling where the Court claimed the right to rule whether EU institutions were acting in conformity with their powers. It was reiterated in the 1995 decision on the banana directive, which asserted the primacy of the basic right to property as guaranteed in the Basic Law over EU law. At the heart of the Federal Constitutional Court's jurisprudence in EU law was a strong institutional incentive to define its role as ensuring the conformity of EU law with the Basic Law and doing so in a manner consistent with the doctrine of judicial activism that it had practised. By 2000, however, there were signs of change, in part consequent on new appointments to the Court (and the departure of Paul Kirchhof, regular rapporteur on European cases since 1987). But perhaps more significantly, and spurred on by public criticisms, the Court identified an institutional incentive to avoid a fundamental clash with the ECJ and other Community institutions at some future point. The banana market decision of June 2000 indicated a new self-restraint and willingness to accept the overriding constitutional role of the ECJ in interpreting Community law.

What emerges from this review of effects on the German polity is the role of institutional incentives to Europeanize and how these incentives have differed. These incentives have been in part shaped by the political context of institutions, and hence it is appropriate to look next at the effects of Europeanization on German politics. The Federal Constitutional Court shows the difficulties of sustaining a practice of coexistence and a difficult process of alternation between co-evolution and contest. The Bundestag illustrates how a measure of co-evolution has complemented rather than overturned a preference for coexistence. The Bundesbank has trodden a track from coexistence, through a measure of contest over the design and timing of EMU, to co-evolution. By contrast, the federal executive combines firmly rooted co-evolution at administrative levels with coexistence and occasional contest at political levels. The major source of contest has come from the bigger and more prosperous Länder, which have had the clearest institutional incentive to redefine the rules of the European game and have drawn the federal government along with them.

Effects on Politics: Manoeuvring within Cultural Constraints

The effects on German politics have been less obvious. Their limited nature in relation to the widening range of policies affected by the EU reflects the strict, historically conditioned cultural constraints at elite and mass levels. The limited effects on German politics in turn have shaped and constrained the Europeanization of the polity. Processes of opinion formation, identity construction and elite–mass interactions have not been notably affected, whether one looks at the party system, interest groups or the media. The prime reasons are to be found in a strong pro-European elite consensus that defines macro-political strategies at home as well as within the EU (constraining polarization about European integration), and in a permissive public consensus. Elite and public consensus might seem precarious in relation to issues such as the loss of the Deutsche Mark and the German budgetary contribution but nevertheless it has proved strikingly resilient.

Though there have been changes in the party system since the early 1980s, notably from a relatively stable two-and-a-half party system to a more fluid five party system, these changes have no clear relationship to Europeanization. European integration has not influenced such party system properties as polarization, fragmentation or coalition stability (Niedermayer, 2003). Parties advocating a national populism, especially on the extreme right, failed to establish a sizeable electoral base, with the European issue remaining highly marginal to electoral behaviour and therefore lacking a mobilizing potential. Even the issue of losing the Deutsche Mark, to which so much symbolism was attached, did not prove a polarizing issue and a successful launch pad for new parties. Issues such as the loss of the Deutsche Mark and Germany's large net EU budgetary contribution were latent issues of contest, but they remained framed within a continuing elite consensus about the overriding German national interest in the integration process and within a permissive public consensus. The result was a lack of centrality for European issues. By 1998–9 the German public had made its peace with the euro. More striking was the greater role of European policy in the content of party programmes and election manifestos. Again, however, even where reforms were advocated, party programmes and manifestos were overwhelmingly pro-European in viewpoint.

For the same reasons the media were not polarized into pro- and anti-European camps; they tended to avoid sensationalized European reporting or centralizing it in editorial commentary, and preferred to domesticate European news in terms of national political figures and their activities (Voltmer and Eilders, 2003). There was no agonizing debate about Europe between or within the parties or within the federal government to draw the attention of the media. In short, the media lacked exciting 'newsworthy' stories about Europe. They also showed little willingness to set the agenda on Europe. Negative reporting was in the context of the more general assessment of the policy performance of the Chancellor and ministers rather than of an attempt to lead on an anti-European agenda.

More complex were the effects of European integration on the major interest groups, especially the business associations. At one level, the market liberalization ethos of the internal market and EMU challenged German traditions of self-regulation and encouraged firms to see less incentive to belong to these associations and more incentive to lobby EU institutions directly (Bührer and Grande, 2000). The EU threatened the cultural basis of German industrial capitalism, noticeably self-regulation, that formed the backbone of the highly organized interest group system. But at another level German business associations were effective players at the EU level compared to their counterparts in Britain and France. This effectiveness reflected above all their organizational capabilities as well-resourced, highly professional multi-level players (Eising, 2003). They had an institutional incentive to transfer their domestic strengths upwards to the EU level and play an influential role within EU policy networks, not least in order to retain membership loyalty. This loyalty was the very basis of their organizational capability. The open question was whether further EU market liberalization would weaken their future organizational capability to sustain this multi-level influence.

Effects on Policy: Managing Veto Players

By far the clearest and strongest effects of Europeanization were demonstrated in public policies. These effects were most evident in regulatory policies, especially associated with the single market and competition policies, and in policies designed to secure economic stability. The EU approximated a form of 'regulatory' and 'stabilization' state (see Dyson, 2000), specializing in the performance of these functions and legitimating itself in an essentially technocratic manner as promoting economic efficiency and 'sound' money and finance. As these values were broadly congruent both with German macro-political strategy for European integration and with domestic ordo-liberalism, they enjoyed a broad-based support in principle. Indeed, the German federal government – led by the Federal Economics Ministry – had strongly promoted the internal market and a tough competition policy regime. It had also backed the Bundesbank in ensuring the 'uploading' of German ideas about 'sound' money (an independent ECB) and 'sound' finance (clear fiscal rules) to the EU.

In practice, however, policy adaptation proved more problematic after the 1990s. In regulatory and competition policies these problems have reflected the complex interaction between the changing nature and direction of policy development at the EU level – putting in question earlier German success in 'uploading' its institutional models, policy preferences and 'ways of doing things' – and entrenched sectoral-level policy structures, discourses and veto players. In stabilization policy the problem has been that fiscal rules have implications for the capacity of the German state to provide policies whose function is distribution and redistribution (for instance, continuingly generous social policies).

In environmental policy Germany has been able to play a strikingly successful leadership role as the Community expanded its competence, in the larger combustion directive, car emission standards, eco-labelling and climate change, for instance. But EU-level policy developments since the 1990s have challenged Germany's rather formalistic style, which relies heavily on detailed substantive regulation, with a 'softer', less interventionist, self-regulatory approach. This approach involved new requirements on Germany to introduce the principle of shared responsibility, to pay more attention to cost-effectiveness of regulation, and to strengthen its procedural measures (notably environmental impact assessment and right of access to environmental information). Also, Germany had institutional difficulties in implementing the EU 'integrated pollution prevention and control' approach embracing air, water and soil. The Länder had a veto position consequent on their key competence in water management and were resistant to the EU's approach and any idea of a national environmental law. On occasion the Chancellor and the Federal Economics Ministry acted as veto players, preventing the Federal Environment Ministry from agreeing to the end-of-life vehicles directive in 2000 and frustrating EU legislation on dangerous chemicals and nature protection. Hence the coexistence and co-evolution of the 1970s and 1980s gave way to a complex of co-evolution and contest from the 1990s.

Competition policy had a similar trajectory of development. Here again Germany had been a policy leader, promoting the idea of a strong rule-based approach to mergers. This idea was institutionalized in, and promoted by, the Federal Cartel Office which took a tough, case-oriented approach in line with traditional German ordo-liberalism. By the 1990s the Cartel Office was fighting a defensive, rearguard action in the face of what it saw as the politicization of merger policy by the European Commission and by the Federal Economics Ministry and the Chancellor's Office. Seen from the EU level, Germany presented a divided picture. The Chancellor's Office and Länder governments appeared as veto players in relation to the Commission's attempt to apply competition policy as a level playing field within the internal market. In so doing they tapped into a well of broad political support. On the other hand, the Federal Cartel Office seemed to be a bastion of old-fashioned competition policy beliefs that acted as a veto player in mobilizing German domestic opposition to a more economics-based approach to merger control.

Two developments were important. First, in developing competition policy within the framework of the internal market the European Commission shifted to a more evolutionary, economics-based approach to merger, which the Cartel Office saw as the abandonment of a rules-based approach in favour of a discretionary approach that offered scope for the consideration of industrial policy goals. Notably the Cartel Office failed to export to the EU level the model of an independent European Cartel Office. It was also unable to prevent the amendment to Regulation 17/62 that shifted competition policy decisively from the formal German *ex ante* notification procedure to a US-style *ex post* control.

Second, within this EU-level context the Federal Economics Ministry and the Chancellor – sensitive to the concerns of German firms, especially in the case of Schröder – were concerned to ensure a strong German corporate presence in a larger and growing European market. The result was what the Cartel Office saw as a politicization of merger policy and its subordination to industrial policy. An example was the Economics Ministry's approval of the giant Eon/Ruhrgas merger in 2002, on the basis that it raised no problem of competition in the European energy market. In doing so, it overruled the Cartel Office. The European Commission chose not to intervene. The federal government was also increasingly sensitive to what it saw as excessive interference by the Commission in pursuing its competition policy. Examples included: an end to the privileges of public-sector savings banks, faster phasing-out of huge coal subsidies, fines imposed on Volkswagen for discriminatory distribution arrangements, an attack on the exclusivity of car distribution schemes, and aid to shipbuilding and steel in east Germany. The accumulation of these cases of tension and conflict led Schröder to a general assault on the Commission for not taking Germany's industrial interests sufficiently into account in its policies.

Sectoral regulation in areas that were earlier exempted from the German competition law regime illustrates how German EU policy positions have been influenced by the specific problems of achieving negotiated compromise in pluralist institutional environments in which potential veto players shape the nature and tempo of reform. It also reflects Germany's relative success in influencing the terms of EU liberalization in different sectors against a background not just of domestic veto players but also of contrasting market conditions. Outcomes could be very different. Thus liberalization of road haulage came as one of the earlier internal market reforms, reflecting the strength of competitive pressures. Here Germany had to adapt quickly. In telecommunications, too, competitive market conditions pushed the agenda of liberalization, especially driven by telecommunications users who wanted lower costs. But Germany was successful in gearing the pace of EU liberalization to domestic difficulties of adjustment. The key here was the shift of strategic direction by Siemens and Deutsche Telekom, both of which had been veto players but recognized that liberalization and the end of their monopoly position was a necessary price for their European and global ambitions. Telecommunications was characterized by co-evolution, with Germany shifting to a greater policy leader role by the late 1990s and adopting a more rule-based approach. A striking outcome was the establishment of a new regulatory authority for telecommunications to replace the Federal Posts and Telecommunications Ministry. Electricity was different partly because market pressures were less intense and partly because veto players such as the Länder and local authorities had much more to lose, notably revenues. Here Germany worked closely with France to control the pace of adjustment and was distinctive in an EU context for preferring negotiated sectoral adjustment over an independent regulatory authority. Until the electricity liberalization directive of 1996 Germany was characterized by coexistence, and thereafter caught up in a dynamic of contest about a stronger rule-based approach versus a negotiated self-regulation that would allow co-evolution. Hence there were pronounced differences in the Europeanization of sectoral regulation.

The most spectacular instance of Europeanization was economic policy. EMU's effects were both wide-ranging and complex, reflecting its three main pillars. First, monetary union represented the transfer of authority to a new supranational authority, the ECB, and the relegation of the once powerful Bundesbank – the so-called 'bank that rules Europe' – in both power and status to a member of the ESCB. This shift did not promise radical policy shifts in the sense that in essentials the ECB had been modelled on the Bundesbank to ensure a continuity of 'sound' money policies. It was independent and committed to ensuring price stability. But there were nevertheless effects. Germany found itself with an ECB monetary policy set with the interests of the euro-zone as a whole in mind that was less appropriate for its own economic circumstances of low growth and stubbornly high unemployment. Between 1998 and 2002 the problem was to some extent alleviated by a weak euro that boosted German exports and hence helped employment and incomes in the manufacturing sectors. Lacking a domestically geared monetary policy, the onus fell on wages policy and on labour-market policies to speed economic adjustment. Between 1999 and 2001 there was success in negotiating and implementing two-year, productivity-based wage agreements. But by 2002 pent-up wage frustrations surfaced in a tougher wage round. More seriously, political resistance to labour-market reforms remained high, with powerful veto players inside the trade unions, within the SPD, within the CDU and within the Federal Ministry for Labour and Social Affairs. It took the scandal at the Federal Labour Office in early 2002 and the subsequent Hartz Commission report to enable the Chancellor's Office to create an atmosphere of crisis that could give momentum to negotiated labour-market reforms. It was, however, by no means clear that these reforms would be sufficient to generate major reductions of unemployment in the context of EMU. The German government was not prepared, however, to call for reforms to the structure or mandate of the ECB which might make it more politically accountable or its mandate more inclusive of other goals, such as growth and employment. That would be to challenge its own creation and to invite severe domestic criticism from those who saw German history as vindicating the need for priority to economic stability.

In the second pillar of fiscal policy, by contrast, the EU – led by German proposals – had established a system of 'hard' policy coordination in the form of the Stability and Growth Pact. Under it member states were required to submit (and gain approval for) national stability programmes that spelt out how they intended to achieve 'close to budgetary balance' over the economic cycle. In 2001 the European Council specified a deadline of 2004 for meeting this objective. The Pact also required that states avoid a budget deficit greater than 3 per cent of GDP. If they broke this requirement, they would be the subject of recommendations for action and ultimately of heavy sanctions. The overall purpose of the Pact was to prevent 'free-riding' by states which, once deprived of the direct exchange-rate constraint, might be tempted to pursue expansionary budgets and offload the costs to other states in the form of higher ECB interest rates. It was also to provide a fiscal flank of 'sound' finance to support the ECB.

Embarrassingly, in February 2002 Germany was threatened with a letter of warning from the European Commission saying that it risked breaching the 3 per cent limit. This was averted by a negotiated agreement in the Council of Economic and Finance Ministers, with Schröder heavily involved because of the high political stakes in an election year. A key result was agreement that the federal government would once again try to negotiate a national stability pact with the Länder and the local authorities that would bind them to budgetary targets consistent with achieving an overall 'close to balance' by 2004 and thereby meeting Germany's commitments. However, there remained a striking difference between the rules and sanctions of the Stability and Growth Pact – which was good enough for the EU in the German view – and the essentially 'soft' fiscal policy coordination that characterized German federalism. The Länder vetoed the idea of a national stability pact with sanctions. By October 2002 (just after the election) it was clear that Germany would breach the 3 per cent limit. The result was another major bout of budget consolidation. A key effect of the Stability and Growth Pact was to reinforce – rather than to create – the domestic political rationale for continuing budgetary consolidation. Schröder and Eichel were careful to distance themselves from fundamental criticism of the Pact, but with the election behind them began to talk of the need for a more flexible interpretation of its provisions.

Perhaps most importantly of all, the Pact reinforced the domestic political status and power of the Finance Ministry. It became an increasingly Europeanized ministry (led by its European division) with an interest in spreading Europeanization to the Länder (through the Financial Planning Council), the Council of Economic Experts and the Bundestag and Bundesrat. From its perspective these bodies were only imperfectly Europeanized and potentially veto players on EMU-related matters. Its influence reached out to constrain the scope for the Defence Ministry to engage in the emerging European security and defence policy and press the case for its reliance on restructuring to release necessary resources. This influence was also felt in terms of pushing the agenda for social policy reforms, notably to pensions and health. In these ways EMU had important indirect effects on German public policies.

More generally in the third pillar of economic policy, especially in policies to promote growth and employment, the EU proceeded by 'soft' coordination. This involved a reliance on guidelines, peer review, benchmarking best practice and policy learning. These processes informed the Macro-Economic Policy Guidelines (Maastricht Treaty), the national employment action plans (Luxembourg process since 1997), the structural reform reports (Cardiff process since 1998), the Macro-Economic Dialogue (Cologne process since 1999) and the Lisbon process (since 2000) for improving the longer-term growth, productivity and employment performance of the EU. This approach has been strongly promoted by the German federal government as consistent with the principle of subsidiarity in economic policy. Thus in 1997 Kohl rejected the idea of the Community being given formal responsibility in employment policy. In its 1999 EU Presidency the Schröder government proposed the Macro-Economic Dialogue as a way of involving the social partners in

EMU in a dialogue and information exchange about optimal policy responses of wages to monetary and fiscal policies.

The overall result of this widening range of EU initiatives was to broaden the circle of German policy actors involved in the process of Europeanization, particularly to include the Federal Ministry of Labour and Social Affairs, the Federal Ministry for Education and Research and the Länder education ministries. In coordinating the German input to the Lisbon process the Finance Ministry was inhibited from being able to make commitments and act as a policy leader by the difficulty of reconciling the plurality of different institutional interests. In labour-market and education policies there was a new interest in benchmarking best practice elsewhere, for instance in the UK; this need was reinforced when in 2001 the OECD's PISA study showed Germany to be falling well behind in international educational league tables of pupil attainment. But this practice was ad hoc, pragmatic horizontal Europeanization with no real connection to EU processes. What was interesting, however, was the tendency to take similar examples: Denmark, the Netherlands, Sweden and the UK. German policy was less introverted and framed in terms of a German model. With that model open to question, or even discredited, domestic policy space was being opened up from within to a wider range of experiences.

The overall effect of EMU was that fewer policy sectors and actors could continue to coexist with Community policy, treating it as marginally significant. Its effects were invading labour market policies, education policies and social policies, especially through the reframing of policies as discourse shifted to how Germany could improve policy performance by benchmarking best practice and drawing appropriate lessons. Here direct and indirect cognitive effects were apparent, strengthening the agenda for promoting vocational education and more precise standard-setting and monitoring in education, trying to retain older people in the labour market and looking at the role of women in the labour market, and encouraging more competition in health and pension policy provision.

From Smooth Adaptation to Punctuated Equilibria

The Europeanization of German governance reveals a paradox in Germany's evolving relationship with Europe and a puzzle about how it might evolve. A substantial degree of stability and continuity is accompanied by a greater measure of conditionality and potential precariousness in this relationship. Up until the 1980s German institutions and policies lived in a condition of equilibrium with the EU. They coexisted, only marginally affected, in a relatively autonomous manner; or they co-evolved with EU policy; or they combined both features. The result was a general picture of accommodation and smooth adaptation. But this equilibrium has been disturbed as deep-seated changes at both the EU level and the domestic level have interacted. Notably, the EU's competences have greatly expanded in the 1980s and 1990s, especially the internal market, competition policy and EMU. They have highlighted the constraining, disciplinary effects of European integration. Europeanization has become more comprehensive and intrusive, with more direct and visible effects of integration on polity, politics and policies. EU enlargement suggests a change in the future character of the Union, with over three-quarters of member states falling into the category of small. This suggests greater difficulties for Germany in shaping both agenda and decision-making than in the past, further accentuating the constraining face of integration. These developments are paralleled by domestic change, notably a more fluid party system, generational change and the complex effects of unification and relative economic decline. In this evolving context fewer institutions and policies can simply coexist with the EU. More typical is likely to be a general pattern of co-evolution, punctuated by mutual challenge between the two levels and episodic contest, with the Länder level as a potential source of tensions. In short, the most probable scenario for German–EU relations seems one of punctuated equilibria.

The high degree of stability and continuity – represented by the ascendancy of co-evolution – is accounted for by a pronounced ideational structuring that is deeply informed by a distinctive historical memory (see Chapter 10). It is also supported by a shared political dynamics of multi-level governance and congruence in modes of governance. These aspects underline the traditional enabling face of integration, showing how it has served to help project German ideas, interests and policy preferences to the European level (Kohler-Koch and Knodt, 2000; Haftendorn, 2001). At the same time, the dynamics of political and policy development at both the EU level and the domestic level have created greater potential for contest. This potential is likely to grow as eastern enlargement alters the balance of power in the EU away from Germany, undermining its potential to act as a 'swing' state in the Council. The capacity for smooth co-evolution is also likely to be eroded from within unless Germany can prevent its decline as a policy model and restore its 'soft' power. In that case, the EU is more likely to act as a transmission belt for Anglo-American ideas about economic and social policies, requiring more radical domestic adjustment both in terms of policy paradigm change and the tempo of change. Europeanization has been linked to paradigm change in sectors such as telecommunications, energy and road haulage. As yet the more politically sensitive areas such as labour-market and social policies have not been affected in such a direct and radical manner. Here the German tradition of social partnership and negotiated change remains intact. More widely – for instance, in EMU, in competition policy and in environmental policy – the major changes have been at the level of policy instruments and their use. Europeanization has the potential to face Germany with much tougher challenges and choices in the future. In such a scenario a 'European' Germany might look more contingent and precarious. European effects would be more polarizing, with fundamental liberalizers more empowered and key interests supporting the consensus model of economic change disempowered by the process. But this scenario raises other questions: can Anglo-American market capitalism retain its model character or will it succumb to crisis, and what would the effects be on the EU's future policies?

9

Foreign and Security Policy

ADRIAN HYDE-PRICE

One of the most significant areas of policy change in Germany since unification has been in its foreign and security policy. Since the early 1990s, a quiet revolution has been under way in German attitudes towards the use of military force as an instrument of statecraft. This has been accompanied by a significant redefinition of Germany's foreign policy role conceptions, with a growing emphasis on its increased 'responsibility' (*Verantwortung*) for international peace and security. This shift in policy is starkly illustrated by the very different response to the wars that began and ended the 1990s: the Gulf conflict of 1991, and the Kosovo War of 1999. In 1991, the newly reunified Germany declined to participate in the UN-backed campaign to liberate Kuwait from Iraqi occupation forces on the grounds that its constitution forbade such 'out-of-area' operations. In 1999, however, despite the absence of a clear UN mandate, Bundeswehr forces participated in 'Operation Allied Force', the intensive aerial campaign waged to forcefully end Serbian repression in Kosovo. Since then, the Bundeswehr has also acted as the 'lead nation' in peacekeeping operations in Macedonia, and joined the US 'war on terrorism'.

This chapter offers a critical exposition and analysis of German foreign and security policy since the mid-1990s, focusing on developments since the coming to power in 1998 of the Red–Green coalition led by Chancellor Gerhard Schröder and Foreign Minister Joschka Fischer. This period has witnessed two major military conflicts (Kosovo and Afghanistan), along with a series of potentially far-reaching changes in Europe's security architecture. These include NATO's enlargement and its strategic redirection, and the launch of the EU's common European Security and Defence Policy (ESDP). In addition, the years since 1998 have seen the beginnings of a process of restructuring of the

Bundeswehr to meet new security demands, and – of particular importance – the emergence of proliferation, 'rogue states' and international terrorism as the primary threats to global peace and security. The period since the late 1990s thus marks the end of the post-Cold War interregnum, and the emergence of a new era in international security, given shape and definition by the events of 11 September. As the new century begins, therefore, German policy-makers are facing a new and uncertain international security environment, which is very different from that envisaged in the heady days following the fall of the Berlin Wall.

Germany and the End of the Cold War

The demise of the East–West conflict transformed Germany's geostrategic situation. From being a front-line state in a divided Europe it became a country 'encircled by friends' (Meiers, 1995, p. 85). With the steady reduction of Cold War military forces in Central Europe, Germany enjoyed an increasingly benign security environment. 'For the first time in history, Germany has – from a military perspective – achieved the status of being absolutely secure!' (Hacke, 1997b, p. 6).

In this transformed security environment, German policy-makers strove to realize their vision of a 'European peace order' based on institutionalized cooperation and non-violent conflict resolution. Germany's approach to the reshaping of European order was deeply coloured by post-war West German strategic culture and the tried and tested instruments of its foreign policy: multilateralism and strategic partnerships (Hyde-Price, 2000, pp. 119–20). Deterrence and the balance of military forces were to be replaced by a system of 'cooperative security', given institutional expression in a revitalized and more robust CSCE (Conference on Security and Cooperation in Europe). Germany was at the forefront of efforts to give this pan-European forum for collective diplomacy a more institutionalized form, a strategy that eventually led to the CSCE's transformation into the OSCE (Organization for Security and Cooperation in Europe). Yet while the OSCE was perceived as an important pan-European body, German policy-makers nonetheless accorded a central place in the new European peace order to the two key organizations of Western Europe: NATO and the EU. These two organizations were to provide the institutional pillars of a stable peace, through their enlargement to the new democracies of Central and Eastern Europe.

Germany's post-Cold War foreign and security policy reflected the ingrained habits and patterns of thought forged during the previous

40 years. The Federal Republic's long and positive experience of *Westintegration* (Western integration) fostered an almost 'reflexive multilateralism' in its approach to foreign relations along with a distinctive foreign policy style. This was characterized by a pronounced *Bescheidenheit* (modesty) and *Zurückhaltung* (reserve) in international diplomacy and the exercise of power, coupled with a preference for a 'European' rather than a national identity. West Germany's distinctive foreign policy also gave rise to a 'civilian power' strategic culture. The concept of a *Zivilmacht*, or 'civilian power', refers to a state which actively promotes the 'civilizing' of international relations. In other words, it seeks to replace the anarchy of the international system (which, by its very nature, breeds power politics and security competition) with new forms of global governance grounded on shared norms and values, multilateral institutions and respect for human rights. Civilian powers seek to constrain and ultimately prevent the use of military force by strengthening the rule of law and the authority of international organizations, above all the United Nations (UN). They are committed to the peaceful resolution of disputes and non-violent forms of conflict management, and strive to build new forms of international order based on cooperation, integration and social justice. To this end, civilian powers are willing to transfer sovereignty to supranational institutions in order to promote international cooperation and integration. Above all, however, civilian powers will eschew the use of military force in pursuit of their national interests, preferring to deploy non-coercive instruments of statecraft. Military force, they argue, should only be used under exceptional circumstances, and then only multilaterally on the basis of a clear mandate from a legitimate source of international authority such as the UN (Harnisch and Maull, 2001).

During the Cold War, Germany's character as a *Zivilmacht* was manifest in its resolute commitment to detente and 'common security' in preference to deterrence strategies involving nuclear war fighting, power politics and East–West confrontation. This *Zivilmacht* strategic culture planted deep roots given the Bonn Republic's efforts to eradicate militarism and authoritarianism. The Bundeswehr was thus established as a German army of a new type, deeply imbued with liberal-democratic values and a respect for constitutional principles. Germany's soldiers were henceforth to regard themselves as 'citizens in uniform' responsible for acts carried out under orders. Above all, the Bundeswehr was to be firmly anchored in multilateral structures through NATO, and designed for strictly defensive purposes. According to this logic the Bundeswehr would have failed in its mission the moment it fired its first shot in anger (Stratman, 1988, pp. 97–8).

Germany and Post-Cold War Security

The end of the East–West conflict radically and irrevocably transformed Germany's security agenda. 'We have slain a large dragon', one commentator suggested, 'but we live in a jungle filled with a bewildering variety of poisonous snakes' (Mueller, 1994, p. 536). Throughout the 1990s, it was evident that the transition from Communism in Central and Eastern Europe was generating a distinct set of security risks and challenges. These emanated from the stresses inherent in the transformation of one-party command economies into liberal-democratic market economies. The turmoil and social dislocation that all too often accompanied attempts at macro-economic stabilization and structural reform threatened to undermine the young shoots of political democratization, and provided fertile ground for populists, xenophobic nationalists and demagogues of all descriptions. As Kurt Biedenkopf, the Prime Minister of Saxony, noted in 1994, the 'threat to our values has not disappeared', but has taken a very different form. 'The prime military threat from the East has been replaced by a global threat created by disorder. Our sovereignty and security are threatened not by atomic weapons, but by the dangerous proximity of chaos and disorder to our highly developed, albeit sensitive, societies' (Biedenkopf, 1994, p. 17).

For much of the 1990s, therefore, Germany's security concerns were focused on the belt of instability running from the Baltic through to the Caucasus and into the eastern Mediterranean. Most of these security concerns were primarily about the social and economic consequences for Germany of instability on and around Europe's borders, not least in terms of large-scale migration. This new security agenda was shared by most European countries but, given Germany's central geographical location (its *Mittellage*), it was particularly vulnerable to crises and instability in the post-Communist east. Many of these new security worries were not a function of the balance of power or traditional geopolitical rivalries, but were part of an expanding 'soft' security agenda. As the Federal President, Roman Herzog, observed in March 1995:

Social, ecological and cultural destabilization present additional security risks, which in the long term are scarcely less dangerous than military threats. Meanwhile the list of these risks has become well known: population explosion, climate change, economically-motivated migrants, nuclear smuggling, the drugs trade, fundamentalists of different colours, genocide, the collapse of state authority. (Herzog, 1995, p. 161)

The Gulf War

Hopes that the end of the Cold War would allow Germany to focus on addressing 'soft' security issues through the multilateral construction of new cooperative security structures were rudely dispelled by two events in the early 1990s: the Gulf War and the violent disintegration of Yugoslavia. Both events placed question marks over the continuing utility of a primarily non-military *Zivilmacht* foreign policy role conception in the face of armed aggression.

The Iraqi invasion of Kuwait in August 1990 provided the first test of united Germany's foreign and security policy. As the USA marshalled a broad international coalition to reverse this aggression, the government of Helmut Kohl argued that it was constitutionally unable to send Bundeswehr troops to fight alongside its allies in an 'out-of-area' operation. Instead, Germany provided substantial financial support for the coalition and acted as its diplomatic cheerleader in international fora. This position was broadly supported by public opinion, although a small but vociferous anti-war movement campaigned energetically against what was portrayed as an 'oil war'. Whilst popular at home, however, the German government's approach to the Gulf War was criticized by many NATO allies as being incompatible with the international responsibilities which unification entailed. In particular, Germany was criticized for its predilection for 'cheque book diplomacy' and its unwillingness to risk Bundeswehr lives in a UN-sanctioned operation.

The Gulf War exposed a tension at the heart of post-Cold War German security policy. On the one hand, Germany favoured multilateralism and cooperation with its allies; on the other, it rejected out-of-area military crisis management operations as incompatible with the *Grundgesetz* (Basic Law) and inappropriate for a *Zivilmacht* seeking to overcome the legacy of past militarism (Duffield, 1998, pp. 219–20). Yet with the end of the East–West conflict, Germany's strategic partners were increasingly acting through multilateral institutions such as the UN in order to undertake military crisis management operations in support of international peace and security. During the Cold War, the tension between being a loyal NATO member and a strategic partner of the USA on the one hand, and a civilian power committed to non-military solutions to international conflicts on the other, was less apparent because NATO's strategic thinking was dominated by deterrence and war prevention. The demise of the East–West conflict has led to new thinking about the use of military coercion by international organizations such as NATO and the UN, thereby exposing a role conflict at the heart of German security policy (Maull and Kirste, 1997, pp. 306–7).

The response of the ruling CDU coalition under Chancellor Kohl was to resolve this role conflict in favour of multilateral commitments and its strategic partnership with the USA. Consequently, the years following the Gulf War witnessed a steady recalibration of German security policy. As former Foreign Minister Klaus Kinkel noted, the government used a 'step-by-step' strategy to deploy Bundeswehr troops in UN-sponsored humanitarian missions 'out-of-area'. Initially these did not involve deployments of troops in combat situations; rather, the Bundeswehr deployed medical and technical support units. Thus, for example, the Luftwaffe (German Air Force) was used in April 1991 to distribute relief supplies to Kurdish refugees, and in July 1992 it participated in the humanitarian airlift to Sarajevo. The aim of these and similar missions was to gradually familiarize the German public with the idea of an 'out-of-area' role for the Bundeswehr, and to prepare the ground politically for humanitarian intervention and military crisis-management. The first 'blue-helmet' deployment of Bundeswehr troops was in Cambodia (1992–3), where Germany contributed a medical unit to the United Nations Transitional Authority in Cambodia (UNTAC). Bundeswehr units were subsequently committed to Somalia (1992–3), again in non-combat roles.

Yugoslavia and the Limits of Pacifism

The most important catalyst for the development of a new German security policy was the violent disintegration of the Yugoslav federation. The outbreak of vicious fighting in this corner of the Balkans – historically Europe's 'powder-keg' – illustrated all too sharply the changed nature of Europe's post-Cold War security agenda. The combination of ethno-national differences, historical animosities, economic hardship and unscrupulous political leaders proved a potent cocktail, and placed complex new demands on Western policy-makers. As Wilfred von Bredow, Professor of Politics at the University of Marburg, has noted, with the end of the Cold War 'international politics has suddenly become considerably more ambivalent' (Von Bredow, 1999). New conflicts have emerged which are not amenable to black-and-white analyses or simple solutions. Faced with a complex and ambiguous international system, he argued, the danger existed of political paralysis. The changed international environment thus placed greater demands on the judgement and negotiating skills of political leaders, who found themselves operating in a context awash with legal and moral dilemmas. All Western states found themselves facing this new and demanding situation after the end of the Cold War. Yet, for Germany, the process of adjustment was even more difficult given the constraints imposed by its *Zivilmacht* role conception. 'Up until this time', Peter Schmidt noted, 'the legitimacy of the German armed forces was mainly based on the fact that alliance and national defence were identical. This context had now been redefined' (1996, p. 212).

Germany's first engagement with the contorted politics of Yugoslavia was not a happy one. In late 1990, Slovenia and Croatia responded to Milosevic's attempt to assert Serbian nationalist dominance within Yugoslav federal structures by pushing for independence. In the face of vacillation and uncertainty on the part of the international community, Bonn declared that it would recognize Slovenia and Croatia by Christmas 1991, even if there were no consensus on this matter in the EU (Crawford, 1995). This perceived assertiveness by Germany was widely criticized, with accusations that Bonn's attempt to play a great power role in the Balkans precipitated the violent collapse of Yugoslavia. Such criticisms were largely unfounded, and arose from a misreading of German motives, which had less to do with great power ambitions and more to do with the normative values underpinning German foreign policy. As Michael Libal (1997) has argued, 'the crucial motives for German behaviour during the first two years of the crisis were rooted in a pervasive pattern of moral and political values', which generated a sense of solidarity with states striving for national self-determination in the face of Communist authoritarianism and military intimidation. Nonetheless, German policy-makers were quick to draw the lesson that they needed to coordinate their foreign policy actions more closely with EU and NATO allies in order to avoid any suggestion of great power assertiveness.

The wars of Yugoslav succession that followed this controversial episode served as the catalyst for defining a new role for the Bundeswehr as part of a wider reassessment of German foreign and security policy. As appalling evidence accumulated of atrocities, ethnic cleansing and mass rape in Bosnia, a growing mood developed in German public opinion – as elsewhere in Europe and North America – that 'something must be done'. It was in this context that the German government, led by Defence Minister Volker Rühe, devised a policy of gradually committing Bundeswehr personnel to multilateral humanitarian and crisis-management operations. The idea behind his 'salami tactics' was to gradually prepare public opinion for an out-of-area role for the Bundeswehr.

The constitutional position on out-of-area deployments was finally clarified by a decision of the Federal Constitutional Court (*Bundesverfassungsgericht*) on 12 July 1994. This followed two earlier rulings by the court. The first concerned the legality of German crews in AWACs (Airborne Warning and Control Systems) aircraft deployed to enforce the UN-mandated 'no-fly' zone in Bosnia. The court ruled that the deployment of AWACs was permissible because failure to participate would have jeopardized the confidence of other NATO members. Later, in June 1994, the court ruled on Bundeswehr participation in the UN Operation in Somalia (UNOSOM II), arguing that it was essential to involve the Bundestag in decisions concerning missions outside the NATO area. The constitutional position was finally clarified by the July 1994 ruling, which stated that Bundeswehr forces could participate in military operations outside the NATO area as long as they took place under UN auspices and were approved by the Bundestag. The constitutional basis for this was Article 24(2) of the *Grundgesetz*, which allowed the Bundeswehr to participate in missions associated with membership of a collective security system.

Although the constitutional position was finally clarified in July 1994, the political conditions governing out-of-area deployments still needed resolving (Dorff, 1997, p. 57). German political leaders began formulating a series of criteria for future deployments shortly after the failure of the UN's Somalia mission. These stressed, *inter alia*, the need for a clear and legitimate international mandate; multilateral involvement; a clear political concept underlying the military operation; a limited time frame; and German involvement in the decision-making process (Duffield, 1998, p. 211). For the German left, however, the catalyst for a fundamental change of attitude on the issue of military intervention was the massacre of Bosnian Muslim males by Serbian forces in Srebrenica in 1995. For many former Cold War peace activists, the deepening tragedy in the Balkans raised questions about the moral and political relevance of pacifism in the face of the new, more complex and ambiguous security agenda (Hubert, 1993).

The pivotal figure in this political reorientation was the prominent Green/Bündnis' 90 politician, Joschka Fischer (Sager, 1996, p. 47). In August 1995 he published an open letter to his party colleagues in which he argued that the Srebrenica massacre made necessary a rethink of the hitherto sacrosanct principle of non-violence. He suggested to his colleagues that the German left would lose its soul if it were to fail to intervene in a situation that could only be described as genocide. He made his position crystal clear: in the event of genocide, it was the political and moral duty of the Greens to support military intervention by multilateral forces, and these forces should include a German contingent (Volmer, 1988, p. 513).

By the mid-1990s, therefore, a significant shift in thinking about German security policy was under way. Prompted by the limitations of chequebook diplomacy and the driven by public concerns about violence in the Balkans, a new consensus about the role and purpose of the Bundeswehr began to form (Dalvi, 1998). Volker Rühe was the primary political architect of the Bundeswehr's new out-of-area role, which was made constitutionally possible by the July 1994 Constitutional Court ruling. The new cross-party consensus around humanitarian intervention was manifest in the large Bundestag majority (543 in favour, 107 against) for German participation in IFOR, the NATO-led force established to implement the Dayton peace accord, signed in November 1995. Indeed, 'the Yugoslav war and the active involvement of NATO troops in the post-Dayton peacekeeping operation proved to be a key catalyst in legitimizing out-of-area deployments of the Bundeswehr' (Calic, 1998, p. 18). The commitment of 4,000 troops to IFOR constituted the largest out-of-area operation in the history of the Bundeswehr, and was thus an important landmark in the evolution of post-unification German security policy (Lantis, 1996; Pond, 1997).

Germany and the Kosovo War

The extent of the shift in German security policy during the first decade following the end of the Cold War was evident from the Kosovo War. Whereas in 1991 the Bonn Government refused to participate in Operation 'Desert Storm' against Iraq, despite the fact that it had a clear UN mandate and enjoyed broad international support, Bundeswehr forces took part in 'Operation Allied Force' against the rump Yugoslav Federation in March 1999. This event constituted a significant landmark in the history of the Federal Republic. For the first time since 1945, German military forces took part in offensive combat missions against a sovereign state. This historic watershed is all the more remarkable because it took place under a Red–Green coalition government, and without a clear UN Security Council mandate. NATO's intervention thus had an ambiguous status under international law (Preuss, 1999), and precipitated the worst crisis in Russia's relations with the West since the end of the Cold War.

Germany's participation in the Kosovo campaign was motivated by three primary considerations: first, a desire to demonstrate its reliability as a loyal NATO ally and strategic partner for the USA; second, a normative impulse to respond to ethnic cleansing and widespread violations of human rights. Such normative considerations are often overlooked in foreign policy analysis, but they can have a very real political force. This is certainly true in the case of Germany, given the legacy of the Holocaust. The brutality of Serbian military and police units was widely equated with the ruthlessness of German military and special police units in the Second World War, and this time most Germans wanted to be on the 'right side': hence the broad public support for the use of military force to stop human rights abuses in Kosovo. The third factor, less openly acknowledged, but no less important, was fear of a new wave of asylum-seekers and refugees, an increasingly sensitive political issue in Germany. Serbian ethnic cleansing in Kosovo threatened to precipitate large-scale migration to the West, which the German government wished to prevent. As Defence Minister Rudolf Scharping commented, the ghastly events in Kosovo posed a fundamental question: 'do we deal with force, murder and expulsion by tackling these problems at their source? Or do we watch passively and wait until their consequences come home to us?' (*Der Spiegel*, 31 April 1999, p. 6).

During the Kosovo war, the Red–Green government pursued a twin-track approach: on the one hand, full support for, and participation in, the NATO bombing campaign; and on the other, intensive diplomatic efforts to find a solution to the crisis. Given its presidency of the EU and the WEU (Western European Union), Germany played a pivotal role in negotiations to find a solution to the war and to bring peace to the wider region. This involved strenuous efforts to involve the UN and Russia in the search for peace. Chancellor Schröder invited UN Secretary-General Kofi Annan to attend an informal EU summit in Brussels in April 1999. At the same time, a steady stream of high-level diplomatic visits was made to Russia in order to engage them in the search for peace. The importance attached to Russia reflected Germany's awareness of the need for Moscow's support in shaping a cooperative European security system, and their concern to minimize tensions generated by both NATO enlargement and the Kosovo War. In addition to the EU and the UN, the German government also attached considerable importance to the G-8 as a forum for hammering out a peace settlement, a strategy which bore fruit at the G-8 summit in Bonn in May 1999 at which a set of 'principles' was agreed for ending the conflict (Hyde-Price, 2001).

As the Kosovo War drew to an end, the German government played a central role, as president of the EU, in developing the initiative for a 'Stability Pact for Southeast Europe'. This was designed to stabilize the region through economic investment and support, coupled with the perspective of developing closer relations with the EU, up to and including membership (Ehrhart, 1999). The Stability Pact was formally launched by EU ministers on 10 June 1999 with the former head of the German Federal Chancellery, Bobo Hombach, as its special coordinator (Hombach, 1999). Alongside its promotion of economic reform, the pact seeks to develop a new pan-European security system under the auspices of the OSCE based on conflict prevention, and to strengthen the process of democratization in the region. This approach to security reflected a long-established German preference for non-military conflict resolution and multilateral cooperation, in keeping with Germany's role concept as a *Zivilmacht*.

In terms of its domestic political consequences, the Kosovo war was important in a number of respects. To begin with, it gave a new sense of unity and purpose to an otherwise fractious Red–Green coalition. It also boosted the domestic political profile of leading government figures, most notably Chancellor Schröder, Foreign Minister Fischer and Defence Minister Scharping. The broad cross-party support in the Bundestag for the bombing campaign illustrated the changed mood in public opinion towards an out-of-area role for the Bundeswehr, with qualified support in favour of the war being given by the CDU, CSU and FDP. However, the large Bundestag majority in favour of participation in 'Operation Allied Force' hid major tensions amongst left-wing pacifist elements in both of the governing parties. Indeed, the Greens seemed in danger of breaking apart as the bombing campaign developed, and only the active intervention of Joschka Fischer kept the party together. The only party to distance itself from the war was the former Communist Party, the PDS. They argued that the bombing campaign was an act of aggression by NATO, led by the USA, against a sovereign state and thus illegal under international law. This pacifist-cum-anti-imperialist stance was designed in part to help the party establish a political basis in the western Länder amongst disillusioned pacifists. At the same time, the PDS's anti-war stance received a positive echo in eastern Germany. Whereas 59 per cent of west Germans believed that NATO's bombs were serving humanitarian ends, only 38 per cent were of this view in the eastern Länder. In the west, 70 per cent supported the participation of the Bundeswehr in the Kosovo operation. In the east, only 41 per cent were in favour, whilst 48 per cent were against. Finally, as early as mid-April nearly two-thirds of east Germans wanted to see an immediate end to the air strikes. The differences between the two parts of Germany reflected the legacy of two distinct socialization processes and underlined the difficulties involved in integrating east Germans into the political culture of the Bundesrepublik.

EU Security and Defence Policy

One major consequence of the Kosovo War was to accelerate the process of developing security and defence cooperation within the European Union. West European unease with the quality and direction of US leadership during the Kosovo crisis, coupled with a belief that they must do more collectively for their own defence, gave a major impetus to European defence and security cooperation. Early indications of a possible breakthrough in this area of European integration came with the Franco–British summit at St Malo in December 1998, when London and Paris committed themselves to deepening European defence cooperation. With encouraging signals emanating from Washington, Germany used the opportunity of its combined Presidency of the EU and WEU in the first half of 1999 to drive forward the process of forging a new European defence capability.

The result was the Cologne European Council's historic decision in June 1999 to build a European Security and Defence Policy (ESDP) within the framework of the EU's Common Foreign and Security Policy (CFSP). The Cologne summit approved the German presidency's 'Report on the Strengthening of Common Defence and Security Policy' which proposed giving the Union credible means for taking autonomous action in response to international crises. At the same time, the former NATO Secretary-General, Javier Solana, was appointed as the EU's High Representative for Foreign Policy and – following a German proposal – as the new Secretary-General of the WEU. The subsequent Helsinki summit in December 1999 built on these decisions by agreeing to a 'headline goal' whereby EU member states would, by 2003, generate military forces capable of carrying out the full range of Petersburg tasks, 'including the most demanding', in operations up to corps level. The proposed European rapid reaction corps was to consist of 15 brigades (50–60,000 troops), with attached naval and air assets, which would be capable of being deployed within 60 days. This force was designed to give the EU an 'autonomous capacity to take decisions where NATO as a whole is not engaged', in order to conduct 'EU-led military operations' including peacekeeping and military crisis-management (Hyde-Price, 2002).

The Cologne EU summit was a landmark event in the history of the European integration process with important consequences for German foreign and security policy. The EU has, since its earliest inception, been central to the institutional embedding of German power in a multilateral framework. Since its inception, the EU has been a 'civilian' organization designed to foster economic, political and social cooperation between its member states. With the decision to create a European rapid reaction corps, the EU has committed itself to establishing an autonomous capability to project military power for crisis management purposes. This transformation of the EU from a 'civilian power' to one capable of using military force for political objectives was only possible because the FRG dropped its reservations about an out-of-area role for the Bundeswehr. The creation of the ESDP was welcomed by Germany, which has long championed European defence cooperation as a complement to NATO. Nonetheless, it does pose some future challenges to German foreign policy given the discord it has subsequently generated in transatlantic relations. The development of a military dimension to the European integration process raises questions about the future of NATO and the US security commitment to Europe, both of which have been at the heart of German security policy since the early years of the Cold War.

NATO and Transatlantic Relations

Throughout the Cold War, the central pillar of German security policy was the NATO alliance and the US security guarantee to Western Europe it embodied. With the demise of the Cold War, NATO lost its primary rationale (deterring the perceived Soviet threat). Nonetheless, as we have seen, German policy-makers were determined to preserve NATO as the core security institution in Europe, both as an insurance policy against Russian recidivism, and as the institutional basis of a new system of multilateral security governance in Europe. The German government thus actively promoted NATO's 'Partnership for Peace' programme with the new democracies of Central and Eastern Europe, and the opening-up of NATO to new members from the region.

As the 1990s drew to a close, NATO appeared to have successfully transformed itself into an alliance capable of addressing the new post-Cold War security agenda. The Partnership for Peace scheme was operating successfully; NATO had developed a new Strategic Concept; a NATO–Russia Permanent Joint Council had been established; CJTFs (Combined Joint Task Forces) had been created to facilitate EU-led operations using alliance assets; a NATO-led peacekeeping force had been deployed in Bosnia; Poland, Czech Republic and Hungary joined the alliance in 1999; and NATO had conducted its first successful military campaign in Kosovo. Germany had significantly contributed to all these developments, and in some cases had played a central role in their success.

However, on closer analysis, there were strong indications that 1999 represented NATO's high point. The Washington summit of April 1999 revealed some fundamental differences between the USA and its European allies on the future role and geographical reach of the alliance. Whereas many in the USA wanted NATO to play a more active role in tackling threats to global energy sources, proliferation and terrorism, the majority of Europeans – including the Germans – favoured a more limited and regionally focused role for the alliance (Pradetto, 1999). The new Strategic Concept agreed at the summit was, in the end, a classic compromise document that sought to shroud underlying policy differences in ambiguous diplomatic formulae. More significantly, the USA had found the experience of fighting a coalition war in Kosovo highly frustrating, and many in Washington were determined never again to find themselves constrained by such multilateral decision-making structures.

As the twenty-first century began, it was evident that there were mounting doubts about the future of NATO. These doubts were part and parcel of wider tensions in the transatlantic relationship arising from disputes over trade and economic relations, approaches to global security threats, regional conflicts (such as the Middle East), environmental policy, and social issues such as gun control and the death penalty. At the heart of these transatlantic tensions was a fundamental difference in foreign policy: whereas the Europeans – and the Germans above all – favoured multilateral and primarily non-military approaches to foreign policy involving patient negotiation and compromise, the USA was increasingly disposed towards unilateralism and the use of coercive power to tackle perceived security threats such as terrorism and proliferation, pre-emptively if necessary. These differences have generated growing uncertainty about the future of NATO. With a further round of eastern enlargement due in November 2002, it was clear that the cohesion of the alliance would inevitably suffer, further weakening its utility in US eyes. The dispute between the USA and the EU over the new International Criminal Court further damaged transatlantic relations, leading to rumblings from the Bush Administration that if European nations refused US requests to grant immunity for US forces from politically motivated prosecutions, America would have to re-examine its commitment to NATO.

Thus, as the twenty-first century begins, it is clear that two of the central pillars of German foreign and security policy – the NATO alliance and the strategic partnership with the USA – are cracking. As we will see below, these cracks became more pronounced during the 2002 election campaign. The mounting tensions in transatlantic relations will force a fundamental rethink in Germany's foreign policy, with implications for its approach to international security. A further impulse for rethinking German foreign and security policy came in the wake of the terrorist attacks of September 2001, which have significantly transformed the international security agenda and the foreign policy of Germany's American ally.

Germany and the 'War on Terrorism'

The terrorist attacks on the Twin Towers of the World Trade Center in New York and the Pentagon in Washington were greeted in Germany by a widespread feeling of shock and horror. The sense of moral outrage deepened when it was discovered that much of the planning for this atrocity took place in Germany, at least three of the terrorists having lived and studied in Hamburg. Speaking to the Bundestag on the following day, Chancellor Schröder noted that 'yesterday the 11 September will go down in history for all of us as a black day'. The atrocities in New York and Washington, he insisted, were directed against 'the civilized community' as a whole. Consequently the Federal Republic would extend 'unconditional – I repeat – unconditional solidarity to the United States, including the deployment of military forces' (Schröder, 2001, p. 153). His call for 'unconditional solidarity' was endorsed by all parties in the Bundestag with the notable exception of the PDS, which once again wanted to profile itself as the only 'peace party' in Germany (Schulz, 2001, p. 924). The Bundestag's decision (by 565 to 40) to 'make available all appropriate military facilities' was facilitated by NATO's decision to invoke – for the first time in its history – the Article V collective security guarantees of the 1949 Washington Treaty. This had an important symbolic and political impact on Germany, even though its practical consequences were marginal.

In the initial period following the terrorist attacks, Germany played an important role in the creation and consolidation of the international alliance against terrorism. Foreign Minister Fischer was the key figure here. He embarked on an intense round of shuttle diplomacy around the Middle East, Central Asia and Pakistan. He also worked assiduously to build a common EU diplomatic response to the terrorist attacks and sought to strengthen the role of the United Nations in the anti-terror campaign. His efforts were complemented by those of Chancellor Schröder, who travelled to the Far East visiting China, India, Pakistan and, on his return flight, Russia. The German government also played a key role in organizing and funding the UN-sponsored conference in

Bonn on the creation of a post-Taliban interim regime. The conference was officially opened on 27 November by Foreign Minister Fischer, and concluded with the signing of the 'Bonn Accords', establishing an interim government led by Hamid Karzai.

The terrorist outrages raised fears in Germany about domestic security and the country's vulnerability to similar attacks. These fears were fuelled by a wave of hoax anthrax letters and – more worryingly – evidence that Osama bin Laden's al'Qaida network had put down deep roots in Germany. It became increasingly clear that al'Qaida had a substantial financial and logistical base in the Federal Republic and, according to informed estimates, was home to up to 31,000 members or supporters of militant fundamentalist Islamic organizations, some of them having links with al'Qaida (Krause, 2001). In this context, it was essential that Otto Schily, the Federal Interior Minister, acted quickly and decisively to address public unease about domestic security, whilst assuring rank-and-file members of the coalition parties that fundamental civil liberties would remain sacrosanct.

Pledging that the government would display 'absolute toughness' against radical Islamists operating in Germany, Schily moved swiftly to introduce 'Security Package I' (*Sicherheitspaket I*), a series of measures designed to strengthen domestic security. Following the unexpected success of Ronald Schill's *Partei Rechtsstaatlicher Offensive* (Law and Order Offensive Party) in the Hamburg Land elections in late September 2001, the Federal Government introduced 'Security Package II' (Golz, 2001). This was much more far-reaching in scope than the first batch of proposals, and significantly shifted the balance between security and civil liberties. These security measures were given final Bundestag approval in December, and led to an immediate crackdown on radical Islamic groups. In addition, the German authorities sought to identify and root out the financial and organizational network of al'Qaida and cognate groups, resulting in the announcement by Finance Minister Hans Eichel in October 2001 that all bank accounts in Germany would be subject to government scrutiny for unusual cash-flow patterns. Eichel also worked closely with his colleagues in the G-8 on a comprehensive action plan to combat money laundering by terrorist groups.

In terms of the military campaign, the invoking of Article V did not result in an active role for NATO, although five AWACs aircraft and their crews – 25 per cent of who were Bundeswehr personnel – were deployed to the USA. This reflected the desire of the USA to retain their operational freedom of action in the 'war on terrorism'. Nonetheless, when the USA launched its long-expected military campaign against al'Qaida and its Taliban hosts in Afghanistan in early October,

Chancellor Schröder declared in the Bundestag that 'active solidarity and responsible action are expected of Germany – and they will be forthcoming. Our solidarity must be more than mere lip-service' (Schröder, 2001). The opportunity to demonstrate this unconditional solidarity came in early November when President Bush made a formal request to the German government for military support. Schröder was quick to respond by offering 3,900 troops, arguing that this decision was made 'in a solidarity I have expressed again and again since the September 11 attacks on New York and Washington'. Following rumblings of discontent from pacifist elements in both coalition parties, the Chancellor decided to link Bundestag approval for the military deployment with a confidence vote. This was only the fourth time in the history of the Federal Republic that this procedural device had been used, and it underlined the seriousness of the threat to the government's stability.

The crucial vote was held on 16 November 2001 and resulted in the government's motion being supported by 336 to 326. This decision was of historic importance because it approved the largest-ever combat deployment of Bundeswehr forces in an out-of-area operation. The forces allocated consisted of Fuchs armoured reconnaissance vehicles; an airborne medical evacuation unit; special forces; transport units; and a naval contingent. The resolution defined the operational area in broad terms as NATO territory, the Arabian peninsula, Central Asia, north-east Africa and adjacent seas. The deployments were to last for 12 months and were to be financed by €15 million in 2001 and €160 million in 2002. The decision to commit Bundeswehr forces to the 'war on terrorism' was a further significant landmark for German foreign and security policy. Chancellor Schröder underlined this in his speech to the Bundestag on 11 October:

> Only ten years ago no-one would have expected more from Germany than secondary assistance, i.e., infrastructure or funds, in the international efforts to safeguard freedom, justice and stability. As I pointed out immediately after 11 September, this era of German post-war politics is over once and for all. Particularly we Germans, who were able to overcome the consequences of two world wars and achieve freedom and self-determination with the help and solidarity of our American and European friends, now have an obligation to shoulder our new responsibilities in full. Let there be no mistake: this expressly includes participation in military operations to defend freedom and human rights, and to establish stability and security. (Schröder, 2001, p. 153)

Although the German government was fully committed to supporting the US military campaign against al'Qaida, it expressed major reservations about extending the war on terrorism to 'rogue states'. These differences became apparent following President Bush's 'axis of evil' speech in January 2002, when he declared that 'our war against terror is only beginning' and spoke of an 'axis of evil' formed by Iran, Iraq and North Korea. These states were accused of developing weapons of mass destruction and, in the case of Iran and Iraq, of supporting terrorists. The USA, he argued, 'would not wait on events while dangers gather'. In particular, Iraq was targeted as an immediate threat to the USA and international security. The Bush Administration's desire to extend the scope of the war on terrorism by launching a pre-emptive attack on Iraq was widely condemned in the German media, and Foreign Minister Fischer spoke openly of his disquiet with US ambitions. These differences were to ignite into a major crisis in transatlantic relations during the Bundestag election campaign of 2002.

The 2002 Election Campaign

Trailing in the polls and facing the prospect of electoral defeat, Schröder decided to campaign on opposition to US policy towards Iraq, describing it as an 'adventure'. 'Under my leadership', he declared, 'there will be no German participation in military interventions'. Warming to this theme, he told cheering crowds at election rallies that 'We will go our special German way'. He rejected military action against Iraq even if sanctioned by a UN Security Council mandate. By playing the Iraq card, Schröder hoped to consolidate his electoral base on the left and appeal to the anti-war sentiment in German population, but his adoption of Bismarckian rhetoric in speaking of a 'special German way' caused concern amongst Germany's neighbours and partners. The implicit anti-Americanism of the SPD–Green campaign was evident from the comments of the Justice Minister, Herta Dauebler-Gmelin, who reportedly compared Bush's tactics to those of Hitler (she was subsequently forced to resign).

The unilateralism of Schröder's 'special German way' not only placed Berlin in direct confrontation with the USA, but also left Germany isolated amongst its European allies, whose attitude to American policy was sceptical but more 'wait-and-see'. For many, the election campaign once again put the 'German question' at the forefront of international affairs. For the first time since 1945, a major transatlantic ally won an election by campaigning against American policy. The outspoken US Secretary of Defense, Donald Rumsfeld, declared that Schröder's campaign 'has had the effect of poisoning the relationship' between the USA and Germany, a view echoed by the National Security Advisor, Condoleezza Rice. According to Washington insiders, President George W. Bush was deeply hurt and angered by Schröder's statements, particularly given the key role his father had played in German unification.

The Red–Green coalition will therefore have its work cut out repairing the damage caused to transatlantic relations and Germany's international standing. Berlin's penance will be long and painful. In an effort to mend fences, Schröder paid his first foreign visit not to Paris, as is traditionally the case with newly elected Chancellors, but to London. His purpose was to ask Tony Blair to use his high standing in Washington to repair bridges between the Bush Administration and the Schröder government. Germany also promised to provide logistical and diplomatic support for US action against Iraq, and offered to take over as lead nation in the international peacekeeping force deployed in Afghanistan.

The consequences of the election campaign for the future are likely to be far-reaching. The anti-war stance of the Greens and SDP was symptomatic of wider European unease with US policy towards Iraq and its pre-emptive national security strategy more generally. Nonetheless, their refusal to countenance military action against Iraq, even if mandated by the UN, has severely damaged transatlantic relations, which will take a long time to heal. Schröder's campaign rhetoric has undone much of the progress made in the 1990s in demonstrating Germany's value as a transatlantic ally and its responsible approach to international security. It has also deepened US suspicions about its European allies' lack of resolve in confronting threats to international order, thereby further weakening NATO and loosening the ties binding America and Europe. Finally, Schröder's Bismarckian rhetoric has generated wider European unease with German unilateralism. Opposition to US policy was couched not in 'European' terms, but as a 'special German way'. This seems to confirm a trend in the late 1990s towards a more assertive and self-interested German foreign policy. Already in 1998, Chancellor Schröder had spoken of the Berlin Republic as a 'self-confident nation' uninhibited by the past which would replace 'chequebook diplomacy' with a clearer focus on German national interests. Germany's foreign and security will henceforth be intensely scrutinized by Germany's neighbours and partners for further indications of unilateralism and assertiveness.

Conclusion

The Kosovo War and Germany's 'unconditional solidarity' with the USA in its war on terrorism illustrated the transformation which German foreign and security policy underwent in the 1990s following unification and the Gulf War. This reflected both German awareness of the need to shoulder their full share of responsibility for international order, and the changed nature of the international security environment. The immediate post-Cold War agenda of anchoring united Germany in multilateral structures and stabilizing Central and Eastern Europe has now been largely superseded by new tasks. These centre on completing the integration of the new democracies into the EU and NATO, and strengthening webs of institutionalized cooperation with countries such as Russia and Ukraine. Germany will continue to focus on developing a stable European peace order, and addressing 'soft' security issues such as transnational crime, migration and environmental degradation. However, German foreign policy will also have to cope with the fact that Europe's established institutional architecture is undergoing a process of far-reaching change. The EU will have to significantly reform its decision-making structures and its key policies as it enlarges to the east. It is also engaged in the historic task of developing a common foreign and security policy, including defence. NATO too is evolving, both through eastern enlargement and the redefinition of its role and purpose. Underlying both these institutional developments are unsettling trends in transatlantic relations – dramatically exposed during the election campaign – which are contributing to a process of continental drift. These trends will place major new demands on German statecraft, and will provide a catalyst for a further significant re-calibration of its foreign and security policy.

Despite the challenges of change in Europe's institutional architecture, Germany's immediate continental security environment remains largely benign. Europe has emerged as a zone of stable peace in an otherwise troubled world, where the threat of war and large-scale military conflict remains remote. However, the terrorist attacks of September 11 and the dangers posed by the proliferation of weapons of mass destruction illustrate the changed nature of international security in an era of globalization. It is increasingly evident that no country, however powerful, can divorce itself from the fate of the wider international system, with its pockets of despair and fanatical hatreds. The security of America and its European allies cannot be insulated from events in the Middle East and Asia. German policy-makers are having to come to terms with the fact that threats to transatlantic security increasingly come not from inside Europe, but from the wider international system. Following September 11, the Federal Republic can no longer afford the comfortable complacency of focusing almost exclusively on its 'near abroad' in Europe, but needs to develop a broader geostrategic perspective.

Since 11 September 2001, a wide-ranging debate on foreign and security policy has been under way in the USA, which has challenged many traditional assumptions. However, Germany, along with most other European countries, retains a strategic culture largely forged during the Cold War. Yet in what is becoming an increasingly complex and ambiguous international environment, old concepts of 'containment' and 'deterrence' may not be relevant. Before the election campaign, Chancellor Schröder demonstrated some awareness of the need for German foreign and security policy to adapt to the new situation, especially in terms of the use of military force. In an interview with *Die Zeit* in October 2001 he argued that over the previous three years his government, 'often somewhat unnoticed', had 'fundamentally changed' German foreign and security policy, primarily by seeking to remove the taboo on the use of military force. His aim, he argued, was to build a 'permissive consensus' for the use of military force as a legitimate instrument of foreign policy. '11 September has changed the world situation', he argued, and the Bundeswehr's participation in the war on terrorism marked a clear watershed for Germany. Whilst earlier interventions had taken place inside Europe, these deployments were taking place outside Europe: 'That is a qualitative difference, but one which arises from the changed role of Germany in the world and the expectations of its partners.' Although the Red–Green government 'has always said that our main focus must be on crisis prevention and management ... this has never been an excuse not to take military action if need be.'

This new, more hard-headed approach to foreign and security policy will only be feasible if the German armed forces are restructured and adequately funded. 'The Bundeswehr', one analyst has noted, 'must overcome its founding charter as a non-interventionist, conscript-based territorial defence force' (Sarotte, 2001, p. 12). Throughout the 1990s, defence expenditure was repeatedly cut in an elusive search for the 'peace dividend', whilst far-reaching military reform was repeatedly postponed. In May 2000, the Red–Green government finally committed itself to a process of defence restructuring, but there are doubts about whether this will give the Bundeswehr a significant capacity to respond to security challenges requiring force projection and out-of-area military crisis management. The public admission in the spring of 2001 that the Bundeswehr was no longer fully operational and that it was unable to fulfil all of its alliance obligations underlines the distance Germany has to travel if it is to be able to shoulder its new-found responsibilities.

The final question to be addressed is whether Germany is still a *Zivilmacht*. Hanns Maull has argued that the Federal Republic remains, at heart, a civilian power, and that this foreign policy role 'may currently be the most convincing model for a world of increasingly globalized international politics'. He also notes, however, that Germany as a civilian power draws on 'a wide spectrum of instruments, including, under certain circumstances, the use of military force – not in the classic sense of war, as an instrument to promote vital national interests, but as a means of pacifying violent conflicts and stopping those who resort to violence' (Maull, 2000, pp. 1–24). With this caveat, however, he seems to be stretching the original concept of a 'civilian power' to breaking point. As the 2002 election illustrates, there is clearly a strong cultural aversion to war in Germany. However, the Bundeswehr has participated in offensive military operations in Kosovo, demonstrating that with decisive political leadership Germans are willing to accept the legitimacy of coercive diplomacy. It is therefore less and less clear what distinguishes Germany from other mature European democracies that, with the partial exception of the UK, share similar reservations about the utility of military force (Everts, 2002). To this extent, one can perhaps speak of a European, rather than an exclusively German, model of 'civilian power', in contrast to the USA and other great powers that are willing to use coercive power in pursuit of national interests. Whether or not this European model of civilian power is appropriate for the new global security agenda of terrorism and proliferation is another matter, and one that will tax German policy-makers in the coming years.

10

Germany and Europe

WILLIAM E. PATERSON

The fall of the Berlin Wall in 1989 led both to a united Germany and the end of the divided Europe in which both Germanies were so deeply embedded. In a divided and bipolar Europe the Federal Republic had played a key role in the integration of Western Europe by pursuing a policy of reflexive multilateralism and a close strategic alliance with France. It was not entirely clear in 1989/90 that this formula could be transferred into the new wider European environment or that this would be the choice of future German governments. It was, however, clear that the future prospects of stability and prosperity in the new Europe would depend disproportionately on Germany. The weakening performance of the German economy now raises questions about how Germany might fulfil this role.

Post-Westphalian versus a Westphalian Future

In the immediate post-unity period there was a vigorous debate about whether Europe's most powerful state would continue to be its most multilateral. This puzzle was answered in contrasting ways by those who adhere to a Westphalian view, which accords states a privileged monopoly position in the international system originally established by the Peace of Westphalia (1648), and post-Westphalians, who focus on the way that the state's monopoly is being hollowed out by integration and globalization. The prevailing political and academic orthodoxy talked of a post-national state where Germany would be the model in a post-Westphalian Europe characterized by ever higher degrees of integration and interdependence. This view assumed that 'the Rhineland position' of ever closer European integration of successive German governments was a constant and that the economic resources of a unified Germany would allow Germany to steer developments in this direction. Counter-intuitively this endorsement of a post-national, post-Westphalian future coincided with the creation of a unified fully sovereign German state.

The German version of the post Westphalian state was characterized by:

- exaggerated multilateralism
- a readiness to pool sovereignity at a European level
- avoidance of explicit reference to national interest
- reliance on 'soft power'
- avoidance of explicit leadership except in tandem with France.

This post-Westphalian view was questioned by academics such as Hans Peter Schwarz and Christian Hacke, his successor in the chair of Political Science at Bonn University (Schwarz, 1994; Hacke, 1997) and conservative newspapers such as the *Frankfurter Allegemeine Zeitung* who, while they accepted the main lines of German European policy, had a much less post-Westphalian view of the European future. In their analysis nation states would remain the key shapers and Germany should pursue a normalization course in which, like Britain and France, it would talk openly of national interests. The post-unity period, in the view of Hacke and Schwarz, represented a new opportunity structure for Germany in which, free from the constraints of semi-sovereignty, it should pursue a post-classical policy analogous to the UK and France.

Germany, in their view, had been disempowered by a European and foreign policy orientation which played down power considerations. Whereas those who held a post-Westphalian view thought that the constraints on Germany were a product of increasing interdependence which affected all states, Hacke and Schwarz saw those constraints as largely contingent on Germany's post-war situation. The reflexive multilateralism which was the policy response of the post-Westphalians to interdependence was in their view contingent on Germany's post-war semi-sovereignty, and should be replaced by an explicit policy of national interest post-unity. Within Europe, Germany would be the central power by virtue of its greater power resources, and a process of European and German normalization would place Germany in the position of central balancer.

In the Kohl period the influence of the Westphalians remained small, although both Hacke and Schwarz were part of a group that met Kohl on a regular basis to discuss external and European issues. The Kohl period was one in which a reconstituted 'Rhineland vision' (Paterson, 1998) of ever deeper integration provided the *leitmotiv* of European policy.

This vision did evolve somewhat and Kohl backed away from his earlier endorsement of a 'United States of Europe', but this development was occasioned more by the difficulties encountered in securing the ratification of the Maastricht Treaties and EMU than any academic analysis. Under Kohl, Germany continued in a post-Westphalian mode. These contrasting views, with their divergent 'futures', were divided by differing conceptions of power in the international system. Those assumptions were, however, often unspoken, a situation which did little to clarify the debate or to demystify German European policy. Now, more than a decade after unity, it is possible to be more definite about German power resources and their relationship to wider European developments.

The Resources of Power

In the immediate aftermath of unity many analysts exaggerated the extent of German power by overemphasizing the impact of enhanced territory and population and ignoring or downplaying the drag effect that integration of the former German Democratic Republic into the Federal Republic would necessarily bring with it, if it were to be brought up to Western standards. One exception to this tendency was Timothy Garton-Ash: 'The State's external dependencies have been decisively reduced, but the external demands on it have significantly increased, and the resources to meet these demands have not grown commensurately' (Garton-Ash, 1994, pp. 72–3).

In estimates of German power, economic power was normally accorded a central status. This was inherently problematic. It is difficult to extrapolate from economic to political power because the political impact of economic standing is notoriously difficult to measure, *inter alia* because economic power (unlike military power) is often in private hands (Paterson, 1996, p. 175).

There were, however, two ways in which German economic resources and institutions did confer power. The first was in the area of institutionalized monetarism: David Marsh was able to refer to the Bundesbank as 'The Bank that Rules Europe' (Marsh, 1993). In effect, European monetary rates were determined by the Bundesbank as a response to conditions prevailing in the German economy. Post-unity this entailed the export of deflationary pressures throughout Western Europe in order to respond to the problems of an overheating German economy. In promoting the move to EMU and the replacement of the Bundesbank by the European Central Bank (ECB), Germany was able to exercise a great deal of power but, once the ECB was established, its capacity to exercise power was much more diffuse. Whilst this, of course, makes the ECB model much more attractive to Germany's fellow member states, the 'One size fits all' character of EMU has been much less comfortable for the Federal government than the 'one bank (the Bundesbank) fits all' formula of the earlier period.

Pre-eminently, economic power has been exercised through budgetary power. Germany has contributed quite disproportionately to the budget of the European Union. In helping to shape the preferences of other member states in a direction congenial to itself, Germany often deployed side-payments in which political obstacles were smoothed over by economic benefits. This policy was increasingly unpopular at a mass level in the Federal Republic. Germany's role as paymaster of Europe was, however, vigorously defended by Germany's political elite who focused on the benefits derived from the European Union rather than the costs of membership. In the latter years of the Kohl government even Chancellor Kohl, however, began to focus on the costs of Germany's contributor role. The continuing problems for Germany's public finances occasioned by the massive transfers to the Eastern Länder has put huge pressure on the Red–Green government to further reduce Germany's contribution. Chancellor Schröder made the reduction of Germany's contribution a rhetorical priority, but at the Berlin summit in 1999 he was only able to secure very modest progress, given French objections to changes in the financing of agriculture. Agriculture reform was again downplayed in a post-election agreement between President Chirac and Chancellor Schröder. The direction is, however, clear. Germany is unwilling and unable to make the disproportionate contribution it once did in order to secure the policies it favours.

Political Power

Germany's political power to shape decisions and preferences in the European Union was partially a reflection of its budgetary power. This was, however, only one dimension. A central dimension was provided by the elite consensus on the desirability of European integration that has persisted since the late 1950s. This elite consensus and the permissive consensus that characterized mass/elite relations in this area, even when the elite took decisions that did not accord with mass preferences (as in the budgetary area) was a major political resource for successive German governments. It allowed them a great deal of discursive space in which to deploy ideational power in a constitutive manner at the European level. This discursive space was essential in the realization of major European policies. Nowhere was it more central than in the achievement of Economic and Monetary Union where the Kohlian vision (Paterson, 1998) was essential in overcoming domestic and external opposition.

This discursive space has depended on the maintenance of elite consensus and the continuance, albeit in a much weakened form, of 'permissive consensus'. Elite consensus has shown some signs of erosion, however. The rhetoric of European policy (Jeffery and Paterson, 2003) is now notably dualistic and important differences of emphasis have emerged between the national and Land level (see Chapter 8 above). Mass support for the European Union has dropped alarmingly. The effect of these developments is that German politicians now have to look over their shoulders at mass opinion in a way that they are not used to in this area, and increasingly they have to stress specific benefits for Germany. This change is reflected in the larger role of the Finance Ministry in the formulation of German European policy and the increasing readiness of the Chancellor to defend specific German interests.

The Advantages of Congruence

In writings informed by the realist tradition Germany's reflexive or exaggerated multilateralism is seen as demonstrating a lack of power, especially when it is accompanied by the absence of strong central coordinating mechanisms in the British or French manner designed to identify and pursue a focused state interest. This perspective fails to resolve the German puzzle as to why a state that talked of shared European interests was so successful both in realizing its own interests and reconstituting Europe in a way that was notably compatible with the interests and institutions of the Federal Republic. The most convincing resolution of this puzzle is provided in the seminal contribution of Simon Bulmer (Bulmer, 1997).

Bulmer reconceptualizes power as deliberate power, indirect institutional power, non-intentional power and reverse image power. Exaggerated multilateralism and institutional pluralism constrain the use of deliberate power but, in the Bulmerian formulation, the other three faces of power (which stress the congruence between the German and the European levels) empower Germany and provide a basis on which Germany was able to reshape the European milieu (Bulmer, Jeffery and Paterson, 2000). A central element of this reshaping was institutional export in which German institutional assumptions become adopted at the European level. Notable examples included the European

Central Bank and the way in which German DIN (industrial standards) dominated the framing of European standards in the Single European Market.

The accretion of power through institutional export can be sometimes a wasting asset, however. Whilst agreement on DIN standards is of permanent and tangible benefit to Germany, the export of instutionalized monetarism through the ECB has resulted in a significant constraint in German power. In the area of competition policy German assumptions were very influential in the framing of European Union policy given French difficulties with competition. In recent years, however, British ideas and assumptions about competition have been much more influential, and successive German governments have been involved in a series of protracted disputes with the European Commission on competition issues.

A major feature of Germany's power at the European level has been in its management of bilateral relationships in a way that empowers German preferences. In pre-unity Germany, the Franco–German relationship played a key role in German European policy. Its role reflected not only the reconciliation imperative but also the perception that unilateral assertion of German power resources was likely to be counterproductive. All member states require allies in multilateral institutions but the Franco–German relationship reflected German singularity, which I have expressed as 'the leadership avoidance reflex' (Paterson, 1993, p. 10). The original perception of the pre-sovereign years, that discriminations and constraints on Germany could only be lifted in alliance with France, firmed into a core elite belief that a manifest strategic leadership role for Germany, however impressive Germany's power resources had become, would remain closed and that this role could only be played in tandem with France. By 1989/90 the relationship had become heavily institutionalized and very strongly underpinned; it normatively provided such an impressive vehicle for collective action that a well known study writes of 'cooperative hegemony' (Pedersen, 1998).

The Red–Green Government

Post-unity under Kohl the Franco–German relationship retained its centrality and exclusivity and EMU, the central project of his post unity European policy, was 'nested' in the Franco–German relationship. There was, however, some alteration in the terms of relationship and the balance of adjustment shifted to some extent on to France.

Under the Red–Green government the shift in the relationship has been much more manifest. It has lost some of its exclusivity. There is now also an alternative discourse of globalization which was reflected in the Schröder/Blair paper (see Chapter 8 above). Whilst Chancellor Schröder was not able to carry through the Schröder/Blair paper, the key point was more that this was an initiative on a central area where the partner was a state other than France. Even in the institutional debate, Franco–German exclusivity is weakening. It is true that Fischer's Humboldt speech (see 'Three elite visions' below) bears the imprint of the Quai d'Orsay planning staff alongside the input of the German Foreign Office, but subsequent contributions to the debate have been more unilaterally German. Chancellor Schröder insisted on his own initiative at Nice on an IGC in 2004, and the adoption of the SPD *Leitantrag* (main resolution) on Europe was choreographed with a visit by Prime Minister Blair to the Party Conference at Nuremberg rather than being closely coordinated at any stage with France. Part of this erosion is, of course, contingent. It was always much more difficult to operate the relationship during cohabitation (i.e., where different parties hold the French Presidency and Prime Ministership).

There are, however, more far-reaching grounds for thinking that, while the Franco–German relationship will persist as the alliance of first resort, the future shape of the European Union will tend to reduce an exclusive reliance on 'the privileged partnership'; Germany, in order to secure its preferences, will have to move towards a system of multiple bilateral alliances, which I have called multiple bilateralism.

The grounds for anticipating a German shift to multiple bilateralism alongside a continuing (though weakened) Franco–German relationship derive from the future shape of the European Union. EMU could be carried by the Franco–German relationship since the EMU-based EU follows a logic of convergence. Enlargement up to 27 members and possibly even beyond in the next decade entails institutionalizing a logic of diversity. In this larger and more complex EU, gridlock is a danger and there is a clear aggregation of a problem with preferences. In an enlarged Europe over a range of issues the Franco–German relationship is unlikely to be the optimal vehicle for collective action it once was. Even in the run-up to enlargement Germany has had to make very unwelcome concessions to France on agricultural financing at the Berlin summit in 1999 and on voting weights at the Nice IGC. Future German governments will have to devise more attractive incentives for other member states than simple prior Franco–German agreement. Continued public finance shortages in Germany suggest that side-payments as a means of securing support will be less available. Taken together, these factors suggest a widening of German bilateral relationships beyond the Franco–German case. An earlier reinvention of the Dutch–German relationship post-German unity was not especially problematic since Dutch preferences on major issues were by that time close to German preferences and did not therefore present a major challenge to the Franco–German relationship. Britain, Poland and Spain will be more difficult partners to accommodate than a Europe based on the Franco–German alliance, but their support will be essential over a range of issues.

Three Futures

There seem to be three possible futures for multiple bilateralism for Germany. One would be to expand the Franco–German core to a *troika* including the UK, and indeed there have been some developments in this direction in practice, especially in the wake of 11 September. The appearance of a directorate is strongly resented by other member states, however, and the degree to which Britain, France and Germany excluded other member states in their consultations about their response to 11 September produced a series of hostile reactions from other member states.

A more likely form of institutionalizing multiple bilateralism is some variation on differentiated integration/reinforced cooperation/flexibility. Here multiple bilateralism is very explicit and preferred/privileged partners are sought for 'coalitions of the willing' to achieve particular ends. Multiple bilateralism in this model is not viewed as a way of dealing with the aggregation of preferences; rather, the assumption is that overall consensus is not attainable and coalitions of the willing are the way to move integration forward.

The implications of differentiated integration for German European policy have recently been spelt out by Josef Janning and Claus Giering, who argued that the more complicated structures associated with enlargement will require targeted balancing. They go on to suggest that Germany should play the leading role:

The European framework conditions for a leadership role for German European policy appear promising. Size, resources and position make Germany a key state of the enlarged European Union, the necessity of political leadership given the weakness of the old role model of federal integration is scarcely contested and the overstretching of the supranational structures of the EU makes their steering by differentiated integrated groups and contributions by individual states imperative. (Janning and Giering, 2002, p. 692)

The final institutional setting assumes that the obstacles in the way of a formalized core, directorate or differentiated EU remain formidable. In such an enlarged EU, consensus building and aggregation of preferences would become a major problem. It is also assumed that the Franco–German relationship would be too narrow. The obvious answer would be for Germany as Europe's central state to construct a range of bilateral relationships. Germany's much stronger power position would allow it to carry out this role in a way denied to the UK by its much weaker position. Were Germany to adopt this stance it would bring it much closer to the UK position since positions would no longer be foreclosed by a prior Franco–German agreement.

The barriers to such a course remain high, however. It would involve a very major departure from prevailing practice which could only be triggered by a major change of elite perceptions. More obviously, Germany's parlous state of public finances would appear to make selective alliances more necessary but there must be some doubt about the readiness to finance the necessary side-payments in the foreseeable future.

Military Power

Military power is traditionally a key element of state power and here, given Germany's recent past, the exercise of power was at its most multilateral and constrained. Alongside the constraints of multilateralism was a strong self-perception as a civilian power. Force should be employed only as an ultimate resort with resources concentrated on soft power as a way of ensuring peace and stability. The protracted conflict in former Yugoslavia has brought about very significant changes in German security doctrine (see Chapter 9 above). It is now possible to envisage the use of hard power over a much wider geographical area and in a much wider range of circumstances. This change in doctrine and in practice in the case of Kosovo and Afghanistan has been very difficult to sustain in practice, however. All states, with the exception of the USA, have reduced military expenditure since the end of the Cold War. In the German case expenditure was already at a low level in comparative terms. The pressures on the military budget given the parlous state of German public finances and the strongly civilian orientation of its citizens make it very difficult to sustain a military budget which can credibly support Germany's increased responsibilities.

The Paradoxes of Power: Towards a Resolution

The picture that emerges from the foregoing analysis is replete with paradoxes. Both post-Westphalians and Westphalians had assumed an increasing prosperity and weight for the German economy, which could be mobilized for their contrasting policy visions. The weakened state of the German economy, especially its public finances, will constrain the wider influence of German European policy whatever policy vision it pursues. The ratification of EMU and the replacement of the Bundesbank by the European Central Bank is, however, a major step in the post-Westphalian direction and deprives the German state of one of its most potent sources of power.

On the use of political power, we have noted the reduction in the discursive space available to the German political elite. That this formerly conferred a huge advantage in the exercise of influence can be seen by contrasting the situation of the Federal Republic with the elite of the UK, where domestic political pressures so narrowed the discursive space as to rob them of almost all influence at a European level. There has been some change in rhetoric with the invocation of national interest now coexisting with still quite ambitious institutional visions for Europe. The congruence between German interests and the European level is not so comfortable as before. As European integration deepens in the economic area it begins to disturb embedded German interests. It has always been the case that specialist German ministers defended these interests vigorously, but in a whole series of issues the Chancellor now takes the lead in defending German interests (Jeffery and Paterson, 2003). The strained state of German public finances has also increased the role of the Finance Ministry in German European policy and given it a harder edge (Bulmer, Maurer and Paterson, 2001). The imperatives of enlargement and the declining utility of the Franco–German relationship are also pushing the Federal Republic along the path of normality (see above).

On the use of military force the Federal Republic is now more Westphalian. 'The most striking differences for other states will be Germany's enhanced security role and a more up-front insistence on German interests on a case by case basis in the European Union' (Paterson, 2000, p. 38). Normalization is, however, constrained by the underlying public attitudes of what is still a civilian society and the low priority given to security spending and a deep commitment to multilateral fora.

EMU apart, the general thrust has been towards very gradual normalization. Germany continues to be an outlier among large member states in its post-Westphalian character and elite enthusiasm for further institutional integration. There has of course also been a change in the position of other member states, most notably Britain, which has accepted EMU in principle and (perhaps even more surprisingly) the idea of a European constitution.

Three Elite Visions

The imminent prospect of enlargement and the indication that European integration is losing much of its attraction for mass publics has precipitated a new debate about the future shape of European institutions at elite level. Institutional reform was largely avoided at the Amsterdam IGC (1997) and very inadequately addressed at the Nice IGC (2000). At Nice a decision was taken to convene an IGC on institutional reform in 2004. In 2002 a Convention was established to focus debate and work out a draft in the run-up to the 2004 IGC.

Fischer

The debate on the future of European institutions has been very heavily influenced by German contributions and, where other leaders have responded, German views have been taken as the reference point. Indeed the debate was launched by a speech of Joschka Fischer, the Foreign Minister, at Humboldt University in May 2000 (Fischer, 2000a). Fischer's position on European issues strongly reflected the values of the Foreign Ministry, traditionally the most pro-European of the Federal ministries.

His European rhetoric has, however, owed a great deal to Kohl. It was essentially historically driven. This could, of course, allow for changes in policy. In the Kosovo crisis the lessons of history were reversed to justify German intervention. Whereas the past activities of German troops in that area had been seen as barrier to intervention, Fischer cleverly invoked the imperative of preventing mass extermination ('Never again Auschwitz!'). In European policy Fischer has been a strong 'integration deepener' and an advocate of close cooperation with France.

The planning staffs of the French and German foreign ministries were very heavily consulted in the preparation of the Humboldt speech. This involvement is reflected in the future-oriented and 'blue skies' quality of the institutional prescriptions which build on neither existing national nor European institutions. The vision is federal but it is very vague about institutional specifics. Either the European Council or a directly elected Commission President will fulfil the government function. There will be a bicameral Parliament in which one chamber will be composed of national representatives and a state chamber modelled either on the US Senate or the Bundesrat. He is in favour of a constitutional treaty which should enumerate a Charter of Rights, a division of competences between the European institutions and a division of competences between the federal construction and the member states.

The federal model is not a simple institutional export with only the Charter of Human rights being obviously inspired by the Basic Law. In this model the balance between state and European level is to be framed on the basis of a lean federation with only recognized federal functions at the European level. The speech did, however, revive the idea of an avant-garde of states committed to a maximal view of integration who would be allowed to press ahead. This idea of differentiated integration had first surfaced at a political level in the Schäuble and Lamers paper of 1994, although it had long featured in academic discourse. It is a view held by those who fear that enlargement will lead to dilution and gridlock. Although Fischer claimed to be addressing the legitimacy deficit, this is only catered for by the first parliamentary chamber. It is clear that the priority is the European Union's capacity to act: 'What we in the EU lack is decision making structures that guarantee swift action' (Fischer, 2000a).

Schröder

Gerhard Schröder represents a much clearer break with the Rhineland rhetoric than Joschka Fischer. In the early period of his government he constantly invoked a normalization discourse in which a new Germany, liberated from the constraints of Germany's past, would be able to stand up for national interests:

> My generation and those following are Europeans because we want to be not because we have to be. That makes us freer in dealing with others ... I am convinced that our European partners want to have a self-confident German partner which is more calculable than a German partner with an inferiority complex. Germany standing up for its national interests will be just as natural as France or Britain standing up for theirs. (Bulmer, Jeffery and Paterson, 2000, p. 109)

In the ensuing period Schröder often invoked German national interests as in his resistance to the liberalization of the European car market in 2002 and a whole series of competition issues which bought him into conflict with the European Commission. Alongside his role as pragmatic and stubborn defender of specific German interests, Schröder was identified with the *Leitantrag* on Europe to the SPD Party Conference in November 2001 (SPD, 2001). The *Leitantrag* is much less 'blue skies' than the Fischer plan. Institutionally the suggestions build on existing institutions. The Commission, somewhat surprisingly given Schröder's difficulties with the Prodi Commission, is to be turned into a strong executive. The European Parliament should be strengthened and given full budgetary authority, and the European Council should be turned into a Bundesrat (i.e., representatives of state governments).

Like Fischer, the *Leitantrag* envisages a written constitution. The two proposals are very similar here apart from the *Leitantrag* talking explicitly of a division of competences between four levels of government from the European to the municipal. At first sight the Schröder plan looks more integrationist than Fischer's but, although the institutional structures are more clearly spelt out, the overall thrust is arguably less integrationist. There is no reference to avant-garde states and, in a number of policy areas including agriculture, structural economic policy and social protection (*Öffentliche Daseinvorsorge*), competences are to be returned to the state and substate level. The *Leitantrag* also contains a strong endorsement of the Lisbon process and the open method of coordination which is based not on the Commission but the European Council, and a great deal of discretion is left for national authorities.

Stoiber

Edmund Stoiber, the unsuccessful Chancellor-candidate of the CDU/CSU in 2002, presented his vision to Humboldt University on November 2001 (Stoiber, 2001). His vision has a British feel to it since it concentrates not on new institutional structures, about which he has relatively little to say, but on what sort of policies a Europe of 27 or 30 members needs to address. He is also much more explicitly and consistently concerned with the question of legitimacy, or *Akzeptanz*. His answer is a much clearer, more explicit division of competences with a much tighter ring-fencing of national competences against European intervention. Although some policy competences, such as internal security, would be better dealt with at the European level, he argues strongly for a renationalization of competences in agriculture regional policy and subsidy controls.

Stoiber is against the creation of a European Constitution, preferring instead to talk of a European basic treaty. In earlier statements he was against a referendum on such a document but by 2001 he argued that 'the acceptability problem' was so great that it would need to be ratified by referendum. The impact of referenda in the Weimar Republic ruled out the use of referenda at the federal level post-1945 and Stoiber's suggestion breaks a key taboo on the exclusive merits of representative government in the Federal Republic.

There is a striking degree of overlap between the Schröder and Stoiber visions. Still much more far-reaching institutionally than British or French assumptions, the policy frameworks now advocated show a considerable retreat from earlier ambitions. Policies and visions are now best viewed as dualistic with ambitious future institutional plans flanked by pragmatic, interest-driven policies.

Reconstituting Europe

Post-unity the instinct of the Kohl government was to deepen rather than dilute integration, and Economic and Monetary Union was the centrepiece of this policy. Externally EMU enjoyed a great deal of support from other member states who viewed it as a way of buying into German monetary stability through the adoption of a Bundesbank model for the ECB, which was to be located in Frankfurt. It also offered other states some voice, an option which they did not enjoy when European-wide interest rates were, in effect, set by the Bundesbank. German fears about the way in which loose budgetary discipline in other member states might undermine the goal of monetary stability were addressed by the Stability Pact of 1996, which was designed to ensure monetary stability even in recession.

Internally there was little enthusiasm at the popular level where support never amounted to more than one-third of those polled. The Bundesbank, unsurprisingly, always entertained considerable reservations. Contrary to his normal political style, where he would wait until the indications were favourable, Chancellor Kohl pursued Economic and Monetary Union with considerable zeal, invoking a rhetoric which equated support for EMU with support for peace and good Europeanism. The European integrationist code was still widely shared among the German elite and Kohl's decision to make EMU a test of Europeanness prevailed against those doubters, including for a time Gerhard Schröder and Edmund Stoiber, who sought to capitalize on public hostility. The ratification of the move to the third stage of

Economic and Monetary Union was seen by the Kohl government as Germany's principal contribution to European-wide prosperity and stability. Kohl had been disappointed by the failure to make significant progress on political union at Maastricht, but comforted himself with the argument that EMU on its own possesses an irresistible integrative logic.

In the event the impact has been mixed. Paradoxically EMU has been most uncomfortable for Germany. Joining at a disadvantageous rate, it has been negatively affected by interest rates designed to reflect pan-European conditions at a time when Germany has a total of 4 million unemployed. It has also looked at times as if Germany's overstretched public finances would lead to it potentially falling foul of the provision of the Stability Pact which had been designed to ensure that other states met German standards. It was only with difficulty and strong support from the UK for Germany that the European Commission was dissuaded from sending Germany a strong formal warning letter on the potential size of its budget deficit in the spring of 2002. After the election in October 2002, Finance Minister Eichel conceded that Germany would overshoot the 3 per cent budget deficit in 2003. The Stability Pact criteria appear very unlikely to be met by France, Germany and Italy, its largest members. This is widely perceived as damaging, but no formula on its replacement has been agreed. There is a now a question mark against what had been the central German precondition for the move to the third stage of EMU.

Germany and the Wider Europe: Enlargement

Alone among the larger member states of the EU, Germany has claimed to be consistent proponent of deepening and widening. Whilst this may have been true at a rhetorical level, at an operational level the Kohl government gave deepening (in the form of EMU) a very clear priority. Great care was taken given the public's lack of enthusiasm not to initiate a debate about enlargement until the move to the third stage of EMU was safely ratified.

Enlargement commands wide support among the German political and economic elite. For the political elite enlargement is seen as the best guarantor of economic and political stability, a condition from which Germany (because of its geographical position) would benefit proportionately. For the economic elite enlargement offers the prospect of a new European division of labour where German firms could outsource the most labour-intensive processes and escape the labour-market rigidities that have so weakened the German economy.

This general endorsement comes with a number of qualifications. Perhaps most importantly at a budgetary level the Federal Republic, like the UK, has given a central priority to containing the costs of enlargement. This concern made the Federal government for a long time unwilling to yield to the preferences of the applicant countries for a fixed timetable since this was seen as likely to create inexorable pressures to settle whatever the cost. The same concern informs the stance of the German and British governments on the weighting of Council votes. Both were determined at the Nice IGC to avoid a weighting of votes in the Council where a coalition of small poor states could outvote the large, rich states.

On institutional questions more widely, the Federal government, here unlike the UK government, has been worried about the potential impact of enlargement on the dynamic of integration. It is this fear which underlies the various visions (see preceding section) and an enthusiasm for differentiated integration and coalitions of the willing in the areas of Justice and Home Affairs and Common Foreign and Security Policy.

The manifest determination of the Kohl government, the manner in which the process was governed by a timetable and the supportive stance of the great majority of European governments left little room for sectoral and territorial interventions into the EMU process. On enlargement, however, these conditions have been reversed. It is not a 'vision thing' as EMU was for Kohl; there is no equivalent fixed timetable, and the attitudes of existing member governments diverge widely. These uncertainties leave a much greater role for sectoral objections. Under Kohl German agriculture prevented meaningful negotiations about that key element of the enlargement dossier. The anxieties of the German trade union movement ensured that freedom of movement of labour became a difficult issue, and an extended transition of seven years is foreseen in relation to Poland.

The lack of enthusiasm at a popular level combined with the fears of some sectoral lobbies to persuade the Schröder/Fischer government to move cautiously on enlargement. Schröder, for instance, insisted that Günter Verheugen, a German Commissioner, take on the enlargement brief in the Prodi Commission. German caution was also motivated by calculations about the need to persuade France. French opposition to reform of the CAP in particular has been a major complicating factor. Rather than tackling this head-on, the German government assumed that French attitudes would be changed by the pressure of the World Trade Organization negotiations and they have failed to exert significant pressure in France. The Central European states, in particular, who had seen Germany as their *Anwalt* (advocate) in the enlargement negotiations, have been disappointed by Germany's cautious though still positive attitude. Disappointment has been greatest in Poland, with whom Kohl had cultivated a close relationship, and the Czech Republic, where relationships have been further soured by statements by the Bavarian government linking enlargement to re-examination of the Benes decrees which legalized the expulsion of the Sudeten Germans in 1946. Polish opinion was enraged by ungenerous EU proposals on agriculture but heartened by the Federal government's defence of the Polish position on future voting weights at the Nice summit. This presented a stark contrast to the failure of the Federal government to take a similar stand on the proposed weighting for Hungary and the Czech Republic.

Despite those difficulties the interest of the German political and economic elite in further enlargement remains strong and the Federal government has endeavoured to reassure its central European neighbours of its continued commitment; the likelihood is that enlargement will proceed in 2004 and that the consequence will be ever closer relations between Germany and its eastern neighbours as it is Germany that will continue to invest in and trade disproportionately with those states.

Germany's impact on the applicant countries is very visible at the level of society and economy. All of the German party-political foundations have a presence in the applicant countries and *Modell Deutschland* has been a very potent model of emulation for the states on its border. Interaction is most visible at the economic level. Germany is the most important trading partner of the Central and East European states on a regional basis but the concentration does not 'lend Germany the power ascribed to either a hegemonic or even dominant state' (Sperling, 2001, p. 402).

Germany is also by far the largest foreign direct investor in the area. While a large number of German firms do not lend themselves to the exercise of deliberate German power given their widely disparate interests and preferences, they arguably provide 'an intangible or soft' form of power for Germany, primarily by transferring German labour, social welfare or even manufacturing practices to Central and Eastern Europe (Sperling, 2001, p. 404).

Germany and Russia

Russia was necessarily a key element in German aspirations to wider peace and prosperity in post-Wall Europe. In the immediate post-unity period vast amounts of German public aid and private investment were poured into the Soviet Union with the hope of encouraging stabilization.

In the absence of settled institutional structures, administrative competence and plausible programmes for economic reform, aid simply disappeared into a black hole. German attempts to interest other leaders in matching German aid to the Soviet Union were similarly unsuccessful.

Throughout the early 1990s there was a strong interministerial dispute between the so called Muscovites and the Warshavistes on the place of Russia in the future security architecture of Europe. The Muscovites, centred on the Foreign Ministry, were concerned not to destabilize the Soviet Union/Russia and were at pains to avoid further loss of face for Russia. They gave the maintenance of stability in Russia a higher priority than the security concerns of the Central and Eastern European states. These priorities entailed resisting the Eastern enlargement of NATO and continuing to give some credence to OSCE, an organization that strongly reflected Russian preferences.

The Warshavistes, by contrast, were fundamentally concerned with the enlargement as far as possible of the existing security community. The Warshavistes, who were concentrated in the Defence Ministry, were strongly in favour of the expansion of NATO to meet the security fears of the Central and East European states. For some time the dispute between the Muscovites and the Warshavistes was unresolved but, after the USA's preference for enlargement became unmistakably clear, Chancellor Kohl threw his weight behind the Warshavistes. Germany, nevertheless, continued to give a great deal of weight to reassuring Russia through what was often called 'sauna diplomacy' between Kohl and Yeltsin.

Relations were further strained by the Kosovo crisis and the German support for Allied intervention. Indeed the protracted conflict in former Yugoslavia had placed a continued strain on the relations since Russia was a consistent supporter of Serbia, while the German position might be characterized as 'anyone but Serbia'. The Federal government, which held the EU Presidency, appointed Martii Ahtisaari, the President of Finland, as the principal peace negotiator partly because he was, *inter alia, persona grata* in Russia. Russia under the German presidency became more deeply involved when the former Russian Prime Minister, Viktor Chernomyrdin, also became a negotiator and Russian troops became involved in peacekeeping measures.

The election of George Bush in 2000 and his proposed missile defence system aroused enormous anger and anxieties in Russia and considerable nervousness in Germany (as in other European states). In the early 1980s Kohl had unmistakably aligned himself four-square with the USA in the crisis occasioned by the stationing of Intermediate Range Missiles. Post-2000, the situation was much less clear. The wider impact of September 11 has been to defuse much of the tension between Russia and the USA as the USA has sought allies in its global anti-terrorism campaign. The changed climate has also allowed closer relations between Germany and Russia to flourish. President Putin, as a former KGB officer in the GDR, speaks fluent German and has laid an especial emphasis on Germany as a partner. In the new situation Russia feels less encircled and is reconciled to the future EU and NATO membership of the Baltic republics. For its part Germany now soft-pedals the issues of possible human rights violations in Chechnya. Kaliningrad/Königsberg has moved up as an issue of importance since the probable membership of Lithuania in the EU will effectively cut Kaliningrad off from Russia. Russia sought German help to waive border regulations in this area but the issue of the external border regimes is one in which Germany has a very high stake in maintaining a consistent and tight policy. Germany has been especially concerned to maintain tight external EU borders since it would be most severely affected by uncontrolled migration and organized crime. This new German–Russian closeness was again evident in the Iraq crisis where Germany has aligned itself with France and Russia against Britain and the United States. How stable this Franco–German–Russian alliance will prove to be remains an open question.

Conclusion

Neither the record of the past ten years nor the foreseeable future completely supports either the post-Westphalian or the Westphalian view of the impact of German European policy. Both schools assumed a central role for Germany. In the post-Westphalian school, Germany would drive Europe towards a post-Westphalian future towards which it is already being pushed by the logic of integration and interdependence. In the Westphalian school Germany's power resources make it the central power. The post-Westphalian view of Germany as driver of European integration reached its apogee under Kohl. It was expressed in Franco–German terms but, although they were singing from the same hymn sheet, the German voice was noticeably louder and there was a general perception that the score owed more to it than to its French counterparts. In this period post-Westphalianism appeared to correspond to the deep structures of the EU, of which Germany appeared to be a decisive shaper, and to the mind-set of the German political elite.

In the longer term the picture is more complex. The weakness in the performance of the German economy has severely compromised

Germany's ability to act as the central player in either a Westphalian or a post-Westphalian sense. Those who believe that Germany will continue to operate as a decisive post-Westphalian player rely on the path dependency created by EMU (Kohl's most signal achievement). The strains associated with the operation of the stability pact do, however, cast some doubt on the strength of this path dependency. This logic of convergence is, however, counter-balanced by a logic of divergence associated with enlargement which will put Germany under pressure to pursue a policy of multiple bilateralism, ad hoc coalitions and interest-driven policies.

In this complex environment the German political elite has retained large elements of post-Westphalianism. The new generation is more comfortable talking in terms of power, but it remains adjectival. Power is legitimized by reference to some desirable state, as in civilian power. In relation to Europe the continued post-Westphalianism (see 'Elite visions') of the political elite is coming under increased pressure from mass opinion which is extremely sceptical about Germany's paymaster role, and which no longer shares even the modified Rhineland vision of the political elite. Mass opinion is in favour of pushing through German preferences without the sort of compromise that has characterized the policy style of all post-war German governments. Unfortunately, whilst mass opinion is in favour of pushing through German preferences it is against the use of budgetary power which has helped make this happen in the past.

The increasingly shrilly expressed mass preferences have also significantly reduced the discursive space which was central to the ability of German governments to put themselves at the centre of European bargains. This is most evident on economic and social issues where domestic pressure fuelled through sectoral and party channels has significantly dented the wiggle room available for German governments. These pressures help explain Germany's weakish implementation record and its new preference for non-binding modes of governance such as the Lisbon process. These sectoral and popular pressures are much less present in the area of Common Foreign and Security Policy (Miskimmon and Paterson, 2003) and institutional vision. Here a lack of political saliency allows the German elite more autonomy, and the constraints are more obviously external. The freedom still available to the German elite on institutional questions was effectively deployed by Joschka Fischer to launch the debate on the institutional future of the European institutions. By utilizing a 'blue skies' approach, Fischer increased his first-mover advantage in dislodging existing preconceptions. The debate began therefore from a different point than it would otherwise have done. Few expect the outcome of the IGC in 2004 to be identical with Fischer's or other German drafts but it will be different from what would have emerged had he not precipitated the debate. Eloquent testimony to this point is given by the new readiness of the British government to talk of a European Constitution, a position unimaginable before Fischer launched the debate.

Germany will remain disproportionately central to the future prospects of stability and prosperity in the New Europe. It will be at the centre of EMU and enlargement; however, its capacity to shape these developments (whilst still impressive) will be compromised by the weakening performance of the economy. In the immediate post-Wall period it seemed obvious to William Wallace that Germany's resources made it a natural hegemon (Wallace, 1991, p. 167) which would drive on integration. Whilst this view may always have been a little overplayed, there is some danger, if Germany's poor economic performance continues, that Germany – in Anne Marie Le Gloannec's phrase – will exercise a 'hegemony of weakness' (Le Gloannec, 1993), which over time might unscramble Germany's European vocation and its unrivalled contribution to the reconstitution of Europe.

11

Towards an Open Society? Citizenship and Immigration

SIMON GREEN

For several decades now, the cluster of issues around immigration and citizenship has figured high on the agenda of domestic politics in Germany. One key reason for their prominent political profile is that successive governments have failed to fully address the consequences of the relatively large numbers of immigrants that Germany has received and continues to receive. However, the last decade has seen policy undergo a number of fundamental changes: not only has Germany's highly symbolic asylum system been reformed, but its restrictive nationality laws have been liberalized to encompass a more inclusive definition of citizenship. More recently, immigration policy itself has shifted tentatively from prevention towards management. Following a brief outline of the main phases of immigration and the political responses to them, this chapter will discuss how and why this transformation has taken place and, in particular, it will ask whether the changes that have been introduced have created a more open, multicultural society.

Phases of Immigration

Although immigration had already been a factor in imperial Germany (Brubaker, 1992), Germany's main experience of immigration dates back to the end of the Second World War. In a first migratory phase, some 8 million refugees and displaced persons from Germany's former eastern territories arrived in the West between 1945 and 1950. This was followed by almost 3 million GDR citizens up until the construction of the Berlin Wall in 1961. Then, between 1954 and 1973, around 9.5 million non-nationals immigrated to Germany, consisting mostly of so-called 'guest workers' (*Gastarbeiter*) from Mediterranean countries, who had been actively recruited to work in German industry on a temporary basis. Almost 4 million of these remained in the country after formal recruitment ended in November 1973, and it is this group which henceforth constituted the rump of Germany's foreign population (*Ausländer*). After 1973, the focus of migration shifted to dependants, as the remaining labour migrants began to bring their spouses and children to West Germany as part of the process of permanent settlement. Even today, the size of this migration remains considerable: over 250,000 dependants entered Germany between 1996 and 1999 alone.

From 1978 onwards, asylum-seekers emerged as a numerically significant source of immigration to Germany. Between 1985 and 2001, some 2.6 million new asylum applications were made, and even though an average of only around 14,000 applications was recognized annually during this period (corresponding to a recognition rate of decisions made of just 8.3 per cent), it must be assumed that many people have stayed on illegally after their claims were rejected. Another important group of immigrants has been the over 4.2 million ethnic Germans from Poland, Romania and most recently the former Soviet Union who arrived in Germany between 1950 and 2001. There have been other smaller groups, including around 90,000 *Gastarbeiter* from Vietnam and Mozambique who were working in the GDR at the time of unification, as well as about 120,000 Russian Jewish immigrants. Finally, several hundred thousand war refugees from former Yugoslavia were granted temporary entry during the 1990s, although by 2000 all but around 40,000 had returned home. All told, West Germany, and later united Germany, has witnessed net immigration (i.e., inflows minus outflows) of non-Germans for all but ten years between 1955 and 1999 (Münz and Ulrich, 1999, pp. 16–20). Between 1991 and 1995, net immigration averaged 335,000 persons per annum, although this fell to just under 60,000 between 1996 and 2000.

By the end of 2001, Germany's non-national population had thus risen to a shade over 7.3 million, representing 8.9 per cent of the population (Table 11.1); it included 1.9 million Turkish nationals, 1.1 million persons from former Yugoslavia and 1.9 million citizens of other EU countries. Of these 7.3 million non-nationals, 55 per cent had lived in Germany for at least ten years, rising to 67 per cent for Turks and 74 per cent for Italians. Roughly 96 per cent of immigrants lived in the west, where they were concentrated in urban areas: cities such as Frankfurt am Main, Stuttgart and Munich all had non-national populations in excess of 20 per cent of their inhabitants. At the beginning of the new millennium, Germany therefore bore many of the hallmarks of a culturally diverse country of immigration.

TABLE 11.1 *Key data for non-national population in
Germany, 1982–2001*

Year	Non-national population	Percentage of total population	Naturalization rate (%)
1982	4,666,900	7.6	0.3
1983	4,534,900	7.4	0.3
1984	4,363,600	7.1	0.3
1985	4,378,900	7.2	0.3
1986	4,512,700	7.4	0.3
1987	4,240,500	6.9	0.3
1988	4,489,100	7.3	0.4
1989	4,845,900	7.7	0.4
1990	5,342,500	8.4	0.4
1991	5,882,300	7.3	0.5
1992	6,495,800	8.0	0.6
1993	6,878,100	8.5	0.6
1994	6,990,500	8.6	0.9
1995	7,173,900	8.8	1.0
1996	7,314,000	8.9	1.2
1997	7,365,800	9.0	1.1
1998	7,319,600	8.9	1.5
1999	7,343,600	8.9	2.5
2000	7,296,800	8.9	2.6
2001	7,318,628	8.9	2.4

Note: West Germany before 1991.
Source: Statistisches Bundesamt; own calculations.

A Contradictory Policy Area

Yet despite the evident diversity in its population, the policy framework has traditionally operated under the assumption that Germany was 'not a country of immigration' (*Deutschland ist kein Einwanderungsland*: Joppke, 1999, pp. 62–99; for an opposing perspective, see Ronge, 2000). This assumption, which first appeared in a strategic policy document in 1977 (see Katzenstein, 1987, p. 239), complemented the historical conception of German nationhood as ethnically and culturally exclusive (cf. Brubaker, 1992; Green, 2000, pp. 105–13). Together, these two self-definitions meant that successive German governments pointedly refused to adopt the kinds of policies common in other countries with similar patterns of immigration, such as formal labour migration mechanisms and quotas, as well as a simple residence and more a inclusive citizenship policy. The notion of Germany as a non-immigration country continued to underpin government policy until the 1998 election, even though by then the realities of globalization meant that the issue for Germany had long evolved from the prevention of immigration to shaping it according to its own interests.

This paradox between large-scale and permanent immigration to Germany and a policy framework based largely on the principle of restriction has been reflected in the confusing patchwork of laws, regulations and non-binding guidelines which apply in this area. Strictly speaking, each of the different sources of migration listed above is a discrete policy issue, with different legal instruments and moral standards in play. Of course, as in other countries, the political boundaries between the various questions are often blurred, especially between asylum-seekers and long-term residents. In the interests of brevity, this chapter will also deliberately oversimplify by restricting itself to using the terms 'immigrants' and 'non-nationals' interchangeably.

The problems created by this contradictory legal framework and the lack of uniform and coherent standards have long plagued the entire policy area. For instance, work permits have traditionally been regulated independently of residence policy. This has meant that, because of Germany's status as a non-immigration country, immigrants could be refused residence permits, even if they were in employment or actually creating jobs through their own business (cf. *Der Spiegel*, 4 March 2002). In particular, the legal incorporation of immigrants, via access to permanent residence status and ultimately citizenship via naturalization, has been very slow. In 2001, only 45 per cent of *Ausländer* possessed a permanent residence permit (nominally available after five years), compared to 73 per cent of immigrants with more than six years' residence.

Moreover, the traditional ethnic and cultural exclusivity of German citizenship effectively ruled out high levels of naturalization of immigrants, despite the CDU/CSU–FDP government admitting in 1984 that 'no state can in the long run accept that a significant part of its population remain outside the political community' (*Bundestagsdrucksache* 10/2071, quoted in Brubaker, 1992, p. 78). The proportion of resident non-nationals obtaining citizenship each year (the naturalization rate) has thus been much lower in Germany than in other European immigration countries, in particular France and the Netherlands. Indeed, throughout the 1980s, Germany's naturalization rate failed to rise above a meagre 0.4 per cent annually (Table 11.1). Its low level was compounded by the fact that the ascription of German citizenship at birth was limited to descent from one parent (and before 1975, solely the father), known as the *ius sanguinis* principle. With 21 per cent of non-nationals in 2001 actually being born in Germany, the otherwise counter-intuitive notion of a 'third generation of *Ausländer*' is thereby made a reality. By contrast, in most other countries of immigration, children of non-national parents born within that country would have been automatically granted citizenship at birth (the *ius soli* principle).

Yet whereas the legal status of immigrants in Germany was unusually restrictive in international comparison, Germany occupied the other end of the spectrum in terms of receiving asylum-seekers. A number of factors combined to make Germany by far the most popular asylum destination in Europe by 1980: its constitutionally guaranteed right to asylum in Article 16 of the Basic Law, the (initially) generous social benefits, a large established immigrant community, the sheer size of the German economy, and the absence of any other possibility after 1973 for labour migrants to enter the country legally. The 2.6 million new applications for asylum made in Germany between 1985 and 2001 thus compared with 0.6 million in France and just 7,500 in Portugal. A gradual, but severe, reduction in the social conditions for asylum-seekers since the 1980s has done nothing to dent Germany's image as an unusually liberal asylum country, even if recognition rates (as noted above) have been anything but liberal.

This combination of issues and historical developments forms the backdrop against which party political disputes over immigration have taken place since 1980. On the one hand, the parties of the left – the SPD, Greens and later PDS – have argued that Germany's immigration history necessitated inclusive residence and citizenship policies, including an overriding humanitarian obligation towards asylum-seekers. On the other hand, the conservative CDU/CSU have maintained that Germany was not a country of immigration, that the burden of integration lay in the first instance with non-nationals, and that the overriding concern in asylum policy should be to prevent misuse by 'bogus' applicants. Of course, when taken on its own merits, the CDU/CSU's logic held good: because Germany did not proactively seek to increase its population through migration, it was not a country of immigration in the sense that Canada or the USA is. But this argument overlooked the pluralistic reality of life in many German cities, as well ignoring the privileged status of ethnic Germans, mainly from the former Soviet Union. Even today this group of people, whose ancestors often emigrated to Russia centuries ago, enjoy the right (albeit now heavily qualified) to immigrate and to receive automatic German citizenship.

These conceptual differences between the parties have meant that immigration is now one of the recurring political issues in modern German politics, even if, as the respected *Politbarometer* polls show, its status in public consciousness has in recent years tended to be more sporadic. The role of hard-nosed electoral calculations should also not be underestimated in party differences: research has shown that, whereas naturalized immigrants vote overwhelmingly for parties of the left, ethnic Germans vote heavily for the CDU/CSU (Wüst, 2002). At the same time, extreme or populist parties in Germany have not been able to capitalize on immigration in the same way as in countries such as France, Denmark or the Netherlands. This is the result of a number of reasons. First, the electoral system, together with the deliberately broad appeal of the CDU/CSU, provides little political opportunity for fringe parties to break into the political mainstream. In addition, the absence of personalities with a genuine mass appeal among right-wing parties has meant that the occasional successes of the *Republikaner* party and the more extreme German People's Union (DVU) at Land elections over the past decade have remained one-off phenomena. Finally, given Germany's past, there is arguably also a moral imperative not to support such parties, which does not exist in the same way in other European countries.

This complex and sensitive policy area has been in flux since the early 1990s. One by one, key issues of immigration and citizenship have been addressed and reformed. The aim of the rest of this chapter is to trace and analyse this transformation in more detail, beginning with the central importance of unification for this policy area. It will then discuss the pressures which led to two critical pieces of legislation in the course of the last decade, both of which addressed a different aspect: the reform of asylum in 1993, which also covered ethnic German immigration, and the reform of citizenship in 1999. The chapter will also address the debate over the introduction of Germany's first ever formal immigration law in 2002. As the chapter will show, the cumulative effect of these developments has been fundamentally to transform the self-perception of Germany as a 'non-immigration country'. Following a brief consideration of Germany's approach to the Europeanization of immigration, the chapter will conclude with a discussion of how and why integration is emerging as the key question for the future.

The Impact of Unification

One of the most striking aspects of Germany's immigration policy is the contrast between its stability prior to unification, and the fundamental policy changes that followed it. Between 1949 and 1989, just one law was passed regulating the residence and legal integration of non-ethnic Germans: the 1965 Foreigners' Law (*Ausländergesetz*). This basically made the granting and renewal of residence permits subject to the 'interests of the Federal Republic of Germany'. As these interests, in turn, explicitly excluded the notion that Germany was a country of immigration, it was unsurprising that the administration implemented the law restrictively, even after changes to the secondary legislation in 1978 introduced some improvements to residence permits (Joppke, 1999, pp. 66–7).

Nowhere is this sense of stability more evident than in citizenship policy. Throughout the period 1949–89, membership of the German citizenry was defined by the *Reichs- und Staatsangehörigkeitsgesetz* (RuStAG) of 22 July 1913, complemented by Article 116 of the Basic Law. Not only did these two provisions grant a guarantee of acceptance to German expellees from the east, but they also served to undermine the legitimacy of the GDR by including all East Germans in their definition of 'German'. Throughout the duration of Germany's division, western politicians of all parties had studiously avoided compromising the legitimacy of West Germany's claim to represent all Germans (the so-called *Alleinvertretungsanspruch*). A key component of this claim lay in the fact that West Germany explicitly adopted a definition of citizenship which included all citizens of the GDR (Green, 2001b, pp. 85–6). Therefore, it was politically not possible to change the 1913 law fundamentally as long as the GDR existed. The only meaningful elaboration of policy was the formulation of the Guidelines on Naturalization in 1977 (*Einbürgerungsrichtlinien*), which also first institutionalized Germany's rejection of dual citizenship. This particular principle was to become crucial in policy discussions during the 1990s, as the CDU/CSU doggedly insisted that the avoidance of dual citizenship be maintained wherever possible (see below).

However, unification changed the framework within which German immigration policy as a whole was formulated (Green, 2001b). The increase in global travel opportunities that accompanied the end of the Cold War, especially in the former eastern bloc, enabled many more people to take up not only Germany's offer of safe haven for political refugees, but also its right of return for ethnic German minorities hitherto trapped behind the Iron Curtain. The end of the GDR also finally made a reform of citizenship policy politically possible.

These changes to both the external and internal parameters for policy formulation have helped produce a marked increase in the number of initiatives in this area since unification. First, a revised *Ausländergesetz* came into force just three months after unification itself, on 1 January 1991, although this had been the subject of painstaking negotiations between the governing CDU/CSU and FDP parties during the whole of the 1980s. The law was presented by the government as constituting a comprehensive modernization of the previous policy regime, even though it in fact represented a formalization of existing administrative practice in many areas (Green, 2003). However, it did introduce a brand-new 'simplified naturalization' procedure (*erleichterte Einbürgerung*) initially limited until 1995 for immigrants either below the age of 23 or with over 15 years' residence. It also set the fees for this procedure at just DM100 (Green, 2001a).

A second area to see fundamental change after unification was the hitherto unrestricted immigration of ethnic Germans (*Aussiedler*). Already in 1987, their number had begun to rise, and in the five years between 1988 and 1992, almost 1.5 million arrived in West and united Germany. In 1990, a law was passed requiring ethnic Germans to apply for entry to Germany *before* leaving their home country, as well as demanding evidence of German language competence as an indicator of cultural membership of this group.

The Reform of Asylum

However, the aspect of immigration which overshadowed all others in the early 1990s was the question of asylum-seekers, and the radical changes to Germany's asylum system which were introduced in the so-called asylum compromise of 6 December 1992. This comprehensive deal between the CDU/CSU, SPD and FDP (but not the Greens) over immigration represented the high point of the sense of crisis that had been brewing in the asylum system since the 1980s (Marshall, 1992, pp. 253–6; Marshall, 2000, pp. 80–96). More immediately, the crisis had been caused by the high absolute numbers of asylum-seekers during the 1980s (averaging about 70,000 annually) and by the rapid increase in applications following unification, (from 193,063 in 1990 to 256,112 in 1991, peaking at 438,191 in 1992). This total represented an all-time European record, and saw Germany take two-thirds of all asylum-seekers in the EU that year.

More than ten years on, it is easy to underestimate the sense of crisis that pervaded Germany in the summer and autumn of 1992. That August, the eastern German city of Rostock was rocked by the worst anti-immigrant riots in Germany's post-war history, and images were flashed around the world of locals applauding as neo-Nazis launched yet another assault on the asylum-seekers' residence in the suburb of Lichtenhagen. Far right parties had scored well at individual *Land* elections in Bremen the previous year, and in the states of Baden-Württemberg and Schleswig-Holstein that spring. Most tragically, neo-Nazis firebombed a Turkish residence in the northern German town of Mölln in November 1992, causing the death of three people.

In the aftermath, millions of Germans took to the streets in the form of candle-light vigils (*Lichterketten*) to express their outrage at such events, as immigration and asylum soared to become the most important issue in the *Politbarometer* opinion polls.

Against this background, there was inexorable public pressure on the parties to act, focusing mainly on the SPD, which had hitherto refused to agree to amending the constitutional asylum provision as demanded by the CDU/CSU (Green, 2001a, pp. 92–5). Faced with increasingly hostile public opinion, the SPD reluctantly agreed to give up its opposition, but in return insisted on a comprehensive deal on immigration policy, to include ethnic German migration and citizenship policy (Figure 11.1).

The effect of these changes, which came into force on 1 July 1993, was significant. In the short term, they certainly achieved the desired drastic reduction in the number of asylum seekers. By 1998, new applications had fallen to below 100,000 for the first time in ten years, although Germany remains one of the long-term favourite destinations for asylum seekers in the EU. Moreover, the deal, in combination with two other key pieces of legislation, effectively drew a line underneath ethnic German immigration, which from then on were termed *Spätaussiedler*. Any person born after 31 December 1992 seeking ethnic German status has to prove that they were disadvantaged because of their cultural identity. In addition, the quota for *Spätaussiedler* was lowered in 1999 to just over 103,000 (Beauftragte der Bundesregierung, 2001).

Asylum Policy	*Other Aspects of Immigration*
• 'Safe Third Country' rule introduced: applicants passing through any countries bordering on Germany are automatically rejected	• A *de facto* quota of 225,000 p.a. on ethnic German immigration • Simplified naturalization procedure due to expire in 1995 changed to permanent entitlement (*Rechtsanspruch*)
• 'White list' of safe countries of origin introduced: applicants from these countries are automatically rejected	• Fees for standard naturalizations dropped from up to DM5,000 to DM500
• Fast-track 'airport procedure' set up in Frankfurt	• Comprehensive reform of citizenship law (RuStAG) promised by CDU/CSU

FIGURE 11.1   *Principal features of the 1992 asylum compromise*

The asylum compromise made a first, albeit tentative, step towards establishing a more comprehensive system of immigration control, not least by establishing a quota for ethnic German immigration in everything but name. It ended the 'state posturing' (Hogwood, 2000) in asylum and ethnic German policy, thereby limiting Germany's exceptionalism in these two areas when compared with other European countries. The further relaxation of citizenship laws also resulted in a long overdue increase in the number of annual naturalizations, which rose from 37,000 in 1992 (0.6 per cent of the foreign population) to 107,000 (1.5 per cent) in 1998.

The Liberalization of German Citizenship

Although the asylum compromise, by ending policies with a high symbolic and moral status which had become politically unsustainable in practice, represented an important first step in the overdue modernization of Germany's immigration regime, this momentum of reform could not be maintained during the thirteenth *Bundestag* between 1994 and 1998. In particular, the promise of a full-scale reform of citizenship, which was part of the overall package, proved empty, as the re-elected CDU/CSU–FDP coalition made little serious effort to fulfil its side of the bargain (Green, 2003). The key reason for this failure lay in the refusal of the conservative majority in the CDU/CSU, led by the hardline Interior Minister, Manfred Kanther, to sanction the introduction of *ius soli*. This would have automatically granted citizenship to children of non-German parents born in Germany, and is a policy common in other countries with a history of immigration. However, it would also have resulted in a sharp increase in the number of dual citizens in Germany, as such children would also routinely have inherited their parents' citizenship. The principled rejection of *ius soli* by the CDU/CSU was therefore at least in part justified by the desire to avoid the increase in the number of dual citizens that this would have created.

Instead, the coalition agreed what can only be described as a messy compromise in the 1994 coalition treaty. The proposal aimed to create a transitional status for third generation non-German children born in Germany, which would be transformed into an entitlement to naturalization upon reaching the age of majority (Joppke, 1999, p. 207). However, the proposal was so complex and impractical that it was quickly disowned by both the FDP and the more liberal elements of the CDU. In early 1996, three younger CDU MPs proposed the introduction of full *ius soli*, with the proviso that the children would have to choose at majority between their German citizenship (ascribed via *ius soli*) and their parents' citizenship (inherited via *ius sanguinis*). This proposal, known as the *Optionsmodell*, was also subsequently adopted by the FDP as official policy.

However, the problem was that the conservative majority among the CDU/CSU was not prepared to contemplate anything which deviated substantially from the *Kinderstaatszugehörigkeit*, and especially not *ius soli* and dual citizenship. In the ensuing stalemate, the conservative elements in the CDU and CSU preferred to play for a 'non-decision' in this area (Green, 2003). Crucially, the lack of political will to reform citizenship represented a huge missed opportunity: between 1995 and 1998, over 400,000 non-German children were born in the country, none of whom at that stage would have gained an independent right to German citizenship until the age of 16.

By contrast, the election of an SPD–Green government in 1998 constituted an absolute caesura in the development of citizenship policy. During their long period in opposition, the SPD and Greens had argued repeatedly that Germany *was* a country of immigration, and that this needed to be reflected in more inclusive citizenship laws. Chancellor Schröder's new government thus made a reform of the 1913 citizenship law (the RuStAG) an absolute priority, even though the SPD's designated Interior Minister, Otto Schily, initially ruled out a full-scale immigration regime for political reasons.

The bill to reform the RuStAG, which was published on 13 January 1999, represented a complete departure from previous policy. It aimed to introduce *ius soli* for the third generation of immigrants (so-called double *ius soli*) and also extended it to children of non-nationals who themselves had immigrated before the age of 14. Most controversially, it proposed accepting dual citizenship in all naturalizations as a matter of course. The intent of this proposal was quite pragmatic: the administrative process of obtaining release frequently took years to complete, with some countries additionally imposing high release fees on their citizens. When combined with the emotional cost of giving up one's citizenship of birth, Germany's rejection of dual citizenship, so the SPD and Greens argued, constituted a major disincentive to naturalization. The CDU/CSU maintained that only applicants who were fully integrated in Germany should be naturalized, and that full integration (by definition) ruled out the formal maintenance of links to another country via dual citizenship.

For this reason, the bill was completely unacceptable to the CDU and especially the CSU, yet it seemed as if the two parties could do nothing to stop it, given that the SPD and Greens also held a slim majority in the

Bundesrat, whose approval (as this was a consent law) would be needed. The CDU and CSU leaders, Wolfgang Schäuble and Edmund Stoiber respectively, recognized that their only chance of defeating the bill lay in ousting the SPD–Green *Land* government in Hesse, where an election was due on 7 February 1999. Without Hesse's votes, the government would not have the absolute majority necessary to pass the bill, and would therefore be forced to seek a compromise with the opposition.

It was with the specific aim of mobilizing the party's supporters in the run-up to the Hesse election that the CDU/CSU launched a unique and highly controversial petition campaign *(Unterschriftenkampagne)* against dual citizenship in January 1999. In adopting what was an unorthodox political strategy in the German context (Cooper, 2002), the two parties had read the public mood well. The voters harboured deep suspicions over dual citizenship, as the enormous resonance of the petition campaign illustrated: indeed, this suspicion transcended party political cleavages, as illustrated by a poll for the magazine *Der Spiegel* (Table 11.2).

Although the CDU/CSU leadership came under intense criticism, not only from the government but also from churches, unions, welfare organizations and even some sections of the party, the tactic was vindicated by the outcome of the Hesse election. For only the second time since 1950, the CDU gained power in the state, and the government was forced to go back to the drawing board with its plans for the citizenship law.

Fortunately for the government, the votes of Rhineland-Palatinate, which had an SPD–FDP government, were enough to reinstate the *Bundesrat* majority, and so Interior Minister Schily wasted no time in beginning negotiations with the FDP. The FDP, in turn, insisted on the *Optionsmodell* for *ius soli*, as well as on dropping the general acceptance of dual citizenship. Although the CDU/CSU continued to

TABLE 11.2 *Public opinion on dual citizenship in Germany, January 1999*

Question: 'Are you for or against the introduction of dual citizenship?' (All Germany, percentage values, by voting intention)

	Total	CDU/CSU	SPD	FDP	Greens	PDS	Extreme Right
For	39	22	49	37	84	41	11
Against	53	71	44	54	14	58	82
Don't care	5	5	5	-	2	-	7

Source: Emnid, in *Der Spiegel*, Issue 2 (1999), p. 23 (author's translation).

- Introduction of *ius soli* for children of non-German parents born in Germany, provided one parent has lived in Germany for eight years and has corresponding permanent residence status
- Option for those children aged ten or under for who would have qualified for *ius soli* at birth, limited until 31 December 2000
- Dual citizenship created by this provision may be retained until age 23, by which time release from the parent's citizenship must be obtained to avoid automatic loss of German nationality

- Reduction of residence requirement for naturalization entitlement from 15 to eight years
- Special provisions for non-national minors dropped
- Introduction of requirement of language skills, plus loyalty to the Basic Law
- While dual citizenship in naturalizations is not permitted in principle, the number of exceptions is increased over the previous law
- Inheritance of German citizenship abroad limited to first generation
- Fees increased from DM100 to DM500

FIGURE 11.2   *Principal features of the 1999 citizenship reform*

oppose the reform on principle, the resulting compromise between the SPD, FDP and Greens passed the parliamentary process without further complications, and the new citizenship law came into force on 1 January 2000. Its key provisions are summarized in Figure 11.2.

Like the asylum compromise, the new citizenship law (*Staatsangehörigkeitsgesetz*, or StAG) brings German policy firmly into the European mainstream, albeit through a process of liberalization rather than restriction (as in the case with asylum). Even so, doubts remain over its effectiveness in delivering the goal of higher naturalizations (Green, 2000). Although the naturalization rate rose from 2 per cent in 1999 to 2.6 per cent in 2000, it fell back in 2001 to 2.4 per cent (cf. Table 11.1 above). Moreover, once net migration levels, live births (excluding *ius soli*) and deaths of non-nationals had been added to naturalizations, the size of the non-German population actually increased in 2001 by just over 20,000. Without a substantial further increase in the naturalization rate, it will therefore take decades to achieve the inclusion of even the majority of Germany's immigrants, the rationale for which had first been acknowledged almost 20 years earlier in 1984. The impact of *ius soli* (which does not count as a naturalization) is also limited: because of the requirement for the (non-German) parents to have not only eight years' residence, but also the corresponding permanent residence status, only between 30 and 40 per cent of their children born in Germany actually gain German citizenship automatically at birth.

Even so, the new law is almost certain to have a long-term positive impact. Irrespective of the problems with gaining citizenship via *ius soli*, it remains to be seen how rigorously the requirement for dual nationals created by this provision to choose between their citizenships will be enforced when the first such cases arise in 2013. In addition, it must be remembered that one-quarter of non-nationals in Germany come from other EU member states, and as a result of their privileged status have little to gain from naturalization. Consequently, the fact that the number of Turks naturalizing has doubled between 1997 and 2000 is particularly important. Finally, the fact that the toleration of dual citizenship has risen from one in seven naturalizations in 1999 to almost one in two in 2000 may itself encourage more immigrants to apply for German nationality.

The Reappraisal of Labour Migration

By 2000, with asylum and ethnic German immigration down to a politically acceptable level, and with a new citizenship law in place, the remaining (and arguably most important) issue was the management of labour migration via a formal immigration regime, as well as the formal structuring of the integration process. The issue was a litmus test of Germany's development towards self-recognition as a country of immigration: without a formal immigration and integration framework to pull the other aspects together, policy would remain as fragmented and uncoordinated as it had been for the previous 40 years.

Although Interior Minister Schily, as noted above, was initially against such an immigration law, even deliberately provoking the Greens in November 1998 by declaring that Germany had exceeded its capacity to take immigration (*Der Spiegel*, 30 November 1998), everything had changed within just one year. At the annual Hannover trade fair in the spring of 2000, Chancellor Schröder announced that up to 20,000 five-year work permits for information technology (IT) specialists were to be made available in what became known as the 'Green Card' initiative.

This constituted a highly significant break with previous policy. The only non-EU labour migration that has taken place since the end of guest worker recruitment in 1973 had been temporary labour from Central and Eastern European countries, mainly to work in agriculture. Not even foreign students finishing their degrees in Germany had generally been given access to the labour market. But now, at the insistence of industry, highly-skilled workers were to be granted this privilege in noticeable numbers, and that at a time when unemployment stood at almost 4 million nationally. The short-term reason for this U-turn lay in the skills shortages that were emerging in key areas of the economy, including engineering and information technology, but also in service sectors such as hotels and catering. Indeed, in December 2001 there were an estimated 1.2 million unfilled vacancies in Germany.

However, the shortages also reflected longer-term developments in the demographic structure of Germany's population (cf. Münz, Seifert and Ulrich, 1997). Not only has the population been getting older, because of increased life expectancy, but it has also been shrinking because of a low fertility rate. This rate measures the number of children borne by each woman, with a community requiring an overall fertility rate of about 2.1 in order to maintain its size without immigration. Yet in 1999, Germany's fertility rate stood at just 1.3 (Münz, 2001; Schmid, 2001). In coming decades, this will have major implications for social policy, and especially for the 'pay-as-you-go' pensions system: the ratio of people of working age to the rest of the population (who are supported by the working population's tax payments), the so-called potential support ratio, is set to halve by 2050. In fact, in order to keep its potential support ratio at the 1995 level of 4.4, a high-profile United Nations report in 2000 calculated that Germany would require annual net migration of almost 3.5 million persons (United Nations Population Division, 2000).

In response to continued pressure from industry, and to the delight of the Greens, the government therefore began to think in earnest about an immigration law. The CDU/CSU had always opposed such a law and continued to do so now: as permanent labour migration from outside the EU had been suspended back in 1973, they argued that the mere existence of an immigration law would simply encourage potential immigrants to come to Germany. Indeed, during the campaign for the North Rhine-Westphalian state election in the spring of 2000, the CDU's candidate, Jürgen Rüttgers, coined the populist slogan 'Children, not Indians' (*Kinder statt Inder*), thereby underlining his position that more attention should be paid to the education of Germany's youth rather than recruiting IT specialists from India. Although the tactic failed to win him the election, it did neatly encapsulate the reservations of many in the conservative camp over permitting new immigration when unemployment in Germany, not least among non-nationals themselves, remained stubbornly high.

In the autumn of 2000, Interior Minister Schily set up a cross-party commission, chaired by a former CDU speaker of the *Bundestag*, Rita Süssmuth, to examine the political and economic options for an immigration law. In reply, the CDU set up its own commission, under the chairmanship of the moderate Minister-President of the Saarland, Peter Müller. While the possibility of a cross-party consensus was initially deliberately talked up by the parties, the publication of the two commissions' reports in June and July 2001 ended such speculation. The fundamental assumptions for each commission were different, mirroring the party-political conceptions of labour migration, even though both argued for the introduction of a points system for regulating high-skilled migration (Hailbronner, 2001). Thus, the Süssmuth Commission, as it had become known, argued that Germany needed immigration, and therefore proposed concrete quotas for up to 20,000 high-skilled migrants per annum. It also argued in favour of formal integration courses along the lines of those pioneered in the Netherlands. By contrast, the CDU commission argued that immigration should not be allowed beyond high-skilled specialists, and thus made no suggestions for general quotas. In addition, both commissions diverged substantially on the issue of minors joining their parents in Germany (*Kindernachzug*), which has polarized party positions in immigration policy for over 20 years. While the Süssmuth Commission wanted to see the existing age limit of 16 brought into line with other EU countries, where 18 is standard practice, the Müller Commission argued that this should be lowered to ten, and preferably six, on the grounds that an immigrant's chances of integration would increase dramatically with the amount of formal education received in Germany.

While the bill for the so-called *Zuwanderungsgesetz* (immigration law), published in November 2001, deliberately avoided any concrete quotas for political reasons, it did adopt many of the Süssmuth Commission's suggestions, including the idea that language integration courses should be offered to all new (and many existing) immigrants and that the system of work and residence permits should be merged. The bill also took the opportunity to go beyond the commission's ideas for a full-scale overhaul of Germany's impenetrable system of residence permits. On the other hand, it made a deliberate attempt to move towards the CDU/CSU, by proposing an age limit of 14 for *Kindernachzug*. But a compromise remained out of reach, even though the number of children potentially affected by reducing the *Kindernachzug* age to 12 was estimated to be no more than 6,000, or just 1 per cent of the total annual migration inflows (Leicht, 2002).

Just like the 1999 citizenship law, the *Zuwanderungsgesetz* thus quickly found itself at the centre of a heated political controversy. At the decisive session of the Bundesrat on 22 March 2002, the SPD, in the absence of its own majority in that chamber, used a procedural sleight of hand to ensure the bill's adoption into law (see *Der Spiegel*, 30 March 2002). The law was subsequently unsuccessfully challenged in the Constitutional Court by several CDU-led Länder, which ruled against it on 18 December 2002, only two weeks before it was due to come into force. Nonetheless, the issues the *Zuwanderungsgesetz* was designed to address remain as pertinent as before, and a renewed attempt to reach a cross-party compromise was begun by the SPD-Green government in early 2003. Germany therefore was well on the way to developing almost a full range of policy tools for the management of immigration. By early 2003 only an anti-discrimination law, which will permit the practical enforcement of existing constitutional provisions for equality (and which is in any case required in the coming years under EU legislation), remained to be introduced in early 2003. It is worth remembering that, at the time of unification, Germany possessed none of these policy instruments.

The Europeanization of Immigration Policy

All the time during the 1990s that Germany was undertaking reforms to its domestic immigration framework, the development of immigration as an area of EU policy was continuing apace. Germany, as one of the founder signatories of the Schengen Accord on border controls in 1985, has long had a prima facie interest in promoting a common European immigration policy. This interest increased considerably in the early 1990s, as the asylum crisis was looming, when Chancellor Kohl had attempted to seek an EU-wide solution to the issue, including a full-scale distribution mechanism between the various member states similar to the one employed by the German Länder. Perhaps unsurprisingly, given that the overwhelming majority of asylum seekers in the EU was heading for Germany, few other member states felt inclined to increase their own share of the EU's asylum seekers in order to help Germany (Marshall, 1992, p. 261). Chancellor Kohl's initiative therefore failed, prompting the government to seek a domestic solution with renewed energy, which ultimately resulted in the 1992 asylum compromise (Henson and Malhan, 1995).

After 1992, Germany's support for Europeanization, while remaining strong in rhetoric, was considerably weaker in practice. With a solution in place that satisfied the demands of domestic politics, Germany could be much more picky in the Commission initiatives it chose to support. In particular, the German position in the late 1990s has prioritized the maintenance of its own (tough) policy 'standards', especially with reference to asylum and family reunification policy. In this respect, the SPD–Green government has continued the policy of the previous CDU/CSU-led government. Indeed, at the Laeken European Council in 2001, Germany was temporarily accused by the Belgian presidency of being the principal hindrance in the development of the common immigration policy agreed at the 1999 special European Council meeting in Tampere (cf. *Frankfurter Rundschau*, 17 December 2001).

Towards an Open Society? Between Integration and Assimilation

Despite all the policy progress made during the 1990s, it has also become clear that the integration of immigrants into German society has so far only been partially successful. In common with other European countries, immigrants in Germany show many of the characteristics of a structurally marginalized population. For instance, unemployment among *Ausländer* in 2000 stood at 16.4 per cent, compared to 7.8 per cent for the western German population as a whole. Surveys showed that non-nationals were not only heavily underrepresented in public service, but also earned lower incomes and had less living space per person than Germans. They also had much lower levels of formal qualifications and, as the OECD's PISA study showed in 2001, generally poor levels of educational attainment. For example, whereas 26 per cent of German school leavers qualified for university entrance in 1999, the corresponding figure for *Ausländer* was just 10 per cent (Beauftragte der Bundesregierung, 2002, pp. 201–3, 342–3, 351–2, 361). In particular, the level of language proficiency has been found to be actually decreasing among younger generations, thereby reducing further the chances available to them: in 2002, some 59 per cent of non-German children in the city of Essen were found not to speak German well, compared to 26 per cent of Germans (*Welt am Sonntag*, 17 February 2002).

This development has thrust the aims, methods and outcome of German integration policy into the political spotlight. Integration means the equal combination of the cultural traditions and values of immigrants with those of the indigenous population to create a new whole. This has been the official policy aim since the late 1970s. It is the dominant paradigm of immigrant inclusion in the EU, in contrast to Australia and Canada, which explicitly define themselves as multicultural societies. Among other things, successful integration depends on a clear definition of what both sides are expected to tolerate.

Integration policy in Germany, however, has tended to be rather idiosyncratic. The degree of cultural diversity which the main parties, were willing to tolerate was in reality quite low. For instance, the 1977 Guidelines on Naturalization, which were agreed in a cross-party consensus to structure an otherwise vague naturalization process (and which remain in force in 2002), explicitly require a very high standard of cultural adaptation by an immigrant, to include the nebulous demand of 'voluntary and lasting orientation towards Germany' (*freie und dauernde Hinwendung zu Deutschland*: cf. Green, 2001a, pp. 30–1). Similarly, until 1998, government policy required that naturalization should only take place once integration had been completed, whereas most other European countries view citizenship as a stepping stone on the way towards this goal. As no objective end to the integration process was set in Germany, this notion simply served to prolong the legal exclusion of immigrants.

In practice, Germany's approach meant that immigrants were expected not to integrate, but to assimilate: that is, to give up the majority of their cultural identity in favour of 'becoming' (not just legally) German (cf. Joppke, 1999, pp. 201–2). Of course, the term 'assimilation' was rarely used, because of its direct association with the Nazi era. Instead, the leader of the CDU/CSU *Fraktion* in the Bundestag, Friedrich Merz, caused a storm when he demanded in the autumn of 2000 that immigrants adapt to Germany's indigenous 'dominant culture' (*Leitkultur*). Applauded for his frankness by conservative politicians, he was condemned by the left for allegedly proposing the forced 'Germanicization' of immigrants. He also prompted an anguished debate among intellectuals of whether such a *Leitkultur* actually existed and, if so, how it might be defined (Klusmeyer, 2001). Similarly, in the summer of 2002, Interior Minister Schily (SPD), no doubt with one eye on conservative voters in the federal election campaign, declared in a newspaper interview: 'The best form of integration is assimilation' (*Süddeutsche Zeitung*, 27 June 2002).

What this means is that one of the major challenges for the political parties to consider in the coming years will be just how much cultural and value diversity Germany can handle. Here opinions range widely. For the conservative majority of the CDU as well as the CSU, Germany should at heart remain a Christian, occidental society. Accordingly, the two parties have also been emphasizing the potential impact on internal security of migration, in particular since the attacks on the USA in September 2001. Some of the CDU, the FDP and most of the SPD prefer a more republican definition of national identity, which emphasizes political, rather than cultural and ethnic membership. At the other end of the spectrum, the Greens and PDS have in the past argued for a highly heterogeneous multicultural society with a 'post-national' identity, although more recently the focus has been on providing a haven for refugees from all over the world (cf. Cohn-Bendit and Schmid, 1992; Murray, 1994; O'Brien, 1996).

This range of conceptualizations of Germany's identity *vis-à-vis* immigration has led to some adventurous ideas by politicians from all parties. Thus, the Greens' and PDS's repeated demands for improving the status of asylum-seekers are simply politically unrealistic; at the same time, the claim by some conservative politicians that Muslims, and in particular Turks, are unwilling or even unable to integrate is equally wide of the mark. In any case, the latter argument is irrelevant, as non-nationals in Germany, even if they do refuse to 'integrate', cannot in practice be expelled in large numbers for both political and legal reasons. The example of 'Mehmet', the alias of a 14-year-old Turkish young offender with a string of convictions, illustrates this point on an individual basis: even though he had been born in Germany and his parents still lived there, the city of Munich attempted to have him expelled to Turkey in November 1998. Ultimately, the expulsion was quashed on appeal to the Federal Administrative Court in 2002, but not before 'Mehmet' had spent almost four years in enforced exile in his 'homeland'.

Conclusion

In managing integration, the only real option for Germany is therefore to open itself more to its non-national population. This will require a much greater societal awareness of concepts such as institutional racism and indirect discrimination, which, in contrast to the UK, have been almost entirely absent from public debate. The alternative is a further retreat of both Germans and non-Germans into their respective cultural environments: already, over 40 per cent of Turkish families speak only Turkish at home (quoted in *Der Spiegel*, 4 March 2002), which almost certainly contributes to the poor command of the German language displayed by many non-German children. Amazingly, it was not until late 2002 that concrete steps towards the inclusion of Islam on the religious education curriculum were taken in some *Länder*: hitherto, Islamic tuition had been provided solely by local communities through unaccredited and unregulated teachers, and (moreover) not in German. Although integration classes are likely in the near future, it remains to be seen how effective these will be, given that the very high costs involved create the incentive to cut corners in order to save money. In the light of such developments, it at least seems certain that the issues of immigration, and especially integration, will not disappear from the political stage in the foreseeable future.

12

The Environment and Nuclear Power

WOLFGANG RÜDIG

'*Deutschland wird Weltmeister*' (Germany will become World Champion). This prophetic statement appeared in whole-page colour advertisements in German newspapers in the spring of 2002: they showed a young man standing with one foot on what, at first sight, looked like a giant football. On closer inspection, the round object turned out to be the top half of the concrete containment structure of a German nuclear power station: the advertisement campaign had been launched by the German Environment Ministry to highlight its programme of phasing out nuclear energy, making Germany 'world champion' because of the speed with which it plans to close down its remaining nuclear stations.

Germany as a front-runner, a pace-setter of environmental policy, if not in the world then at least in Europe, is an image that German ministers have always embraced quite willingly. Environmental issues certainly played quite a major role in German politics over the last decades; in particular, over the question of nuclear power, environmental issues were politicized to a very high degree. The nuclear issue became the main focus of protest politics that first developed in Germany in the 1960s student movement. One of the major results of this process was the formation and development of a strong Green Party. Formed in 1980, the Greens entered local and, after 1985, regional government on quite a frequent basis but had to wait until 1998 before playing a role in federal government.

The 1998 elections thus brought a party to power that had arisen out of the environmental and anti-nuclear movements of the 1970s. It had campaigned from the start for the closure of the entire nuclear industry and a range of other environmental demands such as the introduction of ecological taxation, the promotion of renewable energies and energy conservation, a radical expansion of public transport, and a reform of agricultural policy to promote organic foods. With a new 'Red–Green' regime replacing the Christian-Democrat/Liberal government that had been in power during virtually all of the existence of the Greens, was the result a 'Green revolution' which fundamentally changed the nature of German society?

Environmental policy touches on a vast area of human activities, such as industry, agriculture, transport, energy, housing, water management, and forests. In each of the these areas, institutions, laws and regulations, as well as public perceptions and values, had been formed and developed over many years that had some important environmental connotations. The terms *Umweltschutz* (environmental protection) and *Umweltpolitik* (environmental policy) were unknown in Germany before 1970: they essentially were the result of the creation, by government initiative, of a whole new policy area, in the early 1970s (Hucke, 1985; E. Müller, 1995; Weidner, 1995; Weidner, 1999). The way in which this new policy field developed reflected, however, many traditions that can be traced back to the beginning of the twentieth century and before.

Contemporary German environmental policy is shaped by five main forces: the role of local and state government, federal environmental institutions, the role of the European Union and other international environmental policy arenas, specific traditions of choosing environmental policy instruments, and the role of non-governmental organizations. These will now be examined, followed by a more detailed analysis of the environmental record of the Red–Green government. (For brief overviews of the main developments in English, see Pehle, 1997; Pehle and Jansen, 1998; Jänicke and Weidner, 1997. In German, comprehensive overviews of environmental policy-making developments are provided by E. Müller, 1995; Weidner, 1999; Jänicke, Kunig and Stitzel, 1999.)

Local and Regional Institutions

One key element of German environmental policy is the importance of the local and regional (state) levels which are firmly grounded in the history of German policy-making. Environmental issues were recognized as a policy issue with the beginning of industrialization. In Prussia, a series of administrative rules was issued in the early nineteenth century regarding the licensing of specific industrial processes which included an examination of what today would be called the 'environmental impact' of the plant. While the regulation of air pollution followed the pattern of a state-led regulatory culture, the resolution of water pollution and drinking water supply issues took a variety of forms, reflecting different regional conditions and political traditions, with local authorities taking the initiative in most areas (Wey, 1982; Rüdig and Krämer, 1994).

With the creation of the Federal Republic of Germany in 1949, the Länder were established as key players in environmental policy, and major legislative initiatives in the 1950s and 1960s emerged from the regional level. As the states implement federal legislation in most policy areas, it was also Land administrations that were responsible for making key decisions on individual projects with environmental impacts. It was only after 1969 that federal government developed a strong interest in environmental policy (see below), but the Länder continued to defend their autonomy in this area, resisting successfully, for example, the plan to pass legislative competence in water management to the federal level.

Local and Land politics also became extremely important after environmental and energy issues had become strongly politicized in the 1970s. Particularly after the rise of the Green Party in the 1980s, local authorities and Land governments involving Social Democrats and Greens tried to push forward with radical energy and environmental plans. Much of the effort went into stopping the federal nuclear energy programme that had intensified in the 1970s. Here, even otherwise pronuclear Christian Democratic Land governments turned into opponents of federal policies, as in the case of the CDU in Lower Saxony refusing to license a planned nuclear reprocessing plant in the late 1970s, in defence of Land interests. The policy of using Land government to try to block nuclear development reached its high point after the Chernobyl accident of 1986: state governments run by Greens and Social Democrats began to try everything possible to get nuclear power stations closed down. A policy of administrative harassment was followed in which life was made as difficult as possible for utilities operating nuclear facilities. State governments tried various means to shut reactors, while utilities looked towards the federal government to use its constitutional powers to override decisions by state governments where legally possible. In the end, no state government succeeded in closing down a single nuclear power station (Rüdig, 1990; Rüdig, 2000).

Finally, local and Land governments also were a major motor of policy initiatives on the new global environmental issues that had dominated the agenda since the early 1990s. With society highly sensitized to environmental issues, many local authorities reacted very positively to the Agenda 21 initiative. Of the local authorities who joined the International Consortium of Local Environmental Initiatives (ICLEI), a disproportionately high share came from Germany. Also on climate policy, German local authorities were very active, developing a broad range of initiatives to reduce greenhouse gas emissions, and could thus be seen as the 'real policy leaders' in this field (Huber, 1997, p. 80).

Federal Institutions

Before 1969, there had been few incidents of initiatives from central government. A law on bird protection passed in 1888 was one of the noteworthy exceptions, as were several importance laws passed under the Nazis in the 1930s, such as the first comprehensive nature protection law of 1935 (Dominick III, 1992). After 1949, the main policy initiative in this area was nuclear energy. Regarded as the technology of the future, the Federal Republic developed a national research and development strategy run by a Federal Ministry of Atomic Affairs created in 1956 (Radkau, 1983). Responsibility for other environmental policy areas was located in a range of other federal ministries, from economics to health and agriculture.

It was only after the general election of 1969 bringing to power a 'reform coalition' of Social Democrats (SPD) and Liberals (FDP) that the new policy area called 'environmental policy' was created as a major federal initiative. Environmental policy appeared attractive as a reform project to modernize Germany, following the major initiatives in the USA, culminating in the passage of the National Environmental Policy Act (NEPA) in 1970.

German policy-makers saw 'the environment' as an essentially non-political issue that was separate from the main conflict lines of German politics. To a major extent, the new environmental policy initiative was a public relations event, but it also involved the reorganization of the administrative location of environmental responsibilities at federal level. Prime responsibility for environmental policy was given to the powerful Interior Ministry, a traditional department that carried responsibility of a wide range of state activities, including internal security, the civil service, citizenship, and immigration. Many other government activities with important environmental connotations remained outside its remit, however: the whole area of energy supply remained in the Economics Ministry, for example, and nuclear energy remained the sole responsibility of the Federal Ministry of Research and Technology (BMFT) that had arisen from the old Ministry of Atomic Affairs.

Amongst other institutional innovations the Environmental Protection Agency (UBA) was created. Unlike its US namesake, however, the UBA had no executive functions whatsoever. Its role was mainly to conduct research and provide technical and scientific advice to the ministry, and thus its powers were rather limited. A more important innovation was the creation of a conference of Land environment ministers (UMK), starting in 1972, in an effort to increase the coordination between the Länder as well as between the Federal and Land levels. The UMK has developed into a major policy arena over the years, in particular through the creation of numerous working groups.

While the Land level remained important, the federal government sought to increase the competence of the federal level in a number of areas. In 1972, a change in the Basic Law was passed, giving the federal state legislative powers on air pollution, waste disposal and noise abatement. The most important individual piece of federal legislation was the Federal Emissions Law. Mainly covering questions of air pollution, it was passed unanimously by the German Bundestag in 1974 (Müller, 1995).

The absence of an independent federal ministry exclusively dedicated to environmental policy could be seen as a disadvantage for environmental interests but, allied to a strong ministry of state, environmental issues were promoted quite vigorously in the early 1970s, and again the early and mid-1980s. Environmental policy remained with the Interior Ministry until 1986 when, following the Chernobyl nuclear accident, Chancellor Helmut Kohl decided to create a new ministry, the Federal Ministry for Environmental Protection, Nature Protection and Reactor Safety (BMU). The environmental policy sections of the Interior Ministry provided the core; the main addition was the nuclear safety divisions which had previously been located in the BMFT (Weale, O'Riordan and Kramme, 1991).

The BMU gave environmental issues a higher visibility in government. Following the renewed nuclear debate in the late 1980s, the BMU also had to cope with the impact of German unification and the major environmental problems in Eastern Germany that came under its purview as a result. In the 1990s, the BMU fought a long rearguard action in defence of nuclear power in Germany, trying to keep nuclear power stations open against fierce opposition from anti-nuclear state governments. Apart from a leadership role in international environmental politics, the main domestic initiative concentrated on waste policy. Apart from the provision of separate waste containers for glass, and the separate collection of paper and bio-degradable material, the major innovation was a system to allow the recycling of packaging from plastic and other materials. This was the issue that the government devoted most of its political capital to, devising the so-called 'dual system' in which manufacturers signed up to finance a new recycling system (Pehle, 1998).

EU and International Environmental Politics

A key feature of German environmental policy-making in recent decades has been its leadership role at the European and international level. The 1980s in particular saw Germany pushing forward European environmental policy, focusing especially on the control of air pollution following the emotional rise of 'acid rain' as a domestic policy issue in the early 1980s (Boehmer-Christiansen and Skea, 1991).

German industry found that it proved difficult in the new political climate of the 1980s to resist environmental reforms. Industry did not want to put itself into a positon where it was seen as anti-environmental. At the same time, it was concerned that new environmental regulations were imposing an increasingly heavy burden on it which put it at a major disadvantage regarding its competitors in other countries. But while domestic policy processes became difficult, there was the chance to take the issue on to a different level: the European Union. Either EU policy led to uniformly high environmental standards being adopted throughout Europe, thus imposing a similarly high standard on the industry of other countries, or the EU rejected higher standards, thus effectively killing off costly German demands. German industry thus found it generally beneficial to move the environmental decision-making arena from the national to the EU level (Grant, Paterson and Whitston, 1988).

In other areas, too, Germany played a leading role international environmental politics. In climate policy in particular, Germany pushed for ambitious targets at EU and international level. Germany benefited here from the outcome of German unification: the collapse of East German industry and the closure of polluting power stations gave the new unified Germany a major bonus as 1990 was the baseline for the measurement of the reduction of greenhouse gas emissions. Germany thus dramatically reduced its greenhouse emissions in the early 1990s. The fact that this reduction was the unintentional result of economic collapse in East Germany after unification rather than the result of an active climate policy with substantial sacrifices did not stop German ministers claiming leadership in this field. Germany hosted the 1995 conferences of the parties to the Climate Convention which passed the 'Berlin commitment' that paved the way to the Kyoto agreement in 1997; Germany also arranged for the UN Climate Secretariat to be located in Bonn (Beuermann and Jäger, 1996; Huber, 1997). In other areas, Germany found it difficult to maintain policy leadership at EU level. A number of new policy initiatives dominated the EU environmental agenda in the late 1980s which proved rather difficult to stomach (e.g., the directives on environmental impact assessments and on environmental information). Both required public access to administrative information to a degree that was alien to German administrative traditions. Furthermore, the fact that legislation is implementated by state and local authorities created problems: some German Länder refused to comply or dragged their feet. The EU Commission repeatedly rejected claims by the German federal government that it was not to blame for non-implementation on the grounds that Länder failed to comply (Héritier, Knill and Mingers, 1996).

Policy Instruments

German environmental policy of the early 1970s was heavily influenced by earlier developments in the USA, but it also developed new elements that had an impact on environmental policy debates beyond its own borders.

The key piece of environmental legislation was the Federal Emissions Law that set out a particular German approach to environmental policy: the law was essentially the further development of the industrial plant licensing legislation that had started to develop in Prussia in the early nineteenth century. It concentrated on 'command and control' measures where licensing authorities were enabled to ask companies to fulfil a range of environmental conditions before plants were allowed to be built and operated. In international comparison, the most noteworthy element was the introduction of the principle of *Vorsorge* (the precautionary principle), which allowed the authorities to act in advance of possible adverse impacts that could be expected to occur in the future (O'Riordan and Cameron, 1994). The other important principle was the concept of the *Stand der Technik*, or the current state of technological development. The driving force of improvement was thus technical development, and the law sought to ensure that industry always applied the most modern and efficient environmental protection technology available (Boehmer-Christiansen and Skea, 1991).

To many policy observers, the result of the German environmental policy initiatives of the 1970s were ultimately disappointing. They diagnosed what came to be known as the 'implemenation deficit'.

Despite good intentions, the new legislation was not, or could not, be implemented successfully. This was, to some extent, an outcome of the federal political system which gives state governments as well as local authorities a major political and administrative role. High-flying legislative aims were being ignored by decison-makers at local level who faced many conflicting demands, in particular demands for creating employment and attracting industry to their town or area to generate important tax revenues (Mayntz *et al.*, 1977; Mayntz, 1978).

In the context of an international trend towards 'deregulation' and a reduction of state intervention, the traditional 'command and control' measures typical of the environmental approach of the early 1970s became increasingly unpopular in the 1980s and 1990s. One alternative policy instrument that began to dominate the environmental agenda was eco-taxation. Promoted by economists for decades, German policymakers had remained resistant. By the late 1980s, the idea had found strong promoters amongst some of Germany's environmental think-tanks (cf. von Weizsäcker and Jesinghaus, 1992), and the Greens also began to adopt the demand of ecological taxation as a major policy. While the CDU and Kohl appeared to be willing to consider this idea, the business community and the CDU's coalition partner, the FDP, remained deeply opposed, and the federal government failed to agree on the introduction of ecological taxation in the 1990s. Earlier ideas of introducing a carbon tax as part of an active climate policy were thus abandoned as part of a national policy, with only a commitment to pursue a EU carbon tax remaining which never materialized (Strübin, 1997; Krebs, Reiche and Rocholl, 1998; Reiche and Krebs, 1999).

Instead, the new policy approach that dominated much of the 1990s was the idea of pursuing environmental policy in agreement with industry. In several areas, industry was willing to make a voluntary commitment to achieve specific environmental goals. The government eagerly embraced these offers. In climate policy, voluntary agreements with industry became the key policy (Beuermann and Jäger, 1996; Huber, 1997). In other areas where conflicts arose, the idea of coming to a consensus with industry also became influential. Most pertinently, a number of attempts were made to come to a solution of the nuclear question on a consensual basis, but all talks failed.

Environmental Movements and Interest Groups

One of the most important features of German environmental politics is the high degree of politicization. This is essentially a product of the politics of the 1970s when the anti-nuclear movement became the focus of the radical protest politics of the heirs of the 1960s. Compared with the USA and the UK, Germany did not have well-established environmental interest groups in the 1970s that could have taken up the new wave of protest. There is a long history of environmental groups, but the ideological connotations of the movement with nationalist and anti-democratic tendencies (Dominick III, 1992) and the association of 'nature' with forces such as German romanticism, which were seen to have contributed to the rise of Nazis, made environmental issues somewhat suspect in post-war Germany. Combined with the problems of rebuilding the country after the destruction of the war, this pushed environmental issues very much into the background.

It was only by the the the mid-1970s that movements emerged again to challenge governmental records on the environment, this time dominated by a left-libertarian agenda. The catalyst was protest against (civil) nuclear energy. After years of political consensus regarding nuclear power, local public protest in 1975 catapulted the issue on to the national agenda. The resistance of local populations was important in giving the protest legitimacy; its main national resonance was gained amongst the 'New Left', a heterogeneous group of people influenced by the agenda of the 1960s student movement. The movement had some limited success as it managed to delay the construction for some nuclear power stations by bringing court cases. Its most important success came in 1979 when a protest against a massive combined nuclear re-processing and waste disposal plant at Gorleben succeeded (i.e., the re-processing plant was stopped). More importantly, the political climate for the construction of nuclear power stations became very hostile in Germany and, after the Harrisburg accident of 1979, a de facto moratorium applied to the construction of new nuclear power stations (Burns and van der Will, 1990; Rüdig, 1990; Koopmans, 1995).

The effect of this period on German environmental policy has been profound. Two important changes occurred to the policy field as a result: first of all, environmental groups took centre stage for the first time. In the 1970s, the Federal Association of Citizen Action Groups on Environmental Protection (BBU) became Germany's most prominent environmental group leading the fight against nuclear power, but its relevance faded as other environmental issues, such as acid rain and global environmental problems, became important in the 1980s. Other environmental interest groups have since become the dominant players, in particular the German Association for Environmental and Nature Protection (BUND), which is affiliated to Friends of the Earth International; the German branch of Greenpeace International; the

German Society for Nature Conservation (DNR), a national association of various animal and nature protection groups; and the Nature Protection Association (NABU), the successor of the bird protection associations (Dalton, 1994b; Rucht and Roose, 1999).

The other major innovation was the birth of the Green Party: the first local parties were formed in 1977, in direct response to the protest movements against nuclear power. The federal Green Party, first conceived as a temporary list known as 'The Greens' that contested the 1979 European elections, was formed in January 1980 and combined two strands of parties that emerged out of the anti-nuclear movement. The Green Party went on to enter the Bundestag in 1983 (Frankland and Schoonmaker, 1992). In subsequent years, it became involved in local government and, since 1985, also state government on many occasions, eventually entering federal government in 1998.

The strength of the German environmental movement and the rise of the Green Party profoundly influenced the political agenda of German politics in the 1980s and 1990s. However, from the beginning, environmental groups were kept outside the federal policy-making process. While environmental mobilization was higher than in many other countries, the involvement of environmental groups in the policy-making process was underdeveloped (cf. Richardson and Watts, 1985). The relative exclusion of environmental interests was arguably one contributing factor behind the politicization of environmental issues in the 1970s and the rise of the Greens in the 1980s. In the 1990s, this radical legacy provided an additional obstacle to environmental groups becoming directly involved in the policy-making process, particularly at the federal level (Pehle, 1997; Pehle, 1998).

Environmental Policy under the Red–Green Government, 1998–2002

With the arrival of the Greens in federal government in 1998, the hitherto final chapter of German environmental policy was opened. How many of the past patterns of German environmental policy were changed by the Greens? Their challenge in the past had been radical: they were formed to break the long tradition of federal pro-nuclear policies, aiming ultimately for all German nuclear power stations to be closed down. Greens also demanded the introduction of ecological taxation, and with these two major demands they entered the 1998 electoral campaign and the coalition negotiations with the Social Democrats.

How successful, in fact, have the Greens been? How much were they able to change? In order to understand the role of the Greens in government, the political context in which they entered government will first be examined. Then we will concentrate on the discussion of the Greens' two most important policy goals, ecological taxation and the phasing-out of nuclear power. Finally, how have the Greens done on a range of other issues close to their heart, such as agriculture and transport?

Preparing for Government

The Greens entered the 1998 election campaign from a position of weakness. After a period in the mid-1990s when their opinion poll rating stood at well over 10 per cent, the first months of 1998 showed a fairly steep decline. Blamed for the poor rating was a series of public relations disasters. In March 1998, the Green Party conference had made a demand for the price of petrol to be raised steadily over a period of 10 years to about DM5 per litre: this was about treble the current rate. If the Greens had simply been regarded as a rather colourful, but ultimately insignificant, small protest party, this demand (as similar ones previously) would not have attracted much attention. But as the Greens for the first time were seen as a potential partner in government, the press coverage was huge. In addition, a Green MP proclaimed that airfares also had to rise to take account of the environmental impact of flying: one holiday flight abroad every five years would be quite enough. The popular media presented the Greens as the party who wanted to take away two of the most basic pleasures of ordinary Germans: driving a private motor car and flying to a sunny destination for their holidays. The resulting dip in the opinion polls demonstrated to Green politicians that some of their demands were deeply unpopular with the vast majority of the population.

Once before, in 1990, the Greens had campaigned on global warming and ignored what the people really were interested in (namely, German unification); they had paid a heavy electoral price. This time, they wanted to avoid making the same mistake: in a hasty move, a shorter election manifesto was produced in which the DM5 petrol price did not appear, and nothing was heard again of the idea of making holiday flights dearer. The Greens fought a very difficult campaign, being mainly on the defensive. Their result, 6.7 per cent of the vote, was worse than in 1994, but they had made it into the Bundestag, and with the SPD doing very well, the SPD and Greens together had a majority.

In government, the Greens were painfully aware of their limitations as the small coalition partner with barely 7 per cent support among the population. The Greens had to demonstrate that they could be responsible in government, and it fell to Foreign Minister Joschka Fischer to show the Greens' resolve to stay in government and to take and support difficult decisions, such as on German participation in military actions abroad. With environmental issues not high on the electorate agenda, the Greens having just managed to get into Parliament again, and with Chancellor Schröder having other options to replace the Greens as coalition partners, they knew that their bargaining position was not very strong. Apart from the Foreign Ministry, the Greens had obtained two other cabinet portfolios: Jürgen Trittin, former party co-speaker and leader of the left-wing faction of the party, became Environment Minister, and Andrea Fischer was installed as the new Health Minister. Trittin was thus charged with promoting what many Greens regarded as the key issue on which their continued role in government depended: the closure of the nuclear industry. The other issue that the Greens devoted most attention to was ecological taxation (Rüdig, 2002)

The Eco-Tax

The debate on ecological taxation had raged in German politics for more than 10 years. The Greens had embraced the idea in the early 1990s, but with the increasing importance of the *Standortdebatte* (the debate about Germany as a place of investment in a globalized economy), the Greens felt that they had to modify their tax policy to make it fit in with the desire to improve the conditions under which companies were investing in Germany. The result of this Green debate was the idea that the proceeds of the eco-tax would not, as earlier models had suggested, be used for environmental purposes. Instead, Green policy was to use the proceeds of the tax to reduce secondary labour costs. Over the years, the relative size of these costs for unemployment insurance, pensions and health insurance had risen steadily, and they were blamed for the rise in unemployment as they made it increasingly expensive for employers to take on staff. To use the eco-tax to put more money into the pension system, for example, and thus allow pension contributions to fall, would kill two birds with one stone: the increased price of energy would provide an incentive to conserve energy, with beneficial effects for the environment, and in particular in terms of reaching Germany's ambitious target of reducing CO_2 emissions by 25 per cent by 2005; and the reduction in secondary labour costs would help to fight unemployment.

The SPD could live with the general principle behind the idea. Up for discussion was the size of the tax, and the exact conditions that would apply. In an interview in the election campaign, Schröder had already made a commitment that the resulting increase in petrol prices would not be more than 6 Pfennigs per litre, and this limited the negotiating options the Greens could take. In the end, the agreement reached consisted of the introduction of the eco-tax in three phases. This allowed Schröder to stick to his promise for the first phase and generate substantial savings in indirect labour costs for the full four years of the policy.

The drafting of the necessary tax bill provided more difficulties: industry lobbied successfully for highly energy-intensive industries to be exempted from the tax. Another abnormality that attracted criticism was the fact that public transport, including the railways and local buses and trams, were not exempted. The eco-tax thus increased the cost of public transport as well. The energy tax also was applied to all forms of energy, not only the fossil-fuel generated energy that produced greenhouse gases. And finally, the tax was socially regressive. Only those who were in employment and paid pension contributions were financially better off or saw no difference; but students, housewives, pensioners, and the unemployed, who had no secondary labour costs to pay, still had to pay more for their energy but failed to see any benefits. The financial disadvantage for pensioners became even stronger when, in 2000, the government decided for reasons of budget discipline not to increase pensions in line with average wages but only in line with inflation.

Has the policy been a success? Politically, the eco-tax was never popular. Public opinion polls showed almost universal rejection. Even environmentalists were disappointed as the proceeds did not directly contribute to environmental improvements, and opposition politicians used this to call the tax a misnomer that had nothing to do with the environment. When, in 2000 and 2001, petrol prices started to increase quite sharply due to a rising dollar and world petrol market conditions, a public campaign for the abolition of the eco-tax attracted some support. Lorry drivers staged major protests and blocked off Berlin for one day. In particular the FDP, once the protagonists of environmental policy in the early 1970s, campaigned vigorously for a total repeal of the eco-tax.

In terms of its environmental impact, the eco-tax has been a success: petrol and energy consumption have decreased since its introduction (BMU, 2002). In terms of reducing secondary labour costs, the eco-tax appears not to have made a radical difference, in particular as the downturn of the economy and rising unemployment in 2002 have placed additional demands on pensions and health insurance contributions. Overall, the eco-tax has not brought the great effects that originally were promised. To some, this was predictable as the size of the tax was far too small. For others, the story of the tax demonstrates once again that the electorate does not take kindly to new taxes of whatever kind. The project of slowly increasing energy prices, as proposed by the protagonists of the eco-tax idea, seems politically unfeasible. The government argues that, without the eco-tax, pension contributions would have to be even higher. But this is a rather abstract argument that is difficult to sell, what people see is that they had to pay more tax, and yet pension contributions are still rising and unemployment is back to the levels of the Kohl government. It will be difficult for a future government to sell the idea of ecological taxation to the German electorate again.

Phasing Out Nuclear Power

The second major demand that the Greens insisted on was an end to nuclear power. Back in the 1980s, after Chernobyl, the Greens demanded the immediate shut-down of the nuclear industry, and scenarios were produced by Green think-tanks that such a rapid closure (within a year or two) was indeed economically and technically possible. For the modern Green politician of the 1990s, it was equally clear that the Greens could not possibly hope to implement such a policy. One reason was the German legal system: nuclear operators had been given a licence to run their nuclear power stations. If now their licences were revoked, many legal experts claimed that they could claim compensation. Would the government be prepared to risk a long court case and, if it lost, pay billions of marks in compensation? No, not with Schröder as Chancellor: during his election campaign, he had insisted that any phasing-out would have to be negotiated with the utilities and reached in a consensus.

The Greens knew that they could only enter a government with the SPD if they agreed to this consensus solution. That also meant the end of the 'harassment' tactics at state level. But how long would nuclear stations still have to run before finally being closed down? The SPD did not want any commitment to a specific figure before the negotiations. The Greens concentrated, therefore, on a package which had the reform of nuclear regulation including the end of reprocessing within 100 days, as its key element. That was agreed with the SPD. Then, if no phasing-out had been successfully agreed with the utilities after one year, the government would prepare legislation for a forced phasing-out.

Most Greens were happy with that result, but it quickly turned out to be unworkable. Trittin, appointed to head an Environment Ministry that had previously been a staunch supporter of the nuclear industry, started drafting a new atomic law but immediately ran into trouble. The utilities strongly opposed the ban on reprocessing that he wanted to impose, claiming that the treaties they had signed with France and Britain would require them to pay hefty compensation. Trittin claimed that this was not the case, but it quickly turned out that secret contracts as well as diplomatic agreements existed of which the government had not been aware. Furthermore, the utilities refused to enter any negotiations if the reprocessing ban was imposed. Schröder backed the utilities and humiliated Trittin. This was a clear violation of the coalition agreement between the SPD and the Greens, but the Greens did not want to leave the government over this. Instead, Trittin had to back down completely, and a long period of negotiations started in which the Greens now were on the defensive.

One bargaining chip the Environment Minister retained were nuclear waste transports which had been suspended in 1998 following a scandal about breaches of safety guidelines. With on-site waste storage facilities due to run out of capacity within a few months, nuclear plants would be forced to shut down unless waste transports could resume. However, Chancellor Schröder did not want an open conflict with industry: his whole economic strategy was based on reaching consensus with industry to help him reach his aims of reducing unemployment. He did not want to antagonize industrial interests by making life difficult for the utility industry. By appointing Werner Müller, a former utility manager, to be his economics minister and leaving it to him and Trittin to negotiate the consensus, Schröder had already indicated where his sympathies lay. Given the governments unwillingness to risk conflict, the industry saw no reason to compromise.

It was only towards the end of 1999 that the government could finally agree on restating its willingness to force the utilities into a phasing-out plan by legislation. The internally disputed issue had been under which conditions such legislation would be free from being challenged successfully in the Federal Constitutional Court and free of any claim for compensation. After seeking more legal advice, the agreement finally was that the operating time of all reactors could justifiably be limited by law to 30 years, plus a transition period of 3 years. This 30 + 3 solution attracted major opposition from within the Green Party which eventually agreed to abide by it. With this new negotiating position, supplemented by a willingness to allow a restart of waste transport, negotiations started again in early 2000. In June 2000, Chancellor Schröder could annouce that an agreement had been reached: the agreement was not based on a set time limit for each reactor, but on the total amount of nuclear electricity produced. This was the equivalent of an operating time of 32 years, but industry had the option to close some of its older plants much earlier to give the more recent plants a longer operating life. In terms of the timetable of closures, the agreement meant that no nuclear power station was likely to close before the elections in 2002, and the last nuclear power station was unlikely to be closed down until well into the 2020s (Rüdig, 2000).

All environmental groups, including BUND, NABU and Greenpeace, as well as the local anti-nuclear groups around Gorleben, strongly opposed the agreement. Within the Greens, the 'consensus' was by no means universally welcome, but ultimately the party backed Trittin. Legislation was finally prepared and passed in 2001.

This conclusion of the nuclear issue was painful for the Greens who now saw themselves as being at odds with their erstwhile closest allies in the anti-nuclear movement. Greens now had to defend nuclear waste transports to Gorleben which restarted in late 2000. The compromise allows for waste shipments to The Hague and Sellafield to continue until 2005. In order to store the spent nuclear fuel that otherwise would be shipped abroad, new temporary storage facilities have to be constructed at each nuclear power station.

The consensus left unresolved the question of the final storage of nuclear waste. Work on Gorleben was suspended for three years, and a working group was set up to look for a range of options. Environmental groups were also intended to be part of the working group but, in 2002, they decided to leave in protest at the willingness of the government to grant a licence for another intermediate waste storage facility.

Other Issues

As the Greens pursued the end of the nuclear industry, they were keen to develop alternatives. Funding for renewable energy alternatives were increased, starting with a solar energy programme. The government also favoured wind energy, and passed a law creating more beneficial conditions for the use of combined heat and power (CHP). Apart from making more money available for state subsidies, it is noteworthy that command and control options continued to be shunned: instead, Greens in government followed the pattern already established before, relying on negotiations with industry about voluntary commitments. In the view of the council of environmental experts reporting regularly to the government on environmental policy, there must be serious doubts whether the reliance on voluntary agreements will be sufficient to reach Germany's climate policy goals (Rat der Sachverständigen für Umweltfragen, 2002, p. 242).

The government's own report on the environmental achievements of the Red–Green government lists countless initiatives on a broad range of issues (BMU, 2002), but there were few spectacular successes. The passage of a new Federal Nature Protection Law in 2002 was perhaps the most important achievement, it was one of few measures that attracted the unequivocal support of environmental groups who were given further rights to take legal action in the public interest. Other key policy areas were outside the reach of Trittin: he once unsuccessfully tried to raise the motorway speed limit issue, but the whole transport area remained firmly under the control of the Green's coalition partner.

One issue that one could expect the Greens to focus on was a sustainable development strategy which, arguably, had been neglected by federal policy-makers in previous years (Beuermann and Burdick, 1998). However, the party had concentrated so heavily on the eco-tax and phasing out nuclear energy that this was not an early priority. When the process for the formulation of the strategy was finally started in 2000, it was again firmly placed outside any Green ministerial responsibility and was directly under the control of the Chancellor's Office. A national dialogue was started and, in April 2002, a national sustainable development strategy was finally published (Bundesregierung, 2002). In defence of the Greens, it can be said that they concentrated their efforts on specific policies and laws that made a material difference, rather than on maximizing their impact by drafting another 'programme' full of worthy aims but without any tangible effect.

Internationally, the German Greens also did not quite play the leading role that some had expected. At EU level, the actions of the German environment minister, Jürgen Trittin, were often constrained by decisions of the government. In 1999, for example, Trittin was ordered by Chancellor Schröder to veto a passage of a new directive on the recycling of old cars. Trittin complied, to the dismay of his colleagues on the EU Environment Council and environmental groups. At various climate summits, Trittin was able to play a more positive role: he and his French Green colleague, Dominique Voynet, appear to have played a crucial role in rebuffing the US position at the climate summit in The Hague.

After a very rocky start which saw even Green MPs call for the resignation of Jürgen Trittin, the Green Environment Minister recovered his standing after the conclusion of the nuclear phasing-out agreement. During the two first years, he had been the only Green minister devoting his attention to central concerns of Green environmental policy. The Foreign Minister, and the 'secret' or 'virtual' leader of the Greens,

Joschka Fischer, had not developed any particular environmental initiatives, and the Health Minister, Andrea Fischer, remained bogged down in bitter policy-infighting with the medical establishment which made her few friends. It was after she resigned, together with the SPD Agriculture Minister, over the first cases of bovine spongiform encephalopathy (BSE) found in Germany, that a second source of Green initiatives offered itself. The Greens persuaded Chancellor Schröder to agree to a total reorganization of the Agriculture Ministry, changing it from a department looking after a particular clientele to an active ministry charged primarily with the protection of the consumer. In charge of the new Ministry of Consumer Affairs, Nutrition and Agriculture was Renate Künast, a feisty and popular politician who was co-speaker for the federal Green Party.

Künast's aim was to set in motion a revolution in agricultural policy, the *Agrarwende*. Apart from strict measures to improve food safety standards, she started programmes to develop organic agriculture and also improve the rights of farm animals (e.g., through new regulations on chicken farms).

While Trittin and Künast could thus point to some successes, the Greens had to accept a number of defeats. One particular worry was transport policy. Here, the Greens found it difficult to make any progress. The Social Democrats showed no signs of introducing a paradigmatic change: investment in motorways had a high priority. The aim to stimulate public transport, in particular the railway system, was hampered by the constraints introduced by previous governments: the German railways had been put on a private-sector footing, operating as a private company. The trend was towards closing down lines and concentrating on profitable core businesses, such as high-speed train links between population centres. The Greens managed to mobilize some money from the sale of UMTS licences, but the overall impact seem to be quite limited. More disappointing for the Greens was a change in the discourse on transport: introducing the term 'mobility', the opposition Free Democrats in particular campaigned for more motorway construction. Also the Social Democrats were ready to focus on this issue, making the need to ensure 'mobility' into a key element of their policy. This has put the Greens on the defensive: in North Rhine-Westphalia, for instance, the regional Greens had to give way concerning their objections to numerous motorway projects as a condition of being able to continue as coalition partners with the SPD in 2000.

The only success the Greens could point to in the transport sector was the end of plans to construct a magnetic suspension high-speed train connection between Berlin and Hamburg. The 'Transrapid' project was killed off as the public subsidy was limited on the insistence of the Greens. However, the project appears to have made a recovery with a new project under way in North Rhine-Westphalia, strongly supported by the regional SPD.

Apart from success and failure in specific policy areas, Green politics also stood for a new style of politics. Have the Greens succeeded here? In terms of environmental policy-making, Jürgen Trittin was faced with both the ministry and its whole structure of advisory committees, dominated by pro-nuclear supporters. One of his first decisions was to replace the nuclear advisory committees and appoint 'alternative' anti-nuclear experts to key positions. A Green was also appointed as the new Head of the administrative agency concerned with radiation protection. 'Alternative' experts were also well represented on the working group to find a solution for the final disposal of nuclear waste. The 'inclusive' style mainly applied to representatives of various 'Green' think-tanks, such as the Öko-Institut (Institute for Applied Ecology) which had played an important historical role in challenging the claims of the nuclear industry and developing alternative energy policies for a non-nuclear future. The campaiging groups, such as the BUND, NABU and Greenpeace, remained distant: they had not been directly involved in the so-called consensus talks on nuclear energy, and strongly opposed the results of these talks. Efforts to involve them in other ways generally failed in the energy field: representatives of all environmental groups did not want to be coopted to play a role in the implementation of the nuclear 'consensus' that they passionately opposed.

Evaluation and Outlook

In the general election of September 2002, the Greens managed to increase their share of the vote from 6.7 per cent in 1998 to 8.4 per cent. After many commentators had written off their prospects only a few weeks before the elections, and many academic observers had expressed scepticism about the future of the Greens in government (Lees, 2000; Raschke, 2001), this result could be seen as a surprise. Have the Greens been more successful in government than is commonly realized? One element of their good performance in 2002 which has kept the Red–Green government in power has certainly been the high degree of environmental policy competence that voters ascribe to them. Green voters overwhelmingly see the party as the party of the environment, and with floods in August 2002 raising issues such as global warming, the Greens were well placed to take electoral advantage (Forschungsgruppe Wahlen, 2002).

In the view of the voters, the Greens thus appeared to have done well in office. Their governmental performance increased the public perception of their environmental policy competence. How successful have they been, though, in changing the patterns of German environmental policy-making? Some of the changes have completely reversed decades of policy orientation: never before has a federal environment minister been dedicated to the closure of the nuclear industry. Ecological taxation had not been accepted at federal level before. A move away from industrialized agriculture to an ecologically-oriented, organic agriculture is certainly a revolutionary change for German agricultural policy. Headline policies have certainly changed, but how successfully these policies can be implemented in the future is another question.

Ecological taxation has made a contribution to limiting greenhouse gas emissions, but is highly unpopular and thus difficult to expand in coming years. In the 2002 coalition negotiations, there was no agreement on any further stage of the eco-tax, but only a commitment to consider such a policy at a later date. The eco-tax has not quite brought about the revolution that some had hoped. On nuclear power, no single nuclear power station was closed down in the first period of office. This should change during the second legislative term but, ominously for the Greens, they had to accept that one station due to close in 2003, Obrigheim, will be kept running for a further two years as the result of a personal commitment given to the utility president by Chancellor Schröder. There are some success stories such as major funding for renewable energy sources and animal rights legislation, but they have to be seen in the context of other major policy defeats. Particularly in the area of transport policy, it is very difficult to reconcile the continued decline of rail and public transport and the expansion of the German motorway system, to be used by motorists unhindered by speed limitations, with Green principles. Overall, environmental organizations such as the BUND have come up with positive evaluations of the four years of Red–Green environmental performance, but there remain strong misgivings and disappointment over the nuclear question and the lack of progress in greening the transport system (BUND, 2002).

At international and EU level, a specific Green impact is difficult to identify. Even Green ministers are first of all bound by the national interests they represent, with opportunities to pursue specifically Green policies in conjunction with other Green ministers being very limited. At the other end, at local and regional government, Greens have not been as present in Land governments as in some previous years, with a federal

Green government now facing the prospect of being undermined and opposed by local and regional bodies in just the same way as Greens have previously used the federal structure to oppose federal policies not to their liking. Also, in terms of involving environmental groups and in terms of dominant policy styles, there is perhaps more continuity with Greens in government than change. Furthermore, Greens had to accept voluntary agreements with industry as one major part of the policy repertoire, with other, more traditional, policy instruments remaining mainly off the agenda (the eco-tax being the main exception). In terms of greater involvement of environmental groups in the policy-making process, the nuclear phasing-out negotiations continued the tradition of exclusion. In other policy areas, such as nature protection, this appears to be very different, though. Ultimately, this is a question of power: where there are strong, established interests, such as the utility industry or the car industry, Greens in government find it very difficult to mobilize for radical change. Being and remaining in government imposes restrictions on what Greens can and cannot do. In some cases, thus, being in office could be seen to increase rather than reduce Green powerlessness

Conclusion

Environmental policy is a policy area that has enjoyed a particularly high salience in German politics. Protest movements and the rise of the Green Party ensured that the issue became highly politicized in the 1970s and 1980s. The role of the Greens in local, regional and federal government has underlined the establishment of Green concerns within the political system. While environmental public opinion remains strong, the 1990s and early twenty-first century have demonstrated the limits of a Green revolution. The German electorate would like something done about the environment, but most are not willing to change their lifestyle in a fundamental way or to pay additional taxes for environmental purposes. Thus the Green Party in government has had to limit itself to politically feasible projects and turn its back on the more Utopian views of a Green society that were dominant in its early history.

13

Political Culture and Identity: The Post-Unification Search for 'Inner Unity'

DAVID P. CONRADT

For the rest of the world German unification was formally and successfully completed on 3 October 1990 when the GDR (or East Germany) ceased to exist and, reconstituted into five states or Länder, merged with the Federal Republic. But the social, economic and cultural unification of the once-divided country – what Germans term the 'inner unity' or 'Wall in People's Heads' – is far from complete. The initial hope that at least western-style economic prosperity, the easy part of inner unity, would come to the East within 10 years has not been realized. The former East Germany remains a region dependent on western transfer payments for about 40 per cent of its private consumption, government spending and investment. East Germans, in other words, themselves produce only about 60 per cent of what they consume. Unemployment in the east in 2002 was about 18 per cent (roughly double the western level).

The harsh economic realities of unification are mirrored in the social sphere. Since unification the proportion of easterners who consider themselves 'second-class citizens' continues to rise. Net out-migration from the east in 2001 was almost 200,000 and was heavily concentrated among the younger, better-educated age groups. As a result of this migration of younger families, the number of school-age children in the east has dropped by almost 50 per cent. In one state, Saxony, this means the closing of 350 primary schools.

These economic and social differences have made 'inner unity' an elusive goal. In this chapter we examine the condition of this 'inner unity'. What have we found out about the similarities and differences in the political attitudes, values and beliefs of East and West Germans since unification? Are there now signs of an east–west convergence in political culture, or will persistent and deep regional differences (similar to those found in Italy's Mezzogiorno and the Basque region in Spain) characterize post-unification Germany? Do we have *innere Einheit (inner unity)* (Veen, 1997), or do we still face a 'long, long road' (Bauer-Kaase and Kaase, 1997).

Many analysts consider a nation's political culture – its fundamental political beliefs and values – as a critical factor in the stability or instability of a regime. Such beliefs and values include the level of national identity and pride; social and political trust in core political institutions and processes; political participation; and policy attitudes (i.e., the expectations East and West Germans have of the government). The analytical thread that runs through this chapter is the search for *diffuse* support, the rain or shine attitude or reservoir of goodwill, without which democracies could not survive hard times. We are particularly concerned with the development and level of diffuse support in the old GDR and its relationship to the specific output of the post-unification political system. We know from the 'old' Federal Republic that the development of a high level of diffuse support took at least 20 years (Conradt, 1980). As we shall see below, East German support for the values, processes and institutions of German democracy is more specific, linked to situational factors such as unemployment and perceptions about the economy. Support for democracy is driven by concrete system performance as it was in the early years of the Federal Republic.

Instant (West German-Style) Democrats?

The early investigations of post-unification political culture found great similarities in basic attitudes between the once-divided nation (Weil, 1993; Dalton, 1994a). One study found that: 'the democratic transition in 1989–1990 begins with the East German public expressing strong support for democratic norms and an enthusiasm for the democratic process. East Germans voice support for democratic values that rivals or exceeds the expression of democratic norms in the West' (Dalton, 1994).

How could East Germans have acquired democratic values and attitudes without having had any experience with democratic institutions? The answer was to be found in East Germany's 'vicarious experience of democracy as practised from 1949–1989 in the Federal Republic'.

Dalton (1994a) argued that: 'although we cannot directly test the influence of contact with the West, the political model of the Federal Republic and the transmission of this information to the Eastern public must have played a large role in the creation of support for democratic values in the East'. Thus the citizens of the former GDR were pre-socialized to liberal democracy through their knowledge and vicarious experience of the Federal Republic's development. Since the Federal Republic was more attractive than its own system, the Communist regime was unable to sufficiently socialize new generations. Younger generations anticipated the values of the new regime (i.e., the liberal democracy of the Federal Republic) *before* the revolution. These 'demonstration effects', it was argued, 'can serve as a functional equivalent to a reservoir of legitimation that otherwise takes years to build up'. Support for democracy in post-Franco Spain, for example, grew faster than in post-1945 West Germany (Weil, 1987) because the prestige of foreign democracies was higher. Thus East Germans, according to Weil (1993, p. 209) appear 'to have been born virtually fully democratic'.

If the instant democrats theory is correct, 40 years of Communist education, propaganda and attempted indoctrination had little effect: more important was eastern exposure to West German media and, above all, television. But, as Klingemann and Hofferbert (1994, p.33) contend, 'it strains credulity to think that the furtive and often fictional models provided by television could have overpowered those contained in the entire East German educational and propaganda systems'.

This explanation also adopts a very limited view of socialization in the former GDR. We now know that there are substantial value differences between east and west that are the results of 40 years of division. In spite of their opposition to the one-party dictatorship, which culminated in the 1989 collapse of the regime, East Germans remain far more supportive of socialism as an ideal than West Germans. One question that attempts to tap the impact of socialization under the GDR asks the respondents whether they agreed or disagreed with the statement: 'Socialism is basically a good idea that was badly carried out.' As Figure 13.1 shows, there has been little change in the distribution of responses between the two regions. About 75 to 80 per cent of easterners have consistently agreed with the statement, as compared to about 40 to 45 per cent of respondents in the 'old' Federal Republic. To an extent the eastern responses represent a defence of the GDR's past in terms of an idealized and abstract conception of socialism. When asked in 1998 whether they were satisfied with socialism as it *actually existed*

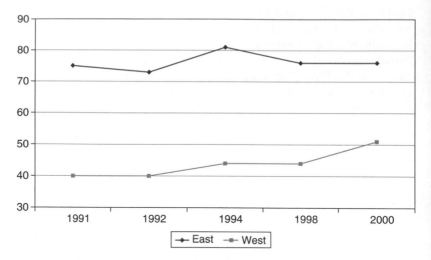

FIGURE 13.1 *'Socialism a good idea, only badly carried out?'* Percentage agreeing, East-West Germany, 1991–2000
Note: Percentage agreeing = % agree fully + % agree basically)
Source: General Social Surveys, 1991–2000.

in the GDR, the support level dropped sharply to only 34 per cent, and only 23 per cent in the same survey considered socialism to be the best form of government. Nonetheless, supporters of the socialist ideal are characterized by lower levels of trust in the institutions of the Federal Republic and a higher level of dissatisfaction with democracy as practised in these institutions. Socialization remains a factor, but one that should not be overestimated. This socialization factor should over time become less relevant. This was certainly the case in West Germany where strong residual support for Nazism and the restoration of the Hohenzollern monarchy was found in early post-war surveys (Boynton and Loewenberg, 1974). This support was, however, concentrated among older age cohorts who had become relatively passive (i.e., their participation rates were well below the already low West German mean). By 1960 this residue had all but disappeared. Thus far, however, there is no such pattern in the east.

There are also a number of political developments in the former GDR that cast doubt on the instant democrat thesis:

1 Substantial support for the former, ruling Communist Party, the PDS, in the new eastern states with practically no support in the west. The PDS thus has a strong interest in maintaining or expanding the current level of east–west differences.

2 The clearly disproportionate amount of xenophobic right-wing violence in the east. According to the *Verfassungsschutz* (Federal office for the protection of the constitution) data for 2000, right-wing violence in the new states occurs at a rate of 2.21 per 100,000 population as compared to 0.95 for the old states. While the west is not immune from such attacks on foreign residents, the frequency of such incidents is much greater in the east. Moreover, there is little evidence of any broad popular support for such behaviour in the west; however, a number of anecdotal reports from the east indicate that many ordinary easterners tacitly support this behaviour.

3 Persistent warnings from mainstream national political figures that the continued relative economic decline in the east, including population transfers, signals the emergence of a German *Mezzogiorno*, a region and economy uncoupled from the west and permanently doomed to second-class status. (Related to this latter sentiment is the very weak representation of the eastern perspective at the very highest levels of state and society. *Easterners*, such as Angela Merkel, become practically mute about the specific problems of the region once they achieve national status.)

One State, Two Cultures?

With these developments in mind other analysts have emphasized the differences between the two countries that are inevitable result of the 40-year division (Minkenberg, 1993; Klingemann and Hofferbert, 1994; Noelle-Neumann, 1994; Bauer-Kaase, 1996; Rohrschneider, 1999). They find persistent east–west differences in (1) the acceptance of democracy as practised in Germany; (2) satisfaction with the performance of democracy in Germany; (3) confidence in the ability of democratic institutions to solve major problems; (4) trust, pride and confidence in democratic political institutions and processes; (5) willingness to abandon democratic principles for dictatorship in times of stress; and (6) policy expectations from government. East Germans are different. They are less satisfied with democracy, less confident about the capability of the democratic system to deal with future problems, less trusting of democratic institutions and less supportive of economic values such as competition and individual responsibility. Freedom is less important to them than economic security and equality. (Economic security was also more important than freedom for West Germans in the post-war (1947–49) period: see Merritt, 1995, p. 339.) But, although less confident and trusting in German-style democracy, they also expect government to do more for them than do West Germans. By margins of 2 or 3 to 1, East Germans want the government to reduce income differences, control wages and salaries, limit prices, and guarantee full employment.

Socialization versus Situation

The two-culture explanation brings the importance of socialization and situation into sharper relief. Is East German identity a result of the legacy of GDR socialism or the product of unification? How much of the easterners' lower level of support for the institutions, processes and values of liberal democracy is a function of their socialization during the 40-year GDR regime, and how much is due to the concrete experiences since unification, above all that of unemployment and the resultant economic and social insecurity?

Situational Differences

There are a number of fundamental differences between the two regions that form the situational parameters within which cultural values have been formed (Zapf, 2000). The first inequality, of course, is in population. West Germany is four times more populous than the former GDR. This means that the probability of an East German interacting with a West German is four times greater than the reverse situation. Easterners are more likely to be reminded of their minority status than westerners of their majority status. Minorities qua minorities will feel disadvantaged, exploited and neglected by the majority. During the unification process, easterners were reminded, in many ways, that they were the 'fifth' wheel; a problem rather than an opportunity for the dominant West German state and society, which really could do quite well without them. The book by Wolfgang Schäuble (1991), *Der Vertrag*, is an excellent example of the paternalistic and patronizing approach to easterners taken by the West German elite. The book is Schäuble's account of the negotiations between the Kohl government and the first (and last) freely elected government of the GDR, which led to the final unification treaty. Schäuble and, we can assume, the West German team, which also included Wolfgang Clement who represented the Länder, left little doubt that the GDR would enter the federation under western terms. This was no merger of equals: the majority was assimilating the minority on its terms.

The second fundamental inequality was economic. The economic potential of the West was at least eight times greater than that of the East (the population being four times as great, and the per capita GDP twice as great). The GDP estimate was soon shown to be overly generous, thus widening the gap. While the transformation of West German political culture after 1945–49 was the result of at least a 20-year process with numerous determinants (Conradt, 1980), one certainly stands out: the extraordinary record of non-inflationary economic growth that started with the currency reform of 1948 and continued until the late 1960s. During this period, average annual GDP growth averaged a phenomenal 7 per cent, inflation a well-contained 2 per cent. The West German economic machine demanded millions of new jobs, far more than the indigenous population could provide, and by the early 1960s there was an acute labour shortage with the subsequent importation of millions of foreign workers. This economic success meant an easy birth and infancy for German democracy. When the inevitable economic downturns occurred, the post-war system was well established through second-order factors such as socialization and the Federal Republic's total integration into the western economic and security systems.

The East German experience, in spite of expectations on the part of some Western politicians, above all Helmut Kohl, of another *Wirtschaftswunder* (economic miracle), has been quite different. Since 1991 West Germans have transferred over a trillion dollars to the East. About 30 per cent of these funds have gone as investments, including infrastructure projects and industrial restructuring. Expenditures for labour market and social programmes have comprised an additional 40 per cent. The remaining 30 per cent has gone to state and local governments through a variety of complex revenue-sharing and tax-distribution programmes. There are some significant trends in these data. The investment portion of the transfers has declined from about DM70 billion annually from 1991 to 1993 to about DM50 billion per year from 1997 to 1999. The consumption share of the transfers (labour market and social programmes) has jumped from DM67 billion in 1991–93 to DM88 billion by 1997–99. The declining level of investments could mean less growth and fewer jobs being in the future.

What has all this money bought? About three million East German pensioners now receive benefits that exceed those of their West German counterparts. Since 1991, over nine million telephone lines have been installed, five million apartments have been brought up to Western standards, 12,000 kilometres of new streets and highways and another 5,000 kilometres of new railway lines have been built. Another DM20 billion has been spent on an environmental clean-up, including sewage treatment plants throughout the region.

The impact of these funds can also be seen in Table 13.1, which presents east–west comparisons for a variety of economic indicators. Per capita GDP has grown from 35 per cent of the western level in 1991 to 62 per cent by 2001. Labour costs (and hence wages and salaries) are up from 48 per cent to 75 per cent of western levels. Unit labour costs in 2001 were down to 110 per cent of those in the old Federal Republic, which represents a substantial improvement in productivity. At least until 1998 investments were higher than the western level, although this has probably declined in the past two years. East Germany's export performance relative to West Germany, however, has improved substantially in the last decade. Finally, by 2001 the number of independent small businesses had grown to about 80 per cent of the western level.

In spite of these massive transfers of capital, which have brought almost all East Germans substantive material improvements in their lives, unemployment and the fear of unemployment remains far higher in the East than in the West. About half of the East German population between 1990 and 1995 was in some way affected by unemployment. They were perhaps (1) currently unemployed and/or (2) long-term unemployed, (3) had lost their jobs in the immediate aftermath of

TABLE 13.1 *Economic indicators*
1991–2001 (East as a percentage of West)

	1991	2001
GDP per capita	35	62
Labour costs	48	75
Labour productivity	35	71
Unit labour costs	141	110
Investments	62	98
Export level (industrial)	52	61
Independent non-manual (*Selbstständigen*)	49	78

Sources: Deutsches Institut für Wirtschaft Forschung, Wochenbericht No. 17 (2002), pp. 19–20; for exports, Federal Statistical Office.

unification or (4) currently feared unemployment or short time. Between 1990 and 1993 over half (52 per cent) of East Germans had experienced one or more of these aspects of unemployment as compared to only 25 per cent of West Germans.

Little wonder that East Germans are no fans of laissez-faire government. Numerous studies over the past ten years have found them to be more supportive of a socio-economic conception of democracy in the form of government guarantees for employment, housing, medical and childcare. Equality in the form of reduced income differences is also a legitimate state priority in the East German view. Westerners, however, generally have a more procedural or liberal conception of democracy. This is a well-known characteristic of West German political culture. In a study conducted in the late 1970s and published in Conradt (1981) well over 80 per cent of westerners saw equality before the law and freedom of expression as absolutely necessary for democracy, but only just over 30 per cent felt that a democracy had to have 'only moderate differences in income'. Defining consensus as agreement that a value was essential for democracy *and* was already realized in the Federal Republic, about three-quarters of the public agreed that the key liberal values of the rule of law, freedom of expression, and political competition had reached this status, but only 5 per cent had such a view of 'moderate differences in income'.

A third inequality involves migration, or the brain drain from East to West. This has been under way since 1945, and by 1961 it amounted to a net loss of 3 million for East Germany, or about one-fifth of its population. The Wall greatly reduced, but did not eliminate, the net loss. Even with the Wall and the sealed borders an additional 400,000 easterners managed to leave between 1961 and 1989. This accelerated with the collapse of the GDR. Hunt (2000) has shown that out-migration since 1989 has been concentrated among the younger, better-educated and ambitious East Germans who are attracted rather than repelled by the greater inequality in the west.

A fourth asymmetry between the East and West Germans involves the disparity in their interest in one another. An interest in West Germany among easterners is far higher than westerners interest in the East. Easterners are three times more likely to visit the West than westerners are to come East. While about one-third of West Germans report that they have friends or relatives in the East, about 85 per cent of easterners have such relationships in the West. This is also seen in the pattern of media usage. Few if any westerners have ever watched East German television, but since the 1970s West German television has been part of the GDR lifestyle.

Finally, the impact of the end of Communism and unification has differed greatly in the two regions. East Germans brought down the Communist state in the autumn of 1989, but West Germans did not fight for anything, either after 1945 or in 1989. Unification has also meant far more economic and social dislocation for easterners than for westerners. Not only the loss of employment, but also the adjustment to western procedures and values was costly to easterners. This can be seen in the 50 per cent drop in marriages and births following unification; these phenomena are usually found only in societies undergoing the traumatic stress of war or depression.

Limitations of Both Theses

Both the instant democrat and two-culture theses are in need of refinement. Before we throw out half a century of research on socialization we must take a closer look at age and generational factors. With the passage of time we should find, as we did in the West German research, increasing differences between age groups in the East and the first signs of convergence among the youngest age cohorts in both regions. There is also the possibility of a selective socialization process in which the residual effects of 40 years of official indoctrination are limited to those who led or managed the GDR regime: party activists, state functionaries, army officers, middle-to-upper level personnel in the socialist economy, the 'socialist intelligentsia', and STASI officers (Roller, 1997). These groups probably constitute about 25 per cent of the East German population (Zelle, 1998). Their level of engagement in the 1990s was expressed above all by their membership in, and support of, the PDS.

Much of this analysis also leaves open the important 'So what?' question. Do these east–west differences have any significance for the long-run stability and performance of the democratic order in post-unification Germany? Does people's stated dissatisfaction with the way democracy functions simply measure public opinion about the government of the day? Is it not normal for a substantial proportion of the citizenry in any democracy to be dissatisfied and to channel that into support for the opposition parties? Or, as long as solid majorities in both regions support the 'basics' (i.e., democratic government), the market economy and Germany's full integration into the European Union and NATO, of what significance are lower levels of trust, confidence and national identity?

There is some support for this argument. In a 2000 survey Hofferbert and Klingemann (2000) find the usual differences between the two regions: in comparison to westerners, easterners prefer equality to freedom, they have more of a substantive than a procedural conception of democracy and they are less likely to be satisfied with post-unification democracy. But Klingemann and Hofferbert go on to demonstrate that the great majorities who are dissatisfied contain this discontent within the boundaries of the established party system. And even for the small minority of non-democrats in both regions, withdrawal rather than support for anti-system movements is the preferred course. They conclude: 'we find little support for the argument that two generations of political socialization under the old [Communist] regime created a political soil infertile for normal democratic politics' (p. 15). Much of their argument hinges on how they classify the former Communists in the East, the PDS. Are they plotting the overthrow of the government? Are they advocating an armed Leninist-style revolution? Hofferbert and Klingemann see them as 'dissatisfied democrats' working within the established framework. As examples of their commitment to the democratic constitutional order they cite the SPD–PDS coalitions in two of the eastern states.

A Third Approach: Performance-Based Convergence/Divergence?

A third approach focuses on the importance of system performance as the key factor in the future development of post-unification political culture. Simply put, it will be concrete policy performance that determines whether there will be convergence or divergence in east–west political culture. A variety of research has already found that the 'attitudes of eastern Germans are more strongly dependent on the perceived output of the political system than is the case in western Germany' (Zelle, 1998, pp. 19–21). This is, of course, similar to the post-war West German pattern (Conradt, 1980; Conradt, 1981). The work of Rohrschneider (1996, 1999) with Berlin elites also finds that among easterners support for the market economy is specific, dependent on their evaluation of economic conditions. Eastern members of parliament basically had a wait-and-see attitude towards core western institutions. While the eastern elites acknowledged the superiority of the economic system, they still did not endorse market values. As in politics, eastern support for the market is 'more performance dependent than among West MPs' (1996a, p. 98).

East German political cultural attitudes are sensitive to the economy. In 1996 some 39 per cent of East Germans, as compared to 17 per cent of westerners, wanted substantial or 'total' change in the democratic system. Among those respondents who had been unemployed during the past 10 years these proportions rose to 45 per cent in the East and 24 per cent in the West. Similarly, about 44 per cent of unemployed West Germans feel that they are receiving less or much less than they deserve, as compared to 68 per cent of East Germans.

The data cited so frequently by the two-culture school, showing eastern support for socialism and/or antipathy for democracy 'as practised in the Federal Republic', is very specific and reflects eastern experience with the post-unification economy and political system and specifically unemployment, loss of status, forced geographic mobility and the *Entwertung* (devaluation) of their identity. These traumatic events are far more likely to have affected easterners than westerners. Thus, like West Germans in the 1950s, their support/non-support is a function of their relationship to the system's output. When and if the post-unification system starts to work for them, their attitudes towards it will become more positive.

Political Culture: Affective Orientations

Among the dimensions of political culture none has received more attention than the affective. It was indeed the central finding of the early work on West German political culture (Conradt, 1980). Germans, unlike the Americans, English and Mexicans, but similar to the Italians, did not feel good about their political institutions and processes. This detachment was interpreted as potentially detrimental to the post-war system in the event of a performance breakdown. Positive affect is also central to the concept of 'diffuse' support, the reservoir of goodwill that can be drawn upon in time of low effectiveness.

In the early studies few differences were found between East and West Germans when general questions about national pride were asked. But, as the data in Table 13.2 show, the *sources* of pride are now different in the two regions. The East German pattern has emphasized the Republic's economic achievements and the former GDR's athletic successes. East German responses are not unlike those found for West Germany in the 1950s. The greatest difference between the two regions is in the area of political institutions as a source of pride. While about 30 per cent of West Germans consider the Constitution or the Bundestag as the single most important source of their national pride, only about one in eight East Germans shared this view. Pride in these political objects has been fairly stable over the 1991–2000 period.

These differences could be the result of several factors. First, they may simply reflect the relative lack of specific experiences with these institutions

TABLE 13.2 *Sources of pride: 1991–2000 (%)*

	West			East		
	1991	*1996*	*2000*	*1991*	*1996*	*2000*
Economic achievements	32	19	21	36	17	21
Democratic institutions[1]	31	34	30	11	11	13
Social welfare state	14	17	16	6	8	9
Athletic achievements	5	8	7	17	25	17
Art and literature	7	10	10	17	23	24
Scholarly achievements	11	12	16	13	16	16

[1] Constitution and Parliament.

Source: General Social Surveys 1991, 1996 and 2000.

that characterizes the East German population. An affective attachment to institutions needs time to develop. Quantitatively, of course, West Germans have had far greater experience. Second, the differences could reflect not the lack of experience of East Germans, but rather the quality of these experiences. The institutions of the Federal Republic are, according to this view, held at least partially responsible for the loss of jobs, status and identity that befell many easterners after 1990. Finally, these differences could be the result of the basically *apolitical character* of unification for many East Germans. Their support for unification was motivated primarily by the economic benefits which they associated with West German democracy, rather than any strong desire to participate in democratic politics. In any case East German pride, like that of West Germans in the 1950s, is focused on non-political objects such as the economy and the social welfare system. These are performance-sensitive areas. Would these pride levels, which are still lower than those in West Germany, persist in hard times? Our approach also posits divergence with declining performance as a real possibility.

Institutional Trust

The 1994 and 2000 General Social Surveys also enable us to explore the institutional trust dimension of political culture. An institutional trust index was constructed from items tapping into the respondent's trust in

Parliament, the courts, local government, the police and the federal government. The scores on the trust index were then regressed against east–west residence, estimations of Germany's economic situation, the 'socialism is a good idea' item, education, age and the respondent's self-position on a left–right scale. In 1994 at the all-German level, east–west residence is the most important predictor of institutional trust. The general economic situation and support for the socialist ideal are also important predictors of institutional trust, while education, age and the left–right variable are generally not significant. In the 2000 survey at the national level significant changes were found. The impact of the east–west variable declined sharply while the condition of the economy factor increased in importance. Indeed, in 2000 the economy, not the region, was the most important predictor of institutional trust.

Satisfaction with System Output: 'Just Desserts'

As we noted earlier, the most obvious structural difference between the two regions is the sharp disparity in economic conditions. Whether measured by per capita income, GDP, or estimates of the national economy the result has been unambiguous: East Germany and East Germans are poorer than their western countrymen. In Figure 13.2 evidence from

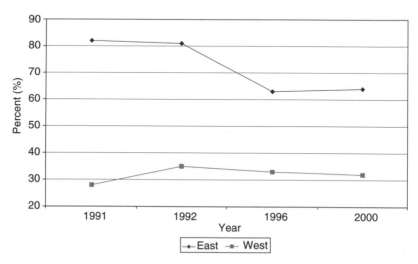

FIGURE 13.2   *Relative deprivation ('just desserts'): East-West Germany,*
1991–2000 (% receiving 'much' or 'somewhat' less than just share)
Note: Question text: 'In comparison to how others here in Germany live, do you believe that you are receiving your just share, more than your just share, somewhat less, or much less?'
Source: General Social Surveys, 1991, 1992, 1996, 2000.

a somewhat different measure, relative deprivation or 'just desserts', is presented. This item asks the respondent whether or not he or she, *in comparison to how others here in Germany are living*, is receiving his or her *just share (gerechten Anteil)*, more than a just share, somewhat less or far less. This variable incorporates the relative and subjective components of economic well-being and has been found to be a powerful predictor of political attitudes, including xenophobia. The results for the two regions since 1991 reveal, as expected, strong differences.

As Figure 13.2 shows, there has been some convergence since 1991. The proportion of East Germans stating that they were receiving their *'just share'* has increased from 18 per cent in 1991 to 36 per cent by 1998. Perhaps more importantly the proportion of East Germans who report that they were receiving 'much less' than their just share dropped to from 36 per cent to 14 per cent.

Specific and Diffuse Support

When asked abstract questions about democratic values such as 'A democracy without an opposition is unthinkable', or 'In every democracy citizens have the right to demonstrate', East Germans have consistently scored as high as (if not higher than) West Germans. When, however, reference is made to democracy 'as found in the Federal Republic', significant differences appear. By July 1991, less than a year after unification, most East Germans were clearly more sceptical about German-style democracy than West Germans; they either stated that there were better forms or they were undecided. Among West Germans there was much less ambiguity. In Table 13.3 we present a similar question from four surveys conducted between 1991 and 2000. This question does not refer to a specific government or policy, but asks the respondents for a general judgement about democracy in the Federal Republic.

TABLE 13.3 *Satisfaction with democracy as it exists in the Federal Republic: 1991–2000 (East–West, %)*

Satisfaction	1991		1992		1998		2000	
	East	West	East	West	East	West	East	West
Strong	34	67	19	48	21	49	23	55
Moderate	48	27	53	38	57	41	56	38
Weak	18	6	28	14	22	10	21	7
Total	100	100	100	100	100	100	100	100

Source: General Social Surveys 1991, 1992, 1998 and 2000.

However, the difference between the two regions drops sharply when respondents in surveys conducted between 1991 and 1998 were asked to judge the 'achievements of the Federal government' (i.e., the Kohl government: see Table 13.4). The very modest correlations between East and West on this item indicate that both East and West Germans, especially by 1992, were reacting in the same way to the Kohl government, but probably for different reasons, such as increased taxes in the West and high unemployment in the East. Clearly, while not an ideal measure of diffuse support, the 'satisfaction' question taps a more general orientation than the 'achievements' question.

What about the relationship between these two items? Is general support for democracy more or less dependent on satisfaction with the government of the day in the East? We should probably expect a closer relationship between diffuse and specific support in the former GDR than in the 'old' Federal Republic. With little experience in democratic politics and with little time to develop a 'reservoir of goodwill', East German attitudes towards democracy in the abstract will be closely related to their concrete experiences with the government of the day. Table 13.5 confirms this assumption. The relationship is stronger in the east than the west and in fact increased between 1991 and 1992. East Germans are more likely to base their general evaluations about democracy on their specific experiences with the Kohl government. Watching West German politics on television is no substitute for actually being governed. While two-thirds of West Germans are satisfied with democracy as it exists in the Federal Republic, only 35 per cent have the same view of the government of the day. In the East the relationship is much closer, with one-third satisfied with democracy and 25 per cent satisfied with the Kohl government. West Germans are thus less likely than East Germans to have their judgements about democracy determined by their experiences with any current government. This finding is confirmed by

TABLE 13.4 *Satisfaction with the achievements of the Federal Government 1991–98 (East–West)*

Satisfaction	1991		1992		1998	
	East	West	East	West	East	West
Strong	25	35	14	21	9	15
Moderate	52	44	52	46	46	46
Weak	23	21	34	33	45	39
Total	100	100	100	100	100	100

Source: General Social Surveys 1991, 1992 and 1998.

TABLE 13.5 *Relationship between specific and diffuse support 1991–98 (East–West Germany)*[1]

	All	East	West
1991	0.41	0.47	0.35
1992	0.42	0.58	0.37
1998	0.37	0.46	0.33

[1] A higher score indicates a stronger correlation.
Source: General Social Surveys, 1991, 1992 and 1998.

Cusack's work (1999, pp. 550–1) with aggregated survey data. He estimates that the reservoir of diffuse support is eight times greater in the West than in the East. Thus poor economic performance would drop support of the system in the west to 40 per cent, but in the east to only 5 per cent.

This pattern of stronger specific support in the east should not come as a surprise. Adherence to abstract democratic values in a new society will suffer in a climate of economic decline and uncertainty. This pattern is not new; it is in some respects similar to that found in studies of political culture during the early years of the Federal Republic (Allerbeck, 1976; Conradt, 1980; Baker, Dalton and Hildebrandt, 1981; Fuchs, 1989; Kaase, 1989). Throughout most of the 1950s positive attitudes towards democratic values, norms and institutions were strongly related to economic well-being (i.e., the economic winners were more supportive of the new democracy than those less well-off). Clear evidence of strong diffuse support was not found in any abundance until well into the 1960s. Even as late as 1965, the year of the Federal Republic's first post-war recession, a drop in system output was related to the rise of the radical right (if not neo-Nazi) National Democrats, a party which in 1969 almost cleared the 5 per cent hurdle.

Signs of Convergence

It has been suggested throughout this chapter that much of the *innere Einheit (internal unity)* problem is largely a function of situation and socialization. Survey after survey since unification has found that East Germans expect the state to do more for them than West Germans. East–west differences are especially large in the area of redistributive politics (i.e., the reduction of income differences, full employment, and

TABLE 13.6 *What should the state do? East–West differences by age 1996*[1]

Age group	18–29	30–44	45–59	60–74	75+
Difference	22	55	74	61	71

[1] Difference in East–West standardized factor scores. A higher score indicates greater East–West differences.
Source: General Social Survey, 1996.

universal healthcare). These differences, however, were found to be strongly related to age. Older East Germans continued to feel strongly attached to egalitarian, socialist ideals, while older respondents in the west generally were less egalitarian. This finding is consistent with a socialization/convergence approach.

A 1996 survey gives us the opportunity to examine responses to a series of questions about what the state should do (i.e., what is the responsibility of government) by age cohort. As expected, there were strong differences between eastern and western responses with the East Germans supporting a stronger state role. These differences, however, were substantially lower among the younger age cohorts. As Table 13.6 shows, the East–West difference among the 18–29 cohort was only about one-third as large as that found among the older age groups. By 1996 this youngest cohort had spent up to one-third of its life in a unified Germany. The psychological costs of abandoning prior beliefs and values or of reconciling them with new values are far lower for them than for older groups. The 1999 Eurobarometer study presented in Figure 13.3 offers further support for generational convergence. The east–west gap in satisfaction with democracy 'as it functions in Germany' is greatly reduced among the youngest age group. This is the group that is closest to the West German level; only 14 percentage points separates the under-30 age cohort as compared to about 30 per cent for the older age groups. These data are, of course, suggestive rather than confirmatory.

Conclusion

After 12 years of unification there are still substantial differences in political culture between the two German regions. Particularly important is the finding that East German support for democracy is still more specific than in West Germany (i.e., there is more of a 'What have

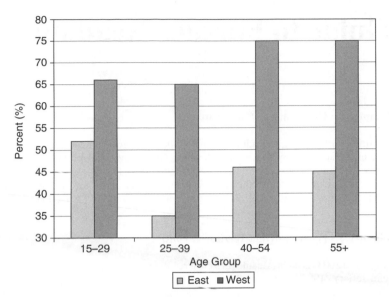

FIGURE 13.3 *Satisfaction with democracy in the Federal Republic, East–West Germany, by age group, 1999 (% satisfied).*
Source: Eurobarometer, No. 51, 55 (March–April, 1999).

you done for me lately?' dimension in the east). But this should not be surprising considering the historical, social and economic gap between the two regions. The lack of concrete experience with institutions and processes also explains the differences in political trust and national pride between the two regions. These differences, however, are not nearly as great as those found in the economic area. There are also signs of decreasing East–West differences among younger age groups, especially those with higher education. This suggests that convergence into a single integrated culture could be occurring selectively.

The results of the 2002 parliamentary elections support the idea of a gradual convergence in political culture. For the first time since unification, the PDS, the former Communists, lost votes at a national election. In 1998 about one voter in four in the eastern states endorsed the PDS; at the 2002 election this declined to about one in six. Perhaps more importantly, the PDS failed to surmount the 5 per cent hurdle and is now represented in Parliament by only two deputies, as compared to 36 in the 1998–2002 Parliament. East Germans appear to increasingly support the approach to their region taken by the national parties.

Guide to Further Reading

Chapter 1   Government at the Centre

Writing in English on the administrative aspects of government at the centre is scarce; the accounts by Mayntz and Scharpf (1975) and Johnson (1983) are now partly dated. For more recent brief analyses see Goetz (1999) and Busse (2001b). There is a richer literature on politics at the centre, often with a focus on the chancellorship. See Padgett (1994); Clemens and Paterson (1998); and Lees (2000).

Chapter 2   Federalism and Territorial Politics

Gunlicks (2003) is an invaluable reference resource on all aspects of the federal system. Jeffery (1999b) provides the most up-to-date and wide-ranging collection of essays on federalism in English. In the German language Sturm (2001) is a crisp introduction, particularly strong on party politics in the Länder and Bundesrat. The standard text is still Laufer and Münch (1997). Männle (1998) is a collection of essays exploring the idea of 'competitive' federalism. The annual *Jahrbuch des Föderalismus*, produced by the Europäisches Zentrum für Föderalismusforschung, reviews the main developments in analysis and practice, including the EU dimension of German federalism.

Chapter 3   Voter Choice and Electoral Politics

Kendall Baker and his colleagues (1981) provide a comprehensive overview of the evolution of public opinion and voting behaviour from the early 1950s to the late 1970s; Anderson and Zelle (1998) and Dalton (2002) update this research. The German language literature on public opinion and voting behaviour is exceptionally rich and sophisticated. For an introduction to this research see Roth (1998), Klein *et al.* (2000) and the edited volumes prepared by Klingemann and Kaase (1998) and Kaase and Klingemann (2001). Finally, a series of books tracks the actions of the parties and the voters through the recent Bundestagswahlen (Rohrschneider, 2003; Conradt, Kleinfeld and Søe, 2000; Dalton, 1996b).

Chapter 4   The 'New Model' Party System

On developments subsequent to German reunification, see Hampton and Søe (1999). For the 1998 election there are two substantial edited volumes to consult (Conradt, Kleinfeld and Søe, 2000; Padgett and Saalfeld, 2002). Lees (2000) gives a rounded account of the Red–Green coalition, as does Hough (2001) for the PDS, prior to its reverse in 2002. On the earlier development of the Greens, the edited collection by Mayer and Ely (1998) is useful. For the recent development of the

German left as a whole, see Padgett (2003). Padgett and Poguntke (2002) bring together various perspectives on the party and political system. On the 2002 election, see Pulzer (2003).

Chapter 5   Policy-Making in a New Political Landscape

For a number of policies information on the Europeanization of policy-making in Germany can be found in Sturm and Pehle (2001). An overview of the Kohl years is provided by Clemens and Paterson (1998) and of the Schröder years by Meng (2002) and Egle, Ostheim and Zohlnhöfer (2003). The liberalization of formerly state-run industrial sectors was discussed by M.M. Müller (2002) and labour market policies by Nativel (2002). The future of the German economy is the topic of Harding and Paterson (2000). For a discussion of higher education policies see Ostermann (2002) and of the economic reforms of the Schröder government, see Harlen (2002).

Chapter 6   Political Economy: The German Model under Stress

Streeck (1997) provides a masterful overview of the German model, its weakness and the potential for reform. Kitschelt (2000) gives an account of the debates over economic reform and the role of political parties in the reform process. Harding and Paterson (2000) contains some insightful chapters on particular aspects of German political economy (see especially Funk, 2000; Timmins, 2000). There are many useful articles in *German Politics*, particularly Harlen (2002) on Schröder's reform agenda, Lütz (2000) on the transformation of the financial sector, Garrett (2001) on mergers and acquisitions and Schröder (1996) on corporate governance. A number of chapters in Crouch and Streeck (1997) and Hall and Soskice (2001) are useful in setting German political economy in comparative context.

Chapter 7   The Welfare State: Incremental Transformation

Clasen and Freeman (1994) provides a systematic English language introduction to the various social policy domains in unified Germany. M.G. Schmidt (1998) is the basic German textbook on social policy for political science students. Also from a political science perspective Alber (2001) and Seeleib-Kaiser (2002) present overviews and analyses of the more recent social policy reforms in English. Lamping and Rüb (2001) give a detailed analysis of the important 2001 pension reforms. Goodin *et al.* (1999) compare the outcomes of social policy in Germany with those in the Netherlands and the USA.

Chapter 8   The Europeanization of German Governance

The best introductions to the literature on Europeanization are provided by Green Cowles, Caporaso and Risse (2001) and Featherstone and Radaelli (2002). For a broad historical overview of Germany and Europe see Haftendorn (2001) and

Kohler-Koch and Knodt (2000). Sturm and Pehle (2001) provide a general introductory analysis and assessment of the Europeanization of Germany, though with more attention to polity and policies than to politics. The most detailed source is Dyson and Goetz (2003). The classic view of smooth adaptation and of how the EU was reinforcing German practices is found in Goetz (1995). For EMU and its effects on Germany see Dyson (2002b and 2003).

Chapter 9   Foreign and Security Policy

For an excellent overview and critical analysis of German foreign policy debates in the early 1990s see Hellmann (1996). Duffield (1998), Banchoff (1999) and Katzenstein (1997) provide good, theoretically informed studies of German foreign policy. Hyde-Price (2000) analyses Germany's role in reshaping European order, focusing on the place of NATO and EU enlargement in German grand strategy. Harnisch and Maull (2001) provide a sympathetic analysis of Germany as a 'civilian power', whilst Rittberger (2001) offers a comparative analysis of different theoretical approaches to the study of German foreign policy. Sarotte (2001) provides a good analysis of German military reform. Volmer (1998) and Hubert (1993) focus on the Greens and foreign policy, while Libal (1997) provides an insider's account of German policy towards the break-up of Yugoslavia.

Chapter 10   Germany and Europe

The most accessible treatment is in Bulmer, Jeffery and Paterson (2000). For those who read German Schneider *et al.* (2001) provides a massively detailed analysis of German European policy. There is no equivalent in English. On the way in which German European policy is changing see Jeffery and Paterson (2003). For a view that stresses continuity see Webber (2001).

Chapter 11   Towards an Open Society? Citizenship and Immigration

With a few notable exceptions, most texts offering a thorough analysis of immigration and citizenship in Germany are in German. Herbert (2001) provides a comprehensive history of migration, while Bade and Münz (2000, 2002) provide up-to-date evaluation of policy developments more broadly. For German citizenship, the work by Brubaker (1992) continues to be a point of reference, and has recently been authoritatively re-examined by Hagedorn (2001). Green (2003) examines the whole field from the perspective of policy-making. Several key texts consider Germany from a comparative perspective, including Joppke (1999), Hansen and Weil (2001) and Bloch and Levy (1999). The internet is a useful source of information for news, data, comment and details of policy, although sites tend to be in German:
http://www.bundesauslaenderbeauftragte.de (best for facts and figures)
http://www.migration-info.de (regular newsletter on migration in Germany and
    Europe)
http://www.bmi.bund.de (website of the German Interior Ministry)
http://www.bamf.de (website of the new executive authority for immigration and
    asylum)

Chapter 12   The Environment and Nuclear Power

For basic overviews of the main developments in environmental policy, see Jänicke and Weidner (1997); Pehle (1997); and Pehle and Jansen (1998). A concise summary of environmental politics of the 1970s and 1980s is provided by Paterson (1989). For analyses of the development of modern environmental politics and policy in its historical context, see Boehmer-Christiansen and Skea (1991), and Blühdorn *et al.* (1995). A useful examination of the legalistic aspects of environmental policy is provided by Rose-Ackerman (1995). For analyses of recent developments and the experience of the Green Party in government, see Lees (2000) and Rüdig (2000, 2002).

Chapter 13   Political Culture and Identity: The Post-Unification Search for 'Inner Unity'

For a general account of German political culture see Conradt (2001b). Maier (1999) provides background on the collapse of the GDR, whilst Flockton and Kolinsky (1999) gives a comprehensive account of the social transformation of eastern Germany since unification. On the emergence of a democratic political culture in eastern Germany see Rohrschneider (1999). For the treatment of gender in the East see Young (1998).

Bibliography

Aberbach, J.D., Derlien, H.-U. and Rockman, B.A. (1994) 'Unity and Fragmentation – Themes in German and American Public Administration', in H.-U. Derlien *et al.* (eds), *Systemrationalität und Partialinteresse. Festschrift für Renate Mayntz*, Baden-Baden: Nomos Verlagsgesellschaft, pp. 271–89.

Adamski, H. (2002) 'Entscheidungsverfahren im Bundesrat: Problemfall Zuwanderungsgesetz', *Gesellschaft-Wirtschaft-Politik*, vol. 51, no. 2, pp. 221–8.

Alber, J. (2001) *Recent Developments of the German Welfare State: Basic Continuity or Paradigm Shift?*, ZeS-Arbeitspapier 6/2001, Bremen: Universität Bremen.

Alemann, U.von, Heinze, R. and Hombach, B. (eds) (1990) *Die Kraft der Region: Nordrhein-Westfalen in Europa*, Bonn: Dietz.

Allen, M. (2002) 'Is German Direct Investment a Substitute for Domestic Investment', *German Politics*, vol. 11, no. 1, pp. 125–46.

Allerbeck, Klaus R. (1976) *Demokratisierung und sozialer Wandel in der BRD*, Opladen: Westdeutscher Verlag.

Amoore, L. (2000) 'The tale of the hare and the tortoise: globalisation and the restructuring of the German model', in R. Harding and W. E. Paterson (eds), *The Future of the German Economy: An End to the Miracle?*, Manchester: Manchester University Press.

Anderson, C. and Zelle, C. (1995) 'Helmut Kohl and the CDU Victory', *German Politics and Society*, vol. 12, pp. 12–35.

Anderson, C. and Zelle, C. (1998) *Stability and Change in German Elections: How Electorates Merge, Converge, or Collide*, Westport, CT: Praeger.

Andreß, H.-J. and Heien, T. (2001) 'Zerfällt der wohlfahrtsstaatliche Konsens? Einstellungen zum Wohlfahrtsstaat im zeitlichen Wandel', *Sozialer Fortschritt*, vol. 50, no. 7, pp. 169–75.

Bäcker, G., Bispinck, R., Hofemann, K. and Naegele, G. (2000) *Sozialpolitik und soziale Lage in Deutschland*, vol. 2, *Gesundheit und Gesundheitssystem, Familie, Alter, Soziale Dienste*, Wiesbaden: Westdeutscher Verlag, 3rd edn.

Bade, K. and Münz, R. (eds) (2000) *Migrationsreport 2000*, Frankfurt am Main: Campus.

Bade, K. and Münz, R. (eds) (2002) *Migrationsreport 2002*, Frankfurt am Main: Campus.

Baker, K., Dalton, R. and Hildebrandt, K. (1981) *Germany Transformed*, Cambridge, MA: Harvard University Press.

Banchoff, T. (1999) *The German Problem Transformed: Institutions, Politics and Foreign Policy, 1945–1995*, Michigan: University of Michigan Press.

Bandelow, N.C. (2002) 'Ist das Gesundheitswesen noch bezahlbar? Problemstrukturen und Problemlösungen', *Gesellschaft-Wirtschaft-Politik*, vol. 51, no. 1, pp. 109–31.

Bastian, J. (1995) 'Brother in Arms or at Arms? IG Metall in 1994: Confronting Recession and Unification', *German Politics*, vol. 4, no. 1, pp. 87–100.

Bauer-Kaiser, P. (1993) 'A Political System After the Shock: The Impact of Unification on the Fabric of Political Orientations in Germany', American Political Science Association, 1993 Annual Meeting, Washington, DC.

Bauer-Kaase, P. and Kaase, M. (1996) 'Five Years of Unification: The Germans on the Path to Inner Unity?', *German Politics*, vol. 5, no. 1, pp. 1–25.

Beauftragte der Bundesregierung für Ausländerfragen (2001) *Migrationsbericht der Ausländer beauftragten*, Bonn and Berlin.

Beauftragte der Bundesregierung für Ausländerfragen (2002) *Bericht der Beauftragten der Bundesregierung für Ausländerfragen über die Lage der Ausländer in der Bundesrepublik Deutschland*, Bonn and Berlin.

Berlin, *et al.* (1999) 'Wer stark ist, würde noch stärker werden,' www. fr-aktuell.de/fr/160/t1600010.htm (viewed on 9 June 1999).

Berry, P. (1989) 'The Organization and Influence of the Chancellory during the Schmidt and Kohl Chancellorships', *Governance*, vol. 2, no. 3, pp. 339–55.

Beuermann, C. and Jäger, J. (1996) 'Climate Change Politics in Germany: How Long will the Double Dividend Last?', in T. O'Riordan and J. Jäger (eds), *Politics of Climate Change: A European Perspective*, London: Routledge, pp. 186–227.

Beuermann, C. and Burdick, B. (1998) 'The German Response to the Sustainability Transition', in T. O'Riordan and H. Voisey (eds), *The Transition to Sustainability: The Politics of Agenda 21 in Europe*, London: Earthscan, pp. 174–88.

Beyme, K. von (1997) *Der Gesetzgeber: Der Bundestag als Entscheidungszentrum*, Opladen: Westdeutscher Verlag; published in an abridged English version (1998) as: *The Legislator: German Parliament as a Centre of Political Decision-Making*, Aldershot: Ashgate.

Biedenkopf, K. (1994) 'Facing the Challenge of Upheaval in Europe', *NATO Review*, vol. 42, no. 3, pp. 15–17.

Blancke, S. and Schmid, J. (2000) 'Die Bundesländer in der aktiven Arbeitsmarktpolitik', *WIP Occasional Paper*, No. 12, Tübingen.

Bleses, P. and Rose, E. (1998) *Deutungswandel der Sozialpolitik. Die Arbeitsmarkt- und Familienpolitik im parlamentarischen Diskurs*, Frankfurt am Main: Campus.

Bleses, P. and Seeleib-Kaiser, M. (1999) 'Zum Wandel wohlfahrtsstaatlicher Sicherung in der Bundesrepublik Deutschland: Zwischen Lohnarbeit und Familie', *Zeitschrift für Soziologie*, vol. 28, no. 2, pp. 114–35.

Bloch, A. and Levy, C. (eds) (1999) *Refugees, Citizenship and Social Policy in Europe*, Basingstoke: Palgrave.

Blondel, J. (2000) 'Introduction', in J. Blondel and M. Cotta (eds), *The Nature of Party Government*, Basingstoke: Palgrave, pp. 1–17.

Blühdorn, I., Krause, F. and Scharf, T. (eds) (1995) *The Green Agenda: Environmental Politics and Policy in Germany*, Keele: Keele University Press.

BMU (2002) *German Environmental Report 2002: Report on Environmental Policy in the 14th Legislative Period*, http://www.bmu.de

BMAS (2002a) *Materialband zum Sozialbericht 2001*, Bonn: BMAS, http://www.bma.de; downloaded 30 July 2002.

BMAS (2002b) *Sozialbericht 2001*, Bonn: BMAS, http://www.bma.de; downloaded 30 July 2002.

BMAS (2002c) *Statistisches Taschenbuch 2002 – Arbeits- und Sozialstatistik*, Bonn: BMAS.

BMFSFJ (1998) *Zehnter Kinder- und Jugendbericht*, Deutscher Bundestag, 13. Wahlperiode, BT-Drucksache 13-11368, 25 August.

BMFSFJ (2002a) *Elfter Kinder- und Jugendbericht*, Deutscher Bundestag, 14. Wahlperiode, BT-Drucksache 14/8181, 4 February.

BMFSFJ (2002b) *Chronologie der familienpolitischen Entscheidungen seit Beginn der Legislaturperiode,* http://www.bmfsfj.de; downloaded 16 May 2002.

BMG (2002) *Bekanntmachung des durchschnittlichen allgemeinen Beitragssatzes der gesetzlichen Krankenversicherung zum Stichtag 1. Januar 2002 und des für versicherungspflichtige Studenten und Praktikanten maßgebenden Beitragssatzes,* http://www.bmgesundheit.de; downloaded 1 November 2002.

Boehmer-Christiansen, S. and Skea, J. (1991) *Acid Politics: Environmental and Energy Policies in Britain and Germany,* London: Belhaven Press.

Boynton, G.R. and Loewenberg, G. (1974) 'The Decay of Support for Monarchy and the Hitler Regime in the Federal Republic of Germany', *British Journal of Political Science,* vol. 4, no. 4 (October).

Brubaker, R. (1992) *Citizenship and Nationhood in France and Germany,* Cambridge MA: Harvard University Press.

BT-Drucksache (1999) *Bilanz der Maßnahmen zum Umzug der Bundesregierung nach Berlin und der Ausgleichsleistungen für die Region Bonn,* 14/1601 (13 September).

Bührer, W. and Grande, E. (eds) (2000) *Unternehmerverbände und Staat in Deutschland,* Baden-Baden: Nomos.

Bulmer, S. (1997) 'Shaping the Rules? The Constitutive Politics of the European Union and German Power', in P. Katzenstein (ed.), *Tamed Power, Germany in Europe,* Ithaca, NY, and London: Cornell University Press, pp. 49–79.

Bulmer, S., Jeffery, C. and Paterson, W. E. (2000) *Germany's European Diplomacy Shaping the European Milieu,* Manchester: Manchester University Press.

Bulmer, S., Maurer, A. and Paterson, W.E. (2001) 'The European Policy Making Machinery in the Berlin Republic: Hindrance or Hand Maiden', *German Politics,* vol. 10, no. 1, pp. 177–206.

BUND (2002) *Vier Jahre Rot-Grün: Eine umweltpolitische Bilanz.* http://www.bund-net.de

Bundesrat (2002) 'Die Arbeit des Bundesrates im Spiegel der Zahlen', at www.bundesrat.de/PdundF/index.html (viewed on 21 August 2002).

Bundesregierung (2002a) *Lebenslagen in Deutschland. Daten und Fakten – Materialband zum ersten Armuts- und Reichtumsbericht der Bundesregierung,* Berlin.

Bundesregierung (2002b) *Perspektiven für Deutschland: Unsere Strategie für eine nachhaltige Entwicklung* (English trans: Perspectives for Germany: Our Strategy for Sustainable Development), http://www.dialog-nachhaltigkeit.de

Bundesministerium für Familie, Senioren, Frauen und Jugen.

Bundesministerium der Finanzen, Referat IV A1 (2002) *Die Ökosteuer – Ein Plus für Arbeit und Umwelt,* September, http://bmwi.de; downloaded 18 November 2002.

Burns, R. and van der Will, W. (1990) *Protest and Democracy in West Germany,* London: Macmillan.

Busse, V. (1998) 'Hierarchieebenen und Gruppenstruktur am Beispiel des Bundeskanzleramtes', *Verwaltungsarchiv,* vol. 89, no. 1, pp. 137–43.

Busse, V. (2001a) *Bundeskanzleramt und Bundesregierung,* Heidelberg: Hüthig, 3rd rev. edn.

Busse, V. (2001b) 'The Structure of the Federal Administration', in K. König and H. Siedentopf (eds), *Public Administration in Germany,* Baden-Baden: Nomos Verlagsgesellschaft, pp. 105–22.

Calic, M.-J. (1998) 'Post-SFOR: Towards Europanization of the Bosnia Peace Operation?', in S. Clement (ed.), *The Issues Raises by Bosnia, and the Transatlantic Debate,* Paris: Well Institute for Security Studies, pp. 10–22.

Cantwell, J. A. and Harding, R. (1998) 'The Internationalisation of German R&D', *National Institute Economic Review*, vol. 1, no. 163, pp. 99–115.

Clasen, J. and Freeman, R. (eds) (1994) *Social Policy in Germany*, New York and London: Harvester/Wheatsheaf.

Clemens, C. (1994) 'The Chancellor as Manager: Helmut Kohl, the CDU and Governance in Germany', *West European Politics*, vol. 17, no. 4, pp. 28–51.

Clemens, C. (1998) 'Party Management as a Leadership Resource: Kohl and the CDU/CSU', *German Politics*, vol. 7, no. 1, pp. 76–100.

Clemens, C. (2000) 'A Legacy Reassessed: Helmut Kohl and the German Party Finance Affair', *German Politics*, vol. 9, no. 2 (August), pp. 25–51.

Clemens, C. and Paterson, W.E. (eds) (1998) *The Kohl Chancellorship*, London: Frank Cass.

Clement, W. (2002) 'Transparenter Föderalismus in Deutschland, handlungsfähige Regionen in Europa', in *Jahrbuch des Föderalismus 2002*, Baden-Baden: Nomos, 15–30.

Coates, D. (2000) *Models of Capitalism. Growth and Stagnation in the Modern Era*, Cambridge: Polity Press.

Cohn-Bendit, D. and Schmid, T. (1992) *Heimat Babylon. Das Wagnis der multikulturellen Demokratie*, Hamburg: Hoffmann & Campe.

Conradt, D., Kleinfeld, G. and Søe, C. (2000) *Power Shift in Germany: The 1998 Election and the End of the Kohl Era*, New York: Berghahn Books.

Conradt, D.P. (1980) 'Changing German Political Culture', in G.A. Almond and S. Verba (eds), *The Civic Culture Revisited*, Boston: Little, Brown, pp. 212–72.

Conradt, D.P. (1981) 'Political Culture, Legitimacy and Participation', *West European Politics*, vol. 4, no. 2, pp. 18–34.

Conradt, D.P. (2001a) *'Political Culture in Unified Germany: The First Ten Years'*, Institute for European Studies, University of California, Berkeley.

Conradt, D.P. (2001b) *The German Polity*, 7th edn, New York and London: Longman.

Cooper, A. (2002) 'Party-Sponsored Protest and the Movement Society: The CDU/CSU Mobilises Against Citizenship Law Reform', *German Politics*, vol. 11, no. 2 (August), pp. 88–104.

Crawford, B. (1995) 'German Foreign Policy and European Political Cooperation: the Diplomatic Recognition of Croatia in 1991', *German Politics and Society*, vol. 13, no. 1, pp. 1–34.

Crouch, C. and Streeck, W. (1997) 'Introduction: The Future of Diversity', in C. Crouch and W. Streeck (eds), *Political Economy of Modern Capitalism: Mapping Convergence and Diversity*, London: Sage.

Cusack, T. R. (1999) 'The Shaping of Political Satisfaction with Government and Regime Performance in Germany', *British Journal of Political Science*, vol. 29, no. 4 (October); pp. 641–72.

Czada, R. (1998) 'Vereinigungskrise und Standortdebatte – Der Beitrag der Wiedervereinigung zur Krise des westdeutschen Modells', *Leviathan*, vol. 26, no. 1, pp. 24–59.

Dalton, R.J. (1994a) 'Communists and Democrats: Democratic Attitudes in the Two Germanies', *British Journal of Political Science*, vol. 24, no. 4, pp. 469–93.

Dalton, R.J. (1994b) *The Green Rainbow: Environmental Groups in Western Europe*. New Haven, CT: Yale University Press.

Dalton, R.J. (1996a) 'A Divided Electorate?', in G. Smith *et al.*, *Developments in German Politics II*, London: Macmillan.

Dalton, R.J. (1996b) *Germans Divided: The 1994 Bundestagswahl and the Evolution of the German Party System*, Oxford and Washington, DC: Berg.

Dalton, R.J. (2000) 'The Decline of Party Identification', in R. Dalton and M. Wattenberg (eds), *Parties without Partisans*, Oxford: Oxford University Press.

Dalton, R.J. (2002) *Citizen Politics*, New York: Chatham House, 3rd edn.

Dalton, R. and Buerklin, W. (1996) 'The Two German Electorates', in R. Dalton (ed.), *Germans Divided: The 1994 Bundestagswahl and the Evolution of the German Party System*, Oxford, UK, and Washington, DC: Berg Publishers.

Dalton, R.J. and Wattenberg, M. (eds) (2000) *Parties without Partisans*, Oxford: Oxford University Press.

Dalvi, S. (1998) 'The Post-Cold War Role of the Bundeswehr: A Product of Normative Influences', *European Security*, vol. 7, no. 1, pp. 25–44.

Deeg, R. (2001) *Institutional Change and the Uses and Limits of Path Dependency: The Case of German Finance*, Max-Planck-Gesellschaft Discussion Paper 01-6, Köln.

Der Spiegel (30 November 1998) 'Jenseits von Schuld und Sühne', no. 48, pp. 22–36.

Der Spiegel (11 January 1999) 'Der Kampf um die Pässe', no. 2, pp. 22–32.

Der Spiegel (4 March 2002) 'Die Rückseite der Republik', no. 10, pp. 36–56.

Der Spiegel (30 March 2002) 'Zwischen Kabarett und Tragödie', no. 14, pp. 26–33.

Derlien, H.-U. (1984) 'Einstweiliger Ruhestand politischer Beamter des Bundes 1949 bis 1983', *Die Öffentliche Verwaltung*, vol. 37, no. 17, pp. 689–99.

Derlien, H.-U. (1996) 'Zur Logik und Politik des Ressortzuschnitts', *Verwaltungsarchiv*, vol. 36, no. 4, pp. 548–80.

Deutsche Bundesbank (2002) 'Kapitalgedeckte Altersvorsorge und Finanzmärkte', *Monatsbericht*, July, pp. 25–39.

Deutscher Städtetag (2001) 'Städte fordern strukturelle Veränderungen in der Arbeitsmarkt- und Sozialpolitik', Press Release 28 August, http://www.staedtetag.de; downloaded 30 October 2002.

Deutschland, Großbritannien und Österreich, Opladen: Westdeutscher Verlag.

Die Zeit (2002) *Eine Zeit-Serie – Die Familie*, Zeitdokument 2/2002, Hamburg: Zeitverlag.

Döhler, M. and Manow, P. (1997) *Strukturbildung von Politikfeldern*, Opladen: Leske & Budrich.

Dominick III, R.H. (1992) *The Environmental Movement in Germany: Prophets and Pioneers, 1871–1971*, Bloomington, IN: Indiana University Press.

Dorff, R. (1997) 'Normal Actor of Reluctant Power? The Future of German Security Policy', *European Security*, vol. 6, no. 2, pp. 56–69.

Duffield, J. (1998) *Political Culture, International Institutions and German Security after Unification*, Stanford, CA: Stanford University Press.

Dunleavy, P. and Rhodes, R.A.W. (1990) 'Core Executive Studies in Britain', *Public Administration*, vol. 68, pp. 3–28.

Dyson, K. (1996) 'The Economic Order: Still Modell Deutchland?', in G. Smith, W.E. Paterson and S.A. Padgett (eds), *Developments in German Politics, 2*, London: Macmillan, pp. 194–210.

Dyson, K. (2000) *The Politics of the Euro-Zone: Stability or Breakdown?*, Oxford: Oxford University Press.

Dyson, K. (2001) 'The German Model Revisited: From Schmidt to Schröder', in S.A. Padgett and T. Poguntke (eds), *Continuity and Change in German Politics; Beyond the Politics of Centrality? A Festschrift for Gordon Smith*, London: Frank Cass, pp. 135–54.

Dyson, K. (2002a) 'The German Model Revisited: From Schmidt to Schröder', in S. Padgett and T. Poguntke (eds), *Continuity and Change in German Politics: Beyond the Politics of Centrality?*, London: Frank Cass, pp. 135–54.

Dyson, K. (2002b) 'Introduction: EMU as Integration, Europeanization and Convergence', in K. Dyson (ed.), *European States and the Euro: Europeanization, Variation and Convergence*, Oxford: Oxford University Press, pp. 2–27.

Dyson, K. (2003) 'Europeanization of German Economic Policies: Testing the Limits of Model Germany', in K. Dyson and K. Goetz (eds), *Germany and Europe: How Europeanized is Germany?*, London: Proceedings of the British Academy/Oxford University Press.

Dyson, K.H.F. and Featherstone, K. (1999) *The Road to Maastricht: Negotiating Economic and Monetary Union*, Oxford: Oxford University Press.

Dyson, K.H.F. and Goetz, K.H. (eds) (2003) *Germany in Europe: How Europeanized is Germany?*, Oxford: Oxford University Press for the British Academy.

Egle, C., Ostheim, T. and Zohlnhöfer, R. (eds) (2003) *Das rot–grüne Projekt. Eine Bilanz der Regierung Schröder 1998–2002*, Wiesbaden: Westdeutscher Verlag.

Ehrhart, H.-G. (1999) 'Stabilitätspakt für Südosteuropa', *Blätter für Deutsche und Internationale Politik*, no. 8, pp. 916–18.

Eising, R. (2003) 'The Europeanization of the Interest Group System and of Interest Groups', in K. Dyson and K. Goetz (eds), *op.cit.*

Everts, P. (2002) *Democracy and Military Force*, Basingstoke: Palgrave.

Esping-Andersen, G. (1990) *The Three Worlds of Welfare Capitalism*, Cambridge: Polity Press.

Estevez-Abe, M., Iversen, T. and Soskice, D. (2001) 'Social Protection and the Formation of Skills: A Reinterpretation of the Welfare State', in P.A. Hall and D. Soskice (eds) *Varieties of Capitalism – The Institutional Foundations of Comparative Advantage*, Oxford: Oxford University Press, pp. 145–83.

Exler, U. (1991) 'Financing German Federalism: Problems of Financial Equalisation in the Unification Processs', in C. Jeffery (ed.), *Federalism, Unification and European Integration*, London: Frank Cass, pp. 22–37.

Fass, T. and Wüst, A. (2002) 'The Schill Factor in the Hamburg State Election 2001', *German Politics*, vol. 11, no. 2 (August), pp. 1–20.

FAZ (2002) 'Herbe Kritik an Wahlprogrammen', 7 May, p. 16.

Featherstone, K. and Radaelli, C. (eds) (2002) *The Politics of Europeanization*, Oxford: Oxford University Press.

Fischer, J. (2000a) 'From Confederacy to Federation – Thoughts on the Finality of European Integration', Speech on 12 May at Humboldt University, Berlin, at http:www.auswaertiges-amt.de/8_suche/index.htm

Fischer, J. (2000b) *Mein langer Lauf zu mir selbst*, Cologne: Kiepenheuer & Witsch.

Fischer, T. and Grosse Hüttmann, M. (2001) 'Aktuelle Diskussionsbeiträge zur Reform des deutschen Föderalismus – Modelle, Leitbiilder und die Chancen ihrer Übertragbarkeit', in *Jahrbuch des Föderalismus 2001*, Baden-Baden: Nomos, pp. 128–42.

Flockton, C. and Kolinsky, E. (1999) *Recasting East Germany: Social Transformation after the GDR*, London and Portland OR: Frank Cass.

Fröhner, R., Stackelberg, M. von and Eser, W. (1956) *Familie und Ehe. Probleme in den deutschen Familien der Gegenwart*, Bielefeld: Maria von Stackelberg Verlag.

Forschungsgruppe Wahlen (2002) *Bundestagswahl: Eine Analyse der Wahl vom 22. September 2002*, Mannheim: Forschungsgruppe Wahlen.

Frankfurter Rundschau (17 December 2001) 'Berlin bremst Ansätze für gemeinsame Asylpolitik aus'.

Frankfurter Rundschau (11 July 2002) 'Keiner weiß, wer den Ausländern Deutsch beibringen soll'.

Frankland, E.G. and Schoonmaker, D. (1992) *Between Protest and Power: The Green Party in Germany*, Boulder, CO: Westview Press.

Franklin, M. *et al.* (1992) *Electoral Change*, Cambridge: Cambridge University Press.

French, S. (2000) 'The Impact of German Unification on German Industrial Relations', *German Politics*, vol. 9, no. 2, pp. 195–216.

Fröhlich, S. (2001) *'Auf den Kanzler kommt es an': Helmut Kohl und die deutsche Außenpolitik*, Paderborn: Schöningh.

Furhmann, N. (2002) 'Drei zu eins für Schröder. Bergmann muss im Hinspiel eine Niederlage einstecken', in K. Eicker-Wolf, H. Kindler, I. Schäfer, M. Wehrheim and D. Wolf (eds), *'Deutschland auf den Weg gebracht'. Rot-grüne Wirtschafts- und Sozialpolitik zwischen Anspruch und Wirklichkeit*, Marburg: Metropolis Verlag, pp. 187–212.

Fuchs, Dieter (1989) *Die Unterstützung des politischen Systems der Bundesrepublik Deutschland*, Opladen: Westdeutscher Verlag.

Funk, L. (2000) 'Economic Reform of Modell Deutschland', in R. Harding and W.E. Paterson (eds), *The Future of the German Economy: An End to the Miracle?*, Manchester: Manchester University Press.

Gaddum, E. (1994) *Die deutsche Europapolitik in den 80er Jahren*, Paderborn: Schöningh.

Garrett, C. (2001) 'Towards a New Model of German Capitalism: The Mannesmann-Vodaphone Merger and its Implications for the German Economy', *German Politics*, vol. 10, no. 3, pp. 83–102.

Garton-Ash, T. (1994) 'Germany's Choice', *Foreign Affairs*, vol. 73, no. 4, pp. 65–81.

Genscher, H.-D. (1995) *Erinnerungen*, Berlin: Siedler Verlag.

Giese, D. (1986) '25 Jahre Bundessozialhilfegesetz. Entstehung – Ziele – Entwicklung', *Zeitschrift für Sozialhilfe und Sozialgesetzbuch*, vol. 25, Part I, pp. 249–58; Part II, pp. 305–14; Part III, pp. 374–82.

Göetz, K. (1992) *Intergovernmental Relations and State Government Discretion*, Baden-Baden: Nomos.

Goetz, K.H. (1995) 'National Governance and European Integration: Intergovernmental Relations in Germany', *Journal of Common Market Studies*, 33, pp. 91–116.

Goetz, K.H. (1997) 'Acquiring Political Craft: Training Grounds for Top Officials in the German Core Executive', *Public Administration*, vol. 75, no. 4, pp. 753–75.

Goetz, K.H. (1999) 'Senior Officials in the German Federal Administration: Institutional Change and Positional Differentiation', in E.C. Page and V. Wright (eds), *Bureaucratic Elites in Western European States: A Comparative Analysis of Top Officials*, Oxford: Oxford University Press, pp. 147–77.

Goetz, K.H. (2000) 'The Development and Current Features of the German Civil Service System', in H.A.G.M. Bekke and F.M. van der Meer (eds), *Civil Service Systems in Western Europe*, Cheltenham: Edward Elgar, pp. 61–91.

Goetz, K.H. (2003) 'Europeanization of the Federal Executive', in K. Dyson and K. Goetz (eds), *op. cit.*

Goetz, K.H. (2003a) 'Executives in Comparative Context', in J. S. Hayward and A. Menon (eds), *Governing Europe*, Oxford: Oxford University Press.

Göhler, G. (1994) 'Politische Institutionen und ihr Kontext', in G. Göhler (ed.), *Die Eigenart der Institutionen: Zum Profil politischer Institutionentheorie*, Baden-Baden: Nomos Verlagsgesellschaft.

Golz, H.-G. (2001) 'Machtworte', *Deutschland Archiv*, vol. 34, no. 6, pp. 921–4.

Goodin, R.E., Headey, B., Muffels, R. and Dirven, H.-J. (1999) *The Real Worlds of Welfare Capitalism*, Cambridge: Cambridge University Press.

Grant, W., Paterson, W. and Whitston, C. (1988) *Government and the Chemical Industry: A Comparative Study of Britain and West Germany*, Oxford: Clarendon Press.

Green, S. (2000) 'German Citizenship in the New Millennium', *German Politics*, vol. 9, no. 3, pp. 105–24.

Green, S. (2001a) 'Citizenship Policy in Germany: The Case of Ethnicity over Residence?', in R. Hansen and P. Weil (eds), *Towards a European Nationality? Citizenship, Migration and Nationality Law in the European Union*, Basingstoke: Palgrave.

Green, S. (2001b) 'Immigration, Asylum and Citizenship in Germany: The Impact of Unification and the Berlin Republic', *West European Politics*, vol. 24, no. 4, pp. 82–104.

Green, S. (2003) *The Politics of Exclusion: Immigration, Residence and Citizenship Policy in Germany, 1955–2002*, Manchester: Manchester University Press.

Green Cowles, M., Caporaso, J. and Risse, T. (2001) *Transforming Europe: Europeanization and Domestic Change*, Ithaca: Cornell University Press.

Grosse Hüttmann, M. (2000) 'Die föderale Staatsfrom in der Krise', in H.-G. Wehling (ed.) *Die deutschen Länder. Geschichte, Politik, Wirtschaft*, Opladen: Leske & Budrich, pp. 277–98.

Grube, N. (2001) 'Föderalismus in der öffentlichen Meinung der Bundesrepublik Deutschland', in *Jahrbuch des Föderalismus 2001*, Baden-Baden: Nomos, pp. 101–14.

Gunlicks, A. (2003) *The Länder and German Federalism*, Manchester: Manchester University Press.

Hacke, C. (1997a) *Die Aussen politik der Bundes republik Deutschlands. Weltmacht-Wider Willen?*, Berlin: Ullstein.

Hacke, C. (1997b) 'Die Neue Bedeutung des Nationalen Interesses für die Aussenpolitik der Bundesrepublik Deutschland', *Aus Politik und Zeitgeschichte*, Bl no. 2, pp. 3–4.

Haftendorn, H. (2001) *Deutsche Aussenpolitik zwischen Selbstbeschraenkung und Selbstbehauptung*, Stuttgart: Deutsche Verlagsanstalt.

Hagedorn, H. (2001) *Wer darf Mitglied werden?*, Opladen: Leske & Budrich.

Hailbronner, Kay (2001) 'Reform des Zuwanderungsrechts. Konsens und Dissens in der Ausländerpolitik', *Aus Politik und Zeitgeschichte* B43/2001, pp. 7–19.

Hall, P.A. (1993) 'Policy Paradigms, Social Learning, and the State. The Case of Economic Policymaking in Britain', *Comparative Politics*, vol. 25, no. 3, pp. 275–96.

Hall, P.A. and Soskice, D. (eds) (2001) *Varieties of Capitalism: The Institutional Foundations of Comparative Advantage*, Oxford: Oxford University Press.

Hampton, M. and Søe, C. (eds) (1999) *Between Bonn and Berlin: German Politics Adrift?*, Lanham, MD: Rowman & Littlefield.

Hank, R. (1999) 'Bündnis Für Arbeit: Macht und Einfluß am Verhandlungstisch', *Das Parlament*, vol. 30, no. 7, p. 5.

Hansen, R. and Weil, P. (eds) (2001) *Towards a European Nationality? Citizenship, Migration and Nationality Law in the European Union*, Basingstoke: Palgrave.

Hartz Kommission (2002) *Bericht der Kommission zum Abbau der Arbeitslosigkeit und zur Umstrukturierung der Bundesanstalt für Arbeit*, Berlin.

Harding, R. and Paterson, W.E. (eds) (2000) *The Future of the German Economy: An End to the Miracle?*, Manchester: Manchester University Press.

Harding, R. and Sorge, A. (2000) 'German Corporatism: Dead or Alive?', in R. Harding and W. E. Paterson (eds), *The Future of the German Economy. An End to the Miracle?*, Manchester: Manchester University Press.

Harlen, C.M. (2002) 'Schröder's Economic Reforms: The End of Reformstau', *German Politics*, vol. 11, no. 1, pp. 61–80.

Harnisch, S. and Maull, H. (2001) *Germany as a Civilian Power? The Foreign Policy of the Berlin Republic*, Manchester: Manchester University Press.

Hartwich, H.-H. (2002) 'Das "Job-AQTIV-Gesetz"', *Gesellschaft-Wirtschaft-Politik*, vol. 51, no. 1, pp. 73–7.

Hay, C. (2000) 'Contemporary Capitalism, Globalization, Regionalization and the Persistence of National Variation', *Review of International Studies*, vol. 26, no. 4, pp. 509–32.

Heath, A. Jowell, R. and Curtice, J. (1985) *How Britain Votes*, Oxford: Pergamon.

Heinze, R.G. (2002) *Die Berliner Räterepublik. Viel Rat – wenig Tat?*, Wiesbaden: Westdeutscher Verlag.

Hellmann, G. (1996) 'Goodbye Bismarck? The Foreign Policy of Contemporary Germany', *Mershon International Studies Review*, no. 40, pp. 1–39.

Helms, L. (1997) *Wettbewerb und Kooperation: Zum Verhältnis von Regierungsmehrheit und Opposition im parlamentarischen Gesetzgebungsverfahren in der Bundesrepublik Deutschland, Großbritannien und Österreich*, Opladen: Westdeutscher Verlag.

Helms, L. (2000) 'The Federal Constitutional Court: Institutionalising Judicial Review in a Semisovereign Democracy', in L. Helms (ed.), *Institutions and Institutional Change in the Federal Republic of Germany*, London: Macmillan, pp. 84–104.

Helms, L. (2001) 'The Changing Chancellorship: Resources and Constraints Revisited', *German Politics*, vol. 10, no. 2, pp. 155–68.

Henson, P. and Malhan, N. (1995) 'Endeavours to Export a Migration Crisis: Policy Making and Europeanisation in the German Migration Dilemma', *German Politics*, vol. 4, no. 3, pp. 128–44.

Herbert, U. (2001) *Geschichte der Ausländerpolitik in Deutschland: Saisonarbeiter, Zwangsarbeiter, Gastarbeiter*, München: Beck.

Héritier, A., Knill, C. and Mingers, S. (1996) *Ringing the Changes in Europe: Regulatory Competition and the Transformation of the State. Britain, France, Germany*, Berlin: Walter de Gruyter.

Herzog, R. (1995) *Die Globalisierung der deutschen Aussenpolitik ist unvermeidlich*, Bonn: Bulletin der Presse- und Informationsamt der Bundesregierung, vol. 20, pp. 161–5.

Hirschman, A. (1970) *Exit, Voice and Loyalty*, Cambridge, MA: Harvard University Press.

Hofferbert, R.I. and Klingemann, H.-D. (2000) 'Democracy and its Discontents in Post-Wall Germany', Discussion Paper FS III–00–207, Berlin: Wissenschaftszentrum.

Hofmann, G. (2000) 'Das System Schröder. Kohls Erbe: Wo die Konsensdemokratie funktioniert und wo sie an ihre Grenzen stößt', *Die Zeit*, 6 July, p. 3.

Hogwood, P. (2000) 'Citizenship Controversies in Germany: The Twin Legacy of *Völkisch* Nationalism and the *Alleinvertretungsanspruch'*, *German Politics*, vol. 9, no. 3, pp. 125–44.

Holmberg. S. (1994) 'Party Identification Compared Across the Atlantic', in M.K. Jennings and T. Mann (eds), *Elections at Home and Abroad*, Ann Arbor, MI: University of Michigan Press.

Holtmann, E. (ed.) (2001) *Zwischen Wettbewerbs- und Verhandlungsdemokratie: Analysen zum Regierungssystem der Bundesrepublik Deutschland*, Wiesbaden: Westdeutscher Verlag.

Holtmann, E. and Voelzkow, H. (eds) (2000) *Zwischen Wettbewerbs- und Verhandlungsdemokratie*, Wiesbaden: Westdeutscher Verlag.

Hombach, B. (1999) 'The Stability Pact: Breaking New Ground', *NATO Review*, vol. 47, no. 4, pp. 20–3.

Hough, D. (2002) *The Fall and Rise of the PDS in Eastern Germany*, Birmingham: University of Birmingham Press.

Huber, E. and Stephens, J.D. (2001) *Development and Crisis of the Welfare State – Parties and Policies in Global Markets*, Chicago: University of Chicago Press.

Huber, M. (1997) 'Leadership and Unification: Climate Change Policies in Germany', in U. Collier and R.E. Löfstedt (eds), *Cases in Climate Change Policy: Political Reality in the European Union*, London: Earthscan, pp. 65–86.

Hubert, H.-P. (ed.) (1993) *Grüne Aussenpolitik: Aspekte einer Debatte*, Göttingen: Die Werkstatt.

Hucke, J. (1985) 'Environmental Policy: The Development of a New Policy Area', in K. von Beyme and M.G. Schmidt (eds), *Policy and Politics in the Federal Republic of Germany*, Aldershot: Gower, pp. 156–75.

Hughes Hallett, A., Ma, Y. and Mélitz, J. (1996) 'Unification and the Policy Predicament in Germany', *Economic Modelling*, vol 13, no. 5, pp. 519–44.

Hunt, J. (2000) 'Why Do People Still Live in East Germany?'.

Hyde-Price, A. (2000) *Germany and European Order: Enlarging NATO and the EU*, Manchester: Manchester University Press.

Hyde-Price, A. (2001) 'Germany and 11 September', in R. Fawn and M. Buckley (eds), *September 11 – World Reactions*, London: Continuum.

Hyde-Price, A. (2002) 'Decision-Making under the Second Pillar', in T. Arnull and D. Wincott (eds), *Accountability and Legitimacy in the EU*, Oxford: Oxford University Press, pp. 99–146.

Jäger, W. (1994) *Wer regiert die Deutschen? Innenansichten der Parteiendemokratie*, Zurich: Edition Interfrom.

Jahreswirtschaftsbericht der Bundesregierung: *Reformkurs fortsetzen – Wachstumsdynamik stärken* (2001) *Bundestagsdrucksache* 14/5201.

Jahreswirtschaftsbericht der Bundesregierung: Vor einem neuen Aufschwung – Verlässliche Wirtschafts- und Finanzpolitik (2002) *Bundestagsdrucksache* 14/8175.

Jänicke, M. and Weidner, H. (1997) 'Germany', in M. Jänicke and H.Weidner (eds), *National Environmental Policies. A Comparative Study of Capacity-Building*, Berlin: Springer, pp. 133–55.

Jänicke, M., Kunig, P. and Stitzel, M. (1999) _Lern- und Arbeitsbuch Umweltpolitik_, Bonn: Dietz.

Janisch, W. (2000) 'Frauen in die Bundeswehr: Wo Europa zuständig ist, hat selbst das Grundgesetz das Nachsehen', _Gegenwartskunde_, vol. 49, no. 1, pp. 87–91.

Janning, G. and Giering, C. (2002) 'Flexibilisierung als Option deutscher Europapolitik', in H. Schneider, M. Jopp and U. Schmalz, _Eine Neue deutsche Europa politik_, Bonn: Europa Union Verlag, pp. 667–94.

Jeffery, C. (1994) 'The Länder Strike Back. Structures and Procedures of European Integration Policy Making in the German Federal System', _Discussion Papers in Federal Studies_, No. FS94/4, Leicester.

Jeffery, C. (1999a) 'From Cooperative Federalism to a "Sinatra Doctrine" of the Länder', in C. Jeffery (ed.), _Recasting German Federalism: The Legacies of Unification_, London: Pinter, pp. 329–42.

Jeffery, C. (ed.) (1999b), _Recasting German Federalism. The Legacies of Unification_, London: Pinter.

Jeffery, C. (2002) 'Uniformity and Diversity in Policy Provision: Insights from the US, Germany and Canada', in J. Adams and P. Robinson (eds), _Devolution in Practice: Public Policy Differences in the UK_, London: ippr.

Jeffery, C. (2003) 'The German Länder and Europe: From Milieu-Shaping to Territorial Politics', in K. Dyson and K. Goetz (eds), _Germany and Europe: A Europeanized Germany?_, Oxford: Oxford University Press.

Jeffery, C. and Hough, D. (2002) 'The Electoral Cycle and Multi-Level Voting in Germany', in S. Padgett and T. Poguntke (eds), _Continuity and Change in German Politics: Beyond the Politics of Centrality?_, London and Portland, Oregon: Frank Cass.

Jeffery, C. and Mackenstein, H. (1999) 'Financial Equalisation in the 1990s: On the Road back to Karlsruhe', in C. Jeffery (ed.), _Recasting German Federalism: The Legacies of Unification_, London: Pinter, p. 329–42.

Jeffery, C. and Paterson, W. (2003) 'Germany and European Integration: Beyond the Stable State?', _West European Politics_, vol. 26, no. 2/April.

Johnson, N. (1983) _State and Government in Germany: The Executive at Work_, Oxford: Pergamon, 2nd edn.

Joppke, C. (1999) _Immigration and the Nation-State. The United States, Germany and Great Britain_, Oxford: Oxford University Press.

Kaase, M. (1989) 'Bewußtseinslagen und Leitbilder in der Bundesrepublik Deutschland', in W. Weidenfeld and H. Zimmermann (eds), _Deutschland Handbuch, Eine doppelte Bilanz 1949–1989_, Bonn: Bundeszentrale für politische Bildung.

Kaase, M. and Bauer-Kaase, P. (1997) 'German Unification 1990–1997: The Long, Long Road', GSA Conference, Washington, DC, 25–28 September, 1997.

Kaase, M. and Klingemann, H.-D. (1994) 'The Cumbersome way to Partisan Orientations in a "New" Democracy', in M.K. Jennings and T. Mann (eds), _Elections at Home and Abroad_, Ann Arbor, MI: University of Michigan Press.

Kaase, M. and Klingemann, H.-D. (eds) (1998) _Wahlen und Wähler: Analysen aus Anlass der Bundestagswahl 1994_, Opladen: Westdeutscher Verlag.

Katz, R. (1999) 'Representation, the Locus of Democratic Legitimation and the Role of the National Parliaments in the European Union', in R. Katz and B. Wessels (eds), _The European Parliament, the National Parliaments and European Integration_, Oxford: Oxford University Press.

Katzenstein, P. (1987) _Policy and Politics in West Germany. The Growth of a Semisovereign State_, Philadelphia: Temple University Press.

Katzenstein, P. (ed.) (1997) *Tamed Power: Germany in Europe*, London and Ithaca, NY: Cornell University Press.

Kersbergen, K. van (1995) *Social Capitalism – A Study of Christian Democracy and the Welfare State*, London: Routledge.

Kitschelt, H. (2000) 'The German Political Economy and the 1998 Election', in D.P. Conradt, G.R. Kleinfeld and C. Søe (eds), *Power Shift in Germany: The 1998 Election and the End of the Kohl Era*, New York and Oxford: Berghahn Books.

Klatt, H. (1991) 'Centralising Trends in the Federal Republic: The Record of the Kohl Chancellorship', in C. Jeffery and P. Savigear (eds), *German Federalism Today*, Leicester: Leicester University Press.

Klein, Markus *et al.* (eds) (2000) *50 Jahre empirische Wahlforschung in Deutschland*, Opladen: Westdeutscher Verlag.

Klingemann, H.-D. and Hofferbert, R. I. (1994) 'Germany: A New "Wall in the Mind"?', *Journal of Democracy*, pp. 5, no. 1.

Klingemann, H.-D. and Kaase, M. (eds) (2001) *Wahlen und Wähler: Analysen aus Anlass der Bundestagswahl 1998*, Opladen: Westdeutscher Verlag.

Klusmeyer, D. (2001) 'A "Guiding Culture" for Immigrants? Integration and Diversity in Germany', *Journal of Ethnic and Migration Studies*, vol. 27, no. 3, pp. 519–32.

Knelangen, W. (2000) ' "Bündnis für Arbeit" oder "Bündnis für Frührentner"? Der Streit über die Forderung nach einer "Rente mit 60" ', *Gegenwartskunde*, vol. 49, no. 1, pp. 93–9.

Knodt, M. and Kohler-Koch, B. (eds) (2000) *Deutschland zwischen Europäisierung und Selbstbehauptung*, Frankfurt am Main: Campus Verlag.

Koch, R. (2001) 'Sozialhilfe – eine zweite Chance, kein Lebensstil', www.roland-koch.de/home_cdu.nsf/$pages/content_sozialhilfe (viewed on 23 August 2002).

Kohl, J. (2001) 'Die deutsche Rentenreform im europäischen Kontext', *Zeitschrift für Sozialreform*, vol. 47, no. 6, pp. 619–43.

Kohler-Koch, B. and Knodt, M. (2000) *Deutschland zwischen Europaeisierung und Selbstbehauptung*, Campus Fachbuch.

König, K. (1985) 'Nationwide Plans and the Planning of Policy at the Central Level of Government: The Federal Republic of Germany', *Verwaltungswissenschaftliche Informationen* (Special Issue 7), pp. 35–47.

König, K. (1989) 'Vom Umgang mit Komplexität in Organisationen: Das Bundeskanzleramt', *Der Staat*, vol. 28, no. 1, pp. 49–70.

König, K. (1991) 'Formalisierung und Informalisierung im Regierungszentrum', in H.-H. Hartwich and G. Wever (eds), *Regieren in der Bundesrepublik II*, Opladen: Leske & Budrich, pp. 203–20.

König, K. (1992) 'Politiker und Beamte. Zur personellen Differenzierung im Regierungsbereich', in K.-D. Bracher *et al.* (eds), *Staat und Parteien. Festschrift für Rudolf Morsey zum 65. Geburtstag*, Berlin: Duncker & Humblot, pp. 107–32.

Koopmans, R. (1995) *Democracy from Below: New Social Movements and the Political System in West Germany*, Boulder, CO: Westview Press.

Korte, K.-R. (1998) *Deutschlandpolitik in Helmut Kohls Kanzlerschaft: Regierungsstil und Entscheidungen 1982–1989*, Stuttgart: Deutsche Verlags-Anstalt.

Korte, K.-R. (2000) 'Solutions for the Decision Dilemma: Political Styles of Germany's Chancellors', *German Politics*, vol. 9, no.1, pp. 1–22.

Korte, K.-R. and Hirscher, G. (eds) (2000) *Darstellungspolitik oder Entscheidungspolitik. Über den Wandel von Politikstilen in westlichen Demokratien*, München: Hanns Seidel Stiftung.

Krause, J. (2001) 'The Consequences of September 11 2001 for Transatlantic Relations', *Newsletter: German Foreign Policy in Dialogue*, Issue 5, http://www. deutsche-aussenpolitik.de/publications/newsletter/issue 5.html, pp. 4–6.

Krebs, C., Reiche, D.T. and Rocholl, M. (1998) *Die ökologische Steuerreform*, Berlin: Birkhäuser.

Kropp, S. and Sturm, R. (1998) *Koalitionen und Koalitionsvereinbarungen*, Opladen: Leske & Budrich.

Lamping, W. and Rüb, F.W. (2001) *From the Conservative Welfare State to Something Uncertain Else: The New German Pension Politics*, Centre for Social and Public Policy, Discussion Paper No. 12, Hanover: Universität Hannover.

Lane, C. (1994a) 'Industrial Order and the Transformation of Industrial Relations: Britain, Germany and France Compared', in R. Hyman and R. Ferner (eds), *New Frontiers in European Industrial Relations*, Oxford: Basil Blackwell.

Lane, C. (1994b) 'Is Germany Following the British Path? A Comparative Analysis of Stability and Change', *Industrial Relations Journal*, vol. 3, pp. 187–98.

Lantis, J. (1996) 'Rising to the challenge: Geman Security Policy in the Post-Cold War Era', *German Politics and Society*, vol. 14, no. 2, pp. 19–35.

Laufer, H. and Münch, U. (1997) *Das föderative System der Bundesrepublik Deutschland*, Bonn: Bundeszentrale für politische Bildung.

Le Gloannec, A.M. (1993) 'Une hegemonie de la Faiblesse?', in Ann Marie Le Gloannec (ed.) *L'Allemagne apres la Guerre Froide. Le Vainqueur entrave*, Brussels: Ouff, pp. 125–30.

Lees, C. (2000) *The Red–Green Coalition in Germany*, Manchester: Manchester University Press.

Lees, C. (2002) '"Dark Matter": Institutional Constraints and the Failure of Party-Based Euroscepticism in Germany', *Political Studies*, vol. 50, no. 2 (June), pp. 244–67.

Lehmbruch, G. (1976) *Parteienwettbewerb im Bundesstaat*, Stuttgart: Kohlhammer.

Lehmbruch, G. (2000) 'Bundesstaatsreform als Sozialtechnologie? Pfadabhängigkeit und Veränderungsspielräume im deutschen Föderalismus', in *Jahrbuch des Föderalismus 2000*, Baden-Baden: Nomos, pp. 71–93.

Leicht, R. (2001) 'Alles Verhandlungssache. Das Kommissionswesen blüht, das Parlament verkümmert', *Die Zeit*, 23 May, p. 5.

Leicht, R. (2002) 'Angsthasen und Panikmacher', *Die Zeit*, no. 14.

Libal, M. (1997) *Limits of Persuasion: Germany and the Yugoslav Crisis*, Westport, CT: Praeger.

Lipset, S. M. and Rokkan, S. (eds) (1967) *Party Systems and Voter Alignments*, New York: Free Press.

Lütz, S. (2000) 'From Managed to Market Capitalism? German Finance in Transition', *German Politics*, vol. 9, no. 2, pp. 149–70.

Maier, C.S. (1997) *Dissolution: The Crisis of Communism and the End of East Germany*, Princeton and London: Princeton University Press.

Männle, U. (ed.) (1998) *Föderalismus zwischen Konsens und Konkurrenz*, Baden-Baden: Nomos.

Manow, P. (1996) 'Informalisierung und Parteipolitisierung – Zum Wandel exekutiver Entscheidungsprozesse in der Bundesrepublik', *Zeitschrift für Parlamentsfragen*, vol. 27, no. 1, pp. 96–107.

Marsh, D. (1993) *The Bundesbank: The Bank That Rules Europe*, London: Mandarin.

Marshall, B. (1992) 'German Migration Policies', in G. Smith *et al.* (eds), *Developments in German Politics*, London: Macmillan.

Marshall, B. (2000) *The New Germany and Migration in Europe*, Manchester: Manchester University Press.

März, P. (2002) *An der Spitze der Macht. Kanzlerschaften und Wettbewerber in Deutschland*, München: Olzog.

Matravers, C. (1997) 'German Industrial Structures in Comparative Perspective', *Industry and Innovation*, vol. 4, no. 1, pp. 37–51.

Maull, H. (2000) 'German Foreign Policy, Post Kosovo: "Still a Civillian Power?" ', *German Politics*, vol. 9, no 2, pp. 1–24.

Maull, H. and Kirste, K. (1997) 'Zivilmacht und Rollentheorie', *Zeitschrift für Internationale Beziehunger*, vol. 3, no. 2, pp. 283–312.

Mayer, M. and Ely, J. (1998) *The German Greens: Paradox between Movement and Party*, Philadelphia and London: Temple University Press.

Mayntz, R. (1978) 'Intergovernmental Implementation of Environmental Policy', in K. Hanf and F.W. Scharpf (eds), *Interorganizational Policy Making*, London: Sage, pp. 201–14.

Mayntz, R. (1980) 'Executive Leadership in Germany: Dispersion of Power or "Kanzlerdemokratie"?', in R. Rose and E.N. Suleiman (eds), *Presidents and Prime Ministers*, Washington, DC: American Enterprise Institute, pp. 139–70.

Mayntz, R. and Derlien, H.-U. (1989) 'Party Patronage and Politicization of the West German Administrative Elite 1970–1987 – Toward Hybridization?', *Governance*, vol. 2, no. 4, pp. 384–404.

Mayntz, R. and Scharpf, F.W. (1975) *Policy-Making in the German Federal Bureaucracy*, Amsterdam: Elsevier.

Mayntz, R., Derlien, H.-U., Bohne, E., Hesse, B., Hucke, J. and Müller, A. (1977) *Vollzugsprobleme der Umweltpolitik*, Stuttgart: Kohlhammer.

Meyer, T. (1998) 'Retrenchment, Reproduction, Modernization: Pension Politics and the Decline of the German Breadwinner Model', *Journal of European Social Policy*, vol. 8, no. 3, pp. 195–211.

Mehl, P. and Plankl, R. (2002) 'Regionale Agrarpolitik in Deutschland – Handlungsspielräume in einem verflochtenen Politikfeld', in *Jahrbuch des Föderalismus 2002*, Baden-Baden: Nomos, pp. 199–210.

Meiers, F. (1995) 'Germany: The Reluctant Power', *Survival*, vol. 37, no. 3, pp. 82–103.

Meng, R. (2002) *Der Medienkanzler. Was bleibt vom System Schröder?*, Frankfurt am Main: Suhrkamp.

Merritt, R. L. (1995) *Democracy Imposed*, New Haven: Yale University Press.

Migration und Bevölkerung (2002) 'Deutschland: SPD und CDU für staatlich organisierten Islamunterricht', issue 8 available via http://www.migration-info.de

Minkenberg, M. (1993) 'The Wall after the Wall: On the Continuing Division of Germany and the Remaking of the Political Culture', *Comparative Politics*, vol. 26, no. 1, pp. 53–68.

Miskimmon, A.J. and Paterson, W.E. (2003) 'Foreign and Security Policy – on the Cusp between Transformation and Accommodation', in K. Dyson and K. Goetz (eds), *Living with Europe – Germany and European Integration*, Oxford: Oxford University Press for the British Academy.

Mueller, J. (1994) 'The catastrophe quota', *Journal of Conflcit Resolution*, vol. 38, pp. 335–75.

306   *Bibliography*

Müller, E. (1995) *Innenwelt der Umweltpolitik*, Opladen: Westdeutscher Verlag, 2nd edn.

Müller, M.M. (2001) 'Die Reform der Betriebsverfassung', *Gegenwartskunde*, vol. 50, no. 1, pp. 93–102.

Müller, M.M. (2002) *The New Regulatory State in Germany*, Birmingham: University of Birmingham Press.

Müller-Rommel, F. (1997) 'Federal Republic of Germany: A System of Chancellor Government', in J. Blondel and F. Müller-Rommel (eds), *Cabinets in Western Europe*, London: Macmillan, pp. 171–91, 2nd edn.

Münch, U. (1998) 'Entflechtungsmöglichkeiten im Bereich der Sozialpolitik. Zur Diskussion um eine Föderalisierung der Sozialversicherung', in U. Männle (ed.), *Föderalismus zwischen Konsens und Konkurrenz*, Baden-Baden: Nomos, pp. 73–8.

Münch, U. (2001) 'Konkurrenzföderalismus für die Bundesrepublik: Eine Reformdebatte zwischen Wunschdenken und politischer Machbarkeit', in *Jahrbuch des Föderalismus 2001*, Baden-Baden: Nomos, pp. 115–27.

Münz, R. (2001) 'Geregelte Zuwanderung: eine Zukunftsfrage für Deutschland', *Aus Politik und Zeitgeschichte* B43/2001, pp. 3–6.

Münz, R. and Ulrich, R. (1999) 'Immigration and Citizenship in Germany', *German Politics and Society*, vol. 17, no. 4, pp. 1–33.

Münz, R., Seifert, W. and Ulrich, R. (1997) *Zuwanderung nach Deutschland. Strukturen, Wirkungen, Perspektiven*, Frankfurt: Campus.

Murray, L. (1994) 'Einwanderungsland Bundesrepublik Deutschland? Explaining the Evolving Positions of German Political Parties on Citizenship Policy', *German Politics and Society*, Issue 33 (Fall 1994), pp. 23–56.

Nativel, C. (2002) *Economic Transition, Unemployment and Active Labour Market Policy*, Birmingham: University of Birmingham Press.

Neidhardt, F. (1978) 'The Federal Republic of Germany', in S.B. Kamerman and A.J. Kahn (eds), *Family Policy – Government and Families in Fourteen Countries*, New York: Columbia University Press, pp. 217–38.

Niclauß, K. (1999) 'Bestätigung der Kanzlerdemokratie? Kanzler und Regierungen zwischen Verfassung und politischen Konventionen', *Aus Politik und Zeitgeschichte* B20/99, pp. 27–38.

Niclauß, K. (2001) 'The Federal Government: Variations of Chancellor Dominance', in L. Helms (ed.), *Institutions and Institutional Change in the Federal Republic of Germany*, Basingstoke: Palgrave, pp. 65–83.

Niedermayer, O. (2003) 'Is there a Europeanization of the Party System?', in K. Dyson and K. Goetz (eds), *op.cit.*

Niedermeyer, O. and von Beyme, K. (eds) (1994) *Politische Kultur in Ost- und West Deutschland*, Berlin: Campus Verlag.

Niejahr, E. (2001) 'Politik gegen Bares. Dosenpfand, Tabaksteuer, Arzneirabatt – Kanzler Schröder macht den Kuhhandel zur Methode', *Die Zeit*, 8 November, p. 25.

Noelle-Neumann, E. (1994) 'Problems with Democracy in Eastern Germany after the Downfall of the GDR', in F.D. Weil (ed.), *Research on Democracy and Society, Vol. 2*, Greenwich, CT and London: JAI Press, pp. 213–31.

Noelle, E. (2002) 'Spannung auf der Zielgeraden: Emotionen bestimmen die letzte Wahlkampfphase', *Frankfurter Allgemeine Zeitung*, 11 September, p. 5.

Norpoth, H. (1983) 'The Making of a More Partisan Electorate', *British Journal of Political Science*, no. 14, pp. 53–71.

Nullmeier, F. (2001) 'Sozialpolitik als marktregulierte Politik', *Zeitschrift für Sozialreform*, vol. 47, no. 6, pp. 645–67.

Oberreuter, H. (1992) 'Politische Führung in der parlamentarischen Demokratie', in K.-D. Bracher *et al.* (eds), *Staat und Parteien. Festschrift für Rudolf Morsey zum 65. Geburtstag*, Berlin: Duncker & Humblot, pp. 159–74.

O'Brien, P. (1996) *Beyond the Swastika*, London: Routledge.

OECD (2001) *Wirtschaftsberichte Deutschland*, Paris: OECD.

Ohr, D. (2000) 'Wird das Wählerverhalten zunehmend personalisierter, or ist dede Wahl anders?', in M. Klein *et al.* (eds) *50 Jahre empirische Walhforschung in Deutschland*, Opladen: Westdeutscher Verlag.

O'Riordan, T. and Cameron, J. (eds) (1994) *Interpreting the Precautionary Principle*, London: Earthscan.

Osborne, D. (1988) *Laboratories of Democracy*, Boston: Harvard Business School Press.

Ostermann, Hanna (2002) 'Rotten at the Core? The Higher Education Debate in Germany', *German Politics*, vol. 11, no. 1, pp. 43–60.

Padgett, S. (1994a) *Adenauer to Kohl: The Development of the German Chancellorship*, London: Hurst.

Padgett, S. (1994b) 'Introduction: Chancellors and the Chancellorship', in S. Padgett (ed.), *Adenauer to Kohl: The Development of the German Chancellorship*, London: Hurst, pp. 1–19.

Padgett, S. (2000) 'The Boundaries of Stability; The Party System Before and After the 1998 *Bundestagswahl*', in S. Padgett and T. Poguntke (eds), *Bundestagswahl '98: End of an Era* London and Portland, OR: Frank Cass, pp. 88–107.

Padgett, S. (2003) 'Germany: Modernising the Left by Stealth', *Parliamentary Affairs*, vol. 56, pp. 38–57.

Padgett, S. and Poguntke, T. (eds) (2002) *Continuity and Change in German Politics: Beyond the Politics of Centrality?*, London and Portland, Oregon: Frank Cass.

Padgett, S. and Saalfeld, T. (eds) (2000) *Bundestagswahl '98: End of an Era?*, London and Portland, Oregon: Frank Cass.

Pappi, F.U. (1984) 'The West German Party System', *West European Politics*, vol. 7, no. 4 (October), pp. 7–26.

Paterson, W. (1981) 'The Chancellor and his Party: Political Leadership in the Federal Republic', in W.E. Paterson and G. Smith (eds), *The West German Model: Perspectives on a Stable State*, London: Frank Cass.

Paterson, W. (1989) 'Environmental Policy', in G. Smith, W.E. Paterson and P.H. Merkl (eds), *Developments in West German Politics*, Basingstoke: Macmillan, pp. 267–88.

Paterson, W. (1993) 'Muss Europa Angst Vor Deutschland Haben?', in R. Hrbek, *Der Vertrag Von Maastricht Inder wissenschaftlichen Kontroverse*, Baden-Baden: Nomos.

Paterson, W. (1994) 'The Chancellor and Foreign Policy', in S. Padgett (ed.), *Adenauer to Kohl: The Development of the German Chancellorship*, London: Hurst, pp. 127–56.

Paterson, W. (1996) 'Beyond Semi-Sovereignty: The New Germany in the New Europe', *German Politics*, vol. 5, no. 2, pp. 167–84.

Paterson, W. (1998) 'Helmut Kohl, The Vision Thing and Escaping the Semisovereignty Trap', in C. Clements and W.E. Paterson (eds), *The Kohl Chancellorship*, London: Frank Cass, pp. 17–36.

Paterson, W. (2000) 'From the Bonn to the Berlin Republic', *German Politics*, vol. 9, no. 1, pp. 23–40.

Pedersen, T. (1998) *Germany, France and the Integration of Europe. A Realist Interpretation*, London: Pinter.

Pehle, H. (1997) 'Germany: Domestic Obstacles to an International Forerunner', in M.S. Andersen, and D. Liefferink, (eds), *European Environmental Policy: The Pioneers*, Manchester: Manchester University Press, pp. 161–209.

Pehle, H. (1998) *Das Bundesministerium für Umwelt, Naturschutz und Reaktorsicherheit: Ausgegrenzt statt integriert?*, Wiesbaden: Deutscher Universitäts-Verlag.

Pehle, H. and Jansen, A.-I. (1998) 'Germany: the engine in European environmental policy?', in K. Hanf and A.-I. Jansen (eds), *Governance and Environment in Western Europe: Politics, Policy and Administration*, Harlow, Essex: Longman, pp. 82–109.

Pierson, P. (2001) 'Coping with Permanent Austerity – Welfare State Restructuring in Affluent Democracies', in Paul Pierson (ed.), *The New Politics of the Welfare State*, Oxford: Oxford University Press, pp. 410–56.

Pielow, J.-C. (2002) 'Öffentliche Daseinsvorsorge als Herausfoirderung für die deutschen Länder und Kommunen – Stand und Perpektive', in *Jahrbuch des Föderalismus 2002*, Baden-Baden: Nomos, 163–81.

Pond, E. (1997) 'Letter from Bonn: Visions of the European Dream', *The Washington Quarterly*, vol. 20, no. 3, pp. 65–74.

Pradetto, A. (1999) 'Zurick zu der Interessen: Das Strategische Konzept der NATO und die Lehren des Krieges', *Blätter für Deutsche und Internationale Politik*, vol. 44, no. 7, pp. 806–15.

Preuss, U. (1999) 'Zwischen Legalität und Gerechtigkeit', *Blätter fur Deutsche und Internationale Politik*, vol. 44, no. 7, pp. 816–28.

Pulzer, P. (2003) 'The Devil They Know: The German Federal Election of 2002', *West European Politics*, vol. 26, no. 2 (April), pp. 153–64.

Radaelli, C. (2000) 'Whither Europeanization? Concept Stretching and Substantive Change', Paper presented to the Annual Conference of the Political Studies Association, London, 10–13 April (see *European Integration online Papers*: 4/8, http://eop.or.at/eiop/texte/2000–008a.htm).

Radkau, J. (1983) *Aufstieg und Krise der deutschen Atomwirtschaft, 1945–1975*, Reinbek: Rowohlt.

Raschke, J. (2001) 'Sind die Grünen regierungsfähig? Die Selbstblockade einer Regierungspartei', *Aus Politik und Zeitgeschichte*, March, pp. 20–8.

Raschke, J. (with Hurrelmann, A.) (2001) *Die Zukunft der Grünen*, Frankfurt a Main and New York: Campus.

Rat der Sachverständigen für Umweltfragen (2002) *Umweltgutachten 2002: Für eine neue Vorreiterrolle*, Berlin: Deutscher Bundestag, Drucksache 14/8792.

Reiche, D. and Krebs, C. (1999) *Der Einstieg in die ökologische Steuerreform*, Frankfurt: Peter Lang.

Reif, K. and Schmitt, H. (1980) 'Nine Second-Order Elections: A Conceptual Framework for the Analysis of European Elections Results', *European Journal of Political Research*, no. 8, pp. 3–44.

Richardson, J.J. and Watts, N.S.J. (1985) 'National policy styles and the environment: Britain and West Germany compared', *IIUG Discussion Paper*, pp. 85–116, Berlin: International Institute for Environment and Society, Science Centre Berlin. Reprinted in W. Rüdig (ed.), *Environmental Policy*, vol. 1, Cheltenham: Edward Elgar (1999), pp. 309–54.

Ridley, F. F. (1966) 'Chancellor Democracy as a Political Principle', *Parliamentary Affairs*, vol. 11, no. 4, pp. 446–62.

Riedmüller, B. and Olk, T. (eds) (1994) *Grenzen des Sozialversicherungsstaates*, Leviathan, Special Issue 14, Opladen: Westdeutscher Verlag.

Rittberger, V. (ed.) (2001) *German Foreign Policy Since Unification: Theories and Case Studies*, Manchester: Manchester University Press

Roberts, G. (2000a) 'By Decree or Design? The Surplus Seats Problem in the German Electoral System: Causes and Remedies', *Representation*, vol. 37, nos 3/4 (Winter), pp. 195–202.

Roberts, G. (2000b) 'Is there Life after Kohl? The CDU Crisis', *Government and Opposition*, vol. 35, no. 4 (Autumn), pp. 419–37.

Rohrschneider, R. (1996) 'Cultural Transmission versus Perceptions of the Economy: The Sources of Political Elites' Economic Values in the United Germany', *Comparative Political Studies*, vol. 21, no. 1, pp. 78–104.

Rohrschneider, R. (1999) *Learning Democracy: Democratic and Economic Values in Unified Germany*, New York and Oxford: Oxford University Press.

Rohrschneider, R. and R. Dalton (eds) (2003) 'Judgment Day and Beyond: The 2002 Bundestagswahl', special issue of *German Politics and Society*.

Roller, E. (1997) 'Sozialpolitische Orientierungen nach der deutschen Vereinigung', in W. Gabriel, Oscar (ed.), *Politische Einstellungen und Politisches Verhalten im Transformationsprozeß*, Opladen: Leske Budrich, pp. 115–46.

Roller, E. (1999) Staatsbezug und Individualismus: Dimensionen des sozialkulturellen Wertwandels', T. Ellwein and E. Holtmann (eds), *50 Jahre Bundesrepublik Deutschland – Rahmenbedingungen, Entwicklungen, Perspektiven*. PVS-Sonderheft 30/1999, Wiesbaden: Westdeutscher Verlag, pp. 229–46.

Ronge, V. (2000) 'Auf dem Weg zum "Einwanderungsland"?', in R. Czada and H. Wollman (eds), *Von der Bonner zur Berliner Republik*, Opladen: Westdeutscher Verlag.

Rose, R., and McAllister, I. (1989) *When Voters Begin to Choose*, Beverly Hills, CA: Sage.

Rose-Ackerman, S. (1995) *Controlling Environmental Policy: The Limits of Public Law in Germany and the United States*, New Haven, CT: Yale University Press.

Roth, D. (1998) *Empirische Wahlforschung: Ursprung, Theorien, Instrumente und Methoden*, Leverkusen: Leske & Budrich.

Rucht, D. and Roose, J. (1999) 'The German Environmental Movement at a Crossroads?', *Environmental Politics*, vol. 8, no. 1 (Spring), pp. 59–80.

Rüdig, W. (1990) *Anti-Nuclear Movements*, Harlow: Longman.

Rüdig, W. (2000) 'Phasing Out Nuclear Energy in Germany', *German Politics*, vol. 9, no. 3 (December), pp. 43–80.

Rüdig, W. (2002) 'Germany', in F. Müller-Rommel, and T. Poguntke, (eds), *Green Parties in National Governments*, London: Frank Cass, pp. 78–111.

Rüdig, W. and Krämer, R.A. (1994) 'Networks of Co-coperation: Water Policy in Germany', *Environmental Politics*, vol. 3, no. 4, pp. 52–79.

Rudzio, W. (1991) 'Informelle Entscheidungsmuster in Bonner Koalitionsregierungen', in H.-H. Hartwich and G. Wever (eds), *Regieren in der Bundesrepublik II*, Opladen: Leske & Budrich, pp. 125–41.

Saalfeld, T. (1998) 'The German Bundestag: Influence and Accountability in a Complex Environment', in P. Norton (ed.), *Parliaments and Governments in Western Europe*, London: Frank Cass, pp. 44–72.

Saalfeld, T. (1999) 'Coalition Politics and Management in the Kohl Era, 1982–1998', *German Politics*, vol. 8, no. 2, pp. 141–73.

Saalfeld, T. (2003) 'The Europeanization of Representation in Germany', in K. Dyson and K. Goetz (eds), *op.cit.*

Sager, K. (1996) 'Grüne Friedens – und Sicherheitspolitik', *Internationale Politik*, vol. 51, no. 8, pp. 43–8.

Sarotte, M. (2001) *Germany Military Reform and European Security*, Adelphi Paper 340, Oxford: Oxford University Press.

Scharpf, F. (1985) 'Die Politikverflechtungsfälle: Europäische Integration und deutscher Föderalismus im Vergleich', *Politische Vierteljahresschrift*, vol. 26, pp. 323–56.

Scharpf, F. (1988) 'The Joint-Decision Trap: Lessons from German Federalism and European Integration', *Public Administration*, vol. 66.

Scharpf, F. W. and Schmidt, V. (eds) (2000) *Welfare and Work in the Open Economy – From Vulnerability to Competitiveness*, vol. 1, Oxford: Oxford University Press.

Scharpf, F., Reissert, B. and Schnabel, F. (1976) *Politikverflechtung. Theorie und Empirie des kooperativen Föderalismus in der Bundesrepublik*, Kronberg: Scriptor.

Schäuble, W. (1991) *Der Vertrag. Wie ich über die deutsche Einheit verhandelte*, Stuttgart: Deutsche Verlagsanstalt.

Schmähl, W. (1999) 'Rentenversicherung in der Bewährung: Von der Nachkriegszeit bis an die Schwelle zum neuen Jahrhundert', in M. Kaase and G. Schmid (eds), *Eine lernende Demokratie – 50 Jahre Bundesrepublik Deutschland*, WZB-Jahrbuch 1999, Berlin: Edition Sigma, pp. 397–423.

Schmidt, M.G. (1996) 'Germany: The Grand Coalition State', in J.M. Colomer (ed.), *Political Institutions in Europe*, London: Routledge, pp. 62–98.

Schmidt, M.G. (1998) *Sozialpolitik in Deutschland – Historische Entwicklung und internationaler Vergleich*, Opladen: Leske & Budrich, 2nd edn.

Schmid, J. (2001) 'Bevölkerungsentwicklung und Migration in Deutschland', *Aus Politik und Zeitgeschichte* B43/2001, pp. 20–30.

Schmid, J. (2002) 'Sozialpolitik und Wohlfahrtsstaat in Bundesstaaten', *Politische Vierteljahresschrift*, vol. 42, pp. 279–305.

Schmidt, M.G. (2001) 'Still on the Middle Way? Germany's Political Economy at the Beginning of the Twenty-First Century', *German Politics*, vol. 10, no. 3, pp. 1–12.

Schmidt, P. (1996) 'Germany Security Policy in the Framework of EU, WEU and NATO', *Aussenpolitik*, vol. 47, no. 3, pp. 211–13.

Schmitt, K. (1993) 'Politische Landschaften im Umbruch', in O. Gabriel and K. Troitzsch (eds), *Wahlen in Zeiten des Umbruchs*, Frankfurt: Lang.

Schneider, H., Jopp, M. and Schmalz, U. (eds) (2001) *Eine neue deutsche Europapolitik*, Bonn: Europa Union Verlag.

Schoen, H. (2000) 'Stimmensplitting bei Bundestagswahlen: Ein Spiegelbild des Verhältnisses zwischen Bürgern und Parteien?', in M. Klein *et al.*, *50 Jahre empirische Washforschung in Deutschland*, Opladen: Westdeutscher Verlag.

Schreckenberger, W. (1994) 'Informelle Verfahren der Entscheidungsvorbereitung zwischen Bundesregierung und den Mehrheitsfraktionen: Koalitionsgespräche und Koalitionsrunden', *Zeitschrift für Parlamentsfragen*, vol. 25, no. 3, pp. 329–46.

Schröder, U. (1996) 'Corporate Governance in Germany: The Changing Role of the Banks', *German Politics*, vol. 5, no. 3, pp. 356–70.

Schröder, G. (2001) 'Statement by the Germany Chancellor, Gerhard Schröder to the German Bundestag, 11 October 2001 in Berlin', *Transatlantic Internationale Politik*, vol. 2, no. 4, pp. 150–4.

Schroeder, W. and Esser, J. (1999) 'Modell Deutschland: Von der Konzertierten Aktion zum Bündnis für Arbeit', *Aus Politik und Zeitgeschichte*, vol. 37, pp. 3–12.

Schulz, W. (2001) 'Unerwartet Harmonisch: Dresdner Bunesparteitag der PDS', *Deutschland Archiv*, vol. 34, no. 6, pp. 924–8.

Schulze, R.-O. (2000) 'Indirekte Entflechtung: Eine Strategie für die Föderalismusreform', *Zeitschrift für Parlamentsfragen*, vol. 31, pp. 681–98.

Schwarz, H.P. (1994) *Die Zentralmacht Europas*, Berlin: Siedler Verlag.

Seeleib-Kaiser, M. (2001a) *Globalisierung und Sozialpolitik. Ein Vergleich der Diskurse und Wohlfahrtssysteme in Deutschland, Japan und den USA*, Frankfurt am Main: Campus.

Seeleib-Kaiser, M. (2001b) 'Globalisation and the German Social Transfer State', *German Politics*, vol. 10, no. 3, pp. 103–18.

Seeleib-Kaiser, M. (2002) 'A Dual Transformation of the German Welfare State', *West European Politics*, vol. 25, no. 4, pp. 25–48.

Silvia, S.J. (1999) 'Reform Gridlock and the Role of the Bundesrat in German Politics', *West European Politics*, vol. 22, no. 1, pp. 167–81.

Silvia, S. (2002) 'The Fall and Rise of Unemployment in Germany: Is the Red–Green Coalition Responsible?', *German Politics*, vol. 11, no. 1, pp. 1–22.

Smith, G. (1990) 'Core Persistence: System Change and the "People's Party"', in P. Mair and G. Smith (eds), *Understanding Party System Change in Western Europe*, London: Frank Cass.

Smith, G. (1991) 'The Resources of a German Chancellor', *West European Politics*, vol. 14, no. 2, pp. 48–61.

Smith, G. (1994) 'The Changing Parameters of the Chancellorship', in S. Padgett (ed.), *Adenauer to Kohl: The Development of the German Chancellorship*, London: Hurst, pp. 178–97.

Smyser, W.R. (1993) *The German Economy: Colossus at the Crossroads*, Harlow: Longman, 2nd edn.

Sodan, H. (2002) 'Föderalisierung der gesetzlichen Krankenversicherung – Verfassungsrechtliche Massstäbe', in *Jahrbuch des Föderalismus 2002*, Baden-Baden: Nomos, 242–51.

SPD (2001) Keynote 'Proposal: Responsibility for Europe', National Conference of the Social Democratic Party of Germany, 19–23 November; http://www.spd.de/english/politics/partycongress/europe.html

SPD, Bündnis 90/Die Grünen (2002) *Erneuerung, Gerechtigkeit, Nachhaltigkeit. Für ein wirtschaftlich starkes, soziales und ökologisches Deutschland. Für eine lebendige Demokratie*, Koalitionsvereinbarung zwischen der Sozialdemokratischen Partei Deutschlands und Bündnis90/Die Grünen, http://www.spd.de, downloaded 24 October 2002.

Sperling, J. (2001) 'Neither Hegemony Nor Dominance; Reconsidering German Power in Post Cold-War Europe', *British Journal of Political Science*, vol. 31, pp. 389–425.

Stamm, B. (1998) 'Wettbewerbsföderalismus in der Sozialversicherung', in U. Männle (ed.), *Föderalismus zwischen Konsens und Konkurrenz*, Baden-Baden: Nomos, 235–42.

Stoiber, E. (2001) 'Cornerstones of the European Reform Process', Speech of the Bavarian Minister-President on 8 November 2001; see http://europa.eu.int/ Inturum/documents/press/sp081101_es

Stratman, P. (1988) 'Arms Control and the Military Balance: The West German Debate', in K. Kaiser and J. Roper (eds), *British German Defence Cooperation: Partners within the Alliance*, London: Jane's.

Streeck, W. (1992) *Social Institutions and Economic Performance: Studies of Industrial Relations in Advanced Capitalist Economies*, London, Sage.

Streeck, W. (1997) 'German Capitalism: Does it Exist? Can it Survive?', in C. Crouch and W. Streeck (eds), *Political Economy of Modern Capitalism: Mapping Convergence and Diversity*, London: Sage, pp. 33–52.

Strübin, M. (1997) 'Ecological Tax Reform in Germany', *German Politics*, vol. 6, no. 2 (August), pp. 168–80.

Sturm, R. (1999) 'Public Deficits. A Comparative Study of their Economic and Political Consequences in Britain, Canada, Germany and the United States', Harlow: Longman.

Sturm, R. (2001) *Föderalismus in Deutschland*, Berlin: Landeszentrale für politische Bildunsarbeit.

Sturm, R. (2001a) 'Divided Government in Germany: The Case of the Bundesrat', in R. Elgie (ed.) *Divided Government in Comparative Perspective*, Oxford: Oxford University Press, pp. 167–81.

Sturm, R. and Pehle, H. (2001) *Das neue deutsche Regierungssystem: Die Europaeisierung von Institutionen, Entscheidungsprozessen und Politikfeldern in der Bundesrepublik Deutschland*, Opladen: Leske & Budrich.

Süddeutsche Zeitung (2002) ' "Ich möchte keine zweisprachigen Ortsschilder haben", Otto Schily (SPD) zum Zuwanderungs- und Integrationsgesetz,' 27 June.

SVR; Sachverständigenrat zur Begutachtung der gesamtwirtschaft-lichen Entwicklung (2001) *Für Stetigkeit – Gegen Aktionismus. Jahresgutachten 2001/02*, Stuttgart: Metzler-Poeschel.

SVR Sachverständigenrat zur Begutachtung der gesamtwirtschaft-lichen Entwicklung (2002) *Zwanzig Punkte für Beschäftigung und Wachstum. Jahresgutachten 2002/03*. Wiesbaden, 13 November 2002, http://www.sachverstaendigenrat.org; downloaded 18 November 2002.

Tegtmeier, W. (1997) *Zur Finanzierung und Finanzierbarkeit sozialer Sicherung bei veränderten Rahmenbedingungen*, ZeS-Arbeitspapier 11–97, Bremen: Universität Bremen.

Thierse, W. (2001) 'Eine Runde der Abnicker? Zum angeblichen und tatsächlichen Bedeutungsverlust des Parlaments', *Frankfurter Rundschau*, 25 June, p. 6.

Timmins, G. (2000) 'Alliance for Jobs: Labour Market Policy and Industrial Relations after the 1998 Election', in R. Harding and W.E. Paterson (eds), *The Future of the German Economy: An End to the Miracle?*, Manchester: Manchester University Press.

Truger, A. (2001a) 'Der deutsche Einstieg in die ökologische Steuerreform', in A. Truger (2001b), *Rot-grüne Steuerreformen in Deutschland. Eine Zwischenbilanz*, Marburg: Metropolis, pp. 135–69.

Truger, A. (ed) (2001b) *Rot-grüne Steuerreformen in Deutschland. Eine Zwischenbilanz*, Marburg: Metropolis.

United Nations Population Division (2000) *Replacement Migration: Is it a Solution to Declining and Ageing Populations*, available at: http://www.un.org/esa/population/publications/migration/migration.htm

Veen, H.-J. (1997) 'Die innere Einheit ist schon da', *Frankfurter Allgemeine Zeitung*, 22 July, 1997, p. 11.

Vitols, S. (1997) 'German Industrial Policy: An Overview', *Industry and Innovation*, vol. 4, no. 1, pp. 15–36.

Vitols, S. (2001) 'Varieties of Corporate Governance: Comparing Germany and the UK', in P.A. Hall and D. Soskice (eds), *Varieties of Capitalism: the Institutional Foundations of Comparative Advantage*, Oxford, Oxford University Press, pp. 331–52.

Vobruba, G. (1990) 'Lohnarbeitszentrierte Sozialpolitik in der Krise der Lohnarbeit', in G. Vobruba (ed.), *Strukturwandel der Sozialpolitik*, Frankfurt am Main: Suhrkamp, pp. 11–80.

Voigt, R. (ed.) (1995) *Der kooperative Staat*, Baden-Baden: Nomos.

Volmer, L. (1998) *Die Grünen und die Anssenpolitikein Schwieriges Verhältns: Eine Ideen Programm und Ereignisgeschichte grüner Aussenpolitik*, Münster: Westfätsches Dampfboot.

Voltmer, K. and Eilders, C. (2003) 'Bringing Europe In? The Marginalization and Domestication of Europe in the German Media Agenda', in K. Dyson and K. Goetz (eds), *op.cit.*

Von Bredow, W. (1999) 'Der Krieg in Kosovo und die Ambivalenz der Eindeutigkeit', *Frankfurter Allgemeine Zeitung*, 26 April, p. 16.

Wallace, W. (1993) 'Germany at the Centre of Europe', in E. Kolinsky (ed.), *The Federal Republic of Germany: The End of an Era*, Oxford: Berg, pp. 167–73.

Wattenberg, M. (1996) *The Decline of American Political Parties*, Cambridge, MA: Harvard University Press, 4th edn.

Weale, A., O'Riordan, T. and Kramme, L. (1991) *Controlling Pollution in the Round: Change and Choice in Environmental Regulation in Britain and West Germany*, London: Anglo-German Foundation for the Study of Industrial Society.

Webber, D. (2001) *New Europe, New Germany, Old Foreign Policy? German Foreign Policy since Unification*, London: Frank Cass.

Webber D. (1992) 'Kohl's Wendepolitik after a Decade', *German Politics*, vol. 1.

Weidenfeld, W. and Lutz, F.P. (1992) 'Die gespaltene Nation. Das Geschichtsbewußtsein der Deutschen nach der Einheit', *Aus Politik und Zeitgechichte*, nos 31–2.

Weidner, H. (1995) *25 Years of Modern Environmental Policy in Germany*, Berlin: Wissenschaftszentrum Berlin für Sozialforschung.

Weidner, H. (1999) 'Umweltpolitik: Entwicklungslinien, Kapazitären und Effekte', in M. Kaase and G. Schmid (eds), *Eine lernende Demokratie: 50 Jahre Bundesrepublik Deutschland* (WZB-Jahrbuch 1999), Berlin: Edition sigma, pp. 425–60.

Weil, F.D. (1987) 'Cohorts, Regimes and the Legitimation of Democracy: West Germany since 1945', *American Sociological Review*, vol. 52, no. 3 (June 1987), pp. 308–24.

Weil, F.W. (1993) 'The Development of Democratic Attitudes in Eastern and Western Germany in a Comparative Perspective', in F.D. Weil *et al.* (eds.), *Research on Democracy and Society: Democratization in Eastern and Western Europe*, vol. 1, London and Greenwich, Conn: Jai Press, pp. 195–225.

Weischenberg, S. (2001) 'Die Macht und die Worte. Gerhard Schröders politische Kommunikation – eine Presseschau', in H. Oberreuter (ed.), *Umbruch 98. Wähler, Parteien, Kommunikation*, München: Olzog, pp. 179–97.

Weizsäcker, R. von (1992) *Richard von Weizsäcker: Converstion with Gunter Hofmann and Werner Perger*,

von Weizsäcker, U. and Jesinghaus, J. (1992) *Ecological Tax Reform*, London: Zed Books.

Welt am Sonntag (2002) 'Man spricht kein Deutsch', 17 February.

Wessels, W. (2000) *Die Öffnung des Staates*, Opladen: Leske & Budrich.

Wewer, G. (ed.) (1998) *Bilanz der Ära Kohl*, Opladen: Leske & Budrich.

Wey, K.-G. (1982) *Umweltpolitik in Deutschland*, Opladen: Westdeutscher Verlag.

Wollschläger, F. (2001) 'Gesetz zur Reform der Renten wegen verminderter Erwerbsfähigkeit', *Deutsche Rentenversicherung*, vol. 56, no. 5, pp. 276–94.

Wüst, A. (2002) *Wie wählen Neubürger? Politische Einstellungen und Wahlverhalten eingebürgerter Personen in Deutschland*, Opladen: Leske & Budrich.

Young, B. (1998) *Triumph of the Fatherland: German Unification and the Marginalization of Women*, Ann Arbor, MI: University of Michigan Press.

Zapf, W. (2000) 'How to Evaluate German Unification?', Study FSIII 00–404, Berlin: Wissenschaftszentrum.

Zehetmair, H. (1998) 'Zur Deregulierung und Neuordnung des Hochschulrahmenrechts', in U. Männle (ed.), *Föderalismus zwischen Konsens und Konkurrenz*, Baden-Baden: Nomos, 243–50.

Zelle, C. (1995) 'Social dealignment vs. political frustration', *European Journal for Political Research*, 27, pp. 319–45.

Zelle, C. (1997) 'Socialist Heritage or Current Unemployment: Why Do the Evaluations of Democracy and Socialism Differ Between the Germans in East and West?', German Studies Association, Washington, DC, September.

Zelle, C. (1998) 'Soziale und liberale Wertorientierungen: Versuch einer situativen Erklärung der Unterschiede zwischen Ost- und Westdeutschen', *Aus Politik und Zeitgeschichte*, nos 41–2 (2 October), pp. 24–6.

Index